MERLEAU-PONTY'S ONTOLOGY

Studies in Phenomenology and Existential Philosophy

MERLEAU-PONTY'S ONTOLOGY

M.C. DILLON

Indiana
University
Press

BLOOMINGTON AND INDIANAPOLIS

Material herein drawn from two of my essays previously published in *Man and World* is reprinted by permission of the publisher. The essays are: "Merleau-Ponty and the Reversibility Thesis," Vol. 16 (1983):365–88 and "Merleau-Ponty and the Transcendence of Immanence," Vol. 19 (1986):395–412.

Manufactured in the United States of America

Library of Congress Cataloging-in-Publication Data

Dillon, M. C.
Merleau-Ponty's ontology.

(Studies in phenomenology and existential philosophy
Bibliography: p.
1. Merleau-Ponty, Maurice, 1908–1961—Contributions in ontology.   2. Ontology—History—20th century.
3. Philosophy, Modern.   I. Title.   II. Series.
B2430.M3764D55   1988   111'.092'4   87-45443
ISBN 0–253–33618–X
1 2 3 4 5 92 91 90 89 88

For R. W. D.

Contents

Conclusion: Abyss and Logos   224

Preface

This text is based on two premises, only one of which will be defended. The first premise, which I simply postulate, is that the history of Western philosophy, albeit an errant history, manifests in retrospect an eidetic necessity in the manner of its unfolding. Thus Plato calls for Aristotle and provides a necessary condition for the possibility of peripatetic thought. And, in a similar fashion, Kant could not have thought as he did without the context provided by the empiricists and the rationalists—as their thinking presupposed the ideas of Descartes, who, in turn, wrote in response to the medieval tradition, and so on. The only way in which we could have arrived at this present, in all its complex particularity, is through the past as it happened. There are, to be sure, competing reconstructions of this history, and even disagreement among historians as to the validity of an ideal of a single history. There are also those who call for destruction or deconstruction of this history in an attempt to mitigate its influence on the present. Here, as everywhere in philosophy, controversy affords the luxury of multiple options. But few, I think, would seriously contest the point at stake, i.e., that present thought is conditioned by past thought.

One consequence of this view is that one understands a piiilosopher's thought better if one interprets it within its historical context, specifically, within the context of its philosophical antecedents. It is for this reason that I begin a book devoted to Maurice Merleau-Ponty by quoting Plato—and then go on to focus the first chapter on Descartes.

The complex of problems addressed here centers around the theme of ontological dualism. It is an ancient theme, but the problems emerging from it that constitute the greatest challenge to contemporary philosophy have their proximal origin in modern thought.

Merleau-Ponty's approach to the problems of ontological dualism is a phenomenological approach. Consequently, the antecedents of this tradition—notably Kant, Hegel, Husserl, Heidegger and Sartre—must also be considered, if only to see how radically Merleau-Ponty departs from the conception of phenomena that has developed through these thinkers. The task he undertakes is to liberate phenomena from their traditional restriction to the sphere of immanence, to restore their transcendence, and thereby to lift the curse of mereness from appearance and return to human opinion the measure of truth it has earned. That task, variously conceived, was also the task of the thinkers just named. The thesis to be defended in these pages is that Merleau-Ponty's thinking differs from theirs to the extent that he succeeds in overcoming the problems that kept them from fulfilling the task.

There is some truth, I think, to the proposition that no genuinely philosophical task ever reaches completion. But that pious homily can also lead to the comfortizing falsity that philosophical tasks should be undertaken only for the sake of exercise, and that the choice among emergent solutions rests finally on personal aesthetics, vogue, and the disposition of one's humors. If that is false, then there must be something that is true.

With this thought, I arrive at the second of the premises mentioned above, the premise of truth, the premise I promised by implication to defend. How? The simple *reductio* on the contrary should, I think, suffice: the proposition that there is no truth self-destructs. As we are constantly reminded these days, however, the premise itself begs its own implicit question: it can be accepted only on the grounds that it posits for itself. One is therefore faced with a choice between a self-defeating pessimism and a self-affirming optimism.

This should not be construed as my defense; it is merely a reflection—on the question of a defense. I shall spend no more time defending truth in general, but move quickly on to defend the specific truths I purport to find in Merleau-Ponty's ontology. At the end of the book, the question of truth arises again. That is the appropriate point for the reader to decide whether the specific case succeeds in establishing the general point. For the moment, I beg indulgence for my optimism.

On it rests the claim I seek to make on behalf of Merleau-Ponty's ontology, the claim that it takes the step whose eidetic necessity will be apparent to posterity. Merleau-Ponty's ontology marks a point of culmination in the development of Western thought which, in turn, establishes the conditions for its own surpassing. If this claim is valid, the ontology articulated by Merleau-Ponty constitutes a phase through which Western thought must pass if it is to progress. It is a matter of chance (which I hope here to influence) whether future historians attribute to Merleau-Ponty or to some currently unknown philosophical clone writing in another idiom the unplugging of the flow of Western thought. The plug is dualism. It has to come out. Merleau-Ponty shows us how.

If this is not generally apparent today, perhaps that is because we have been led to confuse ontology with theology. It is, I agree, a truth of philosophical history that ontology has been grounded in theology. Truth requires a ground: if one seeks an ultimate ground, then ultimately, it would seem, one must fetch up with an ultimate, an absolute. And there are good reasons (grounds) for rejecting absolutes. But the argument that proceeds from the rejection of all absolutes to the rejection of all grounds (and hence all truths) is specious. There are finite grounds, finite truths. It is on the finite ground on which we stand that we must base the truth we need in order to live as long and as well as we do.

A metaphysical inversion has taken place in our time. We who have read Nietzsche have been forewarned; we should have known better. But we have misread Nietzsche—and done him the disservice of invoking his name in the perpetration of the inversion. We seek a ground and find God. Thus the god of philosophy, whose name is *causa sui*, becomes the symbol of the ground, the final guarantor of truth. The ground of truth becomes the province of the absolute. Here is the inversion: God implies ground. Reject god, reject grounds. This is a misuse of *modus tollens*, and not at all what Nietzsche taught. He taught that the godhead is grounded: grounded in human need, human frailty. Recognition of this tolls the knell of god's death. The death throes of the godhead are grounded in the recognition of that truth. But that which gave rise to the birth and death of god did not come into being with god, nor does it pass away with his demise. The ground and our need for it, the birthplace and grave of all godheads, transcends all the symbols it has evoked. One does not need a god to stand on this earth, this ground. That is what Nietzsche taught us. He taught us to be true to this earth.

Nietzsche also taught us to be suspicious of all grounds, especially when they exude the noxious breath of a spirit divorced from its body. I suspect that Nietzsche's nose would twitch at the aroma of the new spirit substance, the new *causa sui*: language detached from both breath and body. But again I encroach on a complex topic that properly belongs where it is to be found: at the end of the book.

Be suspicious of grounds, to be sure, and equally suspicious of proclamations of truth. That suspicion is the ground of the agon of philosophical dialogue, that without which philosophy becomes religion, cant, ideology. But there is an abyss between suspicion of grounds and apriori proclamation of their absence. One may, through default of will, become void of purpose when the godhead, as presumptive source of purpose, defaults; and then, through the inversion of *ressentiment*, take the void as one's purpose. But that is what Nietzsche argued against.

Theology is ontology that has tried, failed, and been tried. But the search for grounds must not be thrown out with the godwater. Pure spirit has failed of purpose. That being the case, we may desist from the mortification of the flesh. Inner worlds have turned out to be as barren as afterworlds; it is time to take stock of this world.

Body. Flesh. World. Body as flesh of the world. These are the terms of Merleau-Ponty's ontology, to which we may now turn to test its truth.

Acknowledgments

This book has been nearly twenty years in the writing. It has grown and shrunk through three major revisions and innumerable modifications. In the course of its gestation, it has passed beneath more gracious and critical eyes than I am able to identify here. The debts I have incurred to teachers and students, friends and family, adversaries, authors, colleagues, typists, librarians, computer wizards, institutions, and editors cannot be described, much less discharged, in these few words, no matter how they are wrought. It does not suffice to name names and say that I am deeply grateful—and fearful of the inevitable and unforgivable omissions—but that is what I shall do.

Karsten Harries guided me through the beginning (hence most difficult) phases of the first draft.

The Foundation of the State University of New York supported my research with four generous grants.

My colleagues in the Department of Philosophy of the State University of New York at Binghamton spurred me in various ways through moments of sloth.

The members of The Merleau-Ponty Circle have renewed me annually for a decade.

And each of the persons named below has touched the manuscript and left a bright mark on it: W. W. Bartley, III, Tom Blake, Irene Byrnes, Susan Cabral, Edward Casey, Jeanne Constable, J. B. Dillon, James Edie, Lisa Fegley-Schmidt, Gloria Gaumer, Amadeo Giorgi, Leon Goldstein, Mary Jane Gormley, Paul Hopper, Jeffrey King, Alphonso Lingis, Glen Mazis, Celia Menard, Parviz Morewedge, Maurice Natanson, Dorothea Olkowski, John O'Neill, Harrison Pemberton, Deborah Pizante, Anthony Preus, Janet Rabinowitch, Elbridge Rand, Emilio Roma, Stephen Ross, Dennis Schmidt, George Schrader, Hugh Silverman, Linda Singer, Lisa Stafford, Kenneth Steiner, Donald Weiss, Rulon Wells, John Wild, Allan Zuckoff, Cheryl Zwart.

Since all philosophizing is limited by the sedimented *Weltanschauung* in the sustenance of which we are all complicit, the responsibility for whatever flaws persist here must be shared in some measure by all of us.

Abbreviations

BN	Sartre, *Being and Nothingness*
BN-F	Sartre, *L'être et le néant*
CAL	Merleau-Ponty, *Consciousness and the Acquisition of Language*
CM	Husserl, *Cartesian Meditations*
CRO	Merleau-Ponty, "The Child's Relations with Others"
EM	Merleau-Ponty, "Eye and Mind"
EM-F	Merleau-Ponty, *L'Œil et l'esprit*
IM	Heidegger, *An Introduction to Metaphysics*
PL	Husserl, *The Paris Lectures*
PP	Merleau-Ponty, *Phenomenology of Perception*
PP-F	Merleau-Ponty, *Phénoménologie de la perception*
PriP	Merleau-Ponty, *The Primacy of Perception*
PW	Merleau-Ponty, *The Prose of the World*
PW-F	Merleau-Ponty, *La Prose du monde*
PWD	Haldane and Ross (ed. and trans.), *The Philosophical Works of Descartes*
S	Merleau-Ponty, *Signs*
S-F	Merleau-Ponty, *Signes*
SB	Merleau-Ponty, *The Structure of Behavior*
SB-F	Merleau-Ponty, *La Structure du comportement*
SNS	Merleau-Ponty, *Sense and Non-Sense*
SNS-F	Merleau-Ponty, *Sens et non-sens*
VI	Merleau-Ponty, *The Visible and the Invisible*
VI-F	Merleau-Ponty, *Le Visible et l'invisible*

MERLEAU-PONTY'S
ONTOLOGY

Introduction

The Problem

Meno: But how will you look for something when you don't in the least know what it is? How on earth are you going to set up something you don't know as the object of your search? To put it another way, even if you come right up against it, how will you know that what you have found is the thing you didn't know?

Socrates: I know what you mean. Do you realize that what you are bringing up is the trick argument that a man cannot try to discover either what he knows or what he does not know? He would not seek what he knows, for since he knows it there is not need of the inquiry, nor what he does not know, for in that case he does not even know what he is to look for.

Meno: Well, do you think it is a good argument?

Socrates: No.

(*Meno*, 80d3–e5)

Merleau-Ponty: Empiricism cannot see that we need to know what we are looking for, otherwise we would not be looking for it, and intellectualism fails to see that we need to be ignorant of what we are looking for, or equally again we should not be searching.

(PP 28; PP-F 36)[1]

Meno's trick argument derives its persuasive force from the common-sense appeal of its underlying premise: either we know something or we are ignorant of it. On the surface, this statement appears to be a straightforward instance of the law of contradiction: either we know X or we do not know X. If this premise is taken to be true, the rest of Meno's argument follows: if we know X, we need not inquire about it; if we do not know X, we cannot inquire about it since we would not know what to look for and could not recognize it even if we were confronted by it. Given this either/or stance with respect to the objects of knowledge, inquiry must be regarded as necessarily futile, an impossible undertaking.

Insofar as philosophy itself depends on the possibility of inquiry, it is incumbent upon Socrates to refute Meno's argument. In order to refute it, Socrates must deny the truth of the premise; that is, he must argue that the either/or asserted by Meno is actually a both/and. That there is a sense in which we both know an object of inquiry and are ignorant of it is the point of the doctrine of anamnesis which Socrates propounds in answering Meno's trick argument. Our cognitive posture with respect to an object of inquiry involves both the prescience of it with which we were born and the ignorance of it (caused by forgetting at birth) which inquiry seeks to dispel.

The mythical trappings which seem to enshroud the doctrine of recollection wherever it appears in the Platonic dialogues have obscured the necessity for including it, or something like it, in any epistemology. Any theory of knowledge which fails to make provision for imperfect knowledge of a thing (i.e., knowing it and not knowing it, having a knowledge of it that is less than perfect) will fall prey to Meno's argument; hence it will not be able to allow for the possibility of inquiry. Moreover, an epistemology that does not include a 'sort of knowing' which, like Plato's anamnesis, permits both knowledge of and ignorance of an object, will be lacking in an even more fundamental respect: it will have to deny the evident fact that there is some degree of opacity attending all objects of human knowledge.

Merleau-Ponty shares with Plato the realization that some account must be given of imperfect knowledge; they agree that something like the doctrine of recollection must form an integral part of any successful theory of knowledge. It is one thing, however, to realize that an explanation of how we 'sort of know' must be given, but it is quite another to deliver that explanation. Here Merleau-Ponty and Plato diverge: where Plato offers a myth-like explanation involving metempsychosis, Merleau-Ponty provides a phenomenological account in terms of prereflective experience. A critical examination of this account will appear in the course of this work.

The problem nexus brought to light by Meno's argument is not confined within the sphere of epistemology. Problems of knowing are at the same time problems of being. To give an account of what it is to know necessarily involves some reference to the nature of what there is to be known. To presuppose, as Meno does, that something can be known so perfectly that there is no need for further inquiry about it is to assume that the nature of that something is such as to allow complete revelation. The intrinsic correlation of knowing and being is even more evident in the case of the second of Meno's two alternatives: the total absence of knowledge with regard to some object. Discourse about things of which one is totally ignorant may be meaningful in some contexts, but paradoxes lie in wait for the unwary. We may talk of being as though it were independent of human cognition, but as soon as we invest being with positive significance (for example, being there, being thus), the content of our speech is already conditioned by factors governing cognition. Insofar as our assertions are to be grounded assertions, it must be possible to know what our assertions purport to know. That is, being, insofar as it is known, must be such as to permit of being known. Put another way, speculative thought about a domain lying utterly beyond the sphere of possible cognition is at most analogical: it describes the humanly unknowable by means of figures and symbols drawn from the sphere of human experience. Such discourse is inherently paradoxical (it speaks about the unspeakable) and must abandon any claim to grounded philosophical truth. Yet it is also a mistake to circumscribe being within the parameters of human cognition: such Protagorean presumption is forgetful of its own finitude and wilfully neglects the reality of the unknown that obtrudes itself daily.

If Meno's argument leads us, with Plato, to the thought of an imperfect kind of knowing in order to resolve the epistemological problems at hand, it might also lead us, with Merleau-Ponty, to parallel thoughts along ontological lines. The thrust of Socrates' response to the dilemma posed by Meno is that philosophical inquiry is indeed a valid and meaningful activity because it is undertaken from an initial posture of imperfect knowledge. The thrust of the dialogue as a whole is that inquiry, the philosophical search for knowledge, is an activity that is sustained throughout life: Socratic ignorance is neither a mere pedagogical device nor a form of false modesty nor an admission by Socrates that he really knows nothing of ἀρετή or virtue, the theme of the dialogue. Socratic ignorance is, rather, an expression of the belief that the ceaseless striving for understanding portrayed in the figure of Socrates instantiates, itself, the human excellence or virtue under discussion. In professing ignorance, Socrates is professing his finitude or his humanity; in the endless search to know, he is exemplifying ἀρετή: the ideal way for man to respond to his finitude.

Granting the epistemological-theoretical and moral-practical points in the dialogue, what are their ontological implications? Given that the quest for knowledge is never-ending and that that ceaseless inquiry presupposes that we remain forever in a state of imperfection with respect to knowing, is it also the case that being betrays something of that imperfection as well? It may be that I depart from Plato here: certainly in the *Phaedo* (80a9–b8) and the *Republic* (478b–d9) the real is defined in terms of perfection (stasis, permanence, completion) and the imperfect realm of becoming is regarded as illusory, less than real. I risk loss of an ally, however, in hopes of making a point. Human reality, the only reality to which we have access as finite beings, is the correlate of human knowledge: what *is* for us is such as to admit of continuous unfolding, continual discovery. If the world of becoming, as the correlate of our imperfect knowledge, were indeed a veil of illusion hiding an immutable realm of being beneath it, then Meno has won the day, we remain in the darkness of total ignorance, and inquiry is futile.

As phenomenologist, existentialist, and psychologist, Merleau-Ponty belongs to a tradition in which an acute awareness of problems arising out of human finitude is a dominant feature. The "enigmas of subjectivity" which occupied the center of Husserl's later writing formed an essential part of Merleau-Ponty's philosophical legacy. Consequently, he too ponders over the "thesis of subjectivity"—what *is* (or being) for man is and can only be what is known by man[2]—and, although his understanding of the correlation of being and knowing differs from Husserl's, his appreciation of that correlation is just as intense and his treatment of the issues relating to it just as thematic as that of his predecessor. Hence, for Merleau-Ponty, epistemological problems are never treated as only that; rather he tends programmatically to search for resolution by looking for the ontological presuppositions underlying the standpoints within which such problems crop up. Accordingly, in this exposition of Merleau-Ponty's ontology, clarification of his understanding of the correlation of being and knowing will be a central concern.

Ontology, the search for the logos or meaning of things, acquires a significance for transcendental philosophy (hence for phenomenology) which is not thematically evident in pre-critical philosophy: although the epistemological subject has never been entirely absent from reflections on the nature of being, the transcendental turn in philosophy intensified reflexivity and brought the thinker to a new awareness of his own role in the constitution of his world. The radical demarcation between internal and external reality, present in philosophy before Descartes but seldom absent from it after him, began to erode with Kant and has been subjected to increasingly critical attention ever since: as what I experience "out there" became more and more closely associated with the cognitive processes going on "in here," the "natural" understanding of being as a continuum of things in themselves began to give way to transcendental reflection, and the thought of being in itself could no longer be taken for granted in a naive way. For the first time, the phenomenon began to assume positive importance (against the predominantly negative connotation it traditionally had as something less than real), and the mere-ness of appearance, the essentially negative definition of appearance in contrast to reality, began seriously to be questioned. In short, it became increasingly viable to accord to phenomena some kind of positive ontological status.

What is it that one refers to when speaking of the phenomenon? There are a number of meanings associated with the term, as Heidegger points out in his discussion of it in *Being and Time*.[3] It is also evident in that discussion that, although the distinctions separating the various meanings may at the start be so subtle as to depend upon a nuance, the implications of those differences are far-reaching. If phenomenology is to provide the logos of phenomena, it would be well to clarify what is meant by 'phenomenon.' And that endeavor leads into the sphere of ontology because one of the points of confusion is that of the relation between the phenomenal and the real.

The reflections upon the thesis of subjectivity, in all its manifold variations, which have been conducted under the heading of transcendental philosophy have led, as remarked, to an increasingly positive understanding of phenomena: that is, since Kant (at least), phenomena have been accorded more and more reality—in various senses of the word 'real.' At the same time, however, these reflections have led to an increasing awareness of human finitude: an awareness of the extent to which man is limited to a circumscribed perspective. Thus a tension is created between the phenomenon as the real (and, as such, transcending man's limited perspective upon reality) and the phenomenon as the object of human experience (and, as such, constituting an immanent reality commensurate with man's finite cognitive powers). Merleau-Ponty was among those who realized that phenomenology, if it is to free itself of naiveté in the matter of its own foundation, must deal with this tension in a thematic way and attempt to provide a sound and consistent understanding of its own subject matter. Hence, like Husserl, Heidegger, and Sartre before him, Merleau-Ponty was drawn into ontology.

In two works already mentioned here, Heidegger's *Being and Time* and Husserl's *The Crisis of European Sciences and Transcendental Phenomenology*, there is evidence of a deep appreciation of the influence of past thought upon present thinking. Both Heidegger and Husserl stress the need to understand the historical antecedents of one's own philosophical milieu. The complex of problems devolving onto twentieth-century philosophy has its ground in a tradition: to the extent that we inherit problems, to that extent we have also inherited the ways of thinking about the world, failures as well as insights, that gave rise to those problems and made the world problematic in those ways. Just as Merleau-Ponty was led by his mentors into the sphere of ontology, so also did they lead him into an appreciation of the need to ground his approach to the problem of ontology in a thoroughgoing critique of the tradition into which he was born and in whose terms he began to think.

The tension underlying the problems confronting phenomenology's attempt to define its subject matter and establish its own ontological foundations—the tension between regarding phenomena as transcendent reality and regarding the phenomenal order as an immanent reality—has its proximal ground in the Cartesian dualism which is, perhaps, tradition's strongest mark on the twentieth century. The antecedents of the radical bifurcation of reality into disparate orders of being, the immanent and the transcendent, certainly stretch back further than Descartes; however, insofar as the era of modern philosophy is taken to begin with Descartes, it is because he marks the point at which the bifurcation in question became the dominant focus for philosophical thought. Accordingly, one finds Merleau-Ponty again following the example of Husserl and his successors, and undertaking a critical reprise of Cartesian thought as an integral part of the development of his own.

Merleau-Ponty's critique of Descartes, and of Cartesianism as it survives in more contemporary philosophy, led him to isolate two strains of Cartesian thought, empiricism and intellectualism, which seem at present to dominate the philosophical climate. Although these two standpoints tend to be antagonistic, even mutually exclusive inasmuch as each defines itself in contradistinction to the other, they share the common Cartesian heritage and can both be explicated in terms of it. Both are products of Cartesian dualism, in Merleau-Ponty's assessment, because the attempt (on the part of empiricism) to find a ground in the transcendent order shares the same foundation as the endeavor (on the part of intellectualism) to bring all issues to rest in the immanent order—in both cases, a bifurcation of reality is presupposed.

Now we have before us the elements constituting the basic structure of this work. There is the problem, posed by Meno, of explaining how it is that the object of philosophical inquiry is both known and unknown to the finite inquirer. As part of the attempt to resolve this problem, there is the task of working out the relations of knowing and being in such a way that the ontological implications of the epistemological resolution are brought into critical focus. As already suggested in these preliminary remarks, however, the problem of relating knowing and being points to the place of their putative intersection, phenomena. Yet so long as 'phenomenon' remains a naive concept, it cannot illumine the ontological-epistemological problematic.

Merleau-Ponty's ontology provides an explication of phenomena in the light of which phenomenology can understand itself—without being naive or dogmatic—as inquiry whose subject matter is the real. The attempt to purge itself of naive and dogmatic assumptions is implemented by means of developing a critical-historical self-awareness. I begin, then, with an analysis of Descartes's fundamental presuppositions and the contemporary standpoints into which these presuppositions have evolved. My endeavor here is to show, in support of Merleau-Ponty's claim quoted at the beginning of this chapter, why empiricism and intellectualism fail to provide a satisfactory basis for resolving Meno's dilemma.

To approach Merleau-Ponty in this way, that is, in the historical context out of which arise the problems to which his own thought is a response, is to coincide in practice with his theoretical assertion that philosophical themes are to be understood against the background of the settings from which they emerge. To set forth an answer in isolation from the questions to which it replies is necessarily to lose much of its relevance and risk distortion of its intent.

Finally, there is another reason for beginning a study of Merleau-Ponty with an analysis of the Cartesian heritage. If Western science, philosophy, and culture are indeed facing the crisis of which Husserl wrote, and if the inadequacy of contemporary philosophy to provide resolution to the life problems now confronting us is responsible for this crisis, then the call is clear: an alternative is needed—a philosophy aware of the mistaken presuppositions which, perpetuated by tradition, have misled our thinking and circumscribed our efforts. If Merleau-Ponty offers that alternative, and I hope to show that he does, then it is important to see it as an alternative generated in response to a certain understanding of its philosophical antecedents. Thus it is necessary to explicate Merleau-Ponty's critical assessment of Cartesianism, old and new, in order to appreciate the view he had of the scope and nature of his task.

Part One

Antecedents and Consequences

ONE

The Cartesian Origins of Empiricism and Intellectualism

1. THE QUEST FOR CERTAINTY AND CARTESIAN METHODOLOGY

There is need of a method for finding out the truth.

(Rule IV, PWD 9)[1]

Reflect, for a moment, on inquiry as the search for truth, the project that defines philosophical man. From the fact that we do have to inquire, we learn of our limitations. We are encompassed by a world that is alien inasmuch as it is unknown and lacking in transparency. Inquiry involves the possibility of error: our propensity to misunderstand our world sets it apart as something different from us. Moreover, even the self is in many respects unknown and alien to itself: we are often confused and dismayed by our ignorance of our own motives and actions. To the extent that we inquire, we acknowledge that world and self, as objects of inquiry, transcend us; we seek to penetrate their opacity, to overcome the world's otherness and our own self-estrangement.

The distinction between appearance and reality, the contrast between the world as it appears to us and the world as it really is in itself, is as old as inquiry itself, and it gives rise to a kind of skepticism which is not much younger. How do we know that what appears to be the case really is the case? Sometimes we err: how do we know that we are not always in error? Lacking the means to distinguish erroneous appearances from veridical ones, skepticism can become rampant and provoke a distrust of all appearances. Reaction to this distrust can—and, in the case of Descartes, did—lead to a quest for certainty: a search for criteria by means of which to determine when we err and when we are in the truth.[2]

The search for truth differs from the search for truth criteria in more ways than those that are immediately obvious. To assert that a statement is true usually suggests that one has some more or less adequate reasons for believing that what is asserted is indeed the case. Ultimately and inevitably it must be left to the critical judgment of the reader or hearer to determine whether (or to what degree) those reasons are adequate or compelling. There need be no explicit prior stipulation about what shall constitute adequate grounds for asserting a statement as a true statement. Furthermore, since the statements in which these truth criteria are set forth may themselves be queried, it is difficult to understand how such stipulations could be rigorously demanded: the specter of infinite regress would seem to haunt those who pursue the demand for explicit truth criteria.

Still, if it were the case that truth criteria could be generated such that to satisfy them would suffice to ground a statement as true, then statements known to meet these criteria would be known with certainty to be true; no future evidence could falsify such statements or create a need to revise them.

The search for truth is an attempt to pierce the opacity of the world, an effort to make our conjectures about the world as accurate as possible. The quest for certainty, on the other hand, is an attempt to eliminate the opacity of the world altogether and make it entirely transparent; an essay to expel all conjecture or supposition from our knowledge. These two endeavors differ and must be kept distinct.

Inquiry or the search for truth presupposes that its objects will always remain to some degree opaque and that error is an ever-present possibility, although both the opacity and the risk of error diminish as we succeed in corroborating our conjectures with more and better evidence. In order to achieve certainty, however, all chance of error and, hence, all opacity must be eradicated completely.

Descartes's rule "to trust only what is completely known and incapable of being doubted" is, therefore, part of a method which is motivated and sustained more by a quest for certainty than by a search for truth. But what criteria will enable us to identify the indubitable? What are the conditions under which we can be certain of our knowledge?

Descartes explicates the conditions for certainty in terms of an absence of the cause of error. The causes of error are poor comprehension of experience and groundless assertions.[3] The responsibility for error lies totally with man: the world does not deceive us; we deceive ourselves about the world. Man is the being that deceives itself. However, if there were a way to avoid miscomprehending experience and making groundless assertions, we could eliminate error by eliminating the causes of self-deception.

Descartes attributes miscomprehension to confusion and confusion to complexity. That is, we fail to comprehend experience because our judgments or propositions about it fuse together, into a complex whole, elements which should be kept separate. Descartes's method, then, requires us to "reduce involved and obscure propositions step by step to those that are simpler, and then starting with the intuitive apprehension of all those that are absolutely simple, attempt to ascend to the knowledge of all others . . ." (Rule V, PWD 14). The irreducible elements of experience, simple intuitions, are not of our making; they are given to us. The possibility of error arises only when we tamper with the given and allow ourselves to combine simple intuitions into complex thoughts or images. Merely by examining a complex image we cannot determine whether the elements constituting it were given to us combined in that way or the combination was the product of our imagination. Thus complex images may be true or false representations and, hence, are subject to doubt.

The simplicity of simple intuitions, however, guarantees that there has been no combination at all, be it given and legitimate or constructed and illegitimate. Error is eliminated by avoiding its prime cause: man cannot deceive himself about the world if he refuses to give credence to anything which might be a construct of his imagination.

Descartes distinguishes imagination and understanding. Imagination is a faculty which either actively works upon or passively receives the images of sense perception.[4] The understanding performs two functions: "self-evident intuition and necessary deduction" (Rule XII, PWD 45). The first includes intuition of simples: given their simplicity, the "least acquaintance" with them ensures exhaustive knowledge of them. The second concerns the "necessary connections" which obtain among simples, for example, that "figure is [necessarily] conjoined with extension, motion with duration," etc. (Rule XII, PWD 42).

Now, "the understanding is . . . alone capable of perceiving the truth," but it can be aided by imagination (Rule XII, PWD 35); or imagination can mislead with its "blundering constructions" (Rule II, PWD 7). Imagination assists understanding by passively entertaining the data, the images, which derive from the senses; it misleads when it acts upon these data and combines their elements in ways that differ from the configuration originally presented to the senses.

The problem that besets Descartes—and, as will be seen, confounds neo-Cartesian dualism to this day—is that it is impossible to determine, merely by examining a complex image, whether the elements constituting it were given to the senses combined in just that way or whether the image was altered in some way by an act of imagination. Since, according to the representational theory of perception operative here, our only access to the transcendent world of things is mediated through these images, we cannot compare the image with the reality it purports to represent. Hence, the possibility of illusion always attends judgments about the world based on sense perception.

In the *Rules* Descartes attempts to avoid this problem by altering the conceptual framework which engenders it. By placing the testimony of the senses in abeyance and restricting our understanding to what is given, "just as it is given," he refuses to make any knowledge claim about "the objects themselves."[5] Cognition is to be based on representations alone: no reference is to be made, nor is any relation to be asserted, to anything they might represent; whereupon Descartes resolves to "treat of things only in relation to our understanding's awareness of them" (Rule XII, PWD 40–

41). But then it follows that we cannot construe that of which our understanding is aware as representational: to regard a mental image as a representation is necessarily to think of it in terms of its relation to something other than our understanding's awareness of it, that is, in terms of the thing it purports to represent. Hence it is valid to conclude that we cannot regard a mental image as a *true* image as long as truth is taken to be correspondence of image and object.

Does this conclusion remain valid when Descartes turns from the analytic movement (that is, the reduction to simple natures) to the synthetic (that is, the formation of complexes based on "deduction" or necessary principles of inference)?

Descartes conceives necessity in terms of analyticity: two simple natures are necessarily connected if the concept of one is implied in the concept of another such that "we cannot conceive either distinctly." "Thus," he says, "figure is conjoined with extension . . . because it is impossible to conceive of a figure that has no extension" (Rule XII, PWD 42).

Descartes's narrow delimitation of knowledge in the *Rules* to simple natures and the necessary connections obtaining among them (Rule XII, PWD 3) renders it impossible to make any knowledge claim about contingent matters of fact. What I can know about the world is reduced to a series of tautologies. If Descartes were thoroughly consistent—if he adhered to his own restriction to "treat of things only in relation to our understanding's awareness of them"—he could not allow himself to claim that, independent of his thought, there exists a thing which has figure and extension.

In a word, Descartes's analytic movement results in an irrevocable restriction to the sphere of immanence. And this, in turn, creates an ontological ambivalence in his work: the transcendent world whose opacity generates error is banished from consideration in the reduction to immanence undertaken to eliminate the possibility of error. The ontology that initiates Descartes's methodology must be abandoned in the process of applying his method. The criterion of clarity restricts the cognitive domain to intuitions which are utterly transparent; hence error is eliminated, but at the expense of the reference to transcendence required for truth. Clarity puts an end to inquiry. The rejection of "merely probable knowledge" puts Descartes in league with Meno: either we know something apodictically, or we relegate it to oblivion. Thus the philosopher may speak with absolute assurance, but not about the world.

In the *Rules*, Descartes's quest culminates in locating the ground of certainty in simple natures, in adopting the standpoint of logical atomism. On this point, however, Descartes confronts a dilemma. If he restricts his cognitive claims to those grounded on the simplicity of atoms, he is reduced to silence: no non-analytic predicate can be assigned to an atom without corrupting its simplicity. If he lifts the restriction, he risks the possibility of error. Underlying this problem is the fact that atoms are logical constructs, creatures of analytic thought.[6] Without some acceptable means of correlating these immanent constructs with a transcendent reality, they remain barren, thoughts about nothing.

Later, in the *Meditations*, Descartes tries to rectify this situation. That is, he tries to find grounds for asserting a correlation between thought, sensation, and "external" reality. Here the goal is to provide thought with the referent which is needed if truth is to have a place in his system; he attempts to achieve this goal, however, without sacrificing the certainty that was the end of his initial quest.

2. DESCARTES AND THE ORIGINS OF MODERN REDUCTIONISM

The principle error and the commonest which we may meet with . . . , consists in my judging that the ideas which are in me are similar or conformable to the things which are outside me. . . .

(Med. III, PWD 160)[7]

In the *Meditations*, Descartes does not forsake the quest for certainty, nor does he abandon his overall strategy: here, as in the *Rules*, he tries to achieve certainty by identifying and eliminating the causes of error. The remaining half of the sentence quoted above harks back to the tactics employed in the *Rules*: ". . . for without doubt if I considered the ideas only as certain modes of my thoughts, without trying to relate them to anything beyond, they could scarcely give me material for error" (Med. III, PWD 160). But, in the *Meditations*, he refuses to "treat of things only in relation to our understanding's awareness of them." Instead, he tries to find a solution to the problem of error by means of a causal analysis of knowledge and perception.[8]

The argument of the *Meditations* opens with a distrust of appearances. That familiar Cartesian theme, which crops up whenever truth is taken to be correspondence of immanent appearance and transcendent reality, is expanded into radical doubt: my senses may deceive me at any time, therefore I shall bracket all evidence derived from them. Then the evil genius is invoked to produce a metaphysical kind of doubting: the demon may deceive me even about the data of intellectual intuition, which include among them the truths of arithmetic and geometry; therefore they too must be bracketed. The possibility that I may be deceived in my intuition of simple natures, that for some reason an idea does not resemble its cause, is expressed in the hypothesis of the evil genius.

It is within this carefully constructed context that Descartes delivers the stroke that altered the course of Western philosophy. Is there a truth which cannot be doubted—for any reason whatever, including the hyperbolic hypothesis of a deceiving divinity? If there is, an analysis of it will reveal the conditions governing its certainty, and those conditions can then be used as criteria to test the certainty of other putative truths. That indubitable truth is, of course, the cogito.[9]

The cogito has already appeared in the *Rules* (Rule III, PWD 7) where it functions as a paradigm of a fact known by intuition whose truth is grounded on its simplicity. In the *Rules*, however, the cogito has the same status as other intuitively grasped simples, such as the truths of geometry, and they have been bracketed in the *Meditations*. Hence, although the cogito remains a simple nature, that no longer suffices to ground its certainty. In the *Meditations*, the cogito exemplifies a criterion for certainty which goes beyond mere simplicity. To explicate this criterion, however, some supporting concepts must first be set forth.

In the *Rules*, Descartes's doctrine of simple natures was insufficient, in itself, to provide an adequate ground for certain knowledge: it had to be supplemented with a rule prohibiting us from asserting "that external things always are as they appear to be" (Rule XII, PWD 44). The need for this rule grew out of Descartes's realization that, although their simplicity precludes the possibility that simple natures might be the products of our imagination, still there is no assurance that that which causes them must resemble them; for example, the thing that causes me to see red may not itself be red.

In the *Meditations*, Descartes contrasts ideas with the causes of ideas in the following way: "Just as [the] mode of *objective* existence pertains to ideas by their proper nature, so does the mode of formal existence pertain to the causes of those ideas ... by the nature peculiar to them" (Med. III, PWD 163). What an idea represents objectively as real may not be formally real; the thing as represented has objective existence, but there may be no thing corresponding to it which exists formally. His refusal to bracket formal reality, as he did in the *Rules*, makes it incumbent upon Descartes to find something such that, if it is objectively real, it must also be formally real.[10]

Most simple natures fail to satisfy this condition (whence the need for rule mentioned above). The cogito, however, does satisfy it. In reflecting upon itself, thought grasps the apodictic truth: I exist. Here objective and formal reality coincide, thus providing at least one certainty which withstands the metaphysical doubt imposed by the demon. Descartes tries to use this coincidence of objective and formal reality as the basis for a general criterion of certainty.[11] That is, Descartes claims that the coincidence of objective and formal reality in the case of the perception "I am, I exist" is guaranteed by its clarity and distinctness; he then makes the general claim that this coincidence must obtain in the case of every perception which is clear and distinct.

The argument, however, does not hold. If clarity and distinctness were indeed sufficient to assure the certainty of our ideas, that is, that these objectively real ideas correspond to formally real things, then there would be no reason to begin with the cogito rather than with any other clear and distinct idea. The indubitability of the cogito must accordingly rest upon some other foundation.

Descartes must find another idea which meets his criterion of certainty, that is, coincidence of objective and formal reality, but which represents something other than himself.[12] Descartes's idea of God fulfills both conditions. Not only does its objective reality coincide with its formal reality (this being established by the ontological argument), but it refers to a transcendent object.

Descartes then goes on to deduce God's benevolence from the perfection intrinsic to his idea of God; and, since God's benevolence eliminates the hypothesis of a deceiving deity, he concludes that he no longer need labor under the restriction of metaphysical doubt: the truths of arithmetic and geometry regain their indubitability. With the lifting of metaphysical doubt, Descartes can again be certain of the truth of anything he knows as clearly and distinctly as he knows the truths of arithmetic and geometry. This leads to an attempt to ground the certainty of simple intuitions (which now appear under the rubric 'clear and distinct ideas') without bracketing transcendent objects or the external world, that is, without violating his original ontology.

This attempt fails. In showing how it fails I hope to spotlight structures of erroneous reasoning that recur in more recent philosophy (which, for that reason, I regard as neo-Cartesian).

Let me begin the critique by taking up the thesis of universal causation: the thesis that explanation consists in causal analysis. This thesis underlies Descartes's conviction that perception and knowledge are the products of causal processes. This belief rests, in turn, on a traditional assumption: *ex nihilo, nihil fit*—nothing comes from nothing; everything must have a cause (Med. III, PWD 162). According to Descartes, ideas, too, must have causes. An idea can be the proximate cause of another idea, but, ultimately, the chain of causes must originate in one of three possible sources: some formally real thing, the imagination, or God. These three exhaust all possibilities. If the formally existent thing is the ultimate cause of the idea, and if neither God nor the imagination intervenes, then the idea must be true, that is, it must correspond to some formally real thing which is its cause. The function of the divine guarantee is to eliminate the possibility that the cause of a clear and distinct idea might not correspond to the idea.[13]

But, by its activity, the imagination does introduce distortions, images of its own fabrication. How is this source of error to be neutralized? Descartes's strategy is to restrain the will, the faculty of judgment or assertion, within the bounds of the understanding, the faculty of clear and distinct perception.[14] That is, if one limits one's assertion of truth to those images perceived clearly and distinctly by the understanding, then one will not fall into error. The clarity and distinctness—that is, the simplicity—of an idea or image guarantees its truth by ensuring that the image is not the product of imagination. Imagination cannot create simple natures (*ex nihilo* . . .); it can only combine them into complex images.

Note, however, that clarity and distinctness can serve only to certify the veracity of our ideas of material things "insofar as they are considered as the objects of pure mathematics" (Med VI, PWD 185). In the *Rules*, Descartes refrained from asserting that simple natures exist apart from our understanding, but here, in the *Meditations*, he conceives them as formally real.

> We must allow that corporeal things exist. However, they are perhaps not exactly what we perceive by the senses, since their comprehension by the senses is in many instances very obscure and confused; but we must at least admit that all things which I conceive in them clearly and distinctly, that is to say, all things which, speaking generally, are comprehended in the object of pure mathematics, are truly to be recognized as external objects.
>
> (Med VI, PWD 191)

That is the thought that evolves into modern reductionism: the objects of science—the things we can truly know—are irreducible quanta which are the products of exhaustive analysis and which lend themselves to the precision of mathematical calculation and processing.

The question that must be put to reductionist analytic thought—both in the case of Descartes and with regard to his contemporary successors—is the question of the relation of these quanta to the reality of everyday mundane experience. They are, *prima facie*, different: the phenomena of ordinary perception are not at all like the objects of pure mathematics. Which has the greater claim to reality? This is one way of posing the central question addressed in this work, and it will take some time to formulate and defend my answer to it. At this stage, the task is to understand the radical nature of the question and its importance for contemporary thought: the question names the issue which separates the school of science-oriented analytic philosophy from the phenomenological movement.

Descartes defines the parameters of analytic philosophy.[15] Specifically, it is his methodology that transforms the epistemological requirement for simplicity into an ontological commitment (a) to constitute the ultimate reality in terms of simples and (b) to remove from serious consideration any aspect of the phenomenal world that cannot be reduced to and reconstructed from simples. This bracketing of recalcitrant aspects of transcendence is both (a) a reduction to immanence and (b) a tacit admission of failure to provide an account of the full range of human experience.

This is manifest in the last pages of the *Meditations* where Descartes asks himself about the extent to which he can give credence to those aspects of his perceptual experience which cannot be incorporated within his *mathesis universalis*. There he argues that nature—the order of things established by a benevolent God—is so arranged that, for the most part, we know enough about worldly things to recognize those which will hurt us and distinguish them from those which are salubrious; "but," he continues, "I do not see that beyond this [nature] teaches me that from those diverse sense-perceptions we should ever form any conclusion regarding things outside of us, without having . . . mentally examined them beforehand" (Med VI, PWD 193). Genuine knowledge is restricted to the reduced sphere of clear and distinct ideas, that is, to simples; and the opinions we have about the complex objects we perceive are subject to error, although they usually suffice to keep us from harm. Conclusion: philosophy, as a rigorous science, must refrain from making claims about the phenomenal world— except insofar as its objects lend themselves to quantification.

Several reductions have taken place in the foregoing account and it is important to note them since, as I shall argue, they have been incorporated into modern empiricism and intellectualism and have contributed significantly to the failures of these two standpoints.

(i) *The knower has been reduced to the role of a spectator.* In both the *Rules* and the *Meditations*, the causes of error have been traced to active faculties within the knower: the imagination and the will. In order to eliminate these causes of error, Cartesian method calls for passivity on the part of the knower. If he exerts no causal influence on the processes of perception and knowledge, then no distortions will occur in the reproductive mechanism that is his mind. *Passivity thus becomes a criterion for certainty in cognition.*

(ii) *Ideas have been reified.* This is a consequence of two related assumptions made by Descartes. The first of these is that everything is governed by causality: he acknowledges no other principle of motivation. Descartes does not exempt ideas from the assumption of universal causation: they, too, cannot spring up *ex nihilo*; they have to be caused by things or other ideas. Descartes regards the interaction of objects and ideas (or ideas and ideas) in the same way he regards that of objects and objects—the same principle of causation governs both. Thus ideas and objects (or things) are rendered homogeneous or, more accurately, ideas are tacitly modelled after things— at least insofar as both are taken to be entities existing within a unitary causal nexus.

The second assumption that leads Descartes to reify ideas is his belief that the ultimate constituents of thought are logical atoms (or the data of intuition or simple natures or clear and distinct ideas). The fact that he conceives certainty in terms of coincidence of (objectively real) clear and distinct ideas with (formally real) things attests to the point in question: ideas and things can be regarded as coincident by virtue of conceiving ideas as like unto things. Descartes speaks of complex ideas as though they were constructed of atomic ideas in the way in which complex things can be built up from simple things. To avoid the error of faulty construction, we must dismantle our ideas until we arrive at the ultimate parts; they are then taken to correspond exactly to the simple things which are their sole causes.

Hence under the reifying regard of Cartesian method, the atoms of thought are conceived as basic elements for consciousness in the same way that extended things are taken to be constituents of the physical world.

(iii) *The world has been reduced to an object for consciousness.* Although Descartes endeavored in the *Meditations* to avoid the bracketing of transcendent objects that he deemed necessary in the *Rules,* his method effectively prohibited success. The Cartesian method is designed to achieve certainty and it attempts to do this by rendering the objects of knowledge clear and distinct to the understanding. Not only the truths of arithmetic and geometry, but external things as well, insofar as they can be known, are to be reduced to clear and distinct ideas.

The thrust of Descartes's argument is to assert that only when I have a clear and distinct perception of it can I be certain that the object I sense corresponds in fact to a formally existing thing and is not the product of my imagination. This assertion can be expressed as a disjunction: either my senses provide me with a clear and distinct perception, in which case I can be certain that it corresponds to an external thing; or my sense perception is obscure and confused, in which case it may have been affected by my imagination and I cannot be certain that there is a formally existing thing corresponding to it. The consequence is manifest: we have knowledge of the external world only insofar as we have clear and distinct perceptions of it.

Clarity and distinctness, however, are incompatible with externality. What is external to me must, by that fact alone, transcend me in some degree: that is why we speak of it as given to me rather than created by me. But what is transcendent is, by definition, not fully known; it is attended by a modicum of opacity—that opacity being phenomenal evidence for its transcendence. Consequently, *insofar as Descartes has reduced the world to that which is known clearly and distinctly, he has denied its externality and transcendence: in short, he has reduced it to an object for consciousness.*

Descartes's attempt to provide a referent for the atoms of thought—but without forsaking the certainty accruing to thoughts by virtue of their simplicity—results in a conception of the world as a continuum of atoms: the ultimate constituents of reality are thus patterned after the ultimate constituents of thought. Descartes is left with two worlds, an inner (or immanent) world and an outer (or transcendent) world, in which the elements of one are identical to the elements of the other: this identity is necessary to allow for the possibility of the coincidence of objective and formal existence (in the case of clear and distinct perceptions) upon which Descartes rests his case for certainty. In the construction of these two worlds, however, Descartes has violated both: he has distorted the ideas of the inner world by reifying them; and he has distorted the things of the outer world by rendering them transparent (that is, depriving them of the opacity which is commensurate with their givenness). Here, once again, one can see how the method designed to fulfill Descartes's epistemological quest for certainty has resulted, through the reductions discussed above, in ontological assumptions which subvert the overall endeavor.

At the root of each of these three reductions is a bifurcation that is the chief feature of all Cartesian thought, present as well as past. In his attempt to achieve certainty by means of clarity and distinctness, Descartes drove an ontological wedge between the spheres of immanence and transcendence. Specifically, he tried to characterize the realm of the subject as a sphere of immanent thought which could be analyzed apart from the things to which that thought refers. Initially, Descartes placed worldly things in a transcendent sphere to which thought had no certain access: hence his move in the *Rules* to disregard such things altogether. There his governing thought was to confine knowledge to the sphere of immanence because he believed, first, that clarity and distinctness were the sole criteria for certainty; and second, that these criteria could be satisfied only within the immanent sphere.

In the *Meditations*, Descartes tried to retain the first, clarity and distinctness as criteria ensuring certainty, but at the same time to regain the reference to an external world necessary for a correspondence model of truth; thus he abandoned the second, the restriction to the sphere of immanence, and attempted to establish a correlation between idea and thing. Given his bifurcated ontology, however, the only correlation he could conceive was that of causality—a mechanical mediation between two mutually exclusive kinds of things, thought and extension. This correlation then required Descartes to reduce perception (and ultimately knowledge) to the status of being the product of a causal relation between things and ideas or between ideas and ideas. In this schema, truth must be regarded as a by-product of the causal influence of reified objects upon reified thoughts.

Once both thoughts and objects have been reduced to thing-like substances, however, they become homogeneous, and the distinction between immanence and transcendence is lost. This leaves Descartes in a dilemma, expressed as follows by Merleau-Ponty:

> When Descartes tells us that sensation reduced to itself is always true, and that error creeps in through the transcendent interpretation of it that judgment provides, he makes an unreal distinction. . . . The 'interpretation' of my sensations which I give must necessarily be motivated, and be so only in terms of the structure of those sensations, so that it can be said with equal validity either [a] that there is no transcendent interpretation and no judgment which does not spring from the very configuration of the phenomena—or [b] that there is no sphere of immanence, no realm in which my consciousness is fully at home and secure against all risk of error.
>
> (PP 376; PP-F 431)

Descartes, of course, in his passion for clarity and distinctness, opts for the first alternative [a] and reduces the world to an object for consciousness.

The consequences of the second alternative [b] would have been equally disastrous: Descartes's fundamental error lies in having made the bifurcation that gives rise to the dilemma.

The excerpt quoted from Merleau-Ponty may serve to relate Descartes's dilemma with Meno's and also to show how both may be avoided. To say that the significance I attribute to my sensations must be motivated is to acknowledge that there must be an element of givenness in perception, and that that givenness presupposes some transcendence of the thing which, in turn, betokens a degree of opacity: my knowledge of the thing can thus never be complete or perfect or clear and distinct. On the other hand, to say that the meaning content of my sensations must also be included within the structure of those sensations is to acknowledge that there must be some transparency in perception, and that presupposes a partial immanence on the part of the object, that is, an affinity between thought and its object: my cognitive posture with regard to the objects of experience can thus never be one of total ignorance or of complete obscurity and utter confusion.[16]

Both dilemmas may be avoided if an account of imperfect knowledge can be given: if, that is, one refuses to take up the either/or stance with regard to knowledge and ignorance that Descartes shares with Meno, and tries instead to show how the both/and position of Merleau-Ponty and Plato can be incorporated into an adequate ontology.

Before undertaking an explication of such an ontology, however, there remains a two-stage critical task: the Cartesian presuppositions tacitly at work within modern empiricism and intellectualism must be brought to light and then it must be shown how these presuppositions led modern thinkers into positions as untenable as those taken up by Descartes.

3. THE CARTESIAN ORIGINS OF EMPIRICISM

Empiricism may be defined—roughly and provisionally—as the philosophical standpoint based on the contention that all knowledge originates in experience. It is a matter of historical fact that Locke's *Essay Concerning Human Understanding* opens with and develops from an attack on the doctrine of innate ideas.[17] It is also historically and critically evident that empiricism tends to adopt a rather narrow interpretation of experience, confining it to perceptual (or, when this frequent distinction is made, to sensory) experience and excluding from consideration such (non-perceptual) forms of intuition associated with pure intellection as those which Descartes described as the "natural light of reason." Although this characterization clearly excludes Descartes from the ranks of empiricists (for the sufficient reason that he did not hold that the origin of all knowledge lies in sense experience) it will nonetheless become clear that empiricism is a variant form of the Cartesianism it seeks to criticize, undermine, and replace.

Empiricism espoused the Cartesian quest for certainty. At the beginning of his *Essay*, Locke declares his purpose to be "to search out the bonds between opinion and knowledge; and examine by what measures, in things whereof we have no certain knowledge, we ought to regulate our assent and moderate our persuasion" (*Essay*, Introduction, sect. 3). Locke's goal is identical to the one set for himself by Descartes: to find criteria by means of which we can demarcate what is true and known to be true (knowledge) from what may or may not be true (opinion) in order that human science might grow by seeking out the former and eschewing the latter.

In order to find truth criteria, empiricism attempts to find an unshakeable ground for knowledge in experience, and in its search for this ground turns to an atomism similar to Descartes's doctrine of simple natures. Not only do many of the Cartesian simples find themselves enumerated in Locke's list of simple ideas,[18] but the generic features of both types of atoms are nearly equivalent.[19]

Both Locke and Descartes stress the absolute inviolability of their atoms and attribute it to the passivity of the mind in cognizing them.[20] For the empiricists, as well as Descartes, error becomes a possibility only when the mind (specifically, the imagination) begins to work upon its contents. But the imagination can only combine ideas; it cannot create them.[21] Hence, the simplicity of the atoms of thought is adequate evidence that the imagination has remained passive; this simplicity thus eliminates that possibility of error. Here again the passive role of the knower in perception tends to reduce him to the status of a spectator. Hume, for instance, uses a telling metaphor: "the mind," he says, "is a kind of theatre, where several perceptions successively make their appearance. . . ."[22]

Empiricists such as Locke and Hume grounded the certainty of simple ideas on their psychogenetic ultimacy—an ultimacy akin to the causal primacy claimed by Descartes in the *Meditations* for the atoms of experience. And that is why Locke felt certain "that the ideas of primary qualities of bodies are resemblances of them, and their patterns do really exist in the bodies themselves . . . " (*Essay*, II, VII, 15). And Hume, abandoning Locke's naive realism for his own phenomenalism—a shift that will be examined shortly—believed it to be certain that all our simple ideas in their first appearance are derived from simple impressions, which are correspondent to them, and which they exactly represent" (*Treatise*, I, I, 1, 4).

Thus the British Empiricists, the Logical Positivists, and most of the sense-data theorists stressed genetic analysis: only if the elements constitutive of an object are traceable to origins in sensation can that object be granted a place in veridical experience. The various statements of the principle of verification, all of which attempt to ground knowledge on observation-statements, are instances of this strain of empiricism.

Empiricism appropriates the Cartesian belief that the intellectual respectability of an idea is grounded in the elements constituting it.

According to most empiricist views, a [rational inquirer] derives all his knowledge from sense observation, stopping the infinite regress of demands for justification . . . with sense observations (sense data) which, it is suggested, are manifestly true, 'incorrigible,' unable to be challenged. . . . For the empiricist the irrationalist is one who entertains notions and theories which cannot be derived from sense observations.[23]

Our knowledge of the atoms of experience is incorrigible because, at this primary level of experience, the purely given elements, since they are simple, cannot yet have been subjected to any of the myriad distortions the imagination is capable of generating with them. The simplicity of the atomic data of sensation, therefore, renders them incorrigible both for Descartes and for the empiricist. Granting this, it still remains to be shown how knowledge of the world can be gleaned from these disparate atoms. The analytic movement from complex perceptions back to atomic sensa has, *ex hypothesi*, provided an absolute ground for knowledge and the criteria which ensure certainty. This must now be supplemented by a synthetic movement: some way must be found to protect our certitude but, at the same time, to sanction those of our cognitions which are complex.

The difficulties attending this synthetic movement are well known and need not be treated at length. Let it suffice here to catalogue them briefly.

Given a realistic ontology, such as those espoused by Locke, Mill, behaviorist psychology, and (in the *Meditations*) Descartes, appeal can be made to a causal theory of perception. Such theories, however, cannot successfully answer the skeptical arguments from illusion. We may assume, on the basis of what Santayana called animal faith, that our complex percepts accurately represent the real things which cause them; but, lacking a way to compare percept with thing, the possibility remains that the percept is an illusion.

A second problem with realist ontologies has been set forth in the preceding section where it was shown that the attempt to guarantee certain knowledge of transcendent things by analyzing them into absolutely simple constituents necessarily fails—because the transparency of the atoms is incompatible with the opacity and givenness intrinsic to transcendent things. Empiricist claims to the contrary notwithstanding, sense-data are not given; they are conceptual constructs.

Such difficulties with realism tend to force empiricists to retreat to phenomenalism. Thus Berkeley and Hume attempt to safeguard certainty by refusing to assert anything about an external world.

As to those *impressions*, which arise from the *senses*, their ultimate cause is . . . perfectly inexplicable by human reason, and *'twill always be impossible to decide with certainty, whether they arise immediately from the object, or are produc'd by the creative power of the mind*, or are deriv'd from the author of our being.[24] Nor is such a question any way material to our present purpose. We may draw inferences from the coherence of our perceptions, whether they be true or false; whether they represent nature justly, or be mere illusions of the senses. (*Treatise* I, III, 5, 84; emphasis added)

Hume's strategy in the passage just quoted resembles Descartes's resolution, in the *Rules*, to "treat of things only in relation to our understanding's awareness of them." Here is further evidence that the presuppositions of Cartesian methodology are present in force at the roots of empiricism. Indeed, the presupposition before us now—that there is an immanent realm of thought which is absolutely clear, distinct, and certain, and which can be considered without having to refer in any way to a transcendent realm—is manifest throughout empiricism; expressions of it can be found in the staunchest (and most naive) of realists: Locke, for instance.[25]

Locke, to be sure, thinks that an inference can be made from idea to "external object" with certainty—on this point he and Hume vehemently disagree—but both Locke and Hume follow Descartes in presupposing that proof of some sort is required before a correspondence between the utterly disparate realms of thought and things can be asserted. Once, however, assent is given to such a bifurcation, the quest for certainty with its demand for complete transparency in the data of cognition leads to a suspension of the thesis of external existence—as is attested by the philosophical progression from Locke to Hume.

Phenomenalism, having performed the reduction which excludes everything beyond atomic data (or that which is based upon simple sensation) from consideration, also encounters overwhelming difficulties when it undertakes the synthetic movement from logical atoms to complex cognitions. Some sort of principle of combination is required to warrant the construction of complexes out of simples and to account for the coherence of our perceptions. Having forsaken all recourse to any realm of transcendence, phenomenalism (and, *a fortiori*, stronger idealisms) must generate principles of combination exclusively from within the sphere of immanence. That is, appeal must be made to the laws governing the operation of the mind. Here, two possibilities arise: either the laws are taken to be *a priori* principles of combination, or they are regarded as *a posteriori* laws, that is, causal laws of (human) nature or psychological laws of association.

Descartes, in the *Rules*, takes the first option. "Deduction is . . . the only means of putting things together so as to be sure of their truth. . . . Mankind has no road toward certain knowledge open to it, save those of self-evident intuition and necessary deduction" (Rule XII, PWD 45).

Hume provides an example of the second. Resemblance, contiguity, and cause and effect "are . . . the principles of union or cohesion among our simple ideas. . . . Here is a kind of ATTRACTION, which in the mental world will be found to have as extraordinary effects as in the natural" (*Treatise* I, I, 4, 12–13).

These approaches to the synthetic movement fall victim to arguments from illusion. Whereas the realistic account breaks down because within it illusion is an ever-present possibility, the phenomenalistic-idealistic account fails because, within it, illusion is never a possibility: so long as the laws governing the operation of the mind remain in effect and access to a transcendent realm continues to be ruled out, nothing can disrupt the coherence of our perceptions.

The brute fact that we do err, that our perceptions do not always follow a pattern of lawful coherence, leads us to regard these laws as inconstant and unreliable. Hume acknowledged the fact of illusion and spoke as though there could frequently be exceptions to the rule of these laws.[26]

Furthermore, Hume introduces an arbitrary epicycle into his psychology precisely in order to save the appearances and make room for error and illusion. The "liberty of the imagination to transpose and change its ideas" (*Treatise*, I, I, 3, 10) is the liberty of chance: it is perfectly inexplicable and, since in Book II of his *Treatise*, Hume seems to adopt the standpoint of causal determinism, it should be stricken from his system on the basis of his own principles and definitions.[27]

The same inconsistency I have documented in Hume must also exist, not only in Descartes, but in all those unwitting Cartesians who appeal to principles of combination grounded exclusively within the sphere of immanence. They all run up against the same dilemma: either all combination of simple impressions is governed by laws, be they logical or natural, in which case the possibility of error and illusion is entirely ruled out; or chance can intervene in the process of combination, in which case the possibility of distinguishing between error and truth is also ruled out. Both alternatives lead to skepticism.

Might there be some way for empiricism to perform the synthetic movement and account for the construction of complex cognitions out of the atoms of experience, a way that does not fall prey to the difficulties attending the various forms of realism, phenomenalism, and idealism that have just been examined? The answer in this question lies in the presuppositions of the Cartesian methodology. Once they have been accepted, the analytic movement which reduced both thought and the world to logical atoms follows inevitably. But, as I have tried to show, the nature of this reduction is such as to preclude the possibility of completing the synthetic movement in which the method was to culminate.

The quest for certainty which is taken over from Descartes by empiricism leads empiricists from the initial profession of an anti-Cartesian viewpoint, through a subsequent reversion to thinly veiled Cartesian principles and, ultimately, to distinctively Cartesian shortcomings. The quest for certainty is the attempt to find an absolutely reliable ground for knowledge. As is evident in his attack on innate ideas, Locke repudiates the rationalism associated with the Cartesian tradition because the self-evident truths of reason held to be innate (imputed to the natural light implanted in us all as the sign of our divine origin) appeared to be corrigible and untrustworthy. Hence, for Locke and those who followed him, God could not serve as the transcendent ground for certainty in human knowledge. Still, Locke's quest led him to look elsewhere in search of something that would serve adequately as a transcendent ground for certainty.

The assumption that the requisite ground must be transcendent, however, is a characteristically Cartesian assumption. It is based on the belief that the origin of error lies within man, hence, that the measure of truth (and the source of the truth criteria needed to guarantee certainty) lies beyond or outside man, that is, in some transcendent sphere.

Whereas Descartes's search for a transcendent ground led directly to God and only in a derivative way to perceptual experience (that is, the validity of the latter had in some way to be assured by the former), Locke appealed directly to experience. I have already asserted that perceptual objects are transcendent and that truth claims, qua *truth* claims, must refer to some transcendent sphere (hence to that extent require something transcendent as a ground). Consequently, I cannot fault Locke on this count. Insofar as the givenness of perceptual objects manifests their transcendence and allows them to provide the referent necessary for an assertion about them to purport to be true, Locke's move in this direction commands assent. He goes astray, however, when he bases perceptual experience upon atomistic foundations.

Like Descartes, Locke attempts to distinguish between the corrigible and the certain in human knowledge, and his intent, again like Descartes's, is to confine his assertions to those which are demonstrably certain. This common motivation led both Locke and Descartes to fasten upon simple impressions (logical atoms, the ultimate products of thorough analysis) as that which could admit of certain knowledge and thereby provide a foundation for extending the scope of certainty in human cognition. The error in both cases is the same: the transformation of perceptual experience from complex objects to atomic elements results in a product stripped of transcendence. As has already been demonstrated, the search for a transcendent ground, when conducted in this way, fetches up in the sphere of immanence; that is, it results in a set of transparent "elements" which are constructs of thought rather than objects of experience. A reduction is performed which, in eliminating the possibility of error, does away as well with the transcendence needed as a ground of truth.

Nowhere is this clearer than in the case of Humean phenomenalism. First, the reduction to simple impressions is coupled with a refusal to make any assertion about some transcendent thing corresponding to those impressions. Then a move is made which is structurally akin, although not identical,[28] to the one made by Descartes in the *Rules*: the synthesis of atoms into complex wholes corresponding to the objects of naive experience is grounded on principles of combination or association originating entirely within the sphere of immanence. In an abrupt reversal, the activity of the subject—initially attributed to the imagination and held to be the source of error—is finally taken as the ground of veridical (re-)constitution of experience. As is borne out by the fact of Hume's ultimate submission to skepticism, the lack of a transcendent ground—either for the basic components of experience or for the principles governing the synthesis of these simple elements into complex wholes—leaves the subject in a world which may be no more than his own dream.

In sum, the empiricist's attempt to ground certain knowledge on an appeal to the transcendence of the objects of sense experience fails because the transformation (reduction to simples) required to render that experience susceptible to certain cognition renders it, at the same time, incapable of functioning as a transcendent ground.

4. THE CARTESIAN ORIGINS OF INTELLECTUALISM

Intellectualism, like its antithesis, empiricism, is another venture in the Cartesian quest for certainty; and, here again, the quest leads to a search for an absolute ground for knowledge. Unlike empiricism, however, intellectualism seeks to ground knowledge in the immanent structures of subjectivity rather than upon the transcendent origins of experience.

The strategy that defines intellectualism has its prototype in Descartes's *Rules*. The basic epistemological problem it seeks to solve is the familiar problem of representationalism: if the subject has access to the transcendent world only by means of its immanent representation, then, in principle, there is no way to compare representation with reality to ascertain whether they truly correspond. The intellectualist solution is to bracket all reference to the transcendent reality and restrict epistemic claims to what is given to the subject only insofar as it is given. Transcendent things have no place in this epistemology; they cannot be objects of knowledge.

Transparency remains the condition for certainty. This condition is met by reduction to immanence and by a movement on the part of the subject to a non-perspectival, impartial vantage. This epistemically privileged vantage is achieved by abstracting away all cognitive influences arising from the particularity of the viewpoint imposed upon the subject by his will and imagination. With the elimination of his individuality, the subject becomes the agency of pure cognition. With the elimination of transcendent objects as possible objects of knowledge, the ground of certainty shifts to the depersonalized pure knowing subject and his immanent data.

As I have tried to show, however, it is self-defeating to attempt to achieve certainty by means of transparency. An object of cognition can be rendered transparent only by depriving it of transcendence—that is, by a reduction to immanence which is incompatible with givenness, other-sidedness, opacity, etc.—and eliminating from consideration what our cognitions are cognitions of. This attempt to guarantee truth undermines itself because it forsakes the referentiality essential to truth.

The task at hand is to show how this self-defeating Cartesian strategy underlies and undermines more recent forms of intellectualism. I have chosen Husserl as exemplar of neo-Cartesian intellectualism for several reasons. Primary among these reasons is the fact that Merleau-Ponty maintains a dialogue with Husserl throughout the course of his philosophical writing. In an essay devoted to Husserl, Merleau-Ponty speaks of "an unthought-of element [*un impensé*] in his [Husserl's] works which is wholly his and yet opens out on something else" (S 160; S-F 202).[29] That "something else" at which we arrive through a critique of the unthought in Husserl might well be conceived as Merleau-Ponty's own ontology. In the same essay, Merleau-Ponty says: "I borrow myself from others; I create others from my own thoughts" (S 159; S-F 201). Just as he finds his own thought in the unthought of Husserl, the Husserl Merleau-Ponty finds reason to praise is frequently an extrapolation of his own philosophy.

In setting forth the standpoint he labels "transcendental idealism," Husserl straightforwardly announces his intention to take over the Cartesian quest for certainty. "The general aim of grounding science absolutely . . . shall indeed continually motivate the course of our meditations, as it motivated the course of the Cartesian meditations" (CM 8).[30] In order to succeed in this quest, the scientist posits for himself the idea of perfectly adequate or apodictic evidence which will serve to ground science absolutely.[31] In pursuing his goal of apodictic evidence, Husserl confronts the same difficulty that stymied Descartes: how can we have apodictic evidence about the existence of transcendent objects? Like Descartes, Husserl is convinced by arguments from illusion that no such evidence will ever be available.[32]

In offering his solution to this problem, Husserl again acknowledges his indebtedness to Descartes. "Following Descartes, we make the great reversal that, if made in the right manner, leads to transcendental subjectivity: the turn to the *ego cogito* as the ultimate and apodictically certain basis for judgments, the basis on which any radical philosophy must be grounded" (CM 18). Husserl's transcendental reduction is essentially a "universal depriving of acceptance" of "all existential positions" (CM 20). 'What is' is reduced to 'what is meant.' It involves a suspension of the naive belief operating with the "natural attitude" that the objects of experience are transcendent things existing in themselves with determinations or properties belonging to themselves. In the *epoché* or transcendental reduction, the systematically meditating philosopher "brackets" all such existential presuppositions and considers the objects he experiences purely as objects of his experience or, in other words, he construes them only as his own *"cogitationes."* "We must regard nothing as veridical except the pure immediacy and givenness in the field of the *ego cogito* which the *epoché* has opened up to us" (PL 9).[33] Thus characterized, the transcendental reduction requires a restriction to the sphere of immanence.

Although Husserl describes his methodology as Cartesian insofar as it is motivated by a quest for certainty which seeks to ground itself in the *ego cogito*, he is also at pains to point out where he departs from the Cartesian program and why. He contends that Descartes operated on the basis of a naive understanding of the ego as a real (or natural) entity existing among the other things constituting the natural world. In this view, the sphere of immanence is conceived in terms of containment: the experience of things consists in the contents (images, thoughts, or the like) entertained, as it were, inside the subject. The ego's thoughts or *cogitationes* (having been reified in the sense explained earlier) are thus regarded as existing within the ego and referring to things existing outside the ego. Repudiating, as he does, this realistic conception of the ego and the equally realistic understanding of immanence as the actual presence of the object of cognition within a real mental process (or ongoing natural event), Husserl redefines immanence in his own "genuine" sense as the sphere of adequate self-givenness.[34] His notion of adequate self-givenness corresponds to what has been called utter transparency above. The *epoché* calls for a withholding of belief from everything lying beyond the sphere of immanence; that is, an exclusion of all that is transcendently posited. It is the transparency or adequate self-givenness of the *cogitationes* within the sphere of immanence that is held to ground the apodicticity Husserl seeks.

From within the standpoint of the transcendental reduction, the world is taken as the subject of the ego's *cogitationes* rather than as a real entity in itself independent of the ego. "The world is for me absolutely nothing else but the world existing for and accepted by me in such a conscious *cogito*" (CM 21). This standpoint is one from which Husserl does not budge, even in works as late as the *Crisis*. "The *epoché* . . . leads us to recognize, in self-reflection, that the world that exists for us, that is, our world in its being and being-such, takes its ontic meaning entirely from our intentional life" (*Crisis* 181).[35]

Notwithstanding the importance of the difference between the meanings they attach to 'immanence,' there is a structural similarity between Descartes's reduction to immanence in the *Rules* and that which takes place in Husserl's *epoché*: in both cases, a quest for certainty leads the thinker to suspend belief in the existence of transcendent entities and to restrict himself to evidence which is absolutely transparent.

Apodictic evidence requires utter congruence of thought with its object. But the transcendence of objects interposes a distance between knower and known. The eradication of that distance is accomplished by a rejection of representational theories of perception which posit a distance in defining cognition. All modes of cognition (that is, modes of "evidence-having") are then defined in terms of absolute coincidence of thought with its object: the object may no longer be construed as transcendent, since it is known with consummate clarity and distinctness.[36] As does Descartes in the *Rules*, Husserl limits the objects of knowledge to the immanent data of consciousness. "Transcendency in every form is an immanent existential characteristic, constituted with the ego" (CM 83–84). It must be granted that this passage—and others like it[37] —admit of various interpretations. One might regard Husserl as intending only to make epistemological claims without committing himself to any ontological assertions. Under this interpretation, his claim that transcendence is an immanent mode of being asserts merely that to regard something as transcendent is to constitute it immanently as having the *meaning* (for me, that is, as my *cogitatum*) 'existing-apart-from-my-conscious-act,' but without making any assertion that it does really exist apart from me.[38]

Notwithstanding these difficulties of exegesis, one point emerges unequivocally: the transcendence of the world of things naively taken for granted within the natural attitude has its ground in a prior constitution of the world of things as transcendent. Again, transcendental subjectivity confers the meaning 'transcendent' upon the world in constituting it. In the natural attitude, however, one is not aware of the constitutive function of consciousness; hence the experience of the world as transcendent is assumed to be grounded in the real transcendent existence of the world rather than in the act of transcendental subjectivity which confers that meaning upon the world.[39] In other words, Husserl regards it as an intrinsic feature of transcendental subjectivity to deceive itself (while in the mode of the natural attitude) about the world insofar as it regards the world as being transcendent rather than as acquiring the (immanent) meaning 'transcendent' from its own intentional constitution of the world. Here Husserl's anthropology concurs with Descartes's: man is the being that deceives itself.

Husserl's reduction to the standpoint of the Transcendental Ego parallels Descartes's reduction to the pure knowing subject: both are attempts to ground objectivity within the subject. Their views of the epistemological subject differ, however, on one fundamental point: Husserl's subject is a transcendental subject and Descartes's is not. Nonetheless, for both philosophers, impartiality is attained by abstracting away from the subject all individualizing features. Husserl calls his pure knowing subject an 'eidos ego' which is equivalent to "any transcendental ego whatsoever," the "transcendental ego as such" (CM 71). The point of view of the eidos ego is impartial because it is pure of the prejudices and interests which color and distort the apprehension of the personal I.[40]

The description of the *epoché* as a shift to the standpoint of an impartial observer free of practical interests and the prejudices inherent within them,[41] that is, as a methodical taking up of the attitude of a disengaged spectator, is another core tenet in Husserl's thought which is not abandoned in his later works.[42] In fact, he comes to characterize the standpoint of the transcendental reduction as one which is taken up permanently (that is, not merely a posture assumed temporarily for the express purpose of philosophizing and later dropped in a return to the natural attitude of ordinary living).[43] Accordingly, one is not surprised to find Husserl saying that the *epoché* involves "a complete personal transformation, comparable in the beginning to a religious conversion," and that it bears "the significance of

the greatest existential transformation which is assigned as a task to mankind as such" (*Crisis* 137). Here again we find a point of contiguity between
Descartes and Husserl insofar as the quest for certainty leads both to seek
freedom from error by a reduction which transforms the knower from a
participant in the world and its concerns into an impersonal and disengaged
spectator.

The comparison at hand of Husserl and Descartes leads to the question
of atomism: are there similarities here as well? Or, to approach the issue
in a deeper and more telling way, is it the case that some appeal to a formless
material substratum (that is, some principle of substantiality conceived either as an atomism, which is the case under consideration here, or as a
monism) is necessary for all forms of intellectualism? My contention that
it is can be substantiated by showing (a) in general, how the primary tenets
definitive of Cartesian intellectualism require the presupposition of logical
atomism, and (b) specifically, how this requirement is reflected in what
Husserl writes.

Intellectualism was characterized earlier as involving the attempt to
ground knowledge in the immanent structures of subjectivity. The relations
asserted in propositions are held to be grounded in the structure of thought
or consciousness rather than in the structure of things or, derivatively, our
experience of things. Thus, for example, Descartes appeals to the principles
of "deduction" to explain the foundation upon which our valid assertions
ultimately come to rest. The question then arises whether the relata are to
be grounded in subjectivity, as well: given that the formal principles underlying the assertion of relations are grounded in the nature of thought,
are we also to regard subjectivity as the ground or creator of the material
elements being related? This would be tantamount to elevating subjectivity
(initially regarded as finite and flawed) to the divine status of creator of
the universe. As seen above, this alternative is rejected in favor of one in
which the material elements of experience are grounded in something
transcending subjectivity: thought is not held to be capable of generating
its material *ex nihilo.* Thus the body of valid propositions constituting human
knowledge is (in this fundamentally dualistic way) grounded formally in
the structure of thought and materially in something other than thought.
Logical atomism follows inexorably: all relations are products of mind,
hence what is not a product of mind is devoid of relatedness or complexity,
that is, is ultimately simple. The material ground of knowledge lies in atomic
data; they are logically irreducible in the sense that they embody no relations.

Husserl's treatment of these issues tends to vary, but it remains within
limits imposed by the fundamental and unchanging principles upon which
his philosophy rests. Meaning, for him, is always constituted meaning, it is
ultimately grounded in intentionality, that is, in syntheses attributed to
consciousness.

It is occasionally difficult to determine what Husserl regards as the basic elements that are synthesized by transcendental subjectivity. The adumbrations which coalesce into a synthetic whole are themselves the product of intentional acts and admit of further analysis into the *"Stoffe"* or "primal contents" or "material data" which do not bear the specific quality of intentionality. These material data are described in terms reminiscent of logical atomism.[44] They provide a means of explicating the aspect of givenness in perceptual experience. However, Husserl also speaks of experience in such a way as to suggest that the given is not atomistic, but is already meaningful (albeit primitively) as it is given. In these contexts, he occasionally describes the given as *Feldgestalten*, that is, as elements in the phenomenal field which present themselves as already *gestaltet*, as having some kind of rudimentary organization of their own.

Upon this point, however, Husserl is faced with a serious problem. If the *Stoffe* of perceptual experience is held to be complex (that is, non-atomistic, already *gestaltet*), then it is already meaningful insofar as it has structure and organization. This clearly conflicts with his core tenet that all meaning is grounded in the constitutive activity of consciousness.[45] Accordingly, Husserl makes a distinction between active and passive genesis (or synthesis) which allows him to explicate the already *gestaltet* nature of the given in terms of intentional activity which is "automatic" (a term suggested by Fink to avoid the *prima facie* difficulties involved in speaking of passive activity) rather than deliberate. Along these lines, Husserl speaks of many levels of constitution, which are distinguished by differing degrees of deliberation, from the explicit syntheses of theory construction to the implicit or automatic syntheses which consciousness performs, as it were, unbeknownst to itself (that is, in the absence of reflective self-awareness). Nonetheless, although Husserl acknowledges that, in the transcendental reduction, there are severe difficulties impeding the project of disclosing in "original self-exhibition" the intentionality operative at remote levels, he never speaks of there being conscious acts which cannot, in principle, admit of systematic disclosure through exhibition in the "self-evidence of inner experience." Indeed, he chides Kant for appealing to "mythical constructions" posited as operating beyond the realm of possible self-exhibition and speaks of "the lack of an intuitive exhibiting principle as the reason for Kant's mythical constructions" (*Crisis*, sect. 30). Consequently, *Feldgestalten*, like all other meaningful unities, must be conceived as deriving their structure (or formal organization) from conscious syntheses: although the constitution involved may be automatic and remote it must, on principle, admit of an intuitive exhibiting.

Logical atomism is as intrinsic to Husserl's transcendental idealism as it is to most other forms of intellectualism. Once meaning (organization, relatedness as such) is relegated exclusively to the formal structures of immanent synthesis, then the matter of experience must be regarded as logically simple and atomistic. The dilemma confronting Husserl may be formulated as follows: either there is a ground of meaning lying beyond the realm of intentionality, or all meaning is grounded in consciousness and the formal structure of constitution. If the former is the case, atomism can be avoided, but only at the price of relinquishing the fundamental claims of transcendental idealism. If the second alternative is chosen (as seems to be the case), then the primal contents or *Stoffe* of experience must be regarded as devoid of intrinsic relations, that is, as perfectly simple or atomic.

Husserl, although he draws the distinction between the material and formal constituents (*hyle* and *morphe*) of phenomena himself, does not tell us much about the material aspect. Perhaps this is because, according to his own account, nothing meaningful can be said about it. Or perhaps it is because it would entail referring to something like the Kantian thing-in-itself, which Husserl explicitly labels as nonsense (CM, sect. 41).

On behalf of Husserl, it might be mentioned that, although logical atomism is a necessary (if unwanted) consequence of the standpoint he adopts, his case for the transparency or utter self-givenness of the elements in question rests not so much on an appeal to their simplicity or logical ultimacy (as is the case with Descartes) as it does upon their immanence.

As a final step in this comparison of Descartes and Husserl, I turn now to the accounts they offer regarding the process of synthesis which both hold to govern the constitution of the world from the discrete elements immanently present to consciousness.

The mind's synthesis of complexes out of simple natures is governed, for Descartes, by *a priori* laws which he groups together under the common name 'deduction.' For Husserl, the synthesis by consciousness of its immanent data is also regulated by *a priori* law: eidetic law.[46] The laws governing the synthetic processes in both the Cartesian and the Husserlian subject are regarded as universal (CM 75). This ensures that the products of synthesis are impartial, not restricted to a particular perspective and, consequently, certain.

Both Descartes and Husserl look upon their laws of synthesis as having the force of necessity.[47] However, neither of them accounts for the ground of this necessity. Husserl attributes it to an " 'innate' Apriori" and Descartes attributes it to the "light of Nature." I infer from this common refusal to proceed any further in the process of explanation that the hypothesis of the pure epistemological subject depends upon two postulates (among others):

(i) Every consciousness is regulated by laws to which there are no exceptions.

(ii) These laws are discoverable and, once discovered, are known (with certainty) to apply universally and necessarily.

The arguments that vitiate Hume's psychology, however, apply here as well. If no element of contingency is admitted with respect to these laws, error and illusion become impossibilities. If, contrary to the claims made about them, exceptions to these laws are regarded as possible, then error and illusion are always possible, and certitude remains forever unattainable.[48]

In sum, then, at least two of the aspects of Cartesian reductionism set forth above would seem to be present in Husserl's transcendental idealism: first, the reduction of the knower to the role of a spectator; and, second, the reduction of the world to an object for consciousness. Also, in the case of Husserl as well as Descartes, these reductions are motivated by a quest for certainty. Hence, insofar as the reductions lead to significant difficulties, there is further evidence for the contention that as it was for empiricism so it is for intellectualism: the quest for certainty conducted along these Cartesian lines produces a set of problems that remain insurmountable.

The thesis here being defended—that the two major standpoints in modern Western philosophy, empiricism and intellectualism, can be traced to a common proximate origin in Descartes—will have been carried if I have succeeded in showing that both standpoints depend, at a fundamental level, upon the Cartesian presupposition that certainty is to be obtained by grounding knowledge in elements whose transparency provides an absolute ground for knowledge.

Furthermore, owing to the fundamental dependence upon a reduction to the sphere of immanence which they share, empiricism and intellectualism tend to collapse into one another. Both ground certainty on the transparency of the data out of which knowledge is to be constructed. Access to these data is described in terms of sense intuition, on the one hand, and intellectual intuition, on the other; but, since both forms of intuition reduce the matter of cognition to immanent data, the differences between them are not crucial.

> We started off from a world in itself which acted upon our eyes so as to cause us to see it [empiricism], and we now have consciousness of or thought about the world [intellectualism], but the nature of this world remains unchanged: it is still defined by the absolute mutual exteriority of its parts, and is merely duplicated throughout its extent by a thought which sustains it. We pass from absolute objectivity to absolute subjectivity, but this second idea is no better than the first and is upheld only against it, which means by it. The affinity between intellectualism and empiricism is thus much less obvious and much more deeply rooted than is commonly thought.
>
> (PP 39; PP-F 49)

The affinity between intellectualism and empiricism here asserted by Merleau-Ponty may be illustrated in still a further way. The reduction they both perform is a reenactment of the Cartesian methodology which results in ontological homogeneity; the heterogeneity distinguishing the realm of the subject from that of the object is lost: subjectivity is reduced to impartiality, objectivity is reduced to transparency, and the two spheres collapse into one.

Consequently, the troubles besetting empiricism also confound intellectualism. The destructive dilemma voiced by Meno and brought to bear against Cartesianism by Merleau-Ponty undermines intellectualism as well as empiricism. Both are caught in the either/or of the learning paradox; neither can admit the imperfect kind of knowledge in whose terms alone meaning can be given to inquiry. The radical bifurcation which sets the immanent data of cognition apart from the transcendent world leaves both empiricism and intellectualism with no way to mediate between knower and known. If the world is completely transcendent, it is completely opaque and cannot be known. If the elements of cognition are entirely immanent and transparent, the degree of opacity and givenness needed to give meaning to externality and transcendence is lost, and truth is sacrificed in a quest for certainty that ultimately defeats itself.

In the case of each of the two standpoints, the nature of the analytic movement back to a ground prefigures the nature of the subsequent synthetic movement. In both cases, the synthetic movement fails in its endeavor to provide a systematic explication of knowledge while preserving the certainty attained in the analytic movement. Although both camps require some doctrine of association, the principles of association and the means of justifying them vary according to the nature of antecedent presuppositions made at a more fundamental level: empiricism is committed to a logic of induction and a belief in the orderly and regular structure of things, and intellectualism is committed to the position that there are *a priori* laws governing the constitution of meaning and being which can be known intuitively and infallibly.

These themes are traceable to major strains in Cartesian thought. The presence of both of these largely antithetical standpoints in Descartes and the fact that the standpoint which dominates a given work never totally excludes the other even within that work (the antithesis always being present in a recessive role in order to endow the thesis with meaning by providing a contrast) attest not only to the subtlety and insight of the thinker, but also to the interdependence of the two points of view.

In fact, neither empiricism nor intellectualism, taken independently, can provide an adequate, or even consistent, philosophical standpoint. Yet, they cannot be brought together into a unitary system because there are elements in each which flatly contradict the other. A third alternative is required: one which confronts the paradoxes generated by the traditional, antithetical conception of immanence and transcendence—and succeeds, where empiricism and intellectualism fail, in the endeavor to resolve the problems generated by the ontological bifurcation which has characterized Western dualism since the time of Plato. My intent, in the pages to follow, is to show that Merleau-Ponty provides this third alternative and thereby lays the ontological foundations for what must, in my view, necessarily be the next step in Western thought.

TWO

The Paradox of Immanence
and Transcendence

1. MENO'S PARADOX AND THE PARADOX OF
IMMANENCE AND TRANSCENDENCE

Merleau-Ponty earned the attention of twentieth-century philosophers by demonstrating the importance of the lived body to a tradition that conceived the best kind of philosophy as that which is generated by disembodied intellect. Philosophers had sought to be angels, and Merleau-Ponty brought them back to earth. For that reason he has been accorded a place in the pantheon of philosophical immortals; but this is the wrong place for him.

Of course, the discovery of his own body is an important and lasting achievement on the part of Merleau-Ponty, and this discovery will receive the consideration it deserves here in due course. What has been missed in the secondary literature on Merleau-Ponty, however, is what led him to the lived body and why he deemed the study of the body philosophically consequential.

Merleau-Ponty's work on embodiment marks the mid-point of a course of development that begins with conceptual problems in psychology and ends—abruptly and before it should have—in the midst of a work on ontology. In that last, uncompleted work, *The Visible and the Invisible*, Merleau-Ponty was working on the concept of the flesh, which he regarded "as an element, as the concrete emblem of a general manner of being" (VI 147; VI-F 193). The body is important, for Merleau-Ponty, because it is a prime exemplar of flesh. And flesh is important because it is the element that unlocks an ontology: it is the element that Merleau-Ponty, before his death, thought would allow him to resolve the ontological problems he had been working on since he first encountered them underlying fundamental issues in psychology.

These ontological problems have a common core: their matrix is the paradox of immanence and transcendence. One specific instance of this general paradox has already been taken up: Meno's learning paradox. And it is the same paradox of immanence and transcendence, in one formulation or another, that guides Merleau-Ponty in his critiques of empiricism and intellectualism. Finally, it is this paradox that defines the nexus of ontological dualism that Merleau-Ponty spent his philosophical life trying to overcome.

The sphere of immanence is traditionally conceived as the sphere of interiority, the sphere of conscious life, the sphere of the given insofar as it is given. Transcendence is conceived as exteriority, the universe of things existing in themselves and independent of consciousness. Conceived in these traditional ways, immanence and transcendence are mutually exclusive, and the lines of demarcation between them impermeable. An object of consciousness is not a worldly thing, and vice versa. A paradox is generated here because cognition requires penetration of this line of demarcation and relations between the two domains: the object of consciousness must somehow capture the transcendent thing and take its measure from it. Yet, given the initial definitions, no mediation between immanence and transcendence is conceivable.

For empiricism, which attempts to ground all knowledge in experience, radical skepticism cannot be avoided; because there is no way to ascertain that the immanent perceptual object conveys reliable information about the transcendent thing, experience may provide no knowledge of the world at all. Intellectualism confronts the problem of skepticism, as it were, from the other side. Once cognitive claims are limited to the transparent sphere of immanence, error becomes an impossibility—because there is no transcendent measure of truth and falsity.

Intellectualism and empiricism, then, represent the two horns of Meno's dilemma. Intellectualism must know everything about its object, or it will not consider it—and empiricism must conclude its inquiry with the admission that what it has learned may amount to nothing. Meno's dilemma and the paradox of immanence and transcendence are both driven by the polarized thinking that results from a misguided application of the law of the excluded middle term.[1]

Yet that middle term is exactly what is required. No epistemology can succeed in mediating what an antecedently adopted ontology has defined as mutually exclusive. The solution to Meno's dilemma requires a middle term between certainty and ignorance, between transparency and opacity. Likewise, the resolution of the paradox of immanence and transcendence requires a middle term, an "element," "a general manner of being" whose being does not preclude, but rather invites, being seen, being grasped, and in some sense of the term, being known. "If the past and the world exist, they must in principle be immanent—they could only be what I see behind me and around me—and in fact be transcendent—they exist in my life before appearing as objects of my explicit acts" (PP 364; PP-F 418). There must be a way to conceive the world as both immanent and transcendent—but that will require reconceiving immanence and transcendence in such a way that they no longer exclude each other.

It may be said that one earns one's place in the history of philosophy by conceiving the thought that will later be seen as constituting the next step necessary to a culture's advancement. Our culture is mired in the polarized thinking that produces the dualisms of mind and body, form and matter, activity and passivity, invisible and visible, etc. In the pages that follow, I will attempt to conceive these dualisms as instantiations of the overarching immanence-transcendence dualism. No doubt their common ground could be conceived in other terms—it matters little—the point is there is a common ground, an ontology from which these dualisms emerge. The next step for our culture is the step that will take us out of the mire of dualist ontology onto another ground. In my view, Merleau-Ponty has taken this step. The task I have set for myself here is to bring others to see his footprint—and the direction in which it points.

2. SARTRE AND THE PROBLEM OF MEDIATION

Mediation. Angels, saints, and Heidegger's poets mediate between men— and gods, the known and the unknown, immanence and transcendence. Kierkegaard argues that, if man and God, like finite and infinite, are incommensurable, the lack of a common measure renders mediation inconceivable. If it is to be achieved, it will have to be by virtue of an absurdity, by means of a transgression of reason. This is, strictly speaking, a logical point: if immanence and transcendence are conceived as mutually exclusive, each being the negation of the other, then mediating between them is impossible. An ontology that defines immanence as radical negation of transcendence cannot be coupled with an epistemology that defines knowledge in terms of a mediation between them; unless, of course, one admits a fundamental contradiction, a logical absurdity, into one's thought . . . thereby transforming philosophy into a magic theater where the price of admission is one's mind.

There is a critique running throughout the *Phenomenology of Perception* in which Merleau-Ponty focuses on the problem of mediation as it appears in Sartre's ontology. The threads of this critique come together in the chapter on "Interrogation and Dialectic" in *The Visible and the Invisible*. In the early critique, Merleau-Ponty shows that Sartre's attempt to mediate being and nothingness necessarily involves him in contradiction; and the later critique demonstrates the failure of Sartre's attempt to raise the contradiction to the level of principle and "neutralize" it by dialectical reasoning.

Since Merleau-Ponty arrives at his own position in large part through his critique of Sartre, the time it will take to review this critique will, I trust, be well spent. Merleau-Ponty is indebted to Sartre, as Kant was to Hume, for awakening him to the need for overthrowing the philosophical assumptions which had become embedded in the Western tradition since the time of Descartes.

Sartre's philosophy rests on a radical ontological dualism: he sets nothingness over against being, emptiness against fullness, consciousness against thing, being-for-itself against being-in-itself.[2] "The thing . . . is that which is present to consciousness as not being consciousness" (BN 174). In the framework of this dualist ontology, Sartre conceives "knowledge as a type of relation between the for-itself and the in-itself" (BN 172). This relation which defines knowledge is the relation of negation, and it has two simultaneous and interdependent moments. The for-itself knows the in-itself as a being which it is not, and the for-itself knows itself as "the reflected negation of this being [i.e., being in-itself]" (BN 180).

> In knowledge . . . the being which I am not represents the absolute plenitude of the in-itself. And I, on the contrary, am the nothingness, the absence which determines itself in existence from the standpoint of this fullness. This means that in that type of being which we call knowing, the only *being* which can be encountered and which is perpetually *there* is the known. The knower is not; he is not apprehensible. He is nothing other than that which brings it about that there is a *being-there* on the part of the known, a presence—for by itself the known is neither present nor absent, it simply is. But this presence of the known is presence to *nothing*, since the knower is the pure reflection of a non-being; the presence appears then across the total translucency of the knower known, an *absolute* presence. (BN 177)

The challenge, of course, is to make sense of this, to understand how the relation between sheer inapprehensible absence (being-for-itself) and absolute plenitude or fullness (being-in-itself) gives rise to knowledge, that is, to the presence of the known.

Being-for-itself or the nothingness that is consciousness is conceived in terms of pure immanence, transparency, and reflexivity. Its prototype is what Sartre calls the "prereflective cogito," a notion that grew out of his critique of Husserl's conception of consciousness in *The Transcendence of the Ego*,[3] and was exhaustively developed in *Being and Nothingness*. The fundamental idea here is that the being of consciousness consists in a relationship to itself which is at the same time a relationship to something that is not itself, that is, the object of which it is conscious. Taking the latter (object consciousness) first, we have a relatively straightforward application of Husserl's notion of intentionality: all consciousness is consciousness *of* something, and that something is its intentional object. This object consciousness is described as thetic or positional. In thetic consciousness, an object is posited as a figure or theme (against a background or within the context of a horizon). Non-thetic or non-positional consciousness is the mode of consciousness appropriate to backgrounds, horizons, or contexts. Now: on to the reflexivity that necessarily accompanies object consciousness. "The necessary and sufficient condition for a knowing consciousness to be knowledge of its object, is that it be consciousness (of) itself as being that knowledge" (BN lii).[4]

Sartre's point here is that there is a difference between being an object and being consciousness of an object. The latter requires both (a) thetic consciousness of the object posited and (b) non-thetic consciousness (of) itself as not being the object posited. This (b) is the prereflective cogito: it is an awareness on the part of consciousness that, whatever object it posits as its object or takes as its theme, it is not that object.

The being of consciousness, being-for-itself (or nothingness) is grounded in the prereflective cogito. Sartre calls it a "non-substantial absolute" (BN lvi). Consciousness is an absolute because its existence, that is, its appearance, is grounded in its reflexivity, that is, in its appearance to itself. It is non-substantial because it exists only in its own awareness (of) itself as not being any thing it posits as an object. Sartre is deliberately paradoxical in speaking of being-for-itself as an absolute: on the one hand, in grounding its own being in its reflexivity or appearing to itself, it meets the traditional definition of *causa sui*; on the other, since there is no consciousness that is not consciousness of an object, consciousness exists only in relation to an object.

Both of the relations constitutive of consciousness, consciousness of an object and consciousness (of) itself, are relations of pure negativity. What it is to *be* an object is to be posited by the for-itself as something it *is not*.[5] And what it is to be consciousness is to be aware (of) itself as *not being* any of the objects it posits.[6]

By contrast with the negativity of the for-itself, being-in-itself is "full positivity." The for-itself is sheer transparency and reflexivity, but the in-itself "does not refer to itself" and is "opaque to itself precisely because it is filled with itself." The in-itself "is what it is" whereas the "for-itself is defined . . . as being what it is not and not being what it is" (BN lxv-lxvi).

Note here that the ontological status of objects is unclear. The being of the object is not being-for-itself. Neither is it being-in-itself, because the object, as known, is determined, bounded, delimited, and being-in-itself is sheer plenitude. What, then, *is* the object, the thing as known? Sartre defines the ontological status of tables and inkwells in terms of presence. And presence is also his definition of knowledge. "Because knowledge is not absence but presence, there is nothing which separates the known from the known" (BN 178). Further on, he says: "The presence of the for-itself to the in-itself . . . is pure denied identity" (BN 178). What are we to understand from this?

There are three central terms to be explicated here: (1) consciousness/nothingness/being-for-itself; (2) plenitude/being-in-itself; and (3) presence/the known/phenomenal object. The relation between the first two gives rise to the third. This is traditional Cartesian thinking: soul encounters thing and an impression is formed. But Sartre redefines the terms: consciousness is nothingness (it does not originate in a substantial ego); what *is* is a plenitude which lacks all definition (differentiation is the result of negation and all negativity originates in the for-itself); and only the known appears as it always has (as objects like tables and inkwells).

In order to account for the emergence of differentiated objects, Sartre appeals to two orders[7] of negation. In first-order negation, the for-itself defines objects by opposing one this (a figure) to the field of undifferentiated thises (background). This act of definition is an act of negation: 'this' is what it is by virtue of *not* being anything else; or again the edge or limit that demarcates a figure by excluding what it is not is, itself, a negativity [*négatité*], something that *is* not. As noted above, the presence of the for-itself to 'this' is one of "denied identity." That is, the for-itself is aware (of) itself as not being the 'this' it posits.

First-order negation culminates in the differentiation of the object from both being-in-itself ('this' is not the undifferentiated plenitude which is in itself) and being-for-itself ('this' is not nothingness).

The second-order negation, which will require further attention later on, is a negation of the negations of the first order. That is, it is a denial (i) that the 'this' is not in-itself (which results in the thesis of the natural attitude, that is, the thesis that the object *is* in itself), and (ii) that the for-itself is not an object (which results in bad faith, that is, the self-deceptive thesis on the part of consciousness that it is an object determined by a set of properties that constitute its essence). It is the second-order negation that results in *situating* the for-itself in a world in which the for-itself loses itself in its fascination with its objects.

Back, now, to the question: what *is* the 'this', the table or inkwell? What is the ontological status of the object that appears, the phenomenal object, the object of knowledge? Neither in-itself nor for-itself, yet somehow related to both, it is the traditional Cartesian immanent object: the object as it appears to consciousness, as it is realized by consciousness.

This follows from Sartre's understanding of knowledge, which he defines as a kind of immanence, as a relation internal to consciousness (BN 121, 172). Whereas some degree of opacity always separates the knower from anything transcendent which he seeks to know, Sartre speaks of "the total translucency of the knower known" relation, and characterizes the "presence of the known as "an absolute presence" (BN 177). Again, he has defined knowledge as intuition, intuition as immediacy or "immediate presence of knower to known" (BN 178), and, finally, this "relation of immediacy which originally unites the knower to the known receives the definition: "pure negativity as the counterpart of a constituting synthesis" (BN 178–9).

Does it follow from Sartre's relegation of knowledge to the sphere of immanence that there is no place in his philosophy for transcendence, or that he must deny that we can know anything that is transcendent? Although one might expect this to be the case, Sartre claims that it is not: he argues for the transcendence of both the self (the ego) and the world. He then defines transcendence in terms of the act of realization.

> The term which seems to indicate [the] inner relation between knowing and being is the word 'realize' . . . in its double ontological and gnostic mean-

ing. . . . *The real is realization.* We shall define transcendence as that inner and realizing negation which reveals the in-itself while determining the being of the for-itself. (BN 180)

Transcendence appears under two general headings in Sartre's writing: the determinate 'this' and the 'all' or undifferentiated totality. He conceives 'this' and 'all' to be correlates, as 'figure' and 'ground' are correlates in Gestalt theory: each is defined in relation to the other (although, for Sartre, the 'this-all' relation is the original source of the 'figure-ground' relation). "The negation constitutive of the this is a negation of externality. Thus we see that determination appears as an external negation correlative with the radical and ekstatic internal negation which *I am*" (BN 183).

The word 'ekstatic' unlocks the meaning of this passage. Consciousness stands beside itself (that is, is ekstatic) by virtue of its temporality. Insofar as its temporal nature sets consciousness beside itself, it disrupts the immediacy of the internal relation of presence in terms of which knowledge has been defined. Thus the temporality of consciousness introduces a mediation between knower and known. More accurately, it introduces a mediation between knower and that-which-was-known or that-which-is-to-be-known (BN 204).

Just as immanence resulted from the immediacy of the presence of knower to known, so does transcendence result from the temporal mediation between knower and known. Thus, reference to a transcendent object (be it ego or inkwell) involves an act of negation which is mediated through time: I am not what I was; this inkwell is what-it-is-not-yet (that is, my anticipations of future adumbrations are constitutive of my present cognitive grasp of an object).

Does the paradox of immanence and transcendence arise in Sartre's account of knowledge, or is his ontology capable of providing him with a means of avoiding it? The answer to this question lies in the strength of his notion of mediation. He begins with a definition of knowledge couched in terms of intuition as an immediate, translucent, absolute relation of knower and known. He then grounds this relation in an act of negation (BN 178). But, as I have sought to show, this confines knowledge within the realm of immanence. Then, with his doctrine that "the real is realization" (BN 180), Sartre introduces a further act of negation which he intends to function as a ground of transcendence. In effect, realization is a negation of immediate presence: the determinate 'this' is not the being revealed in absolute presence. The 'this' transcends immediate presence because, by virtue of the temporality of the for-itself, it is internally related to past and future presences which are not revealed in the immediate presence. That is, the 'this' is determined in the act of negation which posits it as not being any other 'this' in the collection of 'thises' whose ideal limit is the world; the world as an undifferentiated totality serves here as the background out of which the differentiated 'this' emerges as a figure (BN 183).

Temporality, the *"mode of being* peculiar to being-for-itself" or its "intra-structure" (BN 142), is the ground of the plurality of 'thises' whose ideal limit (the totality of thises, the all), in turn, is the ground of the differentiated 'this'. "The appearance of the *this* on the *all* is correlative with a certain way which the For-itself has of being the negation of itself. There is a *this* because I am not yet my future negations and because I am no longer my past negations" (BN 182).

Sartre's notion of mediation, therefore, is grounded proximately on the act of negation termed 'realization' and ultimately on the temporal intra-structure of the for-itself. As such, does it provide him with a foundation strong enough to support an adequate account of transcendence?

It does not. Sartre's inability to produce an adequate account of transcendence can be traced to two major defects in his thinking: the first lies in his notion of temporality, and the second (which is the more serious of the two) lies in his radical dualism.

The 'this' that is realized in the determining act of negation is held to be transcendent because the act of determination necessarily involves a reference to a totality of other 'thises' in contradistinction to which 'this' receives its particularity. The plurality of other 'thises' extends into past and future. Hence, the present realization determines the 'this' in terms of its (negative) relation to other 'thises' which, because they are past and future 'thises,' are not present in the actual presence of the determinate 'this'. Since the determinate 'this' is nothing other than the nexus of negative relations to a plurality of other 'thises' which transcend the present act of realization, Sartre concludes that the determinate 'this' must also be regarded as transcending the act in which it is realized.

This account fails because it neglects a simple but crucial distinction: a genuinely past (or future) 'this' must be kept distinct from a 'this' now posited as having been (or about to be). The former is transcendent and the latter is immanent. In confusing them, Sartre attributes the transcendence of the actually past (or future) 'this' to the immanent 'this' which a present intention posits as in the past (or future). In effect, this confusion is the result of Sartre's reduction of transcendence to an immanent meaning; paralleling this is his tacitly idealistic conception of time; the result is an ontology which tends to construe transcendence as an unmotivated construction produced by the fiat of immanent thought.

To explain: it is possible to distinguish between an immanent construct which is constituted as transcendent (for example, the paranoid's self-induced "belief" in the real existence of a malevolent agency threatening his world) and a perceptual object whose transcendence may be intrusive or even contrary to the anticipations constitutive of one's immanent intention (for example, the pellet of shot which breaks a tooth and disappoints my expectations of a tender bite of pheasant breast). The point of the distinction is to show (to paraphrase Kant) that transcendence is not a predicate, or, in other words, that the predication of transcendence (that is, the constitution of an immanent object as transcendent) must be motivated, and the ground of that motivation must lie beyond the sphere of immanence. On the contrary view, consciousness must be held to be capable of successful self-deception (which Sartre, elsewhere in *Being and Nothingness*,[8] denies is possible). That is, consciousness must be conceived as capable of convincing itself that its own constructs are not its own constructs. If 'this' is experienced as past, as having receded irretrievably beyond me, then it transcends me in a way that a 'this' now posited as a past 'this' does not: the Doppler effect experienced as a source of sound recedes beyond me in space and time cannot successfully be recreated in the immanent sphere by positing an aural past antecedent to the note I currently hear. Yet in grounding the transcendence of the determinate 'this' of a present act of realization in its negative relation to a host of irreal 'thises' posited as temporally bracketing it, Sartre implies that one immanent construct (that is, the determinate 'this' immanently realized now) acquires transcendence in a (negative) relation to a context composed of other immanent constructs (that is, the 'thises' now immanently posited as past and future horizons of the determinate 'this').

No contest is made here with Sartre's underlying insight that its intrinsic relatedness to its temporal horizon (extending into past and future) grounds the transcendence of a present 'this,' but when the constituent 'thises' composing that horizon are conceived as irreal positings rather than as motivated protentions and retentions, the temporal horizon collapses into the present, and past and future reduce to meanings supported by present intentions. Hence the charge made above that Sartre depends on an idealistic conception of time wherein the experience of temporality is grounded in the immanent negation of consciousness (that is, the nihilating activity by means of which the for-itself constitutes given 'thises' as having been or yet to be). The fundamental point at stake here parallels one just made: the transcendence of past and future cannot be reduced to the present positing of an absence as having been or yet to be. Sartre's implicit reduction of time to an immanent structure makes it impossible for him to explain the transcendence of objects appearing in time by appealing to the (immanent) constitution of those objects as inherently involving a reference to the past or future. Once transcendence, either that of the determinate 'this' or that of time, has been reduced to an immanent meaning, the meaning of transcendence is forsaken.

The original distinction between a 'this' genuinely transcendent in time and a 'this' now posited as transcendent, when grasped in the light of the foregoing elaboration, allows one to understand why the paradox of immanence and transcendence arises with such devastating force in Sartre's ontology. As it applies here, the paradox may be formulated as an exclusive disjunction: either the past 'this' is genuinely past and utterly transcendent, in which case it is not present to consciousness and cannot function as a referent for the act of negation which realizes the determinate 'this'; or the negated 'this' is immanent within an intention which posits it as past, in which case the 'this' which is determined in contradistinction to it cannot be regarded as transcendent. The first alternative objectifies time and regards it as a sequence of discrete moments existing in themselves *partes extra partes*. The second alternative collapses time into an eternal present within which past and future are merely correlates arbitrarily assigned by an unmotivated intentionality. Sartre makes use of both: he calls the former "universal" time and the latter "original" or "ontological" time. However, his attempt to bring them together fails: he has defined them in such a manner that there can be no mediation between the transcendence of past and future in universal time and the immanence of past and future in original time.

Notwithstanding these difficulties in his notion of temporality, Sartre's radical dualism alone renders him incapable of dealing with the paradox of immanence and transcendence. In Sartre's view (here summarized by Merleau-Ponty):

> The whole life of consciousness is characterized by the tendency to posit objects, since it is consciousness, that is to say self-knowledge, only insofar as it takes hold of itself and draws itself together in an identifiable object. And yet the absolute positing of a single object is the death of consciousness, since it congeals the whole of existence.[9]

> We cannot remain in this dilemma of having to fail to understand the subject or the object. . . .We must understand how, paradoxically, there is *for us* an *in-itself*.
>
> (PP 71; PP-F 86)

Although Merleau-Ponty does not here identify this dilemma as Sartrean, that is, as a consequence of Sartre's ontology,[10] it should be evident from the preceding analysis of the for-itself and the in-itself that Sartre does, indeed, encounter precisely this dilemma when trying to account for knowledge as a relation between the two. "Everything that exists exists as a thing or as a consciousness, and there is no half-way house" (PP 37; PP-F 48).

Merleau-Ponty's words here echo those of Roquentin in *Nausea*: "I realized that there was no half-way house between non-existence and this flaunting abundance [of being-in-itself]. If you existed, you had to exist *all the way*."[11] Merleau-Ponty doesn't name him, but he is talking about Sartre; and what he says is relevant here because it is just this lack of a "half-way house" between being-in-itself and being-for-itself that eliminates the possibility of mediation and leaves Sartre foundering on the paradox of immanence and transcendence. Sartre is by no means unaware of this problem, but, instead of resolving it, he elevates this basic contradiction in his philosophy to the level of a fundamental principle. "Being is relative to the for-itself in its 'being-there' since the For-itself in its internal negation affirms what cannot be affirmed, knows being *such as it is* when the 'such as it is' cannot belong to being" (BN 217).[12]

Contradiction raised to the level of principle: can this be justified by appeal to dialectic? As noted above, Sartre's dialectic proceeds by means of two orders of negation. The first-order negations are those in which being-for-itself and being-in-itself are placed in a relation of mutual exclusion: the being of the for-itself consists in negation of being-in-itself. The result of the first-order negations is differentiation: definition is introduced into being; 'thises' are constituted against the background of the all; meaning comes into the world through the negations-which-are-positings of the for-itself. The problem here is that the differentiated this, the object present to the for-itself, has no ontological home in the in-itself and remains locked in immanence: being-in-itself is an uncracked plenum which excludes the tracing of nothingness, the not that separates this from this.

But the second-order negation rectifies all this. In the second-order negation, the first-order negations are negated: the not that separates for-itself from in-itself is itself negated, and this self-negation of the for-itself becomes an affirmation of the in-itself. "The For-itself by its self-negation becomes the affirmation of the In-itself" (BN 217). The negation of the in-itself which was the being of the for-itself is now negated, and the for-itself thereby becomes the affirmation of the in-itself. As a result of this second-order negation, something happens to the in-itself: it becomes articulated, differentiated, meaningful—in itself.

> In the quasi-totality of Being, affirmation *happens* to the In-itself; it is the adventure of the in-itself to *be affirmed*. This affirmation . . . happens to the In-itself as the affirmation realized by the For-itself. The affirmation is like a passive ekstasis of the In-itself which leaves the In-itself unchanged yet which is achieved in the In-itself and from the standpoint of the In-itself. All this happens as if the For-itself had a Passion to lose itself in order that the affirmation 'world' might come to the In-itself. Of course this affirmation exists only *for* the For-itself; it is the For-itself itself, and disappears with it. But it is not *in* the For-itself, for it is an ekstasis. If the For-itself is one of its terms (the affirming), then the other term, the In-itself, is *really* present in it. It is outside, on being, that there is a world which discovers itself to me.[13] (BN 217)

It is in the second-order negation, the shift from the original negation to the subsequent affirmation, that Sartre espouses a contradiction as a basic tenet of his philosophy. He begins with an ontological bifurcation which separates consciousness from the world and ends with a world in which consciousness has lost itself. In the beginning being-in-itself is chaos, without definition or meaning. Then there is the upsurge of the for-itself, which adds nothing to being. And in the end, chaos has given way to the affirmation of an articulated world. "It begins by opposing being and nothingness absolutely, and it ends by showing that the nothingness is in a way within being, which is the unique universe. When are we to believe it? At the beginning or at the end?" (VI 66; VI-F 95). If, as Merleau-Ponty goes on to say, Sartre's response is that it doesn't matter because the two are the same, one must object: an undifferentiated plenum is not the same as an articulated world, and a consciousness aware (of) itself as not being any of its objects is not the same as a consciousness which has lost itself in fascination with its world. These are pairs of contradictories, and to affirm, on principle, that they are identities is to affirm a principle of contradiction.

Sartre denies that he is an idealist ("*there is* only being," BN 216) and that he is a realist (" 'there is' being because I am the negation of being," BN 217), but in fact he is both: he can deny realism in the context of his first-order negation because it is an idealism, and he can deny idealism in the context of his second-order negation because it is a realism. As I have argued here and elsewhere, however, it is as an idealist that Sartre does most of his philosophical work, this work being the description of how the for-itself constitutes its world through the negations which are its intentional acts. The world thus constituted is then realized, affirmed as what *is* in itself, but "of course this affirmation exists only *for* the For-itself." "The world," Sartre says, "is human" (BN 218).

Sartre moves from negativity to positivity, from negation to affirmation, from two kinds of being separated by an absolute *not* to one kind of being in which that absolute *not* has destroyed itself. Is this the movement of dialectical thought, thinking that follows the dialectical unfolding of being?

Merleau-Ponty argues that the Sartrean dialectic is "bad dialectic," an empty formal structure which, "against its own principles, imposes an external law and framework upon the content and restores for its own uses pre-dialectical thought" (VI 94; VI-F 128). Good dialectic, or in Merleau-Ponty's terms, "hyperdialectic," is that which understands the profound movement of self-mediation where the process of emergence is grounded in the things themselves, bound always to the concrete contents, and not dictated from above by a supervenient form which imposes its own requirements upon that which it seeks to understand. Sartre's dialectic is static because its formal principle, absolute negation, produces an ambivalence, an oscillation between absolute difference and absolute identity, in which there are only reversals and never developments. Opposed to this is Merleau-Ponty's schema in which ambivalence is replaced by ambiguity and supervenient forms give way to "matter-pregnant-with-form." It is not yet time to develop the notion of ambiguity as Merleau-Ponty's unique understanding of the Gestalt-theoretical "law of *Prägnanz*"; suffice it here to note his critical point that there can be no self-mediation, indeed no mediation of any kind, between two orders defined as mutually exclusive: they can be brought together only by means of contradiction and at the expense of understanding.

Sartre's difficulties are generic for dualism and specific to Cartesian dualism. Taking the matter at hand, dialectical unfolding, one can see that

Sartre has reversed the process of becoming, and that this mistake is generated by a Cartesian reification of the abstract ideal of subjectivity or consciousness. Sartre's dialectic begins with consciousness alienated from the world, faces the problem of how to mediate between the two, and ends with consciousness lost in the world. This places reflective alienation prior to prereflective engagement, which is, at the very least, ontogenetically backwards. Why does Sartre conceive the being of consciousness as initially disjunct from the rest of being? Because, as Merleau-Ponty puts it, his ontology "develops under the domination of concepts such as 'subject,' 'consciousness,' 'self-consciousness,' 'mind,' all of which, even if in a refined form, involve the idea of a *res cogitans*, of a positive being of thought— whence there results the immanence in the unreflected of the results of reflection" (VI 74; VI-F 104). Sartre himself appeals to the classical Cartesian formula for distinguishing consciousness (*res cogitans*) from what it is not (*res extensa*): "it is by and in the extension of the transcendent In-itself that the for-itself makes itself known to itself and realizes its own nonextension" (BN 179).

Sartre's Cartesianism is also evident in his serialized conception of "universal" time which, as noted earlier, regards time as a succession of discrete moments. The dispersed atomic instants of universal time stand in opposition to the immanent unity of "original" or "ontological" time: another basic contradiction which Sartre's dialectic cannot resolve.

Furthermore, the absolute translucency of knowledge as presence is a revivification of Cartesian clear and distinct knowledge; both are putative realizations of the quest for certainty, and both tend to cast the subject in an ambivalent role.

These considerations may help us to see how one *prima facie* difference between Sartre and Descartes dissolves under analysis. On the surface, the Cartesian view that the subject is a non-extended thinking thing would seem to clash with Sartre's description of the subject as no-thing, not-a-thing. In the end, however, they assign to subjectivity basically the same functions: presence to objects and presence to itself (that is, reflection). In defining the subject as no-thing, Sartre does not really deny its substantiality; he merely endows it with a kind of substantiality which differs from the substantiality of things: it is still *substantia*, that which underlies the appearance of things, "that which brings it about that there is a being-there on the part of the known" (BN 177).[14] Correlatively, Descartes reduces the subject to nothing when he argues for its absolute transparency (clarity and distinctness) to itself; this reduces subjectivity to the presence of thought to itself: no longer is there a subject for whom self-knowledge is a task, but merely thought which is translucent to itself and has no secrets from itself. Thus, for both Descartes and Sartre, the subject has an ambivalent status; it is simultaneously substance and nothing. Rather than linger over the fact that this view of subjectivity embodies another fundamental contradiction, I shall only note that the point at stake has been made: Sartre's dualism is a Cartesian dualism. The fundamental features of the for-itself/in-itself bipolarity are structurally parallel to those of the *res cogitans/res extensa* bipolarity.

This dualism is ultimately untenable because it cannot allow for the possibility of knowledge and truth. The ontology precludes a viable epistemology. The putative certainty with regard to immanent contents is spurious because, contrary to the claims for transparency and incorrigibility, the meaning and portent of our own thoughts remain at least as dark and mystified as Freud and Marx have shown them to be. And the radical skepticism with regard to worldly things is equally spurious because, finite and corrigible as it may be, human science is not groundless. The problem for dualism that I have sought to explicate in the works of Descartes and Sartre is the problem of reconciling immanence and transcendence. The problem becomes a paradox when one posits an initial framework—an ontology which conceives immanence and transcendence as mutually exclusive, as separated by a definitional abyss—the terms of which preclude solving a problem whose solution is presupposed in its own formulation: how is it possible that we know what we know we know? Set forth in traditional terms, the problem is that of how the subject, for himself, can know things existing in themselves.

> One cannot . . . conceive any perceived thing without someone to perceive it. But the fact remains that the thing presents itself to the person who perceives it as a thing in itself, and thus poses the problem of a genuine *in-itself-for-us*. (PP 322; PP-F 372)

One way of approaching this problem is to regard it as growing out of a Cartesian tradition of reductionism and reification. We use the terms 'subject' and 'object' to talk about experience: we speak of the perceiving subject and the objects perceived. However, to speak in this manner is already to have abstracted from perceptual experience. What is given in experience after all is neither a subject for-itself nor an object in-itself, but rather a perception.[15] The fallacy inherent in abstraction and analysis lies in our tendency to reify the abstract terms: we speak of such second-order abstractions as subject and object as though they were given in first-order experience. Such is our legacy from Descartes that our language is shot through with locutions which tacitly reify (or realize into first-order existence) the abstractions which should properly be used for second-order reflection upon experience.[16]

Having fallen into this manner of thinking, it is difficult to get out of it. But we must; because once we have adopted a conceptual frame of reference based on the fallacy of reifying abstractions we find it impossible to describe experience in an adequate way. Sartre has just provided an example of this difficulty. Having abstracted being-for-itself and being-in-itself from experience, and then treating them as constitutents of first-order experience, he finds he requires a contradiction to reunite them in the organic integrity of experience as we live it. In the initial abstraction, an irreconcilable polarity was introduced which separates these terms; they were endowed with meanings which are logically incompatible: consequently, once the abstractions were reified, the resulting entities become conceptually incompossible within the unity of concrete experience.

In more general terms, Sartre's troubles spring from his commitment to what Merleau-Ponty calls "analytical reflection" and "objective thought." This commitment may also be expressed as the "prejudice of determinate being" (PP 45n, 51n; PP-F 55n, 62n). The attitude expressed in these phrases is another holdover from Descartes. The quest for certainty is transformed into a quest for that about which we can be certain, that is, determinate being. Analytical reflection provides access to determinate being: it is by analysis that our obscure and confused perceptions are transformed into clear and distinct abstractions. Objective thought is then a form of philosophizing that systematically commits what I have termed the 'fallacy of reifying abstractions': that is, it construes the abstractions generated by analytical reflection as the real, as the ground upon which philosophy begins to work, whereas these abstractions would be more accurately described as the ideal product, the result of a prior process of philosophizing.[17] The point is that systems of objective thought such as Sartre's cannot give an adequate or even consistent explication of perceptual experience because the Cartesian prejudice of determinate being tacitly underlies and effectively (mis-)guides their philosophical efforts.

The problem of mediation emerges from the fallacy of reifying abstractions and its correlate, the prejudice of determinate being—and Sartre provides an excellent example of how this occurs. That which is to be analysed, explained, understood, etc. is always the phenomena of the world we perceive in everyday experience. In the process of analysis/explanation, since it proceeds by means of language, an idealization takes place: the confused, ambiguous, overdetermined richness of perceptual experience is focused, clarified, determined, categorized. Specifically, the phenomenal object, which is perceived by us as in itself, is brought under the categories of consciousness and thing, immanence and transcendence, subject and object. Now we have the problem of mediation: how can we account for the production of the phenomenon in terms of interaction of the underlying realities of consciousness and thing, immanence and transcendence, etc.? The problem is generated by the processes of abstraction, polarization, determination, and reification which give rise to these second-order constructs and mistake them for first-order "underlying realities." The ontological categories are literally misconceived, and they generate the epistemological problems. Once the percept or phenomenon has been torn asunder, bifurcated into polarized and mutually exclusive categories, attempts to reconstruct it will necessarily fail. This problem is endemic to philosophical reflection.

THREE

The Thesis of the
Primacy of Perception

The epistemological thesis of the primacy of perception and its correlate, the ontological thesis of the primacy of phenomena, are two central tenets in Merleau-Ponty's thought which support and inform the entire structure of his ontology. It would be correct, although something of an oversimplification, to say that the course of his thinking is the course of the evolution of these theses, the gradual unfolding of their myriad and far-reaching ramifications. Evolution implies change; hence one will find differences between what Merleau-Ponty says about the primacy of perception in work published in the forties and what he says under the heading of perceptual faith in later work published after his death in 1961. But these differences contain no reversals; they are, rather, differences in emphasis occasioned by the discovery of new implications in the core tenets of his philosophy. My plan is to follow the historical sequence of Merleau-Ponty's developing thought, but only in a loose way; excursions backward and forward in time will be taken when it seems appropriate.

"The perceived world is the always-presupposed foundation of all rationality, all value and all existence" (PriP 13).[1]

The thesis of the primacy of perception immediately identifies Merleau-Ponty as a foundational thinker. The perceived world is the foundation of all claims to truth and validity. This thesis sets him apart from more recent figures in the Continental tradition, currently in vogue, who have emerged from the debate between structuralism and hermeneutics with a new brand of skepticism. For these writers, any appeal to a ground is *ipso facto* a reversion to what Heidegger called "onto-theology." The thoughts that guide their writing might be summarized as follows:

(a) Foundational thinking is thinking that ultimately appeals to a ground.
(b) That ground, to be ultimate, must be conceived as *causa sui*.
(c) The characterization '*causa sui*' uniquely specifies an absolute, the God of Western monotheism.[2]

These propositions support the claim that foundational thinking is necessarily onto-theological thinking. Another set of thoughts is required to support the skepticism that maintains that any appeal to an ultimate ground is necessarily groundless. These thoughts, which might be described as a skeptical version of hermeneutical reasoning, take their departure from a variant of the thesis of subjectivity: all human cognition/thinking/discourse about a ground can refer ultimately only to human cognition/thinking/ discourse about a ground. In a word, human cognition is always mediated by its own limits. Or again, there is an ultimate difference[3] between human thought/discourse and the reality it purports to understand which cannot be overcome. Finally, this skepticism comes to rest in the belief that to be human is to be imprisoned in immanence. Thus any appeal to a transcendent ground cannot, on this view, satisfy the critical query about its own possibility conditions.

I am not yet ready to answer these challenges to Merleau-Ponty's foundational thinking; further groundwork is required. Two important points should be noted now, however. First: the arguments are variations on the now-familiar theme of the problem of immanence and transcendence; and, second, they presuppose a traditionally dualistic ontology as the tacit context that makes the conjunction of immanence and transcendence problematic. To say that any appeal to a ground is ultimately a covert appeal to a godhead as source of that ground is to conceive transcendence in polarized terms, as necessarily beyond the cognitive grasp of man. The latter phase of the skeptical argument makes the same point from the other side of the underlying dualism: the finite intellect of man, being limited by space/time, culture, language, etc., cannot penetrate the context of his own sphere of immanence. At best, he can only de-construct it: that is, make its limits evident as limits. Merleau-Ponty's reply to this skepticism with regard to grounds is, in brief, to point out (a) that the assertion of the existence of the world does not commit one to asserting the existence of a god, and (b) that the limits of our knowledge of this world do not preclude that knowledge from being true. This reply, stated as it is here, can only be an opening gesture: it remains to be seen how it is possible to reconcile the polarized categories of dualist thinking and provide a defensible account of grounded knowledge. However, the selective survey of thinkers from Descartes through the British empiricists to Husserl, Sartre, and the post-Heideggerian skeptics should have made it clear that there is a unity to the complex problematic Merleau-Ponty undertakes to resolve with his phenomenological ontology.

The main thrust of the thesis of the primacy of perception is that the perceptual world is the foundation of all knowledge and action, truth and value, science and culture. It is the ultimate source and the final referent of human cognition. Our concepts seek to measure the perceptual world with a measure that originally springs from it. This reflexivity, which will require further consideration later, is conceived under the headings of *Fundierung* (Husserl's term for the reciprocal founding-founded relationship) in the *Phenomenology of Perception* and "reversibility" in *The Visible and the Invisible*. Relevant here is the point that the notions of *Fundierung* or reversibility allow Merleau-Ponty to conceive the relationship of percept to concept as one of asymmetrical reciprocity or intertwining in such a way that, although they are inseparable correlates, the perceptual world as the founding term retains a genetic priority. There is, as he says, a nascent *logos* in the perceptual world that can be brought to language and which subsequently sediments itself within the field from which it originally emerged.

The thesis of the primacy of perception is properly phenomenological because, as noted earlier, it asserts the ontological primacy of phenomena as its correlate. It is properly phenomenological in a second sense: that is, it points to the phenomenal or perceptual field as the ground and measure of all theorizing, be it labelled philosophy or science. Seen in this way, the thesis of the primacy of perception is a fulfillment of the Husserlian motto "to the things themselves," For Husserl, however, the nature of the thing is derived from the law governing its synthesis or constitution. Merleau-Ponty regards this as an instance of "the experience error," the error of attributing to the phenomenon what antecedently formed concepts (or, in this case, noemata) dictate should be found in it. In this view, the phenomenon is always hard-edged and determinate, always an instantiation of a category. In contrast to this, Merleau-Ponty's thesis of the primacy of perception invites us to attend to the phenomenon as it appears in its richness and multi-determinability, that is, as lending itself to subsumption under a plurality of categories and to placement within a plurality of practical horizons and theoretical contexts. It is this richness of meaning that underlies Merleau-Ponty's thesis of the intrinsic ambiguity of phenomena, a thesis that has been widely misunderstood and one which I shall consider in some depth later on.

The primacy of perception informs Merleau-Ponty's phenomenological ontology/epistemology, as the thesis of the primacy of the subject informs intellectualism and that of the primacy of the object informs empiricism. The ultimate ground for intellectualism is the sphere of immanence, as the ultimate ground for empiricism lies in transcendence. In defining their grounds and defending their claims to primacy, both of these positions state their cases in polarized, oppositional, and polemic terms. Order, meaning, and certainty are grounded within the immanent realm of consciousness, and nothing can be *known* about a world beyond: this is the intellectualist persuasion. Empiricism is the reverse: the order of things is the order of *things*: and error is the consequence of subjective partiality. The structure of argumentation is the same in both accounts: bifurcate reality, then choose sides with a Manichaean fervor—optimism here, pessimism there; certainty on this side, skepticism on that. As I have tried to show, this strategy fails, and the failure is due to the bifurcation and polarization of immanence and transcendence: the *sine qua non* for knowledge and truth, the "in-itself-for-us," is rendered inconceivable. Merleau-Ponty's strategy, implemented in the primacy of perception thesis, is to search for a ground where immanence and transcendence intersect: that is, in the phenomena manifesting themselves in the perceptual field. There is the table. Consider the 'there is'. It is an impossibility outside the context of an intersection of immanence and transcendence.

Two simple diagrams may help to illustrate the main points under discussion here. The first depicts the ontological/epistemological dualism that underlies both intellectualism and empiricism. In the first diagram the appearance (of an object to a subject) is regarded as derivative from an underlying reality. To use an Aristotelian distinction,[4] the appearance is first in the order of knowing (that is, cognition begins with the appearance), but secondary in the order of being (that is, it is grounded in a more primordial reality). For intellectualism, the appearance is veridical if it faithfully adheres to the laws of immanent synthesis, and error is generated when epistemic claims are made about transcendent things. For empiricism, the appearance is veridical if it faithfully adheres to the laws governing things, and error arises with variation from these laws on the part of consciousness.

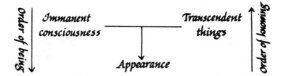

In Merleau-Ponty's ontology and epistemology, there is no opposition between the order of being and the order of knowing: in both orders, the percept or the phenomenon (conceived as immanent *and* transcendent) is primary. This is illustrated in the second diagram. In this view, it is through an act of reflective conceptualization that what is united in the primary reality, the phenomenon, is bifurcated, polarized, and defined in dualist terms as mutually exclusive. These polarized abstractions are then reified and misconceived as ontologically primary (when they are in fact derivative).

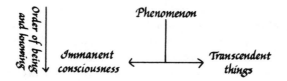

The paradox of immanence and transcendence is a paradox for philosophical reflection, and it disappears as soon as we involve ourselves with the things of the world. We know from the start where we must end: if my philosophy tells me that it is inconceivable for me to know that the desk I am writing on *is* really what I see and touch under my hands, then it is my philosophy that must accommodate itself to the overwhelming argument of the perceptual reality. The challenge is to modify our concepts until they do justice to our percepts. Specifically, the concepts of immanence and transcendence must be reconceived in a manner that no longer makes them mutually exclusive. And the phenomena of phenomenology must similarly divest themselves of the stigmata of illusion: if phenomena are to be conceived as real, they must be distinguished from the traditionally decadent appearance whose dissolution constantly threatens from within.

Reserving the problem of illusion for treatment later, I turn now to the question of how, without contradiction, the phenomena of perception can be conceived as both immanent and transcendent.

At the level of generalities, the answer is easily given. If it is polarized conceptualization that has produced the splitting, then the polarized concepts must be modified or abandoned. The issue becomes more complex, however, at the level of specifics. Which concepts, which terms are at stake? And the answer here must be: all of them. All the traditional distinctions—subject v. object, percept v. sensation, thought v. thing—have grown up from the endeavor of articulating a total vision, a presumptive unity of understanding, an implicit apriori which Western philosophy has been attempting to express and refine since its inception. So: we have here a problem of whole and parts—a whole Idea articulating itself through the manifold hierarchy of ideas. Must we then overthrow the Idea, bracket it, purify ourselves of the preconceptions that surround it? We cannot. We are situated in the midst of its unfolding, and we must begin where we are because there is no *epoché* that could neutralize our cultural antecedents, erase the sediment of centuries, and let us start anew. We must begin with the ideas we have inherited because it is only by investigating their failures and omissions that we open ourselves to the arrival of new ideas. Yet the relation of whole and parts is such that to modify a part is to create a tension in the whole which eventuates in its reconfiguration. Alter the concept of perception and the idea of the subject will shift, as will the ideas of sensation, object, thing, etc. And the overall reconfiguration will then constitute an adventure in the history of the Idea in its errant course in search of the unity which is its enduring goal. Consequently, I begin—or rather continue—here, where we are: confronting the traditional notion of the subject with an idea of perception that sees it for the first time as primary.

If perception is primary, it is not something a subject does: perception is no longer to be conceived as the activity of a soul substance, nor as an accident that it passively sustains. Perception is not something I do or something that happens to me—because the I is a product of reflection and perception is older, more primordial than reflection. Perception is thus prepersonal.

> Every perception takes place in an atmosphere of generality and is presented to us anonymously. . . . So, if I wanted to render precisely the perceptual ex-

perience, I ought to say that *one* perceives in me, and not that I perceive. (PP 215; PP-F 249)

The generality of perception is associated with its anonymity. If the percept is not the private experience of an insular subject *solus ipse*, then it belongs somehow to all bodies capable of perception. Latent in this 'somehow' is Merleau-Ponty's understanding of community and intersubjectivity, which I shall take up in another context. The point at stake here is that perception takes place at a level prior to personal differentiation: 'I see the tree' comes after 'there is the tree' and is founded upon it; again, no matter how divergent our perspectives upon it may be, you and I are seeing the same painting and there are volumes of unspoken concordance presupposed by the page of divergent discourse.

Just as the percept is pre-subjective, so is it also pre-objective. Corresponding to the indeterminacy of the subject there is the indeterminacy of the world and its things.[5] The traditional model in which a determinate thing is perceived from a given angle at a given time by a distantiated subject is here being contested by a model in which there is a phenomenon which unfolds in space/time. A phenomenon unfolds and perception takes place: at this primordial level, no distinction between subject and object has yet surfaced and become thematized. The perception is primary; only later does reflection step back, disengage itself, and transform the world into a spectacle which is viewed from a distance.

Also at stake here is a counter-claim directed against Sartre's position that every thetic perception of an object is necessarily accompanied by a non-thetic awareness (of) not being the object on the part of the subject. Sartre and the tradition insert an ontological abyss in the midst of the phenomenon, an abyss that Merleau-Ponty contends is not there. And yet he must acknowledge that there is an incipient estrangement brewing in perception, that the reflective distantiation which eventuates at higher levels is, indeed, founded—founded in the sense that it is a response to something primordial within the phenomenon which motivates the development of reflection, alienation, and cognitive malaise. To complete this thought, it is necessary to set forth Merleau-Ponty's account of the genesis of reflection, the emergence of the Cartesian cogito from what he initially calls the 'tacit cogito,' but later subsumes under the notion of reversibility. That, too, will be discussed later in this text.

Meno's learning paradox is the paradox of immanence and transcendence: either we know everything or we know nothing; either the object of cognition is immanent and transparent, or it is transcendent and opaque. These are the polarized categories of traditional dualist thought, and they make it impossible to understand how we can know anything of the world in which we dwell. The knowledge which is *de facto* ours becomes a *de jure* impossibility in the dualist conceptual framework because that framework defines as mutually exclusive (being-for-itself v. being-in-itself, consciousness v. thing, immanence v. transcendence) terms which have to be mediated if we are to be able to account for the imperfect knowledge we do have. Sartre's ontology and his dialectic of contradictions provide a paradigm of the problem of mediation.

With Merleau-Ponty's thesis of the epistemological primacy of perception and its correlate, the ontological thesis of the primacy of phenomena, conceptual space is cleared to resolve the paradoxes and problems. The thesis of the incompleteness of perceptual objects, stated just above, provides a basis for the imperfect kind of knowledge needed to answer Meno. Merleau-Ponty also mediates the subject-object bifurcation by pointing to a primordial level of perceptual unfolding which subtends the bifurcation. This is achieved by shifting from conceptions of the subject which construe it as a self-transparent agency underlying perception to one in which the subject appears as a prepersonal power[6] present in perception but remaining anonymous until and unless a subsequent act of reflection posits it as its own. The dualist severing of meaning from thing, value from fact, form from matter of experience is healed by rejecting ontologies in which the sense of the world is ordered from above in favor of an ontology which restores their significance to phenomena and regards the percept as originarily meaningful. Being is prior to thought about being.

> There is a paradox of immanence and transcendence in perception. Immanence, because the perceived object cannot be foreign to him who perceives; transcendence, because it always contains something more than what is actually given. And these two elements of perception are not, properly speaking, contradictory. For if we reflect on this notion of perspective, . . . we see that the kind of evidence proper to the perceived, the appearance of 'something,' requires both this presence and this absence. (PriP 16)

The paradox of immanence and transcendence is grounded in perception insomuch as perception intrinsically embodies both revelation and concealment. But there is no contradiction here; indeed, it is a condition for the givenness of a phenomenon that it withhold itself as well. The contradiction emerges at the level of thought where the revelation and givenness are attributed to an agency whose being consists in estrangement from a world which conceals itself and withdraws. Yet this need not be a contradiction for all thought. A reflection aware of its own frailties, one which attunes itself to the world it seeks to comprehend, and forsakes the illusion of certainty in the hope of discovering some truth—such a thought remains to be thought through: so far, only its outline has been sketched.

FOUR

Ontological Implications
of Gestalt Theory

The *Phenomenology of Perception* is the pivotal work in Merleau-Ponty's development: his earlier work gropes toward it and his later work seeks a deeper understanding of the themes set forth in it. As the title declares, Merleau-Ponty takes up the standpoint of phenomenology in this work, and sets for himself the task of resolving issues of contemporary epistemology and cognitive psychology. Both the issues and the means of approaching them came to Merleau-Ponty within a historical setting, a setting which, for him, was dominated by two convergent lines of thought. On one side, there was the phenomenological movement originating in the work of Edmund Husserl and gaining increasing attention on the Continent through the writings of Heidegger and Sartre. On the other, there was the emergent interest in cognitive psychology surfacing in the work of the Gestalt theorists and the American pragmatist, William James.

I have described these lines of thought as convergent, but at the time Merleau-Ponty was writing his *Phenomenology* they were regarded as divergent, even antithetical. On the one hand, there were the psychologists who were committed to experimentation and empirical methodology as a necessary foundation for their theoretical work. And on the other, there was the anti-scientific bias of Husserl and his followers based on the rejection of psychologism and the charge of naturalism (that is, the charge of operating naively within the nexus of presuppositions constituting the natural attitude). Merleau-Ponty and one other writer, Aron Gurwitsch (about whom I will have more to say later in this chapter), were the first to realize that the antagonism between the two approaches was hindering both, and generating problems that could be resolved by bringing them together. For Merleau-Ponty, the project of reconciling phenomenology and Gestalt theory required establishment of conceptual space in which the polar opposition between Husserl's intellectualism and Gestalt theory's empiricism could be mediated.

In the preceding chapters I have tried to show both the historical and the theoretical antecedents of the opposition between intellectualism and empiricism, and I have tried to unify the various components of this opposition under the general structures of the paradox of immanence and transcendence. I have also attempted, again in general terms, to show how the oppositions constitutive of the paradox can be resolved with Merleau-Ponty's thesis of the primacy of perception and its correlate, the ontological thesis of the primacy of phenomena. Now it is time to move toward greater specificity.

My overall aim in this chapter is to show that the basic tenets of Gestalt theory, if their implications are traced through, presuppose a genuinely phenomenological ontology, that is, one which centers on the thesis of the ontological primacy of phenomena. This will require an exposition of the main themes of Gestalt theory, which, in turn, must be conducted in the context of the problematic out of which the themes emerged. That problem-context, the Gestalt-theoretical critique of perceptual atomism, is entirely germane since it, too, can be subsumed under the general structure of the paradox of immanence and transcendence.

The paradox of immanence and transcendence is a paradox generated by dualistic thought. The dualism at stake now is that of the traditional opposition between the form and the matter of experience. The form of experience, held to be the basis of meaning or intelligibility, is traditionally attributed to mind or consciousness as the ground of the essences or forms which inform experience. Thus, the formal element of experience is associated with the sphere of immanence. The matter of experience is typically located on the other side of the ontological bifurcation in the realm of transcendence. The function of the material elements is to account for the givenness, opacity, and recalcitrance of experience: that is, it is responsive to the idea (associated with the *ex nihilo* argument) that the stuff of experience is not created by mind, but is only informed by it. Now, if the matter and form of experience are conceived as mutually exclusive, then the material element must be regarded as formless, as utterly lacking all meaning, organization, structure, relation, etc. This primal chaos may be conceived monistically as an undifferentiated plenum or pluralistically as a continuum of unrelated atoms. Ultimately, the differences between these views are inconsequential (Sartre, for example, incorporates both in his accounts of transcendence), but that issue is not of present concern. The focus here is on atomism.

1. PERCEPTUAL ATOMISM

Atomism did not begin with Descartes, but it is his version that informs more contemporary versions. I have tried to show earlier how Cartesian simples show up on both sides of the immanence-transcendence opposition; for example, in the minimum perceptible of the empiricist, Hume, and in the hyletic data of the intellectualist, Husserl. In both cases, the attempt is to provide a material substratum for experience upon which the formal structures of mind are seen to work.

The dispute between atomism and Gestalt theory centers on the question of the basic unit of experience. For atomism, the most fundamental element of experience is the product of exhaustive analysis, the irreducible, the atom. For Gestalt theory, the analysis of perceptual experience has to stop at the Gestalt: the most basic unit of experience is that of figure-on-a-background; and if analysis seeks to reduce this fundamental complex into something simpler, it can arrive only at constructs, things which are literally imperceptible.

Merleau-Ponty leaves no doubt about the position he takes on this issue.

> A figure on a ground is the simplest sensible given that we can obtain, [and] this is not a contingent characteristic of factual perception. . . . It is the very definition of the phenomenon of perception, that without which a phenomenon cannot be said to be perception at all. The perceptual 'something' is always in the 'milieu' of something else, it always forms part of a field. A really homogeneous area offering nothing to perception cannot be given to any perception. (PP 4; PP-F 10)

Merleau-Ponty goes on to conclude that "an isolated datum of perception is inconceivable" (PP 4; PP-F 10).

Is this conclusion meant to be taken literally? The challenge to atomism posed here is that of specifying its elements: what is a perceptual atom, what is it that we are to perceive/conceive under this heading?

Hume's notion of the minimum perceptible is one of the classic sources. One puts a spot of ink on a piece of paper and walks back from it: at the point just before it disappears, one beholds the perceptual atom.[1] This, of course, begs the essential question because the ink spot on the paper is a figure on a ground. But it raises another question which is relevant: the question of "thresholds" of perception. This term was introduced into psychology by Herbart in 1824 and subsequently elaborated by Fechner.[2] It was Fechner who sought to arrive at the irreducible quanta of sensation by using experimental and statistical methods to determine the absolute (and differential) thresholds for each of the senses.

The notion of an absolute threshold is relatively straightforward: one detects a stimulus lying above threshold; one does not detect a stimulus lying below threshold. However, as Weintraub and Walker point out, serious difficulties arise when the psychologist tries to establish precisely where the thresholds lie for a given sense.

> When thresholds are measured, no discrete threshold appears. There is always a range of stimulus values—from stimuli so weak that detection is no better than chance, through values detected with increasing probability, to values that are always detected. A 'threshold' is an arbitrarily selected value of the stimulus, such as the intensity of stimulation that is detected exactly 50% of the time. This arbitrary value for the threshold will differ from subject to subject. It will differ with minor differences in the conditions under which the measurements are taken. It will differ with even minor differences in the nature of the response that the subject is asked to make, and it will differ widely between two

widely different responses such as 'accurate verbal report' and a 'significant GSR' [galvanic skin reflex].[3]

To complicate matters, there is the problem of accounting for subliminal perception. 'Limen' is equivalent to 'threshold'; hence subliminal perceptions are those which lie below the threshold of consciousness. This notion refers to cases which some experimental psychologists claim to have observed wherein a subject responds to stimuli of which he is not consciously aware. For instance, measurement of a subject's GSR may show that he has reacted to stimuli even when his verbal report indicates that he was unaware of them.[4]

This brief review of experimental findings attests to the impossibility of accurate quantification of perceptual thresholds. And that, in turn, creates a telling dissonance within the atomist theory between the highly determined concept of an atom and the indeterminacy of relevant experience. This provides further support for the view that no one has ever perceived a sense datum, that the logical atom is a construct which has no equivalent in experience.

There is another set of experimental findings which pertains to the issue at hand. If the figure-ground structure is not elementary in perception, it should be possible to point to perceptual experience which is not structured in that way: the experience, that is, of a pure quality, a ground devoid of figuration. Metzger[5] experimented with subjects seated before a blank wall, Koffka[6] with subjects in a dark room, and Corso[7] with sensory deprivation. Their conclusions were the same: even when, objectively speaking, there is a complete absence of stimulation, the subjects perceived figures against the uniform grounds, figures which either were generated somatically (heart beat, breathing, etc.) or were illusions. These findings support Merleau-Ponty's assertion that "a really homogeneous area offering *nothing to perception* cannot be given to any perception" and leads him on to make a broader claim: "We say a priori that no sensation is atomic, that all sensory experience presupposes a certain field, hence co-existences" (PP 221; PP-F 256).

There are two fundamental dogmas underlying the thesis of the primacy of atomic sensa. (a) All complex sensations are analyzable into a set of determinate and irreducible elements. (b) These elements are the primarily given (complexes are perceived only subsequent to the synthesis or association of the constituent sensa). The preceding arguments have been directed for the most part against (a) the first dogma; they were intended to show that atomism cannot produce its irreducibles, be they regarded as quanta or as qualia: quantitative analysis does not yield an invariant irreducible, and qualitative analysis cannot isolate a pure quality. Consequently, if, as I have argued, the putatively irreducible elements of sensation cannot be given, then it follows *a fortiori* that they cannot be the primarily given. Hence the second dogma (b) falls with the first.

If no one has ever perceived a perceptual atom, then why has it been regarded as the basic unit of perception? The answer to this question is essentially the same for contemporary versions of perceptual atomism as it was for Descartes: the function of the atom is to mediate between percept and thing. The epistemological problem for dualist theories lies in the possibility of a breakdown of correspondence between immanent percept and transcendent thing. If the perceptual atom is conceived as necessarily the same on both sides of the ontological bifurcation, this sameness being guaranteed by its simplicity and irreducibility, then the atom can solve the epistemological problem of mediation.

There are two presuppositions latent in this account that must be thematized and assessed. The first has already been encountered under the coordinate headings of "the experience error" and "the prejudice of determinate being." The second is the constancy hypothesis.

The experience error is the error of making "perception out of things," that is, "what we know to be in things themselves we immediately take as being in our consciousness of them" (PP 5; PP-F 11). The prejudice of determinate being is the presupposition that things are, in themselves, completely and unambiguously determined. Putting this together: if things are determinate and if perceptions of things are confused with things, then perceptions must be taken to be determinate as well. But what I have uncritically referred to as 'thing' here hides another error. 'Thing' in this context is an ideality. The term refers to things as they are "in themselves" or as perceived by an omniscient deity. It is not the thing as we experience it (which is not determinate, but ambiguously determinable); it is the thing *conceived* under the ideal of absolute determination. Not thing, but idea of thing. Now, with this observation, it is evident that the result of coupling the experience error with the prejudice of determinate being is a transformation of perception into thought about things. A reversal has taken place: the concept, itself founded on the percept, becomes the model and measure of the percept. (This reversal is a specific instance of the ontological reversal represented in diagrams in the preceding chapter.) The authentic experience of perception has been obscured, and perceptual reality has been displaced by an idea of reality.

The idea of reality that has dominated Western science since the time of Descartes is one which is governed by quantification or reduction to quanta/ numbers capable of precise manipulation and calculation. As Descartes put it: "all things which . . . are comprehended in the object of pure mathematics are truly to be recognized as external objects" (Med. VI, PWD 191). If the quantum is conceived as the true reality and the percept is to take its measure from that idea, then the percept must be composed of quanta. These are the ontological antecedents of perceptual atomism.

These antecedents make their way into epistemology and cognitive psychology by means of the second presupposition mentioned above, the constancy hypothesis. The constancy hypothesis maintains that there is "a

point-by-point correspondence and constant connection between the stimulus and the elementary perception" (PP 7; PP-F 14). For each point on the
surface of the stimulus, or thing seen, there is a point of stimulation on
the retina. The constancy hypothesis is thus the familiar assertion of a
veridical correspondence across the ontological gap separating immanence
and transcendence coupled with a reduction of both thing (stimulus) and
percept (retinal excitation) to atomic elements.

Problems arise for the constancy hypothesis when determinate stimuli
produce ambiguously determinable perceptions. This can be illustrated
with (A) the Müller-Lyer illusion and (B) a figure used by Gurwitsch[8] in
his critique of the constancy hypothesis.

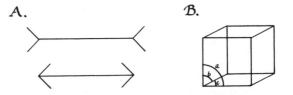

A.   B.

If we look at these figures spontaneously and uncritically, the lines in A appear unequal, and B is seen as a cube in which $\angle a = \angle b = \angle c = 90°$. If
we adopt an objective or analytic attitude, the lines in A are recognized as
equal, and B is seen as a two dimensional figure in which $\angle a = \angle b + \angle c$.
The same stimulus produces different perceptions, hence the strict correspondence asserted by the constancy hypothesis breaks down.

Gurwitsch argues that "the constancy hypothesis always leads to the admission of unnoticed data," and supports this assertion with experimental
findings.[9] In one such experiment, devised by Stumpf and reported by
Gurwitsch,[10] subjects perceive as indistinguishable musical notes which are
close in frequency but objectively different. According to the constancy
hypothesis, the subject must have "heard" the differences (because the notes
were produced by stimuli which objectively differed in frequency), although
they could not notice them.

Although such considerations as these do tend to discredit the constancy
hypothesis, they do not suffice to disprove it. As noted in the discussion of
subliminal perception above, the presence of unnoticed data in perception
can be confirmed by GSR experimentation. And the introduction of ambiguity at the level of perception can be explained by the influence of higher
level processes in the central nervous system which supervene upon the
data. In this way, one can account for the difference between the perceptions of figures A and B above by theorizing that higher level processes
influenced the spontaneous perception but were neutralized in the analytic
or objective mode of viewing the figures.

The constancy hypothesis has the character of a metaphysical assumption. Both Merleau-Ponty (PP 8; PP-F 15) and Gurwitsch[11] refer to the
work of Koehler[12] in which he showed that any attempt to confirm the

constancy hypothesis by means of experimentation required the assumption of the hypothesis in the interpretation of the experiment. If it is to be accepted or rejected, then, the acceptance or rejection must be based on metaphysical grounds. And, indeed, the rejection of the constancy hypothesis by Gurwitsch and Merleau-Ponty ultimately rests on a rejection of the dualism it presupposes.[13] They differ, however, on one crucial point: for Gurwitsch, "the dismissal of the constancy hypothesis can be interpreted as a potential or incipient phenomenological reduction,"[14] and it leads him to replace its dualism with his own neo-Husserlian idealism; for Merleau-Ponty, on the other hand, the rejection of the dualistic atomism underlying the constancy hypothesis leads to the adoption of an ontology based on the primacy of the phenomenon. I will have more to say about this difference in the pages to follow.

The metaphysical issue at stake in the agon between perceptual atomism and Gestalt theory can be formulated in several ways, but they all center around the question of the nature of the relations that constitute the organization of the perceptual field. Atomism is committed to the position that the basic units of perception are not intrinsically related. The underlying idea here is that of simplicity or irreducibility. If a part of a percept is conceived as being what it is only in relation to other parts (as Gestalt theory maintains) then that part is not simple, not irreducible, not an atom. For atomism, relations are adventitious with regard to the identity of perceptual atoms: the atom suffers no change in its perceptual identity if it is shifted from place to place within a percept. This is the issue underlying the controversy between nominalism and realism—a legacy of the scholastics still under probation. And it is also intimately bound up with the form-matter dualism whose antecedents stretch back beyond Aristotle and Plato. If matter and form are ontologically disjunct, then the form of experience (the relations constituting its organization) must be conceived as grounded elsewhere than in its matter (here regarded as discrete and unrelated quanta or atoms).

Perceptual atomism conceives the elements of experience as though they were material quanta. The percept is reified and idealized—modelled upon the abstract idea of the thing in itself. As each material quantum of the thing is conceived to retain its identity in isolation, so is each atom of the percept taken to have an abiding identity which is independent of context. It is the constancy hypothesis that allows this correlation between material quantum and perceptual atom to be made.

But when the attempt is made to account for the synthesis of atoms into percepts, perceptual atomism encounters the same problem that beset Descartes and, later, Hume: the problem of explaining the principles of association, the grounds of the relations which bring the parts together into a whole. This is a problem, as seen earlier, because atomism must conceive its elements as devoid of intrinsic relationships, because the matter of experience is conceived as devoid of form. I shall refer to this as "the problem of organization," and explicate it as a dilemma. Either the synthesis of atoms into a coherent percept is grounded in the relations obtaining among the atoms (in which case the definition of atoms as irreducible quanta has been abandoned), or the relations obtaining in the percept have no ground in material reality (in which case the organization of the percept must be regarded as adventitious). The crux of the issue is whether organization is intrinsic to the perceptual field. If it is, as Gestalt theory maintains, then the analysis of the field into atoms is fundamentally mistaken since the relations constituting that organization are lost in the process of analysis.

If perceptual atomism is to adhere consistently to its definition of atoms as absolutely simple, it must account for the synthesis of atoms by appeal to a supervenient principle of organization. The necessary rules of inference Descartes regarded as based on the natural light of reason, Hume's principles of association, Kant's categories, and Husserl's noemata all serve the same function: they are laws of synthesis designed to explain how the materially based atoms of sensation are organized and take on the forms of perceptual experience. In all cases, the formal principle is grounded in the sphere of immanence and attributed to the activity of mind or consciousness. And in all cases the theories leave unanswered the question of what determines the choice of one formal principle rather than another. Unrelated data can be organized in indefinitely many ways: if the data do not determine how they are to be organized, mind or consciousness must. But then the choice among possible syntheses must be arbitrary because mind or consciousness, being capable of subsuming its data under a plurality of forms, has no basis for deciding which of its schemata to apply.

When the organization of perceptual experience is attributed entirely to the activity of some supervenient immanent agency, experience can no longer be regarded as an origin of knowledge. And the philosophical standpoint adopting this view is forced to extremes: Humean skepticism, Sartrean relativism, or the position held by Kant and Husserl that knowledge is grounded entirely in immanent structures and experience can be viewed as providing only the occasion of learning what one already knew.

The problem of organization is decisive in the contest between perceptual atomism and Gestalt theory. If perceptual atomism adheres consistently to its own premises, it cannot admit that there is any ground in experience for assigning any specific meaning to it. If all meaning ascribed to experience is imposed upon it in an arbitrary way, then experience must be regarded as meaningless. On the other hand, if perceptual experience is held to be intrinsically meaningful, if there is any sense in which we can be said to learn from experience, then perceptual atomism must be rejected in favor of some version of the Gestalt-theoretical "principle of autochthonous organization."

The principle of autochthonous organization maintains that there are intrinsic relations obtaining among the parts of the perceptual whole, that these relations are grounded in phenomena, and that they constitute the perceptual significance or fundamental meaning of phenomenal experience. The claim here is that meaning is intrinsic to phenomena and is not, at the basic levels of perception, imposed upon them by supervenient formal activities grounded in immanent structures. According to the principle of autochthonous organization, the perceptual world is intrinsically meaningful.

This is not to deny the effects of culture, history, language, and other human meaning structures. Nor is it to deny that the conscious activities of predication, categorization, typification, generalization, etc. have some role in the structuring and organization of the phenomenal world. It is, rather, to assert that these effects and activities are founded upon a primordial level of meaning which is intrinsic to perception at its most fundamental level. The issues at stake here regarding the relation of human meaning structures and perception will be taken up later under the headings of expression, sedimentation, and the founding-founded correlation associated with the notions of *Fundierung,* intertwining, and the reversibility of Flesh. At present, the task is to explicate the Gestalt-theoretical theses which provide the necessary groundwork for understanding the later developments in Merleau-Ponty's ontology.

Part of the case against perceptual atomism rests on the point that the figure-ground structure rather than the simple quantum or homogeneous quality constitutes the basic unit of perceptual experience. It was Edgar Rubin who did the pioneer work on the figure-ground relationship.[15] Here is a partial resume of his findings.[16]

(1) When two fields have a common border, it is the figure which seems to have shape while the ground does not.
(2) The ground seems to extend behind the figure.
(3) The figure appears to be object-like (even though it may be an abstract shape) while the ground does not.
(4) The color of the figure seems more substantial and solid than that of the ground.
(5) The ground tends to be perceived as farther away and the figure nearer the observer even though both are . . . at the same distance.
(6) The figure is more dominant and impressive and tends to be remembered more easily.
(7) The common border between figure and ground is called a contour, and the contour appears to be a property of figures.

Rubin's findings were based on experiments with simple figures set against a homogeneous background: an artificial laboratory construct when seen in contrast to the rich heterogeneity of the perceptual world. These findings are also circumscribed within the visual sphere. When the shift is made to the setting of everyday life and perception is taken to include all the senses working together, the terms 'figure' and 'ground' must be replaced with others that are not narrowly limited to vision. Accordingly, the terminology of 'theme' and 'horizon' has largely displaced that of 'figure' and 'ground' within phenomenological discourse on Gestalt theory.

The unity and coherence of themes endow them with stability and identifiability. The unity of a theme or Gestalt is a function of the internal relations among its parts: each part is what it is in relation to the others and to the whole which they all form. This conception of the Gestalt or perceptual theme as a natural or non-arbitrary unity has been formulated in several ways in the history of the development of Gestalt theory. Max Wertheimer called it the "Law of Prägnanz."[17] Koffka expressed it as the "Law of Good Gestalt" as follows: "Psychological organization will always be as 'good' as the prevailing conditions allow. In this definition the term 'good' is undefined. It embraces such properties as regularity, symmetry, simplicity, and others."[18] Another Gestalt psychologist, David Katz, further elucidates the vague notion of goodness in terms of which the law is expressed. Making specific reference to Koffka's formulation, Katz states: "It should be emphasized that 'good' refers to such characteristics as regularity, symmetry, inclusiveness, unity, harmony, maximal simplicity, and conciseness."[19] According to Gurwitsch, the law of pregnance or law of good Gestalt asserts that "the perceived object tends to become the best possible and strongest Gestalt. This strength and this 'goodness' of Gestalt mean, phenomenally, a maximum of stability, clarity, and good arrangement."[20] Although these interpretations of what constitutes goodness in perceptual organization differ in specifics, what they seem to be after is the thought that unity of internal coherence stands as the ideal stasis toward which our perceptual processes strive: the other phenomenal characteristics cited either derive from or contribute to or are synonymous with unity.

Merleau-Ponty develops this notion in a manner that is particularly relevant to the problem of organization. "It is necessary," he says, "that the form and matter of perception be related from the beginning and that . . . the matter of perception be 'pregnant with its form' " (PriP 15). Again: "we must recognize . . . as anterior to any subsuming of content under form the symbolical[21] 'pregnancy' of form in content" (PP 291; PP-F 337). The unity of the Gestalt theme is not constituted by a conscious act of subsuming atomic data of sensation under some immanent form; it is rather the case that the perceptual theme is pregnant with form, that its own autochthonous organization endows it with unity and meaning. I might note here that Merleau-Ponty's thesis of matter-pregnant-with-form recognizes the Gestalt as a dynamic and emergent (rather than static) unity: the meaning of the theme is taken to be diachronic, unfolding through time.

The unity of the Gestalt has to be understood as compatible with an intrinsic ambiguity. Merleau-Ponty's thesis of ambiguity is conceived in opposition to the prejudice of determinate being discussed above, and is based on the Gestalt-theoretical "principle of contextual relevancy." This principle maintains that the meaning of a theme is co-determined (a) by the unity

formed by the internal coherence of its parts, and (b) by the relation between the theme and the horizon that provides its context. Thus, a grey
figure will appear dark against a white background and light against a black
background. Or, again, the meaning of a given word will suffer changes
as it is used in different contexts. Given that themes regularly do appear
in different and divergent contexts, and do so without losing their unity
and identity, it follows that a single theme can take on a multiplicity of
meanings. It is only by attempting to de-contextualize a theme or by forcing
it into one putatively privileged context that it can be made to appear as
univocally determined and unambiguous.

Merleau-Ponty's thesis of ambiguity is not a philosophical throwing up
of one's hands in despair of finding resolution to troublesome problems.
On the contrary, it is a philosophical thesis, grounded on evidence, that is
intended to resolve problems generated by the prejudice of determinate
being. It has antecedents in the Freudian notion of overdetermination and
deep resonances with Wittgenstein's thesis of usage-contextualization and
family resemblance. The ontological point driven home by the thesis of
ambiguity is that Descartes was mistaken in his attempt to correlate clarity
and distinctness in the sphere of immanence (or "objective reality") with
existence in the sphere of transcendence (or "formal reality"). In Merleau-
Ponty's view, it is the ambiguous richness and determinability that attests
to the transcendent reality of a phenomenon: thus, clarity and distinctness
become viewed as characteristics of concepts and idealities which are second-order abstractions founded on the perceptual realities they seek to
categorize.

To conclude this phase of the argument, the point I have attempted to
make is that the understanding of 'phenomenon' underlying Merleau-
Ponty's phenomenology grows out of his Gestalt-theoretical critique of the
perceptual atomism of dualist ontology. Along these lines, I have tried to
show the origins in Gestalt theory of such basic themes in Merleau-Ponty's
thought as autochthonous organization, matter-pregnant-with-form, and
perceptual ambiguity. My overall endeavor continues to be that of providing an ontological explication of phenomena. Here I have attempted to
explicate the phenomenon in terms of the Gestalt. However, it remains to
be seen what the Gestalt *is*. Gestalten have been conceived by different
theorists as natural entities, as ideal entities, and as phenomena. Thus, the
meaning of the term varies in accordance with the ontological commitment
of the theorist. Consequently, I turn now to a consideration of these ontological commitments with two major goals in mind. First, I want to show
why someone like Koffka conceives the Gestalt in naturalistic terms while
someone else, Gurwitsch, proceeding from the same body of theoretical
and experimental information, conceives the Gestalt in idealistic terms.
Then, second, I will argue that neither of these approaches provides an
adequate ontological foundation for Gestalt theory, and that such a foun-

dation can be found uniquely within the context of Merleau-Ponty's phenomenological ontology.

2. NATURALISM AND TRANSCENDENTAL IDEALISM[22]

The historical-conceptual evolution of Gestalt theory proceeds from naturalism to idealism (or from empiricism to intellectualism) and then from those dualisms to the phenomenological ontology. Wertheimer and, following him, Koehler and Koffka adopted the naturalistic standpoint of psycho-physical isomorphism. Merleau-Ponty describes this position as follows.

> The theory of form believes it has solved the problem of the relations of the soul and the body and the problem of perceptual knowledge by discovering structural nerve processes which have the same form as the mental on the one hand and are homogeneous with physical structures on the other. Thus no epistemological reform would be necessary and the realism of psychology as a natural science would be definitively conserved. (SB 134–35; SB-F 145)[23]

Classical Gestalt theory is thus conducted within the standpoint of Cartesian dualism, which it alters only by substituting the Gestalt for the atom and molar processes for molecular processes. Although the principle of isomorphism is held to correlate the psychical processes with the physical ones, it is actually the case here, as it was with Descartes, that the mapping of the psychical onto the physical presupposes a reification of the psychical, a tacit transformation of consciousness to mechanism. As Merleau-Ponty puts it:

> knowledge remains defined, according to the simplest schemata, as an imitation of things; consciousness remains a part of being. The integration of matter, life and mind is obtained by their reduction to the common denominator of physical forms. (SB 135; SB-F 145–46)

As developed by its early proponents, Gestalt theory is a form of naturalism or empiricism.

Then Gurwitsch and Merleau-Ponty come upon the scene and bring with them the transcendental phenomenology of Edmund Husserl. Working more or less independently,[24] they arrive at the conclusion that Gestalt theory cannot remain a naturalism because its own premises, if they are faithfully maintained, require the transcendental turn.[25]

The supporting arguments offered by Gurwitsch and Merleau-Ponty are also essentially the same and derived from the same source: Husserl's critique of naturalism/psychologism. The point of that critique is that natural entities in the objective world (including human physiology and its pro-

cesses) cannot serve as the basis for the phenomena of consciousness because it is through the latter that the former are constituted and known.
In short, since the objective world is constructed on the basis of the phenomenal world, it is a mistake to reverse this order and try to explain the
processes of constitution in terms of the objects constituted.

Although Gurwitsch and Merleau-Ponty concur in their rejection of the
naturalism of classical Gestalt theory, they are in radical disagreement when
it comes to providing the positive account that must follow the critique:
naturalism must be replaced, but with what? The natural thing and the
objective world are not primordial, but founded on a more original order.
Both Gurwitsch and Merleau-Ponty apply the same name to that more
original order: they say that the world of phenomena is the primordial
foundation for the objective world, but they do not understand the basic
term—phenomenon—in the same way. For Gurwitsch, who adheres to the
Husserlian position on this point,[26] the phenomenon is the object as intended by consciousness; it is the product of transcendental constitution;
it is what remains after the *epoché*, the reduction to the sphere of immanence. For Gurwitsch, the rejection of the naive realism underlying the naturalism of classical Gestalt theory leads directly to the adoption of Husserlian
transcendental idealism, that is, it leads to the bracketing of transcendence
or to the transformation of all forms of transcendence into meanings constituted within the sphere of immanence. Gurwitsch locates phenomena in
the sphere of immanence. And that amounts to an unequivocal rejection
of the thesis of the ontological primacy of phenomena because it regards
phenomena as founded upon something more original, that is, the constitutive activity of transcendental consciousness. Since, as I have argued,
this thesis is central to Merleau-Ponty's ontology, the disagreement at hand
is of major consequence and requires investigation.

A general critique of Husserl's transcendental idealism[27] has been set
forth earlier, and the main points of that critique apply to Gurwitsch's
transcendental idealism as well. It does not address the particular issue at
stake here, however: does Gestalt theory, when its genuine presuppositions
are exposed, entail transcendental idealism, or does it rest on the thesis of
the ontological primacy of phenomena? Is the Gestalt properly understood
a phenomenon as Gurwitsch conceives phenomena or as Merleau-Ponty
conceives them? Do we reach the phenomenon only by means of a reduction
to the sphere of immanence or does the transcendence of phenomena rule
out the possibility of completing the *epoché*? In the process of answering
the question, I hope to provide further elaboration of the Gestalt-theoretical
influences upon Merleau-Ponty's ontology.

In his critique of Merleau-Ponty, Gurwitsch clearly identifies the root of
their disagreement: "the existentialist setting of [Merleau-Ponty's] investigations prevents him from performing the phenomenological reduction in
a radical manner."[28] And, indeed, Merleau-Ponty contends that "the most
important lesson which the reduction teaches us is the impossibility of a

complete reduction" (PP xiv; PP-F viii). Gurwitsch is also correct in pointing to the *epoché* as the issue that separates the existentialists from more orthodox phenomenologists, like himself, who adhere more closely to basic Husserlian doctrines.

There are two fundamental moments in Husserl's phenomenological *epoché* which, although they are correlated, can be distinguished: (1) the reduction to the sphere of immanence, and (2) the movement from fact to essence. The first of these, discussed in chapter 1 above, requires suspension of the natural attitude and placing in abeyance all belief in the existence of the transcendent world. The second, sometimes called the eidetic reduction, requires a shift to consider things not as realities but as instances of idealities, as pure possibilities rather than actualities. For Husserl, this second reduction is necessary to fulfill the conditions for genuinely rigorous science. Those conditions, already announced by Descartes under the headings of clarity and distinctness, are apodicticity (that is, the certainty that requires absolute transparency) and univocity (that is, absence of ambiguity). When science is conceived this way, its objects are no longer worldly things, but rather essences: meanings, categories, ideal types, and laws. For Husserl, rigorous science operates exclusively within the sphere of ideality—and must do so in order to meet the standards of atemporality embodied in what he conceives as the very idea of science.[29] Although it is not identified as such by Husserl, this is an ancient idea which is generally attributed to Parmenides: only that can be known which *is*, and that which genuinely *is* excludes coming into being and passing away.[30] The objects of rigorous science must be atemporal essences whose atemporality is ensured by their ideality.

This Eleatic strain in Husserl's thought culminates in the standpoint that meaning (*Sinn*) in general is timeless and ideal. The ancient question of how atemporal meanings become instantiated in the flux of everyday actuality can be addressed by calling upon a central distinction in Husserl's theory of intentionality: the distinction between the *act* of intending (noesis) and the *meaning-content* (noema) of the object intended. The noetic act is real in the sense that it is a temporal event in which hyletic data (or "sensory contents") are synthesized and apprehended by consciousness as an intentional object. The noema, on the other hand, is ideal: it conveys the atemporal meaning which provides the form (*morphé*) according to which consciousness synthesizes its matter or sensory data (*hyle*). Thus, every intentional act (noesis) is an actualization or realization of a timeless meaning.

Gurwitsch adopts the Husserlian thesis of the atemporality and ideality of meaning,[31] and he retains the distinction between noesis and noema—despite the fact that these Husserlian doctrines commit him to a form/matter dualism that runs afoul of the problem of organization—because he regards these doctrines as necessary to answering questions about identification and temporality. That is, Gurwitsch maintains: (a) that it would be impossible to identify an object as the same over a period of time unless the meaning of the object remained constant, and (b) that it would be impossible to account for the experience of duration unless some element of the perceptual field remained invariant against the background of temporal flux. Here, then, is the crux of the dispute between Gurwitsch's idealism and Merleau-Ponty's existentialism: Gurwitsch argues that the refusal on the part of Merleau-Ponty to complete the *epoché* and conceive all meaning as ideal, atemporal, and originating within the sphere of immanence precludes him from providing adequate resolutions to the problems of phenomenal identification and phenomenal temporality. Consequently, I turn now to a consideration of these problems and the relative merits of the viewpoints in conflict.

(a) THE PROBLEM OF PHENOMENAL IDENTITY

Identification over time requires both constancy and change: the person I recognize today is the same person I saw yesterday in a different place in an evolving world. Not only has the background or horizon changed, but the perceptual theme, the person, has also changed in some respects— although in other respects he remains the same. Husserl accommodates this combination of stasis and change within the same perceptual theme identified over elapsed time by distinguishing two elements within the perceptual meaning of themes: there is the "noematic nucleus" or "objective meaning" (*gegenständlicher Sinn*) which remains constant, and the "full noema" which includes both the unchanging noematic nucleus and the changing "thetic characters" or "modes of givenness" (*Gegebenscheitweise*). The invariant noematic nucleus provides the basis for the theme's identity and the modes of givenness account for the changes in the theme's perceptual physiognomy from one horizon to another.[32]

One of the problems that emerge in this account has to do with the law of good Gestalt which maintains that a principle of internal coherence obtains among the parts of a Gestalt such that a change in one part constitutes a change in the whole. Gurwitsch acknowledges this principle and incorporates it in his own standpoint under the heading of "functional significance" of the parts within the whole of a Gestalt-contexture.[33] How, in light of this principle, can a theme retain its phenomenal identity when it has undergone a change in some of its parts (that is, those constituting its thetic character)? The problem is compounded when consideration is given to another Gestalt-theoretical principle: the principle of contextual relevancy which maintains that a change in horizon always entails a change in a theme's perceptual physiognomy.

In Gurwitsch's view, a theme may preserve strict identity through variations in its horizon, hence may be regarded as atemporal, because of "the quite general independence of any theme with respect to its thematic field."[34] Here, however, a distinction must be made between a theme's "inner" horizon and its "outer" horizon.[35] The inner horizon of a perceptual theme grounds its identity through time by remaining constant through changes in the theme's outer horizon. This constancy, in turn, is grounded in the unitary internal structure of the inner horizon: its parts are intrinsically related and interdependent, and cohere to form a whole whose integrity ensures its stability. Underlying the unity and constancy of the inner horizon is the Gestalt principle of internal coherence. The outer horizon, on the other hand, refers to an agglomerate of data which, although "materially relevant" to the theme, do not affect its central and enduring meaning or identity. The principle at work here is that of "material relevancy," Gurwitsch's weakened version of the Gestalt principle of contextual relevancy.

With this espousal of Husserl's distinction between the inner and outer horizons of perceptual themes, Gurwitsch implants a qualitative line of demarcation within the perceptual field. On one side of the line is the unitary theme whose parts are bound together by internal coherence; on the other side there is the loose agglomerate of data which are pertinent, but extrinsic, to the meaning of the theme. The distinction, however, is untenable: to hold that intrinsic relations constitute a theme's inner horizon and extrinsic relations its outer horizon is to hold, contrary to the evidence of experience, that themes are *unambiguously* defined in perception. Gurwitsch's line of demarcation is too sharply drawn; it defines the limits of the theme too precisely, thus leaving no way to explain the difficulty we occasionally experience when we try to determine what it is that we perceive, what is figure and what is ground.

Merleau-Ponty's conception of horizons as matrices of relations and his stronger adherence to the principle of contextual relevancy preclude the drawing of such a sharp line of demarcation. From his standpoint, the relations constituting both the inner and outer horizons of a theme are intrinsic (although they may be weighted differently and vary in importance to the meaning of the theme); to alter either is to alter the theme's meaning. He attributes thematic stability (that is, the constancy of phenomenal meaning that permits us to recognize a theme as the same in diverse perceptions) to "a certain balance between the inner and outer horizon" (PP 302; PP-F 345–49) which is achieved at the point of optimal perception of the theme. For Merleau-Ponty, then, the meaning of a theme and the sameness that grounds recognition depend upon both its inner horizon (internal coherence) and its outer horizon (contextual relevancy). Merleau-Ponty's account (described in greater detail below) thus reflects the fluidity of the phenomenal field, its propensity to shift focus and the resulting *ambiguity* of intentional objects.

Another difficulty with the account of identification offered by Husserl and Gurwitsch has to do with the problem of explicating change in terms of static entities. The thetic characters which are to account for changes in appearance of phenomena are noematic characters; that is, they are meanings and, as such, must be conceived by Husserl and Gurwitsch as atemporal or static. Thus there can be no genuine evolution of perceptual significance; there can be only the illusion of change produced by the rapid running-off of static and atomic frames or moments, each one of which is fixed and immobile. The Eleatic presuppositions of Husserl and Gurwitsch would generate paradoxes for these modern thinkers just as they did for Zeno of Elea.

On the basis of the criticism just presented, one might conclude that Gurwitsch's alteration of the Gestalt principle of contextual relevancy has led him into difficulty. Were he to accept that principle without modification, however, he would have to abandon the thesis of the atemporality of meanings. If the theme is acknowledged to be intrinsically related to the horizon, and if the horizon is regarded as embodying a continuous temporal flux (both Gurwitsch and Husserl do, in fact, espouse this latter thesis) then the meanings of all themes would have to be regarded as reflecting, to some degree, the flux of the encompassing horizon.

Furthermore, in his appeal to the atemporality and irreality of meanings in order to ground a resolution to the problem of identity, Gurwitsch has contradicted the spirit of his own arguments in favor of internal coherence. Gurwitsch takes Husserl to task for regarding the formal element of perception as supervening upon the material element.[36] His arguments are similar to those directed toward the same point earlier in this text: they are based on the problem of organization, and culminate with adoption of the principle of autochthonous organization: "organization must be considered as an autochthonous feature of the stream of experience and of the experiential field in its original form."[37] Yet, this latter principle regards structure and meaning as intrinsically bound to the phenomena manifesting them, and this contradicts in a fairly direct way the thesis that meanings are atemporal, irreal, objective units. Gurwitsch asserts that "no segregation of data may become stabilized unless organization immanent to, and not superimposed upon, experience plays the main part."[38] However, it is difficult to understand how Gurwitsch can maintain that organization is immanent to experience and, at the same time, regard meaning (including the noemata which provide for structure and organization in experience) as atemporal, ideal, and prior to experience. Whereas the principle of autochthonous organization should induce Gurwitsch to hold, with Merleau-Ponty, that meaning is intrinsically bound to experience, his adherence to Husserl's thesis of the atemporality of *Sinn* leads him toward implicit acceptance of the Husserlian notion of supervenience he explicitly rejects.

In sum, then, resolution of the problem of identity by appeal to the atemporality of meaning seems to engender more difficulties than it resolves: not only does it fly in the face of well established Gestalt-theoretical principles, but, in allowing for certitude in identification, it precludes the possibility of error and uncertainty in that sphere. To be sure, critical attention has yet to be paid to Merleau-Ponty's treatment of the problem of identity, but I shall turn to that after having taken up the second of the two claims mentioned above, that is, the claim made by Husserl and Gurwitsch that phenomenal temporality presupposes the atemporality and ideality of meaning.

(B) TEMPORALITY AND IDENTITY

No account of the temporality, especially the duration, of an act of consciousness is possible except with reference to the corresponding identical atemporal noema.[39]

Gurwitsch's argument, "were there nothing identical standing before consciousness, awareness of temporality would no longer be possible,"[40] is based on his interpretation of the description of phenomenal temporality Husserl sets forth in *The Phenomenology of Internal Time-Consciousness.* In that work, time is regarded as ideal: objective time is an extrapolation from originary subjective (or phenomenal) time which, in turn, is constituted by the transcendental ego. Although, as noted, Gurwitsch renounces Husserl's notion of the transcendental ego in favor of a "non-egological conception of consciousness," he nonetheless continues to regard time as ideal, as originating in the transformations in modes of appearance of intentional objects. "Duration consists in, and manifests itself for consciousness by, an incessant transformation of every 'actual now' into a 'having just been an actual now.' "[41] These transformations are attributed to the acts (or noeses) of consciousness as opposed to its meaning contents (or noemata). The argument for the correlativity of temporality and identity, then, goes as follows. An object is preceived as identical when it remains the same through the passage of time; therefore the consciousness of identity presupposes the consciousness of duration. Duration is experienced as the passing of an identical object from the mode of appearance "actual now" to that of "having just been an actual now"; therefore the experience of duration presupposes consciousness of the identity of an object (that is, invariance of its meaning or noema) through changes in mode of appearance. Without this consciousness of identity, there could be no experience of duration because

> there could be only a set of punctiform act-impulses among which one would bear the character of actual presence, whereas the others would be given characters different from one another as well as from that of the former. All these act-impulses, though simultaneously given, would still remain in isolation from one another; at any rate, they would lack the intrinsic relationship to connect them into a unitary act—for the unity of an enduring act is possible only with regard to something identical whose appearance may assume different temporal phases.[42]

In short, consciousness of time presupposes consciousness of an object as identical which, in turn, presupposes atemporality of the meaning of the object.

Merleau-Ponty would take issue with this account on several points. He would deny the ideality of time and the claim that time originates in a sphere of pure immanence (PP 414–421; PP-F 474–481). More to the point, he would deny that strict identity of meaning content is required for consciousness of time. The root issue is this: need there be strict identity in its meaning in order for there to be assertion of sameness or continuity of an enduring perceptual object? Gurwitsch maintains that this identity is necessary for the experience of temporal duration, but he is mistaken. Even if one grants the principle that phenomenal duration requires a differential rate of change within phenomena (something remaining relatively constant in contrast to something changing), that does not require an identical thematic content remaining invariant relative to changes in its mode of givenness. All that is required to produce the experience of change and duration is an emergent/developing/changing theme set against a relatively stable horizon. In fact, it is the nature of horizons to manifest themselves as static relative to thematic foreground activity. This relative stability is a correlate of the generally undifferentiated nature of horizons. And, indeed, it is a salient feature of Husserl's own phenomenology of temporality that the "living now" or temporal foreground stands in essential correlation with a "temporal background" of global or encompassing time.[43]

Lurking behind the issues raised so far is a deeper one which is essential to the question of identity and temporality, but which is difficult to articulate. The issue is whether attribution of identity presupposes an abiding identity of nuclear attributes. Gurwitsch answers in the affirmative, as he must, because he is operating within the sphere of transcendental idealism where phenomenal objects have only the meaning attributed to them in acts of transcendental constitution. Thus, to constitute an object as having a nucleus of abiding attributes is equivalent to that object having such a nucleus. There is no meaning apart from constituted meaning. However, if one regards phenomena in the context of Merleau-Ponty's non-idealistic ontology where they are construed as both immanent and transcendent, then attribution of identity need not entail identity of attributes, and misidentification and uncertainty become conceivable possibilities. The transcendence of phenomena—and the transcendence of global time—makes identification a task at which we can succeed or fail instead of a fiat on the part of consciousness. It also renders enduring identity intrinsically ambiguous: it is both true and false that I am the man I was ten years ago.

By way of concluding this critique of Gurwitsch's account of identification and temporality, let me point out that it is Gurwitsch's antecedent commitment to the reduction, and to the thesis of the ideality and atemporality of meaning that the reduction presupposes, that leads him to interpret the Gestalt theoretical principles of contextual relevancy and autochthonous organization as he does—despite the fact that those principles entail the conjunction of the form and matter of experience rather than the separation implied by the idealization of meaning (or form). Further on this point, I think it is reasonable to conjecture that what induces Gurwitsch to adhere to Husserl's understanding of meaning as ideal and atemporal is the failure on the part of both to recognize the role of language in the constitution of ideality. In brief, it is Husserl's view that empirical languages are all variants of a universal eidetic language, that is, that eidetic structures ground linguistic structures. In this view, any given actual language is an imperfect instantiation of the universal eidetic language. However, as Suzanne Cunningham shows in her book on *Language and the Phenomenological Reductions of Edmund Husserl,* just the reverse is the case. "It is language . . . that makes possible the generalization, idealization, active constitution of experience as meaningful. It is written language that raises experience to an understanding in fully ideal, non-temporal meanings."[44] The written word separates meaning from the world: the sign is then taken as a token for an ideal and atemporal meaning which, through the reversal diagrammed earlier, is mistakenly conceived as prior to and independent of the world from which it was derived. Then, as I have sought to demonstrate in this critique, one is faced with the impossibility of explaining how the ideal and atemporal meaning finds its way back into the world.

In sum, then, it is a failure to understand the role of language in the constitution of ideality that leads to the positing of a sphere of immutable meanings, resident in consciousness and prior to the world of phenomena it is mistakenly held to inform. The thesis of the ideality and atemporality of meaning motivates adoption of the methodology of reduction which further separates essence from fact and meaning from existence. In this context, the phenomena of the perceptual world lose their primacy and are conceived as constituted by the underlying reality of transcendental consciousness. When the principles of Gestalt theory are interpreted within this standpoint, their implications are distorted, and the problems to which they provide solutions (notably the problem of organization) surface again. Overall conclusion: the movement from the early naturalism or empiricism of Wertheimer, Koehler, Koffka, et al. to the idealism or intellectualism of Gurwitsch is a movement that stays within the parameters of dualist ontology and leaves the problems endemic to that ontology unresolved. Now, of course, the burden of proof must be taken up by the other side: how does Merleau-Ponty answer the question of identification and temporality?

3. WORLD HORIZON AND STYLE

The miracle of the real world is that in it significance and existence are one.

(PP 323; PP-F 374)

The first point to be stressed is that Merleau-Ponty's adoption of the Gestalt-theoretical principle of autochthonous organization resolves the problem of organization. There is no question of form supervening upon matter to organize it because "meaning and signs, the form and matter of perception, [are] related from the beginning and . . . the matter of perception [is] pregnant with its form" (PriP 15).

To abandon the doctrine of the atemporality of meaning, however—to regard meaning as grounded in the world and subject to its temporality—is to confront a challenge from the other side of the issue. What of the timeless nature of scientific laws and mathematical relations: do they not constitute a telling counter-example?

It is a consequence of Merleau-Ponty's position that all meanings, both those which are manifest in the flux of the perceptual world and those which are extracted from that world and arrested in language, are subject to historical processes of becoming. This follows from the principle of contextual relevancy. The world horizon as the context of all contexts is a temporal horizon, and its historical unfolding influences all themes, perceptual or linguistic, emerging within it.

The atemporality of mathematical entities and scientific laws is a presumptive atemporality. The laws of science are expressed without temporal qualification, but in the history of scientific development, they have always been modified in the light of discoveries subsequent to their own formulation. The history of science is the history of the evolution of its laws. So is it the case with logic and mathematics: every development in theory carries with it a reconception of elementary relations within the field. For the Pythagoreans, "numbers had shapes and even personalities"; things were numbers and numbers were things.[45] Contemporary quantum theory seems to be returning to some variation of this view—that is, the classical demarcation between number and thing seems to have suffered erosion—and the quanta held to be constitutive of physical reality are sometimes seen as transgressing the laws of logic. My point here is simply that the atemporality attributed to such ideal entities as numbers and laws is always only a putative immutability: the artifacts of language are subject to the processes of becoming obtaining within the world horizon.

The world horizon is defined by its ultimacy or all-inclusiveness: it is that horizon within which all other horizons are nested. "The natural world is the horizon of all horizons, the style of all possible styles, which guarantees for my experiences a given, not a willed, unity underlying all the disruptions of my personal and historical life" (PP 330; PP-F 381). World horizon and style are the unities in diversity that allow Merleau-Ponty to account for identity without freezing time or relapsing into ideality.

The theme-horizon structure grants to the world horizon a unique status among horizons. As the "horizon of all horizons," it is ultimate and all-inclusive because it does not permit thematization. It is characteristic of other horizons that they can be thematized, placed within the context of a more encompassing horizon. But, since every thematization is contextualization within a more encompassing horizon, it follows that there is always a horizon that eludes thematization. It may be that a horizon that functioned as the world horizon at some stage in history subsequently becomes thematized, bounded conceptually, and objectified. Thus, for example, one can speak more or less determinately about the eighteenth-century world or the world of Christian civilization, and one might even claim to be able to speak this way about the twentieth century. But these thematizations presuppose contextualization within an encompassing horizon which remains relatively indeterminate and conceptually elusive. World is Merleau-Ponty's name for what others have called God or *Geist* or Being, and it is as close to an absolute as he ever ventures. But it is not an absolute because it is temporal, it becomes. Its unity is not the unity of immutability: it is the unity of the ultimacy just explained. "The world remains the same world throughout my life, because it is that permanent being within which I make all corrections to my knowledge, a world which in its unity remains unaffected by those corrections" (PP 327–28; PP-F 378). There is one world, one universe, because 'world' and 'universe' name the horizon of all horizons.

It is misleading, however, to conceive the unity of the world horizon entirely on the basis of inference: the unity of the world is a phenomenal unity; the world manifests a unity of style. "I experience the unity of the world as I recognize a style" (PP 327; PP-F 378). The unity of a style is an adverbial unity; it is manifest in the melodic "how" of appearance and behavior. I recognize a person's style in gestures I may never have seen before because they express the *manner* of being that he is. I have difficulty articulating his style in a determinate way because there is no specific invariant, no common quality present, just as there is no common quality present in the games Wittgenstein describes as grouped only by virtue of their "family resemblances."[46]

Speaking now of the style of thematic phenomena (persons, objects, events, etc.), I want to stress the point that it functions as a ground of identification, and does so without having to posit an atemporal core of meaning that remains invariant throughout a given duration of time. It allows one to identify an emergent unity without drawing an ontological line of demarcation between an immutable formal nucleus and accidental material periphery. With the development of the notion of style, essence (in both senses conveyed by the German *Wesen* and the Greek οὐσία) takes on new meaning.

The style of the world differs from the style of persons, things, etc. as horizons differ from themes. I experience the style of the world as a sense of reality, a sense of what might actually occur or come to be and what can only be entertained in modes of fantasy. Traditional metaphysics might be understood as an attempt to think the whole, to articulate the *way* things are, to express the style of the world. But to the extent that its efforts were conducted within the language of themes—that is, to the extent that its discourse was discourse appropriate to themes and not to horizons—it had to fail. To the extent that it undertook to thematize a horizon whose ultimacy precludes thematization, it misunderstood its own intrinsic limitations. (Which, I believe, is why some now speak of the "end of metaphysics" and the overcoming of metaphysical thought, and then turn to other modes of discourse, for example, poetry, to carry on the enduring project of developing and articulating the sense of reality which is commensurate with an era's world horizon.)

The world horizon also functions as a ground of thematic identification. "The horizon . . . is what guarantees the identity of the object throughout exploration" (PP 68; PP-F 82). The world provides an abiding context or framework which establishes a locus in space, time, and meaning whose unity grounds the unity of the diverse adumbrations of the phenomenal theme appearing within it. "I can . . . see an object insofar as objects form a system or a world, and insofar as each one treats the others round it as spectators of its hidden aspects which guarantee the permanence of those aspects by their presence" (PP 68; PP-F 82–83).

Thus, the world is a meaning-grid or meaning-nexus—"an open and indefinite multiplicity of relationships which are of reciprocal implication" (PP 71; PP-F 85)—and it is the enduring location of an object at a particular 'place' in that grid or nexus which allows us to synthesize the changing faces of the object and identify them as faces of the same theme. "We understand by world not only the sum of things that fall or could fall under our eyes, but also the locus of their compossibility, the invariable *style* they observe, which connects their perspectives, [and] permits transition from one to the other" (VI 13; VI-F 29).

Merleau-Ponty's account of identity, in contrast to that offered by Gurwitsch, allows for the possibility of mistakes—and also for the rectification of mistakes. If one thing appears in the 'place' of another, I may confuse them; but if I explore both the worldly relations constituting the place and the manner in which the things appear, I can sort them out. If, for example, someone masquerades as someone else (or, more commonly, as someone other), he might succeed momentarily, but would almost inevitably fail if examined in detail over a period of time. Style and place in the world function as ethological fingerprints.

My intent in this chapter was to explicate the Gestalt-theoretical principles appropriated by Merleau-Ponty, to trace the ontological implications of those principles, and to defend the emergent ontology against challenges from either side of the traditional dualism. I argued that a rough equivalence could be drawn between Gestalt and phenomenon, and that the entity named in this equation must be regarded as both epistemologically and ontologically prior to the perceptual atoms of empiricism and the ideal essences of intellectualism. The underlying issue here, as in the previous chapter, is that of weighing the foundational claims made for ontological grounding in the spheres of transcendence (matter/substance/thing), immanence (form/mind/consciousness), and phenomena (the Gestalt conceived as both immanent and transcendent). The guiding idea is to eliminate the opposition between the immanent or subjective and the transcendent or objective by pointing to a more basic reality, the phenomenon or Gestalt, which embraces both sides.[47] The revolutionary aspect of this manner of thinking consists in reversing the ancient reversal that first posited realities underlying the perceptual world and viewed the latter as derivative, as mere appearance. "The appeal to phenomena as a legitimate source of . . . knowledge precludes in principle treating the *Gestalt* as a lesser or derivative reality" (SNS 84; SNS-F 148–49).

One consequence of this position—which will have to be examined further—might be labelled the thesis of the irreducibility of phenomena. As I have sought to show, attempts to reduce the phenomenon to underlying material or formal substrata necessarily run up against the problem of organization. The principle of autochthonous organization is the positive expression of this thought: the Gestalt organizes itself and generates its own internal coherence; the perceptual meaning, the configuration of parts within the Gestalt contexture, is intrinsic to the sensuous content. Given this irreducibility, this ontological primacy, the Gestalt or phenomenon must be understood as the basic unit of the perceptual world. Since the theme-horizon structure is intrinsic to the Gestalt, however, and since the theme cannot be isolated from its context, it follows that the basic unit of the perceptual world is the world itself—in all its spatial-temporal-cultural-historical fullness—as the ultimate context of all phenomenal themes.

Part Two

The Implicit Ontology of
the *Phenomenology of Perception*

FIVE

The Phenomenal World

The core tenet of Merleau-Ponty's ontology is the thesis of the ontological primacy of phenomena. This thesis is presupposed throughout his work, but never named. Its epistemological correlate, the thesis of the primacy of perception, is named and discussed thematically in Merleau-Ponty's middle period.[1] Ontology is not taken up as an explicit theme until Merleau-Ponty began work on *The Visible and the Invisible*. This gives rise to some problems in interpreting his thought.

There are two major changes that occur between the publication of the *Phenomenology of Perception* in 1945 and the commencement of work on *The Visible and the Invisible* in 1959. The first is a radical change in terminology: terms such as "brute" or "savage being," "the intertwining," "the chiasm," "reversibility," etc. appear for the first time. The second is a change in posture with regard to his earlier work: Merleau-Ponty writes in a working note that "the problems posed in [the *Phenomenology of Perception*] are insoluble because I start there from the 'consciousness'-'object' distinction" (VI 200; VI-F 253). These changes have led some interpreters to speak of a turn in Merleau-Ponty's thinking in which he abandons his earlier standpoint and takes up the task of putting together a new one.

In my judgment, there is not so much a turn as a development in Merleau-Ponty's thought during the last fifteen years of his life. That is, I see a continuity in his thinking rather than a leap to a new position; I see modifications rather than reversals. I think the new terminology was conceived to articulate ideas that were seeking expression in the earlier work, but were held back by the vocabulary of "consciousness," "intentionality," "perspective," etc. that Merleau-Ponty uncritically appropriated from the phenomenological parlance of his time. To be quite specific, I think that the ontological thesis of the primacy of phenomena is the central thesis of both the *Phenomenology of Perception* and *The Visible and the Invisible*, that it is the constant but unfolding thought that unifies the totality of his work, and that the modifications that occur in his writing are in service to the development of this core thought. As I intend to show, this thesis informs the language of consciousness and object in the *Phenomenology*, although this language is inadequate to the idea, and breaks through despite the subtle restrictions imposed by the idiom Merleau-Ponty inherited from Husserl, Sartre, and (to a lesser degree) Heidegger.

The task ahead, then, is to explicate both positions—the ontology implicit in the middle period and the ontology being explicitly developed in Merleau-Ponty's last work—and to demonstrate their unitary foundations in the thesis of the ontological primacy of phenomena. The problems of interpretation mentioned above should now be evident. In the case of the earlier, implicit ontology, there is the problem that stems from the dualistic aura surrounding the language of consciousness and object. My project here, justified by Merleau-Ponty's frequently stated intent to undercut the polarized categories of traditional dualism, is to show how Merleau-Ponty's genuinely phenomenological ontology shines through the obfuscation of a transitional vocabulary that has not managed to catch up to the thought it is after. In this chapter, as throughout this work, I am in search of an interpretation that will be just to Merleau-Ponty's intent, hence I must venture beyond the strictly doxographical.

A similar problem arises in the chapter on the explicit ontology of *The Visible and the Invisible*: because that work was not completed, because Merleau-Ponty might well have altered it significantly before releasing it for publication, because the working notes are rich, confused, and provocatively inconsistent, I shall have to depend on the vector of his thought and my sense of the overriding validity of his central insight to carry me across the aporia in the words he actually left.

1. THE PHENOMENAL WORLD AND THE OBJECTIVE WORLD

Transcendental philosophy since Kant has had to contend with the problem of correlating the human world, the world structured by the categories and culture of finite human subjects, with the world as it is in itself, the so-called objective world. This, of course, is the familiar problem of immanence and transcendence. In the preceding pages, I have tried to show that the two traditional responses to this problem end in failure. The intellectualist attempt to reduce the objective world to the subjective world fails because human categories are inadequate to account for the way things are. And the empiricist attempt to reduce the subjective world to the objective world fails because our understanding of the way things are is always mediated by the categories of finite culture, language, history, etc. Merleau-Ponty's response to this problem, by now a familiar strategy, is to look for a primordial realm which subtends the polarized categories of subjectivity and objectivity. Thus, he will assert that ontological and epistemological primacy belong to the phenomenal world or the perceptual world or the lived world. It is the question of the primacy of the lived world (PP viii; PP-F ii–iii) that confronts us now.

The thesis of the primacy of the lived world, maintained in one formulation or another throughout the *corpus* of Merleau-Ponty's writing, immediately encounters two problems, one historical and one philosophical.

The historical problem arises with Merleau-Ponty's appropriation of one of Husserl's terms: the lived world (*le monde vécu*) of Merleau-Ponty is terminologically equivalent to the life-world (*die Lebenswelt*) of Husserl. The terms invite confusion: one is apt to think that Merleau-Ponty's lived world is the same as Husserl's life-world. Merleau-Ponty abets this confusion by using the terms interchangeably and not distinguishing between them. This is a consequence of his critical/exegetical posture with regard to Husserl. As I have noted earlier, Merleau-Ponty, especially in his middle period, is wont to be uncritical of Husserl, to regard him as a philosophical ally whose standpoint is tending in the same direction as his own. Now, it may well be the case that, had Husserl rigorously pursued the ontological implications of the notion of the *Lebenswelt* he sets forth in *The Crisis of European Sciences and Transcendental Philosophy*, he might have altered his own transcendental idealism (with all its latent solipsism) and arrived at a position similar to Merleau-Ponty's. But the fact is that Husserl never abandoned the reductions or the idealism to which they inevitably lead. Husserl conceives the *Lebenswelt* in the context of transcendental idealism as a constituted cultural horizon. This is ultimately an untenable position if for no other reason than that the primordial sociality of the *Lebenswelt* cannot be generated from within the standpoint of the solipsistic sphere of ownness (*Eigensphäre*) of Husserl's transcendental ego.[2] Conclusion: the lived world of Merleau-Ponty must be conceived within the context of his own phenomenological ontology and should not be equated with Husserl's life-world. The seminal thought—as is frequently the case—was indeed Husserl's, but it is transformed by Merleau-Ponty.

The historical problem is but a prelude to the philosophical problem: is it not *necessarily* a reversion to transcendental idealism or some other form of subjectivism to assert that the objective world is founded upon the perceptual world, that "the whole universe of science is built upon the lived world"? There are two pivotal arguments at work here, one from the side of empiricism, the other from that of intellectualism, which must be critically reviewed. The empiricist argument states, in essence, that the way things are is the way things are and that human attempts to understand the way things are must take their measure from the reality that transcends us and exists in itself independently of us. The rejoinder, emanating from the intellectualist camp, is that all cognition of the way things are is mediated by the finite structures of human subjectivity: we cannot measure the validity of our cognition from the way things are in themselves because we only have access to the way things are for us. Merleau-Ponty's concept of the "in-itself-for-us" is unthinkable within the context of either of the opposed positions. Empiricism understands the need for a transcendent ground for human cognition, and intellectualism argues, on the basis of the thesis of subjectivity, for the need to find a grounding for human cognition in its own immanent structures; but each position conceives itself by means of excluding its opposite, hence neither position can respond consistently and adequately to the need to understand the grounding of human cognition as both immanent and transcendent.

Yet there are profound difficulties in the attempt to conceive an in-itself-for-us which brings together the spheres of immanence and transcendence. The factual reality that the tree I perceive exists independently of me becomes problematic when I attempt to explain how I can know this to be the case. The dualist categories of traditional epistemology and ontology, firmly sedimented in our conceptual space, render the obvious fact theoretically inexplicable.

This is by now a familiar problem, but it must be taken up again because it underlies the issue before us: the conflicting claims to primacy on the part of the phenomenal world and on the part of the objective world. This issue can be schematized with a variation of the diagram used earlier.

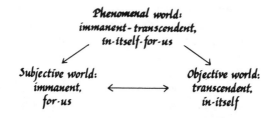

My claim is that the phenomenal world is ontologically and epistemologically prior to the worlds of subjectivity and objectivity which dualist thought posits as primary reality. I claim, with Merleau-Ponty, that the idea of an objective world is founded upon the phenomenal world of perceptual experience. The challenge to be taken up here is that of responding to the charge that this claim constitutes a reversion to some form of subjectivism.

The crux on which the dispute between empiricist objectivism and Merleau-Ponty's phenomenological epistemology/ontology turns is the thesis of subjectivity. This is the thesis on which all forms of intellectualism rest, and it states that the only world we can ever perceive or conceive is a world constituted on the basis of the subjective structures of perception and conception: the only reality to which we have access is an immanent reality. There is a fundamental truth—or half truth—in this thesis which Merleau-Ponty acknowledges (PP 320: PP-F 370). There is an ineluctable immanence to all phenomena, including the phenomena of reflection as well as the phenomena of perception, which derives from their presence, their manifestness. Although it is mistaken to say, as Kant did, that all my experience is *my* experience, because there is experience which is primordially anonymous and experience that is irreducibly *our* experience; still there is a germ of truth in Berkeley's idealism: the phenomenal world is permeated with humanity, and this is a condition for its self-manifestation. We are here at one limit of human cognition: every phenomenon we experience, conceive, imagine, etc. is in some way touched and limited by that disclosure.

In attempting to explicate how the presencing of phenomena affects them, one is tempted to trade on the distinction that is here being questioned; that is, the distinction between the thing as it really is in itself and the phenomenon as it manifests itself to us. But that is precisely the mistake that thrusts us back into dualism: the point is that "the thing as it really is in itself" refers to a way in which we think of the thing, or perceive it, or incorporate it into the praxis of our lives. The perception corresponding to "the thing as it really is in itself" would have to be an infinite perception: a perception of the thing from all sides and throughout the history of its being. This is not a possible human perception. An epistemological limit has here been reached, as most would readily concede.

This limit is a correlate of what I shall call the thesis of finitude (to keep it distinct from the intellectualist thesis of subjectivity). This thesis maintains that phenomena are circumscribed by such basic aspects of finitude as spatiality, temporality, sexuality, cultural sedimentation, and so on. It is finitude that makes perception/cognition of "the thing as it really is in itself" an impossibility for us. Everything that makes us less than gods functions as well to prevent us from attaining the divine omniscience that is the correlate of the ideal of objectivity.

The epistemological consequences of the thesis of finitude are relatively straightforward, but what of its ontological consequences? Shall we make the limits imposed by our finitude constitutive of things themselves? And if we do, is this not a reversion to transcendental idealism? This is a radical challenge. It names the most serious of the issues underlying the current schism between Continental and Anglo-American philosophy. At the time of this writing, the philosophical leadership on both sides of the schism is focusing attention on problems associated with language, and this may be seen as a movement in the direction of reconciliation. But Continental thinkers conceive language within the context of transcendental idealism as that which constitutes an immanent human reality beyond which we cannot penetrate. Opposed to this intellectualism is the empiricism of contemporary Anglo-American philosophy in which language is conceived as a mirror or representation of a transcendent reality or as an objective reality itself. Continental thought has directed its attention to anthropology, sociology, economics, history, psychoanalysis—in short, it has fastened on the human sciences—in order to account for the structuring of language which, in turn, is taken as constitutive of the only reality we will ever be able to know. The "new" psychologisms/historicisms/structuralisms which are modifications of the earlier reductionisms of Freud, Marx, and Lévi-Strauss share an attitude which I have called "post-hermeneutic pessimism" which centers on the belief that language constitutes a horizon of meaning, a circle or sphere of understanding which we cannot break through. Anglo-American philosophy takes its models from the "hard sciences," preeminently physics, and strives for an objectivity in language that is responsive to the objective nature of the physical world itself. The fundamental issue on which the two camps take up opposing sides is the ontological question posed above: do the limits of finite human cognition constitute the limits of reality?

There are two approaches to this question, and both are necessary to provide a satisfactory answer. Since the question is an ontological question, it must be answered at the level of ontology, in terms of a general theory of being. This is where I shall begin—and where I shall end in the chapter on Merleau-Ponty's explicit ontology. Between these end points, I shall take up the second, more specific approach and pose the question in the context of the thematics of intersubjectivity, embodiment, language, and truth.

The range of possible responses to the ontological question is circumscribed by conclusions already drawn. On one side, the transcendence of the world has to be acknowledged: we do not constitute reality, not even the sphere of human reality. One correlate of the thesis of finitude is the thesis that a world exists which transcends our attempts to reduce it to the categories of our own thought. On the other side, these very limits to our thought preclude the presumption of defining reality in terms of the infinite cognition which is the correlate of the ideal of objectivity: to say that reality is as an omniscient god would perceive it, is to understand the real in terms of the incomprehensible. The challenge is to steer between these extremes, and yet to be just to the legitimate claims to validity on both sides.

The standpoint taken by Merleau-Ponty is that the phenomenal world is the real world: reality is conceived in terms of phenomenality. The phenomenal world is equated with the perceptual world, and perception becomes the touchstone of the real. These assertions have already been set forth. The question at issue now is whether the differences held to obtain between the phenomenal world and the objective world tacitly amount to reducing the former to an immanent structure. What, then, are these differences, and what are their ontological implications?

Partiality is a key difference. The tree that manifests itself phenomenally does not manifest itself from all sides and at all times at once: it adumbrates itself through space and time. For objective thought, which is characterized by Merleau-Ponty as *"la pensée de survol"*[3] or thought that ranges over all space and time, this spatio-temporal unfolding is collapsed, and the real tree is conceived as encompassing the entire series of adumbrations. Where are we to locate the real: in the partial adumbration or in the completed series? Recalling the standpoint set forth in earlier discussions of temporality (chapter 2, 2 and chapter 4, 2a above), specifically, the standpoint that phenomenal time is transcendent and irreducible to the processes of immanent constitution, it is evident that the objective thought of the total series of adumbrations is ideal rather than real, a presumptive synthesis, since it includes moments that are no longer and moments that have yet to be. However, if we atomize time and segment space, we are left with a view of the tree from position P_1 at time T_1, a literally one-sided and instantaneous view that is clearly inadequate to the real tree. Neither alternative, neither the totality nor the isolated adumbration, can be taken as disclosing the real.

Between these artificial extremes is the tree manifesting itself through the thickness of the present. The presencing of the tree is forever incomplete, since it trails a past and portends a future, but it also has closure since it forms a unitary Gestalt. The reality is this full moment of the tree's history, this phase of its becoming. The partiality in question belongs now to the tree and is attributable to the fact that the tree, like everything else in the world, becomes. Indeed, instead of its partiality undermining its reality, the reverse is now seen to be true: it is a mark of the real to become, to unfold, and in that process what is manifest in the present as real displaces what has been and portends what will be. Then are past and future moments unreal? No: the past is really what has been and the future is really what will be, but references backward and forward in time take their reality quotient from the evidence to be found in the thickness of the passing moment.

Partiality: the term is ambiguous—a perception is partial when it is incomplete, but it is also partial when it is biased, prejudiced, slanted by attitude and predisposition. The two meanings are related because both the partiality of bias and the partiality of incompleteness are results of limitations in space and time: attitudinal orientations are affected by place and time (this culture, this language, this century, etc., as opposed to some other), by the moment in the evolution of world and species (this bodily configuration, this archaeological residue, etc.), and by all the accidents of a given segment of history. Drawing now upon the Gestalt-theoretical principle of contextual relevancy, we may understand partiality as a consequence of inclusion within the horizon of a given lived world which then functions as a general context to impart meaning to the perceptual themes emerging within it. And this raises again the question of immanence and transcendence, subjectivity and objectivity. Given that every phenomenon emerges within the horizon of a lived world—hence is disclosed with an intrinsic partiality (in both senses of that term)—what can we conclude? Is this partiality to be attributed to subject or object? Or can we distinguish between objective and subjective components of partiality?

The cumulative weight of the arguments presented so far makes it evident that to attribute the partiality of phenomena to the subject perceiving it is to appeal to some version of the thesis of subjectivity; hence it would constitute a lapse into the categories of dualist thought. To be consistent with the thesis of the ontological primacy of phenomena, one must conceive the phenomenon as autochthonous and not as deriving its character from the agency of some underlying reality. In "Indirect Language and the Voices of Silence," published in 1952, Merleau-Ponty argues that a painter, for example, cannot say "what comes from him and what comes from things"—"because the distinction has no meaning" (S 58–59; S-F 72). Locke's distinction between primary and secondary qualities, that persistent thought that we can separate the object's contribution to the percept from the subject's, must finally be laid to rest.

And that means that partiality must be conceived as intrinsic to the phenomenon, as an elementary aspect of its manner of presenting itself, and that we must not attempt to reduce it to a function of the transcendental activity of conscious intentionality. In the *Phenomenology*, Merleau-Ponty says that "subject and object" must be conceived "as two abstract 'moments' of a unique structure which is *presence*" (PP 430; PP-F 492). And later, in *The Visible and the Invisible*, he makes the same point in a different way.

> There can be no question of fitting together passivity before a transcendent with an activity of immanent thought. It is a question of reconsidering the interdependent notions of the active and the passive in such a way that they no longer place us before a philosophical antinomy. (VI 43; VI-F 67)[4]

Partiality is an attribute of phenomena which derives from the spatio-temporal character of the lived world.

The objective world is a world conceived according to the ideal of impartiality. Thus it differs from the phenomenal world which, as I have claimed, is the real world. Does this then mean that the objective world, the world that is the correlate of the "hard sciences," is unreal? Does Merleau-Ponty's phenomenological ontology require us to regard the world of physics as a product of the physicist's imagination which has unaccountably acquired an immense pragmatic/instrumental value?

The anti-scientific/anti-technological bias of Continental philosophy since the time of Husserl had led such thinkers as Heidegger, for example, into an ontological *cul-de-sac* where consistency requires an affirmative answer to questions in the vein of the one just posed. But Merleau-Ponty came to philosophy with an extensive background in scientific methodology and a healthy respect for its ability to generate truth. And his affinity with American pragmatism is strong enough to preclude his ever adopting a position which implies the unreality of the objective world of science. For Merleau-Ponty, the objective world is not unreal; it is abstract and ideal.

The objective world is abstract and ideal in one sense because it is a construct. It is constructed of hypothetical entities, conceptual and mathematical idealities, and tested in artificial environments where recalcitrant data are eliminated by experiment design or "corrected away" in statistical manipulation. The objective world is an ideal unity of the multiplicity of models generated in the various sciences for purposes of prediction, explanation, and mastery. Success in the fulfillment of these purposes attests to the validity of scientific idealities; that is, it demonstrates the validity of thinking of the world in those ways in order to fulfill those aims; but the limits of that validity do not stretch far beyond the limits of the purposes.

The phenomenal world, by contrast, is not an ideal unity of abstract models, but the real unity subtending those models. The reduced worlds of the various sciences are extrapolations from the phenomenal world which remains their ground and measure: the worlds of science originate in the lived world and their validity is measured by their applicability in and to the phenomenal world which functions as their ultimate referent.

The objective world is ideal in another sense: the sense in which objectivity functions as a regulative ideal for all claims to theoretical validity. Partiality is taken as a task, as something to be overcome in the process of theoretical growth and consolidation. The telos of objectivity is the generation of a theoretical world capable of resolving differences grounded in partiality. Objectivity is here the correlate of universality: the goal of reconciling the differences between man and man, culture and culture, by working toward the ideal of a truth which can accommodate all times and places. Merleau-Ponty describes this regulative ideal as one of his objectives.[5] This objectivity in service to universality, this obligation to a history oriented toward the reconciliation of differences grounded in partiality, must, however, be understood for what it is: a telos, a goal that regulates our efforts, an ideality we project, and not a reality that antecedes its own accomplishment.

The objective world is an ideal variant of the phenomenal world. It is an end posited by thought troubled by its own partiality. It is the name for a universal validity that once was conceived through the symbols of divinity and is now conceived through the optimistic projections of science. Objectivity is a responsibility we assume; to take it as a character of the real is to collapse time, ignore ambiguity, and presume a vantage that does not exist.

2. THE PHENOMENAL WORLD AND THE SUBJECTIVE WORLD

Perhaps the greatest challenge to the thesis of the ontological primacy of phenomena is that posed by the argument from illusion. If the phenomenal world is equated with the perceptual world and asserted to be the real world, and if illusion and hallucination are acknowledged to occur within the perceptual world, then it would seem that one is forced to grant reality to illusions and hallucinations. It is the threat of such a *reductio* that brings Merleau-Ponty back to the questions of illusion, perceptual error, dream, schizophrenic delusion, etc. throughout the *Phenomenology* and again in the opening pages of *The Visible and the Invisible*. The project in this section is twofold: (a) the argument from illusion will be taken up with the intent of showing that the phenomena of illusion do not undermine phenomenological ontology, but on the contrary cannot be understood apart from it; and (b), at the same time, an attempt will be made to find a place for subjective worlds within the phenomenal world (as in the preceding section the objective world was found to be a variant of the phenomenal world).

The thesis of the ontological primacy of phenomena maintains that phenomena are real. The phenomenon is here understood to be what manifests itself or presents itself in perception. Illusion, as it is understood in the context of skeptical arguments, is taken to be an instance in which what is manifest is not real, hence it functions as a counter-example to the thesis at stake. The possibility of perceptual error, taken to be intrinsic to perception, serves to surround perceptual faith with doubt: if I was mistaken then, I may be mistaken again. There is no way to determine, merely by examining or attending to a percept, whether it is illusory or not—that is, whether it faithfully represents its object or not—hence the percept must be regarded as an appearance whose relation to reality is problematic.

This version of the argument from illusion presupposes a dualist ontology. The percept is taken to be an immanent representation which is ontologically disjunct from the transcendent thing it purports to represent. In this framework, the difference between valid percepts and illusions consists in the nature of the relation between percept and thing, but that relation is nowhere apparent in the percept: a valid perception of a tree does not look any different from an illusion; both purport to represent the tree in the same fashion, and only the presence/absence of the tree determines the validity of the perception. And that presence/absence cannot be ascertained from the percept. Hence: radical skepticism, because there is no other access to the thing apart from perception by means of which one can tell whether the thing is really there or not, or determine the degree to which the percept represents the thing as it is.

Since, under this dualist representational model, one can never determine whether a perception is valid, neither can one account for illusion. The fact is that the discovery of illusion presupposes a manifestation of truth. "We know that there are errors only because we possess truth, in the name of which we correct errors and recognize them as errors" (PP 295; PP-F 341). The very experience of illusion depends upon its rectification— a rectification which takes place in the perceptual sphere—and this could never occur within the dualist representational model. This appeal to the argument from illusion undermines its own foundations.

The phenomenon of illusion is equally devastating to intellectualist accounts of perception—that is, to those accounts offered within the context of an ontology which defines reality in terms of immanent appearance. Here again illusion is rendered inconceivable: not because skepticism banishes truth, but because apodicticity banishes error. In order to do justice to the phenomenon of illusion, perceptual error and its subsequent correction, truth and falsity must be understood as interdependent and inseparable correlates which are coeval in the perceptual world.

Here the challenge posed by illusion takes on greater stature. To account for illusion, both truth and error must have a place within the phenomenal world. Truth has always been associated with reality, but not so error and falsity. In Western ontologies, error has typically been conceived as originating exclusively within the human sphere: man is the origin of error and falsity, evil and sin. Truth is the correlate of what *is*; falsity is correlated with what *is not*. How can what *is not* be conceived as intrinsic to the phenomenal world when that is conceived as the locus of the real?

Merleau-Ponty does not dwell on the metaphysical aspects of this issue, so neither shall I. Suffice it to say that the traditional ontologies that confront this problem confront it because they espouse a being/non-being dualism which conceives truth and falsity, goodness and evil, etc., as mutually exclusive. The metaphysical problem of the non-being of error can be resolved by abandoning the dualist being/non-being ontology in favor of one based upon the primacy of becoming. This, in my view, is a metaphysical consequence of Merleau-Ponty's understanding of time and accounts for the compatibility of his thinking and the general tenets of process philosophy. In any case, the doctrine of partiality set forth in the preceding section, which implies the primacy of becoming, can accommodate the problem of the reality of error and provide the context for a positive account of illusion.

It is only when phenomena are conceived as temporally dynamic, as unfolding through time, that illusion can be properly understood. One relevant point has already been made: the phenomenon of illusion is necessarily bound up with that of correction, and the correction takes place within the same perceptual dimension as the initial illusion. It is not the case that there is a discontinuity between the illusory percept and the correcting percept; for the illusion to be an illusion, there must be a unitary phenomenon that reveals itself first in one mode and then in another. If I mistake a tree for a person during a walk in the woods, the tree that ultimately reveals itself must be identified with the person it displaces. Here, then, is a phenomenon of succession: an anthropomorphic tree in the process of manifesting itself as such.

But: is there genuinely an illusion here? If the correct description of the earlier perception is closer to an interrogation than a declaration, closer to "Is that a person over there?" than "That is a person," does this warrant being called an illusion? If I am not surprised, disappointed, somehow shaken—disillusioned in a strong sense of the term—can I be said to have suffered an illusion in the first place?

Distinctions must be drawn here between casual mistakes or deflated expectations and the pathology of hallucination, systematic distortion, genuine para-noia, etc.: the divergence of degrees of error is wide enough that qualitative lines are drawn to demarcate the normal from the abnormal. Everyone has experienced illusion of some kind, but some kinds of illusory experience lead to institutionalization. Merleau-Ponty was well aware of these distinctions, yet he regularly overlooks them by incorporating ordinary perceptual error and pathological hallucination (together with dreaming, primitive animism and mythic consciousness) in the same general discussion of illusion.[6] The reason for this, I think, is that there is a general structure encompassing a continuum of illusory experience from the ordinary to the pathogenic. Where a given experience should be placed along this continuum might be regarded as a function of temporality and commitment: thus, the ordinary is separated from the diseased as a fleeting assent to a momentary presence is separated from an abiding and open-ended commitment to a distorted vision of things. Corresponding to this spectrum of degree of duration and commitment, there is a spectrum of degree of credulity and surprise. Our surprise at the discovery of an illusion is porportional to our acceptance of the illusory as real. But that acceptance, as magicians know, is hard to sustain. We are accustomed to living in the midst of ambiguity and we are tacitly on guard against deception. Our gaze is as much a questioning as it is an opening, and our very survival as a species attests to our ability to see things as they are. Hence, it is unusual to be taken in for very long or with any considerable degree of credence. When an illusion is sustained—for instance, when we live through the excitement of a movie or dramatic production—this is achieved through our complicity: we suspend disbelief and live the experience in a subjunctive manner. It is, then, a general structure of illusion that sustained duration is predicated upon complicity; hence attenuated credulity. This, in turn, raises the question whether the sustained duration of pathological forms of illusion indicates complicity on the part of the patient. "For the most part, patients distinguish between their hallucinations and their perceptions" (PP 334; PP-F 385), and "do not believe in their hallucinations in the sense in which one believes in perceived objects" (PP 335; PP-F 386).

Merleau-Ponty makes the same point about primitive peoples who dwell within a "mythical consciousness" (PP 292; PP-F 338). And dreaming, similarly, is a reversion to "the subjective sources of my existence" (PP 284; PP-F 328) which is seldom confused with waking experience.

The evidence summarized here forces one to question traditional conceptions of illusion. Specifically, it contests the point on which all the arguments from illusion turn—that is, the claim that the fact of illusion undermines the credibility of perception and demands a disjunction between phenomenality and reality. Quite the reverse is the case. The subjective world of illusory reality, like the objective world in contrast to which it is defined, is a variant of the phenomenal world and is discernible as such (PP 343; PP-F 395.) The patient sustains his subjective world by a systematic denial of the phenomenal world which continually threatens to obtrude and displace the phantasms of the diseased and irreal world. While it is true that the patient's commitment to his illusion is not entirely voluntary—"modern pathology shows that there is no strictly elective disturbance" (PP 125; PP-F 146)—it is also true that he is complicit in it, since denial necessarily betrays an awareness of that which it negates.

The general structure of illusion, evident throughout the spectrum from ordinary to pathological experience, is such as to support rather than undermine the thesis of the reality of the phenomenal world. To evidence already presented in support of this conclusion, (a) that perceptual error is discovered on the occasion of its correction and (b) that hallucination does not command the same credibility as the perceptual world, two further considerations may be added. First: in presenting itself as a valid perception, the illusion makes use of and depends upon the grounded belief in the phenomenal world (PP 297; PP-F 344), just as the lie can only take place upon a ground of truth. And as it is with lies, so it is with illusions: they open up "a horizon of possible verifications" which is our abiding foothold within the real. The second point is closely related. "The difference between illusion and perception is intrinsic, and the truth of perception can be read off only from perception itself" (PP 296; PP-F 343). To be sure, "it is of the nature of illusion not to present itself as such" (PP 295; PP-F 341); that is, illusions must dissemble, must present themselves as what they are not, must mimic reality—but there can be imitation only if there is an original, and the imitation can never bear scrutiny. There is a richness of the real which derives from its transcendence, permits exploration, and unfolds harmoniously, whereas illusions are thin and melt under the inquisitive eye.

The truth brought to the surface by analysis of the range of phenomena loosely grouped under the heading of illusion is that the phenomenal world is neither objective nor subjective. The structures of partiality and multi-contextuality discussed earlier render the world ambiguous. Both derivative worlds are parasitic upon that ambiguity: the objective world, responding to one kind of anxiety, is the projection of the ideal of a clarity that would dispel the phenomenal world's ambiguity; and the subjective worlds, responding to different anxieties, feed off the richness of the phenomenal world and its ability to accommodate a variety of interpretations. But the fact of the matter is that the phenomenal world can neither be collapsed into an eternal and infinite presence nor be stretched into an indefinite plurality of incompossible dreams. The patient's very refusal to awaken into the public sphere that appeals to him and demands from him a re-sponse-ability he finds too onerous to bear betrays an implicit awareness within him of the encroachment of the real, the weight of the impending realization he exhausts himself in fleeing.

But how does the real encroach? In what manner does the phenomenal world resist the endurance of illusion? Or, to state the problem in another way, is there here a covert appeal to a furtive objectivity? If the truth of perception can be read off perception itself, does this not reintroduce an objective measure and reestablish an appearance/reality distinction in the midst of the phenomenal world?

The perplexity expressed in these questions can be resolved by recalling Merleau-Ponty's critique of the thesis of determinate being. His critique consists in showing that the determinacy maintained by that thesis to obtain among things prior to their ambiguous manifestation and independently of that presencing is, in fact, not the *terminus a quo*, not the original state of things, but rather the *terminus ad quem*, the end toward which their unfolding tends. Phenomena are not originally determinate, but they admit of determination. Determinacy is the result (rather than the condition) of a tendency toward resolution and constancy within the phenomenal field.

This tendency toward resolution has already been mentioned (toward the end of the preceding section) under the heading of the reconciliation of differences that serves the goal of universality. In the present context, the relevant doctrine is Merleau-Ponty's notion of optimal perception. The specific question to which this doctrine responds is the question of a phenomenal measure which gives rise to the ideal of objectivity: how is it that the small thing in the distance and the thing that usurps the total visual horizon close up are identified and assigned a given size that is held to be constant throughout changes in distance and angle of vision? How can the illusions of perspective be resolved in the phenomenal domain without appealing to a spurious notion of a determinate in-itself?

> For each object, as for each picture in an art gallery, there is an optimum distance from which it requires to be seen, a direction viewed from which it vouchsafes most of itself: at a shorter or greater distance we have merely a perception blurred through excess or deficiency. We therefore tend towards the maximum of visibility, and seek a better focus as with a microscope. (PP 302; PP-F 348)

Merleau-Ponty describes this optimal perception as "privileged" and says that it "assures the unity of the perceptual process and gathers into itself all the other appearances" (PP 302; PP-F 348). The unity of the object and of the perspectives upon it, the synthesis of its adumbrations, is thus to be attributed to the manner in which the phenomenon unfolds (PP 17; PP-F 25), and need not be assigned to a preexistent determinate in-itself (as empiricism would have it) or to an ideal and unlearned appresentation (as intellectualism must have it).

As noted earlier, Merleau-Ponty is here, in the *Phenomenology of Perception*, working through an inherited terminological framework which uses and hence tacitly reinforces the subject-object bipolarity he was attempting to overcome. Hence, the doctrine of optimal perception allows an interpretation in which the subjective processes of perception are seen as accommodating the demands of an objective in-itself. Under this interpretation, the perceptual process—including the entire lived body with the motility that both initiates and resolves problems of perspective and viewpoint—is seen as an "I can" that is responsive to a scenario that is determinately what it is, as it were, in the eyes of God. Thus, it is my uneasiness with my perspective on the artwork or my viewpoint within the natural landscape that sets my body in motion in search of the vantage that will reduce my tension and bring the spectacle into focus. The measure of the unity I seek is, under this imperative, an objective (that is, goal) rather than a phenomenal measure.[7]

The proper response to such conflicts in interpretation, both with regard to phenomenal themes in general and with regard to Merleau-Ponty's doctrines concerning these themes, is to seek an appropriate context. Taking the latter—the conflict in interpreting Merleau-Ponty's doctrine—first, the appropriate context is his work considered in entirety. The notion of optimal perception is, as just stated, an instance of the recurring idea that phenomenal themes tend toward resolution and constancy. This, in turn, has foundations in the law of good Gestalt and the principle of autochthonous organization, both of which have been shown earlier to exclude dualistic interpretation. The Gestalt is "auto-figurative": the phenomenon of resolution cannot be explained by appeal to the immanent activity of a subject, the transcendence of an in-itself, or their interaction. The notion of optimal perception must be seen as an instance of Merleau-Ponty's thesis that the matter of perception is pregnant with its form. This interpretation is vindicated in Merleau-Ponty's last writing where my perception of the worldly thing is no longer viewed as the action of my body in response to the demands of a world from which I am separate, but rather as a moment in the self-revelation of the flesh of the world. "One can say that we perceive the things themselves, that we are the world that thinks itself—or that the world is at the heart of our flesh" (VI 136; VI-F 179). This thought, which will receive the explication it requires in part three, is already surfacing in the *Phenomenology* where Merleau-Ponty seizes upon a line from Valéry and says that "I am not *set over against* [the blue of the sky] as an acosmic subject," but rather "it 'thinks itself within me'" (PP 214; PP-F 248). I am, thus, not separate from being, but rather "a fold" in being where being touches itself through me (PP 215; PP-F 249). Whence I conclude: (a) that the nondualistic Gestalt-theoretical understanding of the doctrine of optimal perception just set forth is more apt than the account which trades on the subject-object bipolarity, and (b) that the subject/object discourse of the *Phenomenology* is already giving way, within that very work, to the concepts and terminology of *The Visible and the Invisible* which are more adequate to the ontology seeking articulation throughout Merleau-Ponty's writings.

As it is with the resolution of Merleau-Ponty's text, so it is with the resolution of the text of worldly things: the phenomenon demands an appropriate context and then resolves itself within the context it calls for. At work here is the principle of contextual relevancy, but now with a further development. As set forth earlier, that principle maintains that the meaning of a given theme is in part determined by the context in which it presents itself. Given the nesting and overlapping of contexts, there is an ambiguity, lack of determinacy/unity, intrinsic to all phenomenal themes. Here, then, is a source of illusion and another ramification of partiality which can be described using the concepts of perspective and subjectivity, but which ultimately requires a genuinely phenomenological explanation, an explanation, that is, which is consonant with the thesis of the ontological primacy of phenomena. The demand on the part of phenomenal themes for unity and completion is a demand for proper contextualization: the full Gestalt, the phenomenon striving to overcome its own partiality, must be accorded its due and understood in its integrity as theme-within-horizon. Each theme demands its own place in the world, the lived world which stands as its ultimate context, and exerts its own force in seeking that place by withholding its plenitude until it finds its home. The fact of worldly becoming precludes finality or rest, and stands in direct correlation with the dynamic and evolving nature of things. Hence ambiguity/partiality/illusion—the imperfection/deficiency around which all the discourse of subjectivity is centered—remains inevitable as described earlier in this section under the rubric of the thesis of finitude.

The doctrine of optimal perception must, then, be understood in relation to the phenomenon of contextualization. It is not the case that the tree manifesting itself under optimal conditions reveals all its secrets. It is rather the case that the privileged perception is the one that is most adequate to the nature of the interrogation directing the perceptual query. Thus the same tree or the same painting may call for a series of optimal percepts—this distance for this revelation, that focus of the microscope or spectroscope for that revelation—but, in each instance, the measure of what is optimal cannot be placed exclusively in either subject or thing, but belongs in the chiasm that subtends both. To each context, each interrogation, there is a privileged perception, but these contexts themselves demand unification and call for resolution within the all-encompassing unity of the world. Interrogation stands in essential correlation to becoming: there is an open-ended process pointed toward determination and unification which approaches an ever-receding finality, but will not attain it as long as time remains a finite unfolding. To posit that end as the beginning is a mistake of the objectivist thesis of determinate being. But to forsake the end, to abandon the goal of universality in a retreat to the partial view that happens to be one's own is equally a mistake: the apodicticity of incorrigible subjectivity is an illusory solace for the abandonment of truth.

> The truth is that neither error nor doubt cut us off from the truth, because we are surrounded by a world horizon which the teleology of consciousness invites us to resolve. (PP 398; PP-F 456)

SIX

Consciousness

It is possible to read the history of philosophy as the history of a failure that has just begun to recognize itself as such. It begins somewhere in the prehistory of primitive animism where every thing had a soul or spirit permeating its material being. That spirit had to be named to be appeased, to be reckoned with. But the spirits, the immaterial essences, were released as they were baptized: to name them was to free them from the things in which they dwelled. Things became inanimate. All things but one: man. So the wise ones—the witch doctors, priests, and shamans: the philosophers—set out to release the last spirit, to name it and free it from the world. Buddha, Socrates, Christ: the liberators of the soul. The way of genuinely being a self and the way of genuinely not being a self have this in common: they try to capture the thinking thing with words, with cant and incantation, thereby to emancipate it from subjection to all things and return it to the peace of its own unworldly *Wesen*. Descartes, Kant, Husserl: the deifiers of the soul. The soul, now as consciousness, became first *causa sui* and then cause of the world: a thing necessarily apart from all things. Neitzsche, Heidegger, Sartre: the defilers of the soul. The cause of itself and all things fell from grace and back into the world where it appeared as the cause of nothing, itself nothing, still not a thing. Merleau-Ponty inherited the soul as Being and as Nothingness and set out alone to do what none before him—or since him—could think to do: first he made the soul a thing, a body, and then he incarnated all things into Flesh. His successors have yet to appear. Those who follow him in time are still resisting incarnation: they are still trying to make the Flesh become word; they are still seeking to obtain release from the world by transforming it and themselves into a text. The text is the latest in the vicissitudes of *Geist*.

Sedimentation (PP 130; PP-F 152) is the settling of culture into things. In our culture, the separation of the animate and the inanimate has permeated all things; it is, perhaps, the most deeply entrenched of all dualisms; it permeates our language, our thought, and the things themselves. There is no *epoché* capable of freeing us in one act of reflection from millennia of sediment; it is, rather, the work of a lifetime to perform the askesis required to dig out from under the conceptual weight of the dualist tradition. To think the thought that consciousness is worldly all the way through is, for the psychologist, to abandon the psyche and, for the philosopher, to reverse the direction of his other-worldly vocation.

In the *Phenomenology of Perception*, Merleau-Ponty undertakes the task of incarnating consciousness and bringing it back into the world. But the consciousness whose inner structure is world-structure is still given its traditional name, and that name attaches it to philosophical world-history: the Socratic self, the immortal soul beset by carnal passions, the Cartesian cogito, the historical *Geist*, the transcendental ego, the nothingness of self-transcendence. These all have their truth which cannot be forgotten, but must be accommodated in the thought that would re-place them in the world. So Merleau-Ponty works through the language of consciousness, infiltrates it, dismantles its infrastructure, and forces it to collapse from its own ponderous ineptitude. But he is not an alien ideologue equipped with preformulated doctrines of subversion; his doctrines, on the contrary, are evolutionary, and must be formulated as he proceeds. Where he makes a hole, he must find a way to fill it. One can see divided loyalties in his prose, in the surprises that make his sentences so awkwardly telling. "The acts of the *I* are of such a nature that they outstrip themselves leaving no interiority of consciousness" (PP 376; PP-F 431). The traditional immanence of consciousness here is denied in the same statement that posits it. Yet this is no mere Sartrean revelry in contradiction. This is a man of spirit searching for the meaning of spirituality, and gradually awakening to the realization that psyche, anima, soul, spirit, ego, consciousness are worldly phenomena, that the words refer to a certain manner or style of being flesh, that there is no immaterial, invisible, immutable soul substance or *res cogitans* temporarily resident in the body and animating it, that this region of being is also the product of abstraction, polarization, and reification.

Yet, consciousness regularly appears in the *Phenomenology* as the subject of sentences and actions. "We describe consciousness as involved through its body in a space, through its language in a history, through its prejudices in a concrete form of thought" (PP 399; PP-F 457). How is this consciousness to be conceived? How is it to be reconciled with the thesis of the ontological primacy of phenomena? How can the basic term of transcendental idealism be given positive content within the context of a radical critique of intellectualism?

The scheme of the reply has already been set forth: "The problems posed in [the *Phenomenology*] are insoluble because I start there from the 'consciousness'-'object' distinction" (VI 200; VI-F 253). 'Consciousness' cannot function as a basic term in an ontology that succeeds in overcoming dualism. 'Consciousness' does function as a basic term in the *Phenomenology*. Ergo. . . . But this is simple-minded. 'Consciousness' in the *Phenomenology* is a term seeking its own dissolution. It is an illuminating impediment in the development of Merleau-Ponty's ontology.

To be more specific: consciousness appears in the *Phenomenology* under two main headings, the tacit cogito of prereflective experience and the

Cartesian cogito of explicit and thematic experience. The tacit cogito is anonymous or prepersonal. "Every perception takes place in an atmosphere of generality and is presented to us anonymously. . . . I am no more aware of being the true subject of my sensation than of my birth or my death" (PP 215; PP-F 249). This anonymous perception is not accompanied by an 'I think,' but yet it has—must have—a reflexive character. "All thought of something is at the same time self-consciousness, in the absence of which it could have no object" (PP 371; PP-F 426). Here is the problem that keeps Merleau-Ponty within the language of consciousness and object. To perceive a thing is not to coincide with it, to be it. The presencing of a phenomenon requires a distantiation, a space between the here of perception and the there of the phenomenon; and there has to be an awareness, albeit tacit, of the here for the there to appear as such. This distantiation and tacit reflexivity, which is necessary for perception or the presencing of phenomena, is explicated in the *Phenomenology* under the heading of the tacit cogito, hence within the context of a consciousness-object distinction. Subsequently, in *The Visible and the Invisible*, the same requirement for distantiation and reflexivity will be explicated under the heading of the reversibility of the flesh, a framework which does not trade on the consciousness-object distinction. As will become apparent, it is essentially the same account in both works: there has been no reversal, no *Kehre*; rather, there has been a development in which Merleau-Ponty has found language more adequate to his thought and to the phenomenal world.

The challenge Merleau-Ponty faces is that of accounting for the phenomena traditionally explained by appealing to the immanent structures of an unworldly transcendental consciousness without making that appeal. Paramount among these phenomena are (1) reflexivity or the Cartesian cogito, (2) perspective or the isolation and privacy that have generated the classical problems of solipsism, and (3) transcendental constitution or the centrifugal function of projecting meaning into the world and instituting it there. I shall take up the first of these themes in this chapter, reserving the second and third for treatment in forthcoming chapters on intersubjectivity and language.

1. THE TACIT COGITO AND THE PRIMORDIALITY OF THE UNREFLECTIVE[1]

Merleau-Ponty devotes the first thirty of his forty-page chapter on "The Cogito" (PP 369–409; PP-F 423–468) to a series of arguments and examples designed to demonstrate the primacy of perception to thought.

The relation . . . of reflection to the unreflective, . . . of thought to perception is this two-way relationship that phenomenology has called *Fundierung*:[2] *the founding term*— . . . the unreflective, . . . perception—*is primary* in the sense that the founded term is presented as a determinate or explicit form of the founding term. (PP394; PP-F 451; emphasis added)

Two points are relevant here: (a) perception is associated with the unreflective, and (b) that domain is conceived as foundational to the domain of thought and reflection. Perceptual experience takes place in an unreflective modality. As Merleau-Ponty says in another place, "if I wanted to render precisely the perceptual experience, I ought to say that one perceives in me, and not that I perceive" (PP 215; PP-F 249). The point is that the "I" which emerges only with reflection is absent from perceptual engagement in the world, rendering that experience anonymous or general:[3] the phenomenon presences itself to anyone who would witness it. This is consciousness at the foundational level; other modes of consciousness (reflection, deliberation, predication, hallucination, dreaming, etc.) are founded upon it. "All consciousness is, in some measure, perceptual consciousness" (PP 395; PP-F 452). Here, then, is the basis for an equation—consciousness = perception = phenomenal presencing—that would seem to allow Merleau-Ponty to drop one of the terms, consciousness, and evade the spectre of dualism that haunts it. "The certainty of vision and that of the thing seen are of a piece" (PP 399; PP-F 457); no separation between percept and phenomenon seems to be required: why then infect the percept with the germ of consciousness and expose phenomenology to the malaise of incipient ontological bifurcation?

The answer to this question has already been stated. "All thought of something is at the same time self-consciousness, in the absence of which it would have no object" (PP 371; PP-F 426). Phenomena must be conceived as both immanent and transcendent: transcendence alone is incapable of presence and givenness, and the requisite immanence is articulated in the *Phenomenology* in the terminology of subjectivity and consciousness. "What is evident to us [*nos évidences*] is certainly fact, but is inseparable from us," hence we must define "being as that which appears to us and consciousness as a universal fact" (PP 397; PP-F 455). The requirement fulfilled awkwardly by the language of subjectivity and consciousness is, as stated earlier, the requirement for the tacit reflexivity which is essential to perception. The percept, hence the phenomenon (unlike the thing-in-itself) must be "a being which recognizes itself," must include "knowledge of itself." This reflexivity intrinsic to perception is the tacit cogito.

> The tacit *cogito*, the presence of oneself to oneself, being no less than existence, is anterior to any philosophy, and knows itself only in those extreme situations in which it is under threat: for example, in the dread of death or in the look of another upon me. (PP 404; PP-F 462)

Sartre's influence is manifest here. Merleau-Ponty's tacit cogito is modelled upon Sartre's prereflective cogito and serves the same function of distinguishing percept from thing-in-itself. But the prereflective or tacit cogito is a curious structure: it is a self-consciousness which is unaware of itself in its fascination with the world. When it does become aware of itself— under the look of another or threat of death—it is no longer tacit, no longer prereflective. "The tacit *cogito* is a *cogito* only when it expresses itself" (PP 404; PP-F 463)—but it is tacit only on condition that it not express itself. How can a cogito be prereflective, be tacit? There seems to be a contradiction in terms here.

The missing term that resolves the contradiction, for Merleau-Ponty, at least, is the lived body.[4] The body is preeminently immanence and transcendence: it is the subject of perceptual experience and a possible object of perception. Indeed, it is only because it is a worldly object that it can perceive worldly objects: pure consciousness cannot *touch* anything. The body can touch things, but it can touch things only to the extent that it is touched *by* things: to touch something is necessarily to feel the touch of the thing on oneself—an anaesthetized finger does not properly touch, it only bumps up against things, precisely because it cannot feel. Here, then, is the genuine tacit cogito, in the reflexivity intrinsic to bodily perception, but it is misnamed cogito, for it is not a thought; it is, rather, our primordial contact with things.

> If, reflecting on the essence of subjectivity, I find it bound up with that of the body and that of the world, this is because my existence as subjectivity is one with my existence as body and with the existence of the world and, finally, because the subject which I am, taken concretely, is inseparable from this body and this world. (PP 408; PP-F 467)

As is apparent from this text, there is an unresolved tension in the account of unreflective or perceptual consciousness Merleau-Ponty sets forth in the *Phenomenology*. On the one hand, consciousness is incarnate in the body, hence is a worldly phenomenon. On the other, consciousness of a thing implies consciousness of itself or reflexivity, and that presence to itself or subjectivity verges on an invisible realm of immanence existing, as it were, behind perception and serving as its transcendental condition. This tension is not resolved in the *Phenomenology*, but the resolution set forth in *The Visible and the Invisible* in terms of the doctrine of reversibility of flesh is clearly foreshadowed in the earlier work. The reversibility thesis (which is somewhat counter-intuitive when stated in capsule form, as is necessary here) holds that the flesh of the world perceives itself through our flesh which is one with it. Just as the worldly thing must touch my body for my body to touch it, so, in general, must my perception of the world be correlated with my own perceptibility. The reversibility thesis satisfies the reflexivity requirement without reverting to the traditional language of subjectivity and consciousness. The point I want to stress here, in defense of my claim that there is a continuous development from the *Phenomenology* to *The Visible and the Invisible* rather than a reversal or turn, is that the reversibility thesis is already surfacing in the *Phenomenology*, although it is obscured by the traditional language of that work. In stating that "it is through my relations to 'things' that I know myself" (PP 383; PP-F 439), Merleau-Ponty expresses one of the two essential moments of the reversibility thesis. Then, further on in the text, he makes a statement that encompasses both moments. "In one respect I comprehend the world, and in another it comprehends me. It is necessary to say that it is in the same respect . . . and this is finally because I am situated [in the world] and because it comprehends me" (PP 408; PP-F 467). The verb used three times in this passage is '*comprendre*.' I have rendered it as 'comprehend,' but it could also be translated as 'understand.' There is a deliberate play on the two meanings: I can understand the world only because I am comprehended by it, because the flesh of my body is enveloped by and situated in the flesh of the world. "We are nothing but a view of the world" (PP 406; PP-F 465); "We are the world that thinks itself" (VI 136n; VI-F 179n).

If we are the world that thinks itself, then the thinking of the world is not separate from the world; and if reflexivity is intrinsic to the thinking of the world, it does not require the establishment of an ontological category demarcating another kind of being disjunct from worldly being. The human body, a worldly being, has developed the capacity to thematize the reflexivity inherent in the ability to perceive which it shares with all organisms.

The explicit ontology of *The Visible and the Invisible* centers around the element of flesh, as the implicit ontology of the *Phenomenology* centers around the thesis of the primacy of phenomena. Neither 'flesh' nor 'phenomenon' should be conceived as resurrecting the traditional category of substance (VI 147; VI-F 193–94). These basic terms, 'flesh' and 'phenomenon,' name a way of being (*une manière d'être*) which subtends the polarizing distinctions of language (body v. spirit, visible v. invisible, etc.) at the level of ontology, but readmits them all at the level of empirical taxonomy. Merleau-Ponty's ontology is a radical rejection of dualism, but it is not a traditional monism. There is one manner or style of being which all things share, but this is compatible with the existence of many kinds of things. It is not the case that rocks, plants, and animals are different compositions of a single fleshly or phenomenal being; it is the case that they reveal themselves primarily through perception, through that intertwining of perceiver and perceived—that elementary reversibility—which is prior to their differentiation into subject and object, consciousness and matter.

Nor is this a reversion to Berkeley's *esse est aut percipi aut percipere*, for that *aut . . . aut* preserves the ontological disjunction of subject and object Merleau-Ponty seeks always to undercut. Perceptual revelation does not bring things into being, nor does absence/latency/undiscoveredness betoken non-being. Rather, the thesis of the ontological primacy of phenomena and its correlate, the thesis of the epistemological primacy of perception, maintain simply that the phenomenal world is the real world and that it is revealed primarily in perception. This is to privilege, among the many senses of 'real,' the one associated with phenomenal manifestation, and to regard the others as deriving their legitimacy by reference to it. The question at issue here, the question of the reality of consciousness, is resolved by understanding the phenomenon designated by the term as a worldly structure: specifically, as the structure of reversibility which becomes thematic in the case of human bodies but which governs the capacity of perception in all organisms and which requires as a condition for the ability to perceive a coincidence of *percipi* and *percipere*.

Further explication of the reversibility thesis will be reserved for part three, which is devoted to Merleau-Ponty's explicit ontology—because that is its proper context and because it presupposes an analysis of the lived body which has not yet been provided. Nonetheless, it should now be evident that Merleau-Ponty's account of the tacit cogito anticipates the reversibility thesis which succeeds it, and is already well on the way toward the goal of reaching an understanding of perceptual experience which is consistent with the doctrine of the ontological primacy of phenomena, despite the fact that it is couched in the language of consciousness. The task before us now is to return to the notion of consciousness articulated in the *Phenomenology* and trace the process through which the tacit cogito becomes explicit.

2. THE CARTESIAN COGITO AND THE GENESIS OF REFLEXIVITY

The true *Cogito* does not define the subject's existence in terms of the thought he has of existing, and furthermore does not convert the indubitability of the world into the indubitability of thought about the world, nor finally does it replace the world itself by the world as meaning. On the contrary it recognizes my thought itself as an inalienable fact, and does away with any kind of idealism in revealing me as 'being-in-the-world.' (PP xiii; PP-F viii)

The traditional conception of consciousness takes the Cartesian cogito as its paradigm, and Merleau-Ponty accepts this to the extent that he defines "the essence of consciousness" as "my actual presence to myself" and regards this, "the fact of my consciousness," as "an inalienable fact" (PP xv; PP-F x). But, as is evident in the passage quoted above, Merleau-Ponty does not take the indubitability of the cogito as a model for philosophical certainty and retreat, as Husserl did, into the reduced sphere of immanence. The cogito places the fact of thought beyond doubt, but the thought that is thereby uncovered takes place in the world, not behind or above it, and finally must be conceived as a worldly phenomenon, that is, as a phenomenon grounded in the world, motivated by worldly events, and not as a spontaneous upsurge of nothingness generated *ex nihilo*.

The primary difference between the tacit cogito and the Cartesian cogito is the difference between the anonymity or generality of the former and the personal or individual nature of the latter: the corporeal reflexivity of the one is latent and unexpressed, whereas the explicit reflexivity of the other is thematized in language and thought. The tacit cogito is silent: it sees the world and does not thematize its seeing. The explicit cogito speaks: it thematizes its relations with things and posits itself in the statement, 'I think.' The genesis of the Cartesian cogito is the genesis of thematic self-awareness: through it a self comes into being which is grounded in the body but later transcends it. The birth of the Cartesian cogito is the birth of a personal soul, spirit, psyche, anima. It is the development of a particular perspective aware of itself as such and aware, as well, of its peculiarity, the differences that alienate it from the other perspectives of other selves. It is with the emergence of explicit self-consciousness that the problems of solipsism begin to surface and bring with them the projects of love and hate, communion and conflict.

In lecture notes for a course given in 1950–51, "The Child's Relations with Others,"[5] Merleau-Ponty traces the stages through which the infant passes in the genesis of his awareness of others as other, that is, as distinct from himself. This is a complex process which cannot be recapitulated here, but the pattern of the development is a progression from earlier stages of "syncretic sociability" in which the infant does not distinguish his perspective from those of others but assumes a kind of ubiquity, through phases in the construction of a "corporeal schema" associated with recognition of his own specular image, to arrive at a primitive sense of himself as a being with his own separate identity. In composing my own commentary[6] on Merleau-Ponty's work in this area, I was struck by the correlation—already suggested by Sartre's doctrine of the look—between the cognitive emergence of the self-other distinction and the emotional experience of alienation and estrangement. It is the phenomena of shame, punishment, rejection, and the like which motivate the erosion of syncretic sociability or prepersonal communality and enforce the correlative awareness of forlornness, isolation, and alienation which are the birthpains of selfhood. In my later work on sexuality,[7] I encountered the same correlation during adolescent phases of maturation and individuation: with the emergence of a sexed (as opposed to merely gendered) body-image and the concurrent claim to increased freedom, both of which serve to shame and alienate the changeling, there is an apex of self-consciousness, a never again equalled intensity of reflexivity which manifests itself in the myriad forms of embarrassment, shyness, self-objectification, etc.

Several points are relevant here. First: the Cartesian cogito, that is, thematic self-awareness, is not merely the theoretical act of a disinterested thinker; it is, rather, an existential cogito in which thought is cast back on itself in recoil from traumatic worldly events. I am forced out of a taken-for-granted communal outlook into awareness of an essential solitude. Second: the explicit cogito is not primordial; it is founded upon the primitive (and correlative) structures of corporeal reflexivity and syncretic sociability. The tacit cogito only becomes explicit under threat and in the upheavals that fragment a shared social perspective. Third: the cogito described by Descartes as the act of *res cogitans* is originarily a corporeal phenomenon which is predicated on the development of a discrete body-image as the foundation of the I discovered in reflection. The look of the other impinges on my incarnate person, not on the spiritual self or invisible psyche (which is an abstraction posited and reified at a later stage of development). Fourth: the cogito to which Descartes gave voice was accurately identified by him as a thought haunted by anxiety and doubt. Doubt, like the kindred shame, is one of the essential ways in which I discover that *my* world may not coincide with *the* world: the discovery that my world may be different from the worlds of others (or the ideal unity of the world in itself) is the discovery of the unique perspective which is my self. Once I discover it, I cannot doubt my finitude—although I was not born with this awareness and may spend my entire life in flight from it.

As shown by Merleau-Ponty in his writing on the role of the specular image in the genesis of self-awareness, the experience of the cogito is an experience of self-objectification: I discover myself in the mirror only when I identify myself with the body-image I see over there, apart from myself. This is also an intrinsic moment in Sartre's doctrine of the look: I find myself only when I am caught up in the gaze of another and experience myself from the alien vantage of an other. There is an essential paradox here—reflection, my explicit consciousness of myself, is the taking up of a distanced perspective on myself—my most intimate experience of myself is an experience of self-alienation or self-transcendence. Here is the root of the contradiction around which Sartre's ontology centers. "The for-itself is what it is not and is not what it is" can now be translated to read: "incarnate consciousness discovers its own identity in the process of self-estrangement." The self reflected upon is an object posited as different from the subject reflecting. From my vantage *here*, I see my body-image *there* reflected in the mirror and feel myself bifurcated: I am not the body-object that is the ground of my identity.

The manner in which Sartre responds to this paradox places him in the midst of a long tradition of spiritualism. He is one who defines the spirit (now called subjectivity or consciousness) in opposition to the body. The spiritual self or soul discovered in the process of reflection—in the process of coming of age which coincides with the intense reflexivity of adolescence and the time of a cross-culturally apparent rite of spiritual passage (bar mitzvah, confirmation, etc.)—this spiritual self is the subject that defines itself in conflict with the body-object it seeks to exclude and transcend through acts of ascetic denial and mortification of the flesh. The spirit is born of shame, shame of the body, which is an internalization of the look of the culture at large which refuses to accept the sexuality of the changeling now becoming manifest in publicly visible secondary sexual characteristics. The changeling is a social and spiritual outcast who gains readmission to the community in a ritual designed to reinforce his reflective self-alienation.

Merleau-Ponty's account of reflection allows us to rectify this mistaken praxis by reconceiving the cogito on which it is based. The dualistic scheme whereby subjectivity defines itself by excluding the body object is replaced by a model of corporeal reflexivity: the awkwardly named tacit cogito of the *Phenomenology* and its refined version, the reversibility of the flesh, provide another model of reflection, another ground for the cogito which expresses itself in language and thought. No longer need I be imprisoned in the forlorn subjective self that defines itself as not being the worldly thing, the worldly other, the worldly body I see in the mirror; now I can be flesh that perceives itself by perceiving its world, that touches itself in touching others, that sees *itself* in the mirror. The difference between Merleau-Ponty's explicit cogito and the cogito that Sartre and others take over from Descartes is the difference between my experience of myself as incarnate in this body which is situated in a social world, and my experience of myself as alienated from all the objects I experience as objects (including my own body and the bodies of others). Again, it is the difference between experiencing myself as being ambiguously both subject and object of reflective thematization and experiencing myself as a subject which is essentially (that is, ontologically) set apart from all objects.

The point here is that the bodily 'I can' includes not only the ability to move, grasp, perceive, etc., but also the ability to think. Thought must be conceived as an extension of the body's perceptual powers, a development of the reflexivity that is latent in perception. But this power of reflective thematization is also a power of transformation: it transforms the world by introducing an 'I' into it. 'There is the tree' becomes 'I see the tree' and a world of subjectivity grows up to mirror the world of things. Then, as set forth earlier in this chapter, there emerge the problems of understanding how the worlds of subjectivity and objectivity are related. It is in this manner that reflection, the act that brings philosophy into being, simultaneously brings into being the traditional problems of philosophy. Yet, as Merleau-Ponty teaches, if it is a primative form of reflection that generates the problems of philosophy, then it requires a sophisticated form of reflection to solve those problems: in *The Visible and the Invisible*, he calls for a "hyper-reflexivity" that thematizes and thereby neutralizes the distortions introduced by reflective thinking. The distortion at issue here is the reification of subjectivity: if reflection transforms the world by introducing an I, a thinking thing, then a further reflection can make itself aware of that fact and go on to understand that I as the product (rather than the condition) of thought.

Here the role of language is crucial. Recall a passage quoted earlier: "the tacit *cogito* is a *cogito* only when it expresses itself" (PP 404; PP-F 463). When the tacit reflexivity of perception is expressed in language, it becomes the cogito, the 'I think.' The I of subjectivity, the reified agent of thought, comes into being through language, and the resulting grammatical habit becomes the basis of a philosophical prejudice.[8] When the genesis of the I is understood, the I can return to the perceptual world and take up its proper abode in the lived body. Speaking of the Cartesian cogito, Merleau-Ponty says the following: "The certainty which we have of reaching, beyond expression, a truth separable from it and of which expression is merely the garment and contingent manifestation, has been implanted in us precisely by language" (PP 401; PP-F 459). The I born of reflection and sedimented in language is an expression of corporeal reflexivity.

Of paramount importance here is the ontological significance of Merleau-Ponty's transformation of the Cartesian cogito. No longer does it function as apodictic evidence for the existence of a world of consciousness apart from or behind the phenomenal world.

> Evidence is never apodictic, nor is thought timeless. . . . The certainty of ideas is not the foundation of the certainty of perception but is, rather, based on it —in that it is perceptual experience which gives us the passage from one moment to the next and thus realizes the unity of time. In this sense, all consciousness is perceptual, even consciousness of ourselves. (PriP 13)

"All consciousness is perceptual, even the consciousness of ourselves"— these words, spoken in 1946 shortly after the publication of the *Phenomenology of Perception*, vindicate the thesis of the ontological primacy of phenomena. Thought—even the paradigm of immanence, the Cartesian cogito—emerges from the phenomenal world of perceptual experience and remains tied to it. The I that I think is an expression of the tacit reflexivity manifest in phenomena, a symbolic development of the body image in mirrors and the eyes of others.

Yet thought is not an illusion. This, I take it, is the point of Merleau-Ponty's frequent allusion to the "inalienable *fact* of consciousness": we do have the capacity to distance ourselves from our selves, other selves, and the world. This capacity for alienation is grounded in the processes of self-objectification explicated above in terms of the development of the specular image and the phenomena of shame. When the adolescent suffers through the trauma of coming-of-age, he has at his disposal the grammar of 'I-you-they' already implanted in his speech and ready to take on deeper symbolic meaning. 'I' now becomes the emblem of a multileveled and ambiguous mode of being in the world. I am the body at one with itself, others, and world when I am engaged in team sports. I am also the other whose face in the mirror is sprouting whiskers and pimples. And I am the self whose significance is simultaneously built up and torn down in the look of peers and parents, guys and girls. I—the grammatical sign, the overdetermined symbol—is now a question.

The answer to that question is to be found in the world that motivates it. Thought and its synthetic unity, the subject of Descartes's reflection, arises in the world and from the flesh of the world that is our body. In these few pages, I have tried to sketch something of its genesis, the process whereby the reflexivity of perception becomes thematized, named, and reified. The purpose of this account was to make the phenomenon of re-flexivity manifest as a worldly phenomenon—something grounded in phe-nomenal unfolding—and to show that spiritualism, the various doctrines based on the reification of consciousness, can itself be understood as an errant development of phenomenal reflexivity, the product of worldly in-terrogation seeking to still its own anxiety by thinking itself out of this world.

SEVEN

Intersubjectivity

The Primordiality of
Pre-Personal Communion

For the 'other' to be more than an empty word, it is necessary that my existence should never be reduced to my bare awareness of existing, but that it should take in also the awareness that one may have of it, and thus include my incarnation in some nature and the possibility, at least, of a historical situation. The Cogito must reveal me in a situation, and it is on this condition alone that transcendental subjectivity can, as Husserl puts it, be an inter-subjectivity. (PP xii-xiii; PP-F vii)

If one takes the Cartesian cogito as one's philosophical foundation, as Husserl did, then the alter ego becomes a problem that cannot be solved. The Cartesian cogito, thought reflecting thematically on itself, functions as the paradigm of what it is to *be* a conscious subject and how it is possible to *know* a conscious subject. But these two aspects coincide in the Cartesian cogito in such a way that, if one accepts the paradigm, then the *only* way to know a conscious subject is to be that conscious subject reflecting on itself. The coincidence of formal and objective reality which grounds the certainty of the cogito is limited to first person experience (or performance) of the cogito: because I cannot witness your cogito, I cannot know that you exist as a thinking thing. Consequently, if one defines human being as *res cogitans*, the only human being I can be certain is a human being is myself. Solipsism is intrinsic to Cartesian thought.

If solipsism is the result of identifying the humanity of myself and others with the thought each experiences within himself but which is private and invisible to anyone else, then solipsism can be overcome by redefinition: to be human is to be a human body and exhibit human behavior; since both body and behavior are public and visible, I can see your humanity and you can see mine. My body is the ground of my identity for myself, hence it can function as the ground of my identity for others, and your body plays the same role for you, me, and the others who dwell in our world. Furthermore, the isomorphism of our bodies provides a basis for mutual understanding: I understand the behavior of your hands as I see them from the outside because my hands are similar to yours and I know them from the inside. Indeed, I discover my bodily capabilities as an infant through mimetic responses to the corporeal behavior of others. The infant's experience of other bodies guides its kinesthetic understanding of its own. There is a problem of other minds because others are conceived as minds; as soon as others are regarded as incarnate in their bodies, the problem disappears—but only to emerge again at a different level.

Solipsism is not merely a philosophical mistake; it is rather an aspect of human life that has been misunderstood by philosophers and psychologists theorizing within ontological standpoints incapable of doing justice to the full range of human experience from alienation to solidarity, from forlorn isolation to reciprocated love. While it is true that traditional forms of solipsism arise from a wilful neglect of the lived body, it is also true that these extremist accounts are responsive to a well-grounded segment of human experience: my body may be shaped in the same fashion as yours, but it is my body, not yours, and I experience it in a way that I cannot experience yours. A genuinely adequate theory of intersubjectivity must be able to accommodate both privacy and communion within a unitary and coherent view of human experience. The problem is not to disprove solipsism; it is rather to establish its limits and show what lies beyond.

The classical text on intersubjectivity in the phenomenological tradition is the fifth of Husserl's *Cartesian Meditations*.[1] It is, in my judgment, a noble failure. It fails—has to fail—because it is written within the brackets of a radical *epoché* and conceives its task as moving from the standpoint of immanence and reflective solitude to arrive at the phenomenon wherein the transcendental ego recognizes its counterpart in an alter ego. Given the point of departure to which Husserl is committed, the destination cannot be reached. Yet, if one departs from the standpoint of a more adequate ontological framework and follows the course charted by Husserl, one will arrive (as did Merleau-Ponty in "The Child's Relations with Others"[2]) at the goal. The nobility of Husserl's effort is twofold: the validity of his reasoning demonstrated, by an unintended *reductio*, the falsity of his premises and thereby opened the way for another approach from a different direction. As I hope now to show, it was Husserl's failure—or rather his unintended success in showing that as long as phenomenology was practiced as transcendental idealism it would remain locked within solipsism—that pointed the way for Merleau-Ponty to arrive at a phenomenology of intersubjectivity.

The "Fifth Meditation" begins with a novel development of the *epoché*, a reduction to the *Eigensphäre*, or "the sphere of ownness." Husserl describes this reduced sphere in two ways: initially (sect. 44), he characterizes it as the residuum when everything alien has been bracketed; subsequently (sect. 46), he describes it positively as everything that belongs to the transcendental ego's own self-experience (including his entire stream of subjective processes). In the first characterization, Husserl argues that the objectivity of the world is bracketed, since the meaning of 'objective' is 'capable of being experienced by others as well as myself' and every inference to otherness has to be placed in abeyance. Then, in the second characterization, he says that the entire world is retained in the reduced sphere, but is retained as the correlate of the transcendental ego's self-experience. Husserl attributes to this transcendental self-experience a founding originality: everything within the sphere of otherness (that is, the other ego, the objective world, etc.) is founded within the sphere of ownness. "Within and by means of this ownness the transcendental ego constitutes . . . the 'objective' world, as a universe of being that is other than himself—and constitutes, at the first level, the other in the mode: alter ego" (CM 100).

The strategy of the "Fifth Meditation" is to show how the alter ego makes his appearance within the reduced sphere of ownness, and then to show how the objective world is constituted as a world of intersubjectivity, that is, as a world that is intrinsically experience-able by others. The major problem Husserl faces is that of explaining how the meaning '*other* ego' can be constituted in the sphere of ownness: if, as he claims, the sphere of ownness is primordial and foundational, and if all sense of alienness or otherness is initially absent from this sphere, then it is difficult to see how the sense of otherness can emerge within it. Again, if the world and all its contents are experienced by me as correlates of *my* conscious life, then how do they acquire the significance of being correlates for subjectivities other than my own when I have as yet no direct experience of any subjectivity other than my own (and, moreover, can never have any such experience)?

The answer to this question is that the experience of the alter ego as alter ego is an impossibility within the sphere of ownness: the problem Husserl defines is insoluble within the framework of his definitions. Husserl takes the Cartesian cogito as his philosophical foundation, but, for precisely those reasons set forth at the beginning of this section, he cannot account for the everyday experience of others as other egos: the only consciousness I can experience as a consciousness is my own. "Among the bodies belonging to this [reduced] 'nature' and included within my peculiar ownness, I then find my *animate organism* as *uniquely* singled out—namely as the only one of them that is not just a body but precisely an animate organism" (CM 97). The *Eigensphäre*, "distinguished by being essentially the *founding* stratum" (CM 96), includes but one anima, one consciousness, my own; and none other can ever be experienced originally[3]—hence there is no way to account for the origin of the meaning 'alter ego.'

The conclusion to be drawn here is that there can be no resolution to the problem of other minds unless one acknowledges that the phenomenal world is, at the most primordial level, a communal world, that is, that others are experienced originally as animate organisms like myself. What Merleau-Ponty says about the transcendental reduction in general holds true especially in the case of the reduction to the sphere of ownness: the lesson we learn from it is that it cannot be carried through to completion; it is impossible to experience the world merely as the correlate of my own consciousness.

But that is not the only lesson to be learned from the fifth of the *Cartesian Meditations*. If we neutralize Husserl's brackets and place the reduction to the *Eigensphäre* in abeyance, his account of our own experience of other egos retains much that is valid and enlightening. As we shall see, Merleau-Ponty draws heavily on Husserl's account in the development of his own.

At the core of Husserl's account of the experience of someone else are the notions of "analogical apperception" and "pairing." Analogical apperception falls under the general heading of "appresentation." When the front of a physical object is evidentially present to me in perception, its back is co-presented, co-intended or apperceived by me. I am motivated by the present aspect of the object to constitute the object as having other aspects not now present but included within the totality of the object as intended. These other aspects are appresented. In the case of physical objects, I can verify the appresented aspects by moving around the object: what was initially appresented can then become an originary presentation. In the case of the other, it is his body that is evidentially present and his consciousness or subjectivity that is appresented. I am motivated by what is originarily presented, his body, to apperceive the conscious aspect needed to round out the totality of the intentional object, that is, to constitute the other's body as an animate organism located over there apart from my absolute here. Husserl calls this an *analogical* apperception to indicate that I attribute to the other's body there what I experience in my body here, that is, a field of sensation, a conscious life, a capacity for reflection, etc.

Although he uses the term 'analogical apperception,' Husserl is careful to point out that he is not putting forward another version of the traditional arguments from analogy. I do not deliberately predicate of the other's body a quality of subjective experience extrapolated from my own life. My " 'analogizing' apprehension of that body as another animate organism . . . would be . . . a certain assimilative apperception; but it by no means follows that there would be an inference from analogy. Apperception is not inference, not a thinking act" (CM 111). Husserl was well aware that appeal to analogical inference cannot solve the problem of how I come to see other bodies as loci of subjectivities/viewpoints other than my own. Of course, once I am capable of this recognition, I may use analogical reasoning to think myself into another's viewpoint in a thematic exploration of the empathetic identification, but, as Merleau-Ponty argues,[4] analogical inference begs the fundamental question of how the other is primally instituted as alter ego.

There is a crucial difference between my apperception of the back of a physical object and my apperception of the consciousness of another human body: whereas I can bring the apperceived side of the object into my perceptual field and achieve an original presentation that fulfills the apperceptive intention, this is not possible in the case of my apperception of the other's subjectivity. The "apperceptive transfer from my animate organism" is carried out in "a manner that excludes an actually direct, and hence primordial, showing of the predicates belonging to an animate organism specifically, a showing of them in perception proper" (CM 100–11). This difference raises a question about the motivation of the apperceptive transfer: since I have never properly perceived another's consciousness (as I have perceived the backs of physical objects), what is it that leads me to attribute an interiority to his organism?

The answer to this question and the key idea in Husserl's account of intersubjectivity is the notion of *pairing*. "*Ego* and *alter ego* are always and necessarily given *in an original 'pairing'*" (CM 112). An association is formed (which Husserl places under the problematic heading of "passive synthesis") between my body and his which constitutes them as a pair, as phenomenologically founding "a unity of similarity." This synthesis is conceived according to the same general structure of any plurality formation in which similar data become "prominent and simultaneously intended."

> In case there presents itself, as outstanding in my primordial sphere, a body 'similar' to mine—that is to say, a body with determinations such that it must enter into a phenomenal pairing with mine—it seems clear without more ado that, with the transfer of sense, this body must forthwith appropriate from mine the sense: animate organism. (CM 113)

I see the other as animate as soon as his body enters my perceptual field because, passively and without deliberate thought, I see his body as like unto my own. This association is either strengthened or abandoned according to whether his subsequent behavior harmoniously fulfills the expectations constitutive of the meaning 'animate organism' or is discordant with them.

Notwithstanding the problematic aspects of this account—to which I shall return shortly—there are two important positive points I want to stress. First: Husserl, despite his commitment to a philosophy of immanence (with all the prejudices of spiritualism that go along with it), has been forced to acknowledge the crucial role of the lived body in the foundation of all sociality and objectivity. Second: he fastens, with the notion of pairing, on the phenomenal origin of intersubjectivity. Merleau-Ponty appropriates the idea and, thematically acknowledging his indebtedness to Husserl, develops it in the context of his own ontology under the heading of "transfer of corporeal schema."

> I can perceive, across the visual image of the other, that the other is an organism, that that organism is inhabited by a 'psyche,' because the visual image of the other is interpreted by the notion I myself have of my body and thus

appears as the visible envelopment of another 'corporeal schema.' . . . Husserl said that the perception of others is like a 'phenomenon of coupling.' The term is anything but a metaphor. In perceiving the other, my body and his are coupled, resulting in a sort of action which pairs them. This conduct which I am able only to see, I live somehow from a distance. I make it mine; I recover it or comprehend it. Reciprocally I know that the gestures I make myself can be the objects of another's intention. It is this transfer of my intentions to the other's body and of his intentions to my own, my alienation of the other and his alienation of me, that makes possible the perception of others. (CRO 118)

I have quoted Merleau-Ponty at length here in order to substantiate the fact that his notion of transfer of corporeal schema is deliberately intended to describe the same phenomenon that Husserl calls pairing. The notion undergoes a transformation, however, when it is placed in the context of Merleau-Ponty's phenomenology of perception. There are many significant differences—for example, the originality of the phenomenon can be explicated in terms of autochthonous organization instead of passive synthesis; Husserl's claim that my body is always sensuously prominent can be explicated in terms of Merleau-Ponty's tacit cogito or corporeal reflexivity; and so on—but the main difference under which all the others can be arrayed is a difference in starting point.

Husserl's account of pairing is placed within the context of isolated immanence, the sphere of ownness that he regards as primordial, whereas Merleau-Ponty places the transfer of corporeal schema within a context of syncretic sociability, a context defined as prior to any distinction of perspectives or differentiation between what is mine and what is other. The logic of Husserl's meditation leads him to the brink of recognizing the primordiality of syncretic sociability, but prior ontological commitments draw him back to the thesis of the primacy of the *Eigensphäre*.

Remember that Husserl gives two successive descriptions of the sphere of ownness. In the first (sect. 44), he characterizes it as excluding everything dependent on any sense of otherness; "it is non-alien [*Nicht-Fremdes*]" (CM 95). This characterization depends upon the very sense of otherness it seeks to exclude. Or, again, it trades on the correlative nature of ownness and otherness, and defines the one by exclusion of the other. But Husserl is speaking here of a level of consciousness, a quality of awareness, and orientation of the *cogitatio*: and, for that reason, it cannot be a pure experience of ownness if it includes awareness of the alienness it seeks to exclude. To perceive my experience as my own is to live in a sphere where the own-other distinction is thematically operative. Hence, this first characterization of a sphere of ownness purified of any sense of otherness is self-defeating. This is why Husserl goes on to offer a second characterization (sect. 46) of the *Eigensphäre* "to bring out its positive characteristic, or the positive characteristic of 'the ego in his ownness' " (CM 101). Indeed, he explicitly acknowledges that his first characterization conceives ownness in terms of the otherness it excludes (CM 101), and then proceeds to describe the "original self-experience" taking place in the sphere of ownness without making explicit reference to any sense of alienness or objectivity. Just as one can explicate any concrete object and unfold, "in a concatenation of particular intentions, the object's very own determinations [or] 'internal' determinations" (CM 101), so can one unfold, in a series of self-given intuitions, the internal determinations constituting the unitary stream of subjective processes constituting my own conscious life. In either case, no reference beyond "the particulars making up its ownness" is required to explicate the unity in question. In this way, he attempts in the second characterization of the sphere of ownness to circumvent the contradiction embedded in the first.

Husserl may be correct in claiming that one can isolate a phenomenon—be it a phenomenon of object-perception of one of self-perception—and describe it without referring to other phenomena which differ from it. But he is mistaken in assuming that I can entertain an intuition *with a reflective awareness of it as my own, as given only to me*, without thereby tacitly positing an alien consciousness which is incapable of experiencing this intuition which is my own: own and other are correlates, and neither can be invoked without tacit reference to the other.

What Husserl is seeking in his second characterization is a primordial level of experience that is prior to the reflective distinction between what is privately mine and what is publicly shared by others. Recall that his intent is to describe a quality of experience prior to the entry of the alter ego. He says that he can retrieve the experience in which the world as an "objective transcendency" is constituted as "external" and "alien" by tracing the processes whereby it is founded on the appearance of the alter ego as the origin of alienation. And he says that he can uncover the ordered strata of constitution by means of "static analysis" (CM 106), that is, without appealing to a temporally extended genesis: as transcendental ego, I can perform a reduction that will make originally present an experience of the world prior to its objectification, prior to the alienating presence of the alter ego. This, however, is quite mistaken. As Merleau-Ponty shows in "The Child's Relations with Others," the world prior to the emergence of the other is (a) not a world I experience as my own: it is a world in which there is an indistinction of perspectives, a world from which the mine-alien or self-other distinction is absent. Furthermore, (b) this world of syncretic sociability is an infantile world which corresponds to a quality of experience that is lost[5] with the development of the reflective awareness of perspectival differences between my experience and that of others: if the world of syncretic sociability is to be retrieved, it cannot be done by meditative reduction and static analysis; rather, it requires a genetic phenomenology, an ontogenetic investigation that is the phenomenological counterpart of developmental psychology. And this investigation, as demonstrated in the essay at hand, requires empirical as well as intellectual-logical foundations:

one must investigate the phenomenon of syncretism where it shows itself (that is, in the behavior of infants) precisely in order to offset the intrinsically distorting nature of reflective analyses.[6]

Were Husserl to have rigorously pursued the goal of describing the sphere of experience prior to the appearance of the other as other in a positive way—that is, without depending upon the self-other distinction—he would have had to abandon the characterization 'sphere of ownness,' and that would have entailed abandoning the entire strategy of reduction around which the "Fifth Meditation" is constructed. No wonder, then, that he recoiled. Merleau-Ponty, however, was not committed to the methodology of reduction, hence was able to follow the inner logic of the self-other dialectic. He also had the advantage of a broad and deep background in cognitive and developmental psychology, hence enjoyed the benefits of empirical research that Husserl discounted on a priori grounds for being conducted within the natural attitude.

By way of transition to the explication of Merleau-Ponty's account of intersubjectivity and the use he makes of Husserl's notion of pairing, let me point to a difficulty endemic to the kind of description now being attempted. If syncretism names a quality of experience that is exclusively infantile, then the attempt on the part of an adult to think himself into the infant's experience is fraught with peril because there is no concrete experiential ground against which to measure theoretical conclusions, and there is a constant danger that categories of adult experience will be inappropriately applied to infant life. For example, while Piaget may be correct in describing the growth out of infancy as a process of "de-centering" (CRO 110–11), it would be incorrect to describe the infant as "ego-centric," since ego-centricity is an adult phenomenon and presupposes the development of an 'I-consciousness' which marks the passage out of infancy. For the adult to think himself into the infant's situation, he must think himself out of his own: that is, he must guard against the tendency, intrinsic to reflection, to find a cogito everywhere it looks—precisely because it projects one into every situation it attempts to reprise. Merleau-Ponty's doctrine of hyper-reflection, described earlier as reflection which keeps itself aware of its own limitations, is one way to counter this danger. Another, all too frequently ignored by philosophers, is to attend to the concrete phenomena themselves, to measure one's theoretical findings against their ultimate ground and final referent: the perceptual world.

The basic points of Merleau-Ponty's genetic phenomenology of intersubjectivity have already emerged in the critique of Husserl. Primary among these is the point that Merleau-Ponty traces the development of the child's relations with others from a starting point prior to any distinction between self and other. This recasts the entire problematic. Traditional accounts presuppose, as Husserl did, that conscious life begins in a sphere of ownness characterized as a nascent solipsism or self-centeredness. Merleau-Ponty, on the contrary, describes infantile conscious life in terms of syncretism or indistinction of perspectives; thus, for him, the problem is not 'how does the infant begin to recognize others as other consciousnesses?' but rather 'how does the infant learn to differentiate himself and others as separate beings within a sphere of experience that lacks this differentiation?' Again, it is not a question of how the infant transcends an aboriginal self-centeredness, it is rather a question of how he learns to distinguish his experience of himself from his experience of others, that is, how he transcends syncretism.

One of the phenomena Merleau-Ponty cites in his description of syncretic sociability is that of the "contagion of cries" among babies which occurs in the first three months of life and subsequently disappears (CRO 124). If, in a nursery, one infant begins to cry, the others will begin to cry as well. The infants have not yet learned to distinguish the discomfort another is experiencing from their own somatic states, hence they react to the existence of pain in their syncretic world regardless of the fact that they may themselves be somatically comfortable. The phenomenon of the contagion of cries indicates that the first phase in life is one of "pre-communication, in which there is not one individual over against another but rather an anonymous collectivity, an undifferentiated group life" (CRO 119). The "foundation of syncretic sociability" is "transitivism" (CRO 135), that is, the immediate assimilation of others' experience and the infant's own. Viewed from the outside, adult perspective, this involves the infant's attribution of his experience to the other in a kind of projection and the introjection evident in the contagion of cries (although this language of "projection" and "introjection" presupposes a separation or alienation which is foreign to the infant's experience).

In the first phases of life, infants exhibit a striking capacity for mimesis: they will respond to a smile by smiling and, as Merleau-Ponty notes in the *Phenomenology*, if one playfully pretends to bite an infant's finger, it will open its mouth to return the gesture (PP 352; PP-F 404–405). This mimetic behavior cannot be explained by appeal to analogy because the relation between the smile the infant perceives externally and the internal motor functions it must perform to produce a smile is not one of similarity. How, then, can it be explained? The foundation for Merleau-Ponty's account lies in the notion of "corporeal schema."[7]

The notion of corporeal schema can best be understood by contrasting it with a competitive notion in classical psychology, that of "cenesthesia," which refers to "a mass of sensations that would express to the subject the state of his different organs and different bodily functions" (CRO 114).[8] To maintain that the infant experiences his body cenesthetically is to conceive the infant as experiencing his body as an object which he perceives through sensations of his own bodily states. These sensations are regarded as internal and private, that is, as constituting a sphere of impenetrable ownness. Thus, the doctrine of cenesthesia encounters two serious objections: (1) it reduces the infant's body to the status of object, something he senses or witnesses rather than lives through; and (2) it places that primordial bodily experience in a domain of absolute privacy which makes it inconceivable for the infant to perceive another's body in any way akin to the way he perceives his own.[9] Classical psychology's doctrine of cenesthesia is the empirical correlate of Husserl's conception of the sphere of ownness and is subject to the same critique: both views render the phenomenon of pairing inconceivable, and neither view can explain how someone imprisoned in his own somatic sphere could ever acquire the idea that the other bodies he sees are sensate for themselves as his is for himself.

The notion of corporeal schema, on the other hand, allows one to conceive the infant as experiencing his body by *living* it. His body is neither purely subject (in which case it would be invisible to him) nor purely object (in which case it could not serve his primitive intentions); it is rather the ground of a style of interacting with the environment. The coporeal schema must be understood adverbially, as a manner of being and doing by means of which the infant can see what he does. Were this not the case, it would be impossible, for example, for the infant to develop deliberate prehensile abilities: to be able to reach out and grasp something, he must both see his hand in juxtaposition to a manipulable object and live through his hand as agency of his exploration. Here, then, is the primordial experience of corporeal reflexivity, the aboriginal experience of body-in-relation-to-world-and-itself that (unfortunately) became known as the tacit cogito.

Since the corporeal schema is intrinsically visible, it is not hidden within a private sphere of ownness. There is an overlapping of the infant's experience of his body and his experience of other bodies: he sees others doing what he sees himself doing, and *vice versa*. The notion of corporeal schema renders mimetic behavior conceivable and provides a theoretical foundation for the phenomena of transitivity. In short, pairing—now understood as transfer of corporeal schema—becomes a vital inevitability instead of a conceptual impossibility.

The transfer of corporeal schema, the immediate (that is, reflexive-but-unreflected) perceptual linkage through which we recognize other beings as like unto ourselves, is the phenomenal ground of syncretic sociability, pathetic identification, or, in a word, intersubjectivity. A better word would be 'intercorporeality'[10] because the problem of other minds is really a problem of other animate organisms: at the most basic levels, human communion is a communion of flesh and not a relation between isolated subjects.

It should be noted here that the difference between Merleau-Ponty's account of transfer of corporeal schema and Husserl's account of pairing, the difference that grounds the success of the one and the failure of the other, is a difference in ontology. Husserl's Cartesian ontology is predicated on a radical disjunction between immanence and transcendence, a disjunction which is exacerbated by the reductions which depend on it. The body, for Husserl, can only be the body as experienced within the sphere of immanence (that is, within the *Eigensphäre*); the body as natural object existing among other natural objects in the natural world must be placed in abeyance and cannot function as a datum in phenomenological description. Hence the coincidence of body-as-subject and body-as-object, which is intrinsic to the notion of corporeal schema and renders a transfer conceivable, is precluded from the outset *despite the fact that the phenomenon of pairing depends on it.* In Merleau-Ponty's ontology, however, immanence and transcendence are inseparable aspects of phenomena; this allows for the explication of the phenomenon (that is, pairing or transfer of corporeal schema) which Husserl discovered but could not make intelligible. This point will be developed further in chapter 8 (below) on the lived body; here I need only point out that it is the ontology implicitly at work in Merleau-Ponty's middle period, an ontology struggling to formulate itself in the midst of the uncongenial linguistic/conceptual framework bequeathed by tradition, that allows Merleau-Ponty to reorient the classical problems of intersubjectivity and open the way toward resolution.

Transfer of corporeal schema founds transitivism which, in turn, is the foundation of syncretic sociability: the infant lives in a confusion of perspectives and does not distinguish himself from others. Does this mean that the distinction is false and ungrounded? If the world were entirely what we make of it, if the only reality were a constituted reality as intellectualism or pure transcendental thought must have it, then we would never arrive at the experience of privacy, distantiation, isolation, etc. But the fact is that the world transcends us and cognitive development is required to accommodate phenomenal realities, such as the reality that human bodies are separate and distinct from one another. The infant must learn to distinguish himself from others; he must develop a sense of his own identity as distinct from those around him; he must suffer through the experiences of alienation that will lead him into the adult world where it is true both that we identify with others and that each of us is alone.

Merleau-Ponty's account of the infant's development of personal identity is couched in terms of "body image" and "specular (or mirror) image." The body image is at once an externalization and an objectification of the corporeal schema. In order for the infant to see himself as a separate being, he must learn to see himself 'from the outside' as a body like the other bodies he sees—but different from them insofar as it is his own. There is a paradox here in that the infant must experience self-objectification or self-alienation in order to gain a sense of himself as a self. My body-image is my image of myself: as image, it is object; as myself, it is the subject I am. For it to function as the ground of my self-identity, it must be both object and subject at the same time. Once again, the importance of the requisite ontological foundations for understanding this phenomenon becomes apparent; once again, the basic term in the psychogenetic account is corporeal reflexivity. If I am to perceive my body as my body, I must perceive it in relation to other bodies and other things, and recognize it as the body that immediately enacts my intentions. As explained earlier, corporeal reflexivity is necessary for object-manipulation: in order to grasp the thing I must see my hand as object, live through it as subject, and tacitly identify the two aspects. This tacit identification subtends the corporeal schema. In order for me to develop a thematic body image, however, the tacit identification must become explicit: I must thematize my body-as-object as the body-subject I am. The body image is thus the thematization of the corporeal reflexivity underlying the corporeal schema. Or, in other terms, it is an intermediate thematization, a mediating step, between the tacit cogito and the Cartesian cogito. The tacit cogito is prethematic corporeal reflexivity; the body image involves thematic corporeal reflexivity; and the Cartesian cogito is thematic reflexivity that short-circuits and ignores its corporeality, mistakenly conceiving itself as pure interiority.

To explain the transition from the prethematic corporeal reflexivity of the corporeal schema to the thematic corporeal reflexivity of the body image, Merleau-Ponty draws upon the notion of the specular image, the image of the infant in the mirror. At the beginning of this transition (at about six months of age), the infant does not seem to recognize himself in his specular image; at the end (sometime after the first year of life), the recognition is achieved—although "this does not mean that the system of correspondence between the image of the body and the body itself is complete or that it is precise" (CRO 130). The concrete phases in this process are interesting, but need not be explicated in detail here;[11] it is the latent logic of the development that is of present concern.

The specular image *is* a thematic, external, objectified body image. Thus it provides a tangible referent in the psychogenetic process. (It may or may not be the case that the experience of self-identity or the process of achieving it was altered by the historical emergence of the mirror as a familiar cultural object—I leave this point moot.) In achieving the recognition, in learning to identify that image in the mirror over there as an image of himself, the infant has taken several significant steps in his developing awareness of his situation with regard to self and others.

(1) He has left the realm of syncretic sociability. He can witness another infant's crying without being drawn into it. Subsequent experiences of syncretism (orgiastic unification, team spirit, class consciousness, etc.) will be qualitatively different and episodic rather than abiding. However, the sense of fundamental human community, based on the enduring phenomenon of transfer of corporeal schema, will remain as a permanent experiential possibility (unless it is interrupted or distorted by some intervening pathology).

(2) The recognition of himself in the specular image is a first step in the open-ended process of self-individuation. It helps to found his body image which is the primordial ground of his sense of his own persona. As his body changes, so will his sense of himself. But emotionally ambivalent life passages—adolescence, illness, somatic degeneration in mid-life, the approach of death, etc.—will engender ambivalence in the body image as

ground of his identity. As explained earlier, there is an alienation from the body in adolescence when rapid somatic change creates discordance between the hitherto familiar sense of selfhood and the peculiar qualities which suddenly alter his physical and social being. A persona may develop which, in varying degrees of explicitness, identifies itself in opposition to its body. "I am not my body" is a sentiment of denial—a recoil from sexuality or appetite or death or any of the other figures of finitude—that has been expressed over a wide spectrum of humanity from the fearful virgin to the ascetic to the other-worldly Socrates. But, in all such cases, the denial is self-deceptive and implicitly reaffirms the fact that selfhood originates in the reflexivity of the flesh.

(3) The objectification and externalization of the corporeal schema implicit in the recognition of the specular image is a thematic discovery of oneself from a distanced vantage. The infant becomes other for himself; he can now see himself as another would see him. The initial spatial distance grows into a more complex psychic distance. Following infancy, second-person dialogue with himself and third-person analysis of himself become possible as the child develops the capacity to see himself from the viewpoints of possible personae which he can take up. Pride and shame, conceit and guilt—all the attitudes of reflexivity—are now open to the individual who has learned to stand apart from himself and judge himself. As Merleau-Ponty, citing Lacan, points out, the formation of an ego identity "is the acquisition not only of a new content but of a new function as well: the narcissistic function" (CRO 136). That function contributes to the formation of an ideal image of oneself or, in psychoanalytic terms, the development of a super-ego.

(4) The process of self-recognition is at the same time and necessarily an opening into the dialectic of self-other relations. Here the three preceding points culminate in the founding of intersubjectivity. It is the other who alienates me from myself and thereby introduces me to myself. The other is the locus of the external perspective upon myself. Here I depart somewhat from Merleau-Ponty: he attributes the experience of self-alienation to the encounter with the mirror;[12] I think that the mirror encounter recapitulates an earlier self-alienation that facilitates recognition of the specular image but proceeds from encounters with other persons. The significant other (probably Mother, but perhaps another close figure) introduces a fissure in the matrix of syncretic sociability by obtruding into the infant's world a perspective that violates the one he has lived and implicitly taken as universal. An alien will withdraws the breast, exhibits disgust at the comfortable pillow of fæces, speaks sharply, or rudely disturbs the infant's somatic state. Otherness is experienced as an alien force, a disrupting presence, a disappointment of vague somatic intentions and anticipations. The very experience of birth is an expulsion into an alien world and an introduction into the presence of otherness.

Sartre writes of the look of another as alienating. Merleau-Ponty writes of a look of completion the effect of which can be observed among infants at two or three months of age—that is, well before the infant is capable of experiencing alienation.[13] While concurring with this claim that the affirming look is older or more primordial than the threatening look, I want to suggest that the experience of self-objectification, the development of an alien perspective upon oneself that occurs after the first half year of life, is consequent upon the experience of a look/voice/physical presence which disrupts syncretism by obtruding a quality of otherness into the infant's world and sundering the integrity of its presumptive universality. This experience of otherness would thus provide existential space for self-objectification.

It is, as Merleau-Ponty notes (CRO 129), easier to see what mirrors do in the case of others, where both the other person and his image in the mirror are visible as perceptual objects which can be compared, than it is to see how the mirror functions in the case of oneself, where a relation must be perceived between the dissimilar experiences of one's body as lived and one's body as seen. For that reason and on the basis of empirical evidence, Merleau-Ponty asserts that the infant "distinguishes much more quickly between the other's specular image and the reality of the other's body than he does in the case of his own body" (CRO 127). In order for the infant to see himself mirrored as he sees others mirrored, "he must displace the mirror image, bringing it from the apparent or virtual place it occupies in the depth of the mirror back to himself, whom he identifies at a distance with his introceptive body" (CRO 129).

Presupposed in the accomplishment of this task is the taking up of a distanced/other/alien perspective on himself. The infant must thematically associate his lived body here with its visual image there. In short, he must enact with his specular image the same transfer of corporeal schema that he has already experienced in his relations with others—but with two important differences: (a) the association must now be thematic, and (b) he must see the image as an image of *himself*, that is, see himself as distinct from others. This difference (b) presupposes an *operant* awareness (that is, a lived awareness rather than a conceptual understanding) of his being as separate from others. As I have suggested, the path toward this awareness of self-other difference has been prepared by the affective intrusion of otherness that cracks the solidarity of syncretism.

Recognition of the specular image is not an instantaneous achievement, but a gradual and phased process: the infant manifests a range of behaviors toward his specular image (amazement, fascination, playful interaction, rejection, etc.) before they consolidate into a stable pattern of self-recognition. And, indeed, the quasi-reality of the mirror image is never entirely shed, even in adult life. But, once his behavior does consolidate, then the infant has succeeded in seeing himself as distinct from others and from the distanced vantage of another: corporeal reflexivity has become thematic and a primitive body image has been formed.

The result of this development that bears directly on the issue of intersubjectivity is that the transfer of corporeal schema, the foundation of human communion, has now been dramatically altered in structure and significance. Communion is now communion across a distance rather than syncretic participation in undifferentiated oneness. The infant is now ambiguously same and other to others and to himself. Perspectival differences have insinuated themselves into his world. Parturition has ramified and the symbols of weaning multiply rapidly. Archaic desire, oneiric longing for unity/completion, and its correlate, the teleology of integration, now emerge as latent forces around which subsequent intentions will form. The alienation from self and other, the burden of individuation, is an awakening into finitude. It is certainly not a complete awakening, but it is the first in a lifelong series of thematizations through which the human condition will become manifest.

Whether it is the mirror or the other's look that awakens me to my finitude,[14] the fact is that, once I have experienced self-objectification, I am henceforth vulnerable to the other's gaze—and to my own thematically critical reflection. Sartre was right in describing the threat of the other's competitive perspective as a fundamental mode of our being-with-others. But he was mistaken in conceiving it as the phenomenon in which I originally experience the subjectivity of others. His mistake lies in his failure to understand the threatening/shaming/objectifying look as *founded* upon the original transfer of corporeal schema, as a disruption of the primordial state of syncretic sociability. Nor is this an inconsequential mistake: by founding the entire sphere of intersubjectivity on negation, Sartre commits himself to a profound pessimism in his understanding of human relations. Because "conflict is the original meaning of being-for-others," all attempts to create human solidarity and erotic unification culminate in an irresolvable dialectic of dominance and submission: love is necessarily a vain pursuit.

Sartre's failure, however, is not merely the result of a one-sided and incomplete understanding of the look; it is, rather, the inevitable consequence of adopting a neo-Cartesian ontology predicated on the bifurcation of being into mutually exclusive spheres of immanence and transcendence. For Sartre, as for Husserl and Descartes before him, humanity resides in the immanent sphere, in pure interiority, in a subjectivity that can be known only through first-person reflection. As Merleau-Ponty analyzes the Sartrean account,

> If the other is really the other, that is, a For Itself in the strong sense that I am for myself, *he must never be so before my eyes*; it is necessary that this other For Itself never fall under my look, it is necessary that there be no perception of an other, it is necessary that the other be my negation or my destruction. (VI 79; VI-F 110)

The other as human subject can never be seen by me because the other's subjectivity does not admit of embodiment within the context of Sartre's ontology. The other's body, both for himself and for me, can only be an object. Reflexivity, within this neo-Cartesian ontology, belongs exclusively within the domain of immanence. There can be no corporeal reflexivity, no merging of subject and object within the flesh, hence the human subject the other reflectively is (for himself) can never be visible to me. And since the same is true with regard to his perception of me, I can only be an object for him, and it is only through my objectification under his gaze that his humanity indirectly manifests itself in my shame.

I shall reserve further discussion of this critique for the following chapter on embodiment, and conclude this section with a brief resume of the consequences of Merleau-Ponty's account of embodiment.

The main point I hope to have established in this section is that Merleau-Ponty's account of intersubjectivity vindicates his ontology. It is plainly the case that traditional ontologies render the everyday fact of human recognition, pathos, and communication inconceivable. If humanity is conceived in terms of consciousness, consciousness conceived in terms of immanent reflection, and that reflection conceived as absolutely private and inaccessible to others, then the humanity of others will be forever invisible to me and mine to them, thus forcing the absurd theoretical consequence that we can never experience one another's humanity or even arrive at the idea of an alter ego. The other hypothesis (which I have not taken up in these pages), that consciousness is a myth about occult qualities and human beings are only organic mechanisms which are fully explicable in terms of natural causality—that is, the reductionist position known as physicalism—is equally untenable because, in conceiving consciousness as epiphenomenal, it denies the reality and efficacy of human communion: love and hate, pride and guilt, intention and desire, in sum, the entire sphere of motivation and choice, freedom and responsibility, must be regarded as illusory and inconsequential, and these very words, as I write them, the necessary if remote effects of a cosmic big bang. If I am only a cogito, I am absolutely alone; if I am only mechanical meat, I cannot be alone because the concept has lost all meaning. The conclusion that must be drawn is that the dilemma is ill-conceived, that the ontology that grants being only to mutually exclusive domains of unextended thought and unthinking extension must be rejected, and that we must learn to understand that we are flesh. Our flesh is originally corporeal reflexivity, a body whose ability to touch depends on its own tangibility as its ability to see depends on its own visibility. This is the phenomenal body, the body conceived as phenomenon within the context of the thesis of the ontological primacy of phenomena. As phenomenon, the body I live is both immanent subject and transcendent object of my experience, and that is how you see me, because my subjectivity is incarnate in the body you see. But this is not to say that your vision of me coincides with my own. The simple fact that my body is separate from yours grounds a difference in the manner in which we experience each other's bodies and our own. Indeed, I perceive the otherness of the other's body coincidentally with the dawning of my recognition of my body as my own. This was the point of the discussion of the specular image: the process through which I become aware of myself and recognize myself in my thematic body image is essentially correlated with the process through which I recognize that you are a separate self. Note that the incorrigibility traditionally associated with first-person experience disappears in Merleau-Ponty's account. I must discover myself, learn to recognize myself in the behavior of my body as I see it reflected in the mirror and eyes of others. I am not transparent to myself, as I would necessarily be were I only a cogito (PP 352; PP-F 405). Merleau-Ponty's point here is that I can see the other as a personal being, the same kind of being as I am, because I am opaque to myself as he is to me, because self-transparency is neither a condition for selfhood (as it is in the Cartesian tradition) nor even a possibility. Yet nothing in this account forces the conclusion that I experience your body exactly as I experience my own. I may suffer your pain by witnessing it in your behavior, but it is your pain, the pain of another body separate from mine, and there are both qualitative and physiological differences between your pathos and my response to it. Here is the basic truth obscured by the polemics of solipsism: I live my body as you live yours, but they are separate bodies; if one dies, the other may still live for a while longer; one may eat while the other goes hungry. The transfer of corporeal schema which is the ground of our communion remains a transfer, an exchange across the space that separates us. We may be close in physical space or in psychic space, or we may be removed and estranged from each other—harmonious attunement is a human possibility and, at the other end of the spectrum, so is brutalization and dehumanization—but, although we must dwell in the same world, we cannot occupy the same space at the same time.

In the context of Merleau-Ponty's ontology, love between human beings becomes philosophically conceivable for the first time because—for the first time in the history of Western ontology—it allows us to understand how it is possible for human beings to recognize each other as such and develop at a personal level the pre-personal communion that is our birthright.[15]

EIGHT

The Lived Body

Kant's transcendental turn introduced the hypothesis that has governed Continental philosophy from his time until ours: if the categories of human understanding cannot be found in the transcendent world of nature, then they must be sought in the immanent sphere of transcendental consciousness. Since Kant's time, the transcendental sphere has grown to encompass more than theoretical understanding; now it includes political praxis, archaic desire, everyday involvement in the world found ready-to-hand, self-transcendence through symbolism, and, above all, language. But, although the transcendental sphere now accommodates practically all the structures of human culture, it is still a sphere of immanence—as it must be if it is to serve the transcendental function, that is, the function of organizing the manifold of human experience according to the necessities of finite existence. Kant transported the fundamental principles of intelligibility from the transcendent world to the sphere of immanence, and they have remained there ever since, at least for Continental thought. In the Anglo-American tradition, another aspect of Kant's thought has predominated: philosophy has taken its models from natural science and, for that reason, has until recently remained committed to the transcendence of the natural world. Now, however, it seems that the polemics of estrangement between Anglo-American and Continental philosophy are reluctantly giving way to an uneasy rapprochement: both traditions are seeking to ground their thought in language (although their conceptions of language and methods of inquiry remain divergent). This, in my judgment, is a step in a positive direction, but one which also goes astray. The gain in the recent linguistic turn derives from the fact that language essentially incorporates elements of both immanence and transcendence, hence will force abandonment of dualist ontologies as a condition for resolving its enigmas. But the linguistic turn errs insofar as it construes language as an ultimate ground and refuses to take up the question of its own origins and grounds. Indeed, the current deification of language—that is, the commitment to take language as the *sui generis* origin of meaning—effectively precludes resolving the immanence-transcendence bifurcation, perpetuates dualism, and leaves language ensnared in the domain of immanence. It is apparent in contemporary philosophy, as it is in the culture at large, that the refusal to look beyond the hermetic circle of immanence has kept us within the artificial sphere of the all-too-human.

I write this to introduce Merleau-Ponty's account of the lived body. Yet, the lived body is certainly a human body. How, then, does it free us from the sphere of the all-too-human?

Merleau-Ponty's thinking on the subject of the lived body is dynamic and evolutionary. It took him from physiology to ontology, from concrete problems in cognitive, developmental, and abnormal psychology to wider philosophical concerns about consciousness and intersubjectivity, and fetched up with the doctrines of flesh and intertwining. What was initially a thematic answer to thematic questions became ultimately an exemplar, the emblem of a general philosophical orientation, the phenomenon whose intrinsic demands portended a revolution in phenomenology. To be specific, the problems associated with the thesis of psycho-physical isomorphism in classical Gestalt theory, on one hand, and the problems presented by the case of Schneider,[1] on another, led Merleau-Ponty to reconceive the body in terms that were neither exclusively mechanistic nor entirely intentional but somehow incorporated both. Then, confronting the sources that had motivated him to take up a phenomenological approach to physiology and human embodiment, notably Husserl and Sartre, Merleau-Ponty found both that the lived body was crucial to resolving traditional epistemological problems concerning perception and illusion, intersubjectivity and solipsism, etc., and that the accounts of the human body offered by his mentors were lacking. The phenomenon of the lived body, as explicated by Husserl and Sartre, had also to be reconceived because neither of these two phenomenologists had succeeded in reconciling the body as mechanism with the body as vehicle of intentional behavior. But this failure turned out to be a consequence of fundamentally misconceived ontological commitments. The phenomenon of the lived body was misconstrued because phenomena, themselves, had been misconceived: the ontological foundations of phenomenology had to be reconceived. In sum, the phenomenon of the lived body became, for Merleau-Ponty, the clue to a new ontology.

Merleau-Ponty's ontology delivers phenomena from the sphere of immanence and restores the transcendence which was lost in the transcendental turn and not retrieved in the linguistic turn. The lived body, although human, is not all-too-human because it is a phenomenal body, an organism that retains its inherence within the world. In the context of Merleau-Ponty's ontology, it becomes possible for the body to be conceived as capable of both conscious reflexivity and corporeal reflex. Indeed, Merleau-Ponty shows that each capacity depends on the other, that the immanence or subjectivity of the body is inconceivable apart from its transcendence or thingly nature. The ontology predicated on the thesis of the ontological primacy of phenomena and the conception of phenomena as both immanent and transcendent is an ontology which is adequate to the task of accounting for all the aspects of the lived body.

Merleau-Ponty's account of the lived body is far too extensive for me to attempt to survey its many facets. Instead, I have selected two concrete issues that I hope will serve to substantiate the ontological theses at stake in this work. The first issue grows out of a quandary over how to explicate dysfunctions associated with two fundamental bodily actions, pointing and grasping, and the second centers on the controversial matter of double sensation.

1. POINTING AND GRASPING: THE SPATIALITY OF THE LIVED BODY

Merleau-Ponty takes up the issue of pointing and grasping in the chapter of the *Phenomenology* entitled "The Spatiality of One's Own Body and Motility" (PP 98–153; PP-F 114–72), and discusses it in relation to the familiar case of Schneider. Although the sources he cites most frequently are Gelb and Goldstein,[2] it is reasonable to assume that he was familiar with Heidegger's treatment of *zeigen* (pointing, showing, indicating) in the well-known section of *Being and Time* devoted to "Reference and signs."[3] In any case, he follows the strategy employed throughout the *Phenomenology*: an analysis of the failure of empiricist and intellectualist attempts to account for Schneider's difficulties provides a contrasting background for the exposition and defense of his own account. This and related texts serve my purpose because they demonstrate the ontological thesis I am seeking to substantiate, namely that the functioning of the lived body resists comprehension as long as its mind is conceived as disjunct from its flesh and the spheres of immanence and transcendence are regarded as mutually exclusive.

Schneider displays an inability to perform tasks of an abstract and theoretical nature. He is capable of grasping (*greifen*) various objects which are immediately present and significant to him within the practical context of a concrete project, but he cannot achieve a sufficient level of disengagement from the exigencies of the practical domain to enable himself to point (*zeigen*) at objects or to adopt any proto-theoretical cognitive posture toward things which is not a direct response to the demands of the moment or the requirements of the environment (PP 103; PP-F 120).

A patient, asked to point to some part of his body, his nose for example, can only manage to do so if he is allowed to take hold of it. If the patient is set the task of interrupting the movement before its completion, or if he is allowed to touch his nose only with a wooden ruler, the action becomes impossible. It must therefore be concluded that 'grasping' or 'touching,' even for the body, is different from 'pointing.' (PP 103; PP-F 120)

The problem is to explicate this difference and to explain how a point on my body can be available for grasping but not for pointing (PP 104; PP-F 120).

Other cases are cited in which patients capable of the movements of grasping are incapable of those of ostension. As the data accumulate, this distinction between grasping and pointing is broadened and ultimately subsumed under the more general distinction between concrete behavior (of which grasping is an instance) and abstract behavior (of which ostension is an instance). The rationale for this shift is as follows.

The patient who cannot point to his nose can take out his handkerchief and blow his nose. The bodily movements involved in the two acts are similar; what distinguishes them is the concrete and practical significance of the one as opposed to the abstract and formal nature of the other. Merleau-Ponty brings up additional cases in which orders to perform abstract movements (for example, touch your forehead in the manner of a salute) cannot be carried out—until they are incorporated into the context of a concrete and practical task. In the instance involving saluting, the patient enacts the role of a soldier; he adopts the whole demeanor of military bearing and, within this context, renders the salute.

The difficulty encountered by empiricism in its attempt to provide a physiological and causal explanation of such cases as these arises from the fact that it is a difference in significance which distinguishes the movements a patient can perform from those he cannot, rather than some physiologically specifiable difference in stimuli. The inability to perform abstract movements in these cases is, indeed, related to the malfunctioning of a given organ or set of organs as the result of injuries, but it cannot be reduced to that without ignoring the crucial differences in context (that is, practical as opposed to formal, concrete to abstract) which serve to demarcate the limits of the patient's abilities.

The point at stake here is that no exclusively mechanical or physiological explanation can do justice to the phenomenon in question: the significance a perceptual object has is not reducible to its causal effects upon a sensor. This is further supported by the fact, cited by Merleau-Ponty, that "an excitation is not perceived when it strikes a sensory organ which is not 'attuned' to it" (PP 75; PP-F 89). Perceptual significance is as much a function of anticipations as it is one of sensuous data—yet these anticipations, as *meanings* can have no place in a mechanistic world.

Intellectualism, on the other hand, can explicate the difference between pointing and grasping in terms of the categorial attitude which is necessary for the abstract movement but not for the concrete (PP 120–21; PP-F 140–41). Consciousness is conceived as intentionality, defined by intellectualism as a function of representation which subsumes the sensuous contents of experience under given forms thus providing them with meaning. The normal subject can perform abstract movements because his consciousness projects a context of meaning which provides the orientation for his gesture; he can point and the patient cannot because he represents space as meaningfully structured, as admitting of different possible directions, whereas the patient is immersed in immediacy, can only respond to the actual and cannot represent to himself the possible. Accordingly, intellectualism accounts for the difference between the normal and the pathological by means of the presence or absence of intentionality: lacking the necessary condition, the intentional sense-giving presupposed by abstract movement, the patient can only respond to stimuli insofar as they trigger conditioned reflexes in a practical and concrete domain.

Albeit true that abstract movement is rendered comprehensible by means of the categorial function of intentionality, the difference between the normal subject and the patient cannot be explained in terms of the presence or absence of that function. In performing his concrete movements, the diseased subject displays a purposiveness in the rhythm, coordination, and flow of the various actions constituting the whole gesture. He is, indeed, limited to the concrete and practical, but the practical is practical only by virtue of its teleological structure or purposiveness, and purposiveness is incompatible with the absence of intentionality. Hence the need to speak in terms of degrees rather than presence or absence of the categorial function of intentionality.

For intellectualism, however, "consciousness . . . does not admit of degree" (PP 121–22; PP-F 141). Therein lies the difficulty of intellectualism: its initial identification of consciousness with the sphere of immanence and its characterization of that sphere as a pure sense-giving activity leave intellectualism with but two mutually exclusive alternatives to draw upon in the attempt to explain such cases as those presently at hand.

> Either movement is movement for itself, in which case the 'stimulus' is not its cause but its intentional object—or else it disintegrates and is dispersed in existence in itself, and becomes an objective process in the body, whose phases are successive but unknown to each other. (PP 122; PP-F 141)

Restricted to these alternatives, intellectualism cannot account for the difference between the normal and the pathological because the intentionality which is evidently present in the former is not completely absent from the latter. Once this is granted, the ground of the distinction is lost.

Merleau-Ponty's positive account is responsive to the need, just illustrated, for some standpoint capable of comprehending both the physiological stimuli of empiricism and the intentional objects of intellectualism. More specificallly, what is needed is an understanding of spatiality that can accommodate the valid aspects of the empiricist and intellectualist accounts without being limited by their mutual exclusion.

Space is objectified by both empiricism and intellectualism. Objective space is a continuum of homogeneous points. Be the structuring of space (for example, its three-dimensionality, its unity as a continuous manifold, etc.) regarded as grounded in the nature of space as a transcendent reality or in the formal necessities governing consciousness, both empiricism and intellectualism regard the body as something located in a space whose fundamental structures are independent of it. Objective space may acquire practical significance, but that significance is held to be derivative and explicable in terms of physical or intellectual processes operating within a continuum whose essential characteristics have been determined beforehand. Neither empiricism nor intellectualism grants to the motility of the body any original function in the structuring of space. Opposing himself to the assumption of the primordiality of objective space, Merleau-Ponty argues in favor of the primacy of lived space.

Although it comes buried under a wealth of detail, the structure of Merleau-Ponty's explication of lived space is relatively simple. First, he shows that practical space is bodily space: it is oriented around both the physical structure of the body and the projects undertaken to fulfill the needs of the body. Thus, near and far, accessible and inaccessible, within reach and out of touch, etc., can be described in term of bodily motility, which includes both the body's physical capacities and limitations, and the body's self-fulfillment or frustration in its pursuit of its goals. The crucial point here is the claim that the body has its own intentionality, one which is prior to and independent of any symbolic function, categorial attitude or intelligible condition of consciousness conceived as representation (PP 137–39; PP-F 160–62). Within this framework we can understand bodily motility as consisting of movements that are both immediate (in the sense that they are not mediated by thematic or reflective conscious acts of deliberation or decision) and, at the same time, purposive (hence intentional). For example, the lightning movement wherein the lid closes to protect the eye is performed long before the threatening particle is taken as a conscious theme.[4] In short, Merleau-Ponty's claim is that "the body is an expressive space." Nor is it merely one space among many; rather "it is the origin of the rest, that which projects significations beyond itself and gives them a place" (PP 146; PP-F 171).

The difference between pointing and grasping can be understood in light of the difference between the theoretical, abstract space in which the former takes place and the practical, concrete space of the latter. The patient who can scratch his nose easily but point to it only with difficulty is circumscribed within a spatial continuum articulated by immediate needs. The space in which he can operate effectively is defined in terms of heterogeneous and qualitatively distinct locations (for example, where it itches, where it hurts) and not in terms of coordinates measured quantitatively within a continuum of homogeneous points (for example, so many units from an origin along given planes).

Empiricism is correct in claiming that bodily movements are motivated, that they are responsive to a transcendent state of affairs and are not purely self-initiated fiats of an immanent agency, but fails to see that the attempt to explain them simply as responses to physiological stimuli is reductive and inadequate. Processes occurring in objective space cannot be regarded as stimuli. Only within the context of praxis do events have the significance required to provoke a given kind of directed response. The physical space of empiricism lacks practical structure: any teleological dimension would have to be superimposed. But, the claim for the priority of objective space rules out the possibility of explaining the genesis of a practical ordering. Bodily movement would be reduced to sheer mechanics initially devoid of purposiveness and incapable of ever developing it, since the intentional structures of purposiveness cannot be generated out of a purely mechanistic physiology. Hence no ground could be offered for the distinction between grasping and pointing: both would be mechanical reactions to physical causes and there would be no way to explain how one function could be retained when the other is lost.

Although intellectualism can account for the purposiveness of bodily movement in terms of the intentional structuring of space, it fails to realize that the structures of practical space cannot be reduced to the categories of a disembodied consciousness. If all intentional structuring is held to be the product of the categorial function of consciousness, then the ground of the distinction between practical and theoretical organization of space is lost and with it goes the possibility of explaining how one could survive the injury that curtailed the other. Furthermore, there is no way left to explain bodily movements which are purposive, but conducted in the manifest absence of any thematic conscious representation. The categorially structured space of intellectualism is objective space insofar as it is conceived independently of the needs, involvement, and point of view of the body.

Granting to Merleau-Ponty that bodily intentionality is original, primordial, and the ground of the practical structures of lived space, it remains for him to trace from this origin the genesis of the symbolic or categorial function of conscious intentionality and the correlative structures of theoretical space. Here the motility of the body plays a crucial role: Merleau-Ponty's claim is that bodily space embodies a tension (in that, by virtue of motility, each 'there' can become, hence potentially is, a 'here') which motivates its transformation into universal space and, ultimately, into objective or theoretical space (PP 102; PP-F 119). By way of substantiating this claim, he embarks upon a detailed analysis of motility which endeavors to show how the possibilities grounded in the tension just mentioned become thematized, explicitly recognized, and grasped reflectively. This is the generation of the 'I can' (that is, these possibilities are ones I can actualize) and, in turn, it provides the foundation for a spatial orientation in which space appears as the horizon for a multiplicity of possible movements, expressions, projects, etc. This constructed space provides the background for abstract movement. That is, by virtue of the possibilities opened to it by thematization of the 'I can,' consciousness is liberated from the immediacy of the bodily projects made in response to the concrete and given context, and may now undertake movements in the human space of potentiality (as opposed to the physical space of actuality).

The third step in Merleau-Ponty's account of lived space fastens on the "centrifugal" (PP 111; PP-F 129) nature of abstract movement. The central notion in this step is that of sedimentation: movements which are initially deliberate choices of thematized possibilities may subsequently become automatic. The gesture, for example, of lifting an eyebrow, originally a difficult, forced, and artificial affectation, may become sedimented in one's repertoire of expressions; it is then performed easily and automatically thereby taking on the natural grace of a familiar acquisition. The learning process set forth here in terms of sedimentation provides a means of explaining the kind of phenomena variously known as conditioned reflex, habituation, and the like.

Merleau-Ponty uses the Husserlian term '*Fundierung*' to describe the relations between (a) the space of actuality and (b) that of possibility, (a) given contexts and (b) constructed horizons, (a) concrete spatiality and (b) abstract spatiality, etc. In each of these pairs, there is a kind of reciprocity: whereas the second (b) is derived from, grounded (or founded) upon (a) the first (which is regarded as prior, primordial, "originary"), by virtue of the process of sedimentation, the second returns, as it were, to the first and informs it. Although *Fundierung* involves reciprocity, it is not a symmetrical relation: the found*ing* term (a) grounds the found*ed* (b). Accordingly, the bodily intentionality instantiated in the first terms of the pairs listed grounds the categorial intentionality instantiated in the second terms.

The distinction between grasping and pointing rests upon that between bodily and categorial intentionality. A grasping movement may be a simple motor project involving bodily intentionality but no conscious mediation; pointing, on the other hand, requires the categorial function since it is a symbolic gesture. However, the intentional categories originally requisite for pointing may subsequently become sedimented in the *normal* subject's world horizon, in the space in which he lives. This accounts for the fact that a normal subject may perform pointing movements with the same ease and lack of reflective deliberation that characterize his grasping movements. The normal subject lives in a spatial context structured both by practical exigencies and by theoretical possibilities. When a bodily injury incapacitates a person to such an extent that his recovery is incomplete and it is discovered that he has regained the ability to grasp but cannot perform the movements of ostension as a normal person would, one must account for his degeneration in the terms of a departure from normal spatiality.

Pathological spatiality it not to be understood as simple reduction in or restriction of normal spatiality. The patient's capacities are restricted, to be sure, but what makes his behavior pathological (as opposed to primitive or undeveloped) is the attempt his body makes to compensate for its losses by "substitution behavior" (PP 77–78, 107–109; PP-F 92–93, 125–27). The cases treated above involved patients whose injuries or diseases severely restricted their abilities to operate effectively in the realm of possibility. The problem here is not so much one of conceiving or intellectually apprehending the abstract possibilities open to them, it is rather that these possibilities were not sedimented in their spatial horizons as bodily options. The patient who had difficulty saluting clearly understood the command (as indicated by his subsequent behavior); his problem lay in executing it. The transition from the intellectual comprehension of a task to its bodily achievement, which is effected so easily by normal subjects, was thwarted in his case, not because he was physically incapable of the movements (here again his ability to perform the movements is attested by his subsequent behavior), but because that particular ensemble of movements was not demanded by the concrete exigencies of his environment. To carry out his task, the patient resorted to substitute behavior: he deliberately projected himself into an imaginary context in which the gesture was a sedimented possibility. Two points arise here which bear on the problem of discerning the genuinely pathological aspects of the patient's behavior: first, he found it necessary to deliberate, to work thematically at a task a normal subject would have executed without conscious effort at problem solving; secondly, what was lacking to him, what he had to provide for himself, was an enabling context, environment, or horizon, His behavior was abnormal in that, unlike the normal subject, he had to make the conscious effort of substituting an imaginary and constructed context for his actual context.

In normal subjects, to be sure, the genesis of spatiality proceeds from (a) the level of the immediate responses of bodily intentionality to concrete needs within the actual context to (b) that of the realization and sedimentation of increasingly abstract and theoretical possibilities. The diseased subject is not to be understood as reverting to earlier or more primitive stages in the normal process of development. It is rather the case that he creates a (pathological) style of his own by means of which he tries to approximate normal activity directed toward typical goals within the limited parameters of his own afflicted capabilities.

The types of pathological cases relevant here are ones in which the patient has both an intellectual grasp of the tasks required of him and the basic abilities of bodily movement: what is lacking is a frame of reference (that is, the constructed and sedimented structures of abstract spatiality) in which the two can be coordinated. The patient cannot, therefore, be understood as suffering from a purely physical disability (as empiricism would have it) because he can perform the physical movements; but neither can he be regarded as incapacitated in a purely psychical way (as intellectualism claims) because he can understand the goals to be achieved. His inability to carry out such orders as saluting or pointing to a part of his anatomy stems from the absence of a matrix in which the process of movement and the "thought as a representation of movement" can flow together (PP 110; PP-F 128). The result of this absence is the substitution behavior in which the patient tries, with varying degrees of awkward success, to achieve the ends he conceives by the means of which he is capable.

Properly speaking, then, the injuries and diseases being considered here have resulted in degeneration of the lived worlds of the afflicted subjects. Schneider's wound damaged his world. It was not merely a physical injury, as an empiricist might claim, and its consequences cannot be explained in that reductive way. More than the brute fact of the injury is needed to explain Schneider's affliction; the *meaning* of the wound must be considered if its consequences are to be understood. Nor, similarly, can intellectualism explain Schneider's difficulties strictly in terms of debilities occurring to his psyche or consciousness (his *body* was wounded, after all). Instead, the import of Merleau-Ponty's contention that having a body is equivalent to having a world is growing in clarity: to be incarnate is to be in the world and of the world; it is to be part of the domain it surveys. Merleau-Ponty's concepts of motor intelligence and corporeal intentionality are designed to show that the flesh is intrinsically purposive and that its purposes are grounded in its worldly needs.

The ontological implications of the foregoing account may be easily seen. The reason that the concepts of corporeal intentionality and lived space (the concepts needed to understand both normal and pathological cases of pointing and grasping behavior) have been lacking hitherto is that dualistic ontological presuppositions have engendered a false dichotomy which requires one to choose between mechanical explanation couched in physiological terms and teleological explanation couched in terms of intentionality, but denies the possibility of combining the two (PP 124; PP-F 144). By demonstrating the inseparability of consciousness and embodiment, Merleau-Ponty discredits the ontologies that conceive them as mutually exclusive and provides further validation for his own.

2. DOUBLE SENSATION AND MERLEAU-PONTY'S CRITIQUE OF SARTRE

Classical psychology understands the body as a thing, but as a thing with unique properties that differentiate it from other things. Among these properties is the capacity for double sensation: that is, when I touch one hand with another, I have the double sensation of touching and being touched. Both Sartre and Merleau-Ponty take up the issue of double sensation, and in both cases the manner in which they handle it has powerful and far-reaching implications for their ontological standpoints and for their treatments of the phenomenal body. They concur in rejecting the traditional psychological account—neither wants even to appropriate the term—because they both reject the idea that sensation is to be understood as a property that, in being predicated of animate bodies, essentially defines them. But their agreement ends there: on no other point are they so radically opposed, hence no other point will serve so well to contrast and thereby explicate these two phenomenological accounts of the lived body.

First, Sartre:

> To touch and to be touched, to feel that one is touching and to feel that one is touched—these are two species of phenomena which it is useless to try to reunite by the term 'double sensation.' In fact they are radically distinct, and they exist on two incommunicable levels. (BN 304)[5]

The "two incommunicable levels" of which Sartre writes are two of the three "ontological dimensions of the body" which he states constitute three distinct "orders of reality." The first ontological dimension of the body, "the body as being-for-itself" or as "facticity," designates the body as subject, the body as it touches itself or other things (BN 306–39). The second ontological dimension of the body, "the body-for-others," designates the body as object, the body as it is touched by others (BN 339–51). The third ontological dimension of the body designates the order of reality in which "I exist for myself as known by the other" (BN 351–61) and feel myself objectified by his subjectivity.

Why does Sartre draw such radical lines of demarcation and characterize these three aspects of bodily experience as distinct and incommunicable orders of reality? The distinctions purport to be phenomenological; that is, he presents them initially as though they were grounded in the phenomenal differences in which my body appears to me, to others, and to myself as mediated by the look of the other. But, as I shall try to show, they are dictated by antecedent ontological commitments.

Sartre takes up the question of the body in part three of *Being and Nothingness*, that is, in the context of the ontology articulated in the first two parts. This ontology, as explained earlier (chapter 2, 2), commits him to the conception of consciousness or being-for-itself as nothingness whose relation to all its intentional objects (that is, all the objects it perceives, remembers, imagines, or cognizes in any way) is fundamentally one of negation. Recall, as well, that the relation of the for-itself to the objects it intends necessarily involves the relation to itself that Sartre calls the prereflective cogito. In intending an object, the for-itself defines the object by negation: 'this' is what it is by excluding other 'thises'; 'this' is determined by differentiation from the 'all,' the undifferentiated totality that serves as its background. When the for-itself posits 'this' as its object, it also and necessarily is aware (of) itself as not being this intentional object. The being of consciousness, being-for-itself, resides in the prereflective cogito; consciousness *is* this nonthematic relation to itself, this awareness (of) itself as not being any of the objects it thematically intends.

This view of consciousness commits Sartre to a strange and conflicted understanding of the body. He cannot ignore the body because it is an essential requirement for any account of perception and intersubjectivity:

without bodies, we could never perceive or come to know any-thing or any-body. But the body is palpably an object and, for Sartre, consciousness as the agency of knowledge *is* its awareness (of) itself as not being an object. Sartre confronts this difficulty, as philosophers are wont to do when they are in trouble, by drawing a distinction. He distinguishes between the body as knowing/perceiving and the body as known/perceived (BN 328–29).

As knower or perceiver or subject of its intentional acts, the body is inapprehensible and does not belong to the objects in the world. This is the "first ontological dimension of the body," the body as it is *for me* (BN 329) when I live through it toward other things, "the body as being-for-itself." When consciousness is immersed in the world and fascinated by the objects it posits, it is not conscious *of* its body; rather it exists its body in a non-positional modality: "non-positional consciousness is consciousness (of) the body as being that which it surmounts and nihilates" (BN 330). The body as subject is thematically conscious *of* the objects it posits, but only non-positionally conscious (of) itself. In its first ontological dimension, "the body belongs . . . to the structures of the non-thetic self-consciousness" (BN 330). Yet Sartre denies that it can be identified with the prereflective cogito. He is forced to this denial because the prereflective cogito is sheer immanence, unclouded by the opacity attaching to all forms of transcendence, and he has already described the body at the level of the first ontological dimension as "facticity." This, too, is necessary because it is only as facticity that the body can perform its function of situating consciousness in the world. Already, then, the aura of self-contradiction surrounds Sartre's account of the body: the body as subject is inapprehensible, not a worldly object—yet, as facticity, it is situated in the world.

As known/perceived, at the level of "the second ontological dimension," the body is seen as an object. This is "the body for others": either my body as it appears to the other or the other's body as it appears to me; for Sartre, these are equivalent (BN 339). When the other's body is posited as its thematic object, consciousness is non-thematically aware (of) itself (via the prereflective cogito) as not being that object. The other's being-for-me is that of an object which I transcend; it is an object to which I assign meaning, an instrument available for my utilization. Likewise, my being-for-the-other is also that of an object which he transcends. Because I am an object for him and he is an object for me, the relations between our bodies are purely external: as body, the other is an object in the world for me, a 'this' among 'thises.' On this point, Sartre and Merleau-Ponty are strongly at odds: whereas Merleau-Ponty conceives the foundation of intersubjectivity in terms of the transfer of *corporeal* schema, Sartre contends that "the other exists for me *first* and I apprehend him in his body *subsequently*. The other's body is for me a secondary structure" (BN 339). In the context of Sartre's ontology, the other's body can only be an object for me, hence cannot function to reveal his subjectivity.

Sartre attempts to avoid the solipsism consequent upon this view by means of his doctrine of the look: I become aware of the other's subjectivity through my experience of being objectified under his gaze. My body appears to the other as his appears to me—as an object posited by consciousness in the thetic mode—and I experience this objectification as a threat to my own free subjectivity. The other's perspective on me and my scene, the world as I constitute it, necessarily conflicts with my own, and I feel myself transcended/surpassed by his subjectivity. For Sartre, then, there is no possibility of syncretism and no residue in adult life of the indistinction of perspectives characteristic of infantile experience: the other is aboriginally an alien and alienating presence.

Sartre must be challenged here. If the other exists for me first through his look and it is only subsequent to this that I apprehend him in his body, then his body can play no role in my experience of his look. This is *prima facie* absurd: only a body can manifest the presence of a look.

Sartre's "third ontological dimension of the body" refers to my experience of my body as objectified by the other's look (BN 351). At this level, "my body is designated as alienated" (BN 353): I am alienated from my body because the other assigns it a meaning I cannot know, and yet this is a meaning for which I am somehow responsible. I experience my body in its being for the other through the various modalities of shyness, embarrassment, shame, etc.; that is, I experience my facticity in the eyes of the other.

The resumé of Sartre's account of the body is intended to demonstrate two points: (a) it is a logical extension of the position he takes with regard to the issue of double sensation (as that position is preordained by his ontology); and (b) it renders a large segment of bodily experience inexplicable. Sartre argues that I can either see objects through my eyes and touch objects with my hands at the level of the first ontological dimension, or I can see my eyes as objects (for example, in a mirror) and touch my hand as the object of tactile exploration at the level of the second ontological dimension, but I cannot see the seeing or touch the touching. My body as subject is ontologically disjunct from my body as object. "Either it is a thing among things, or else it is that by which things are revealed to me. But it cannot be both at the same time" (BN 304). It cannot be both at the same time because the body as subject "belongs . . . to the structures of the nonthetic consciousness" (BN 330) and, as such, must include an awareness (of) not being any of the objects it posits, in this case, the body as object. When, at the level of the third ontological dimension, I attempt this perception of my own body, I find that I am alienated from it: not only is the body, as object, other to me, the subject who sees/touches it, but this body-object appears to me already sullied by the look of others. My perception of my body as object is already mediated by a point of view I can intend only emptily, by a secret I cannot share. The act of nihilation which posits my body as object places an insurmountable *not* between consciousness/

interiority/subjectivity and the body which is its exterior/facticity/point-of-entry-into-the-world.

But, if this were truly the case, my body could never be the object of shame. If I am *not* the body objectified by another's look, if I am *not* the body I see through his eyes, then I can feel no shame at the exposure of that body to objectification; it is other to me. The phenomena of shame and alienation require that I be both subject and object of my experience. In a mode of fundamental ambiguity I must be both the object of shame I perceive through the eyes of an other and also the subject who is witness to this shaming objectification and complicit in the act.

Furthermore, if Sartre's account were correct, I could never have learned to do what I am doing now—writing words on paper with a pencil. To learn to write, I must be able to see my hand and live through it, I must be able to watch my fingers, respond to the pressure they feel, and dwell in them kinesthetically. If I were not both subject and object of my bodily acts, I could never catch a ball, or even pick one up. The ensemble of bodily activities grouped under the category of grasping presupposes that I am able to see what I am doing.

Just as Sartre's account of double sensation is driven by his ontology, so is this the case with Merleau-Ponty, and the differences in their accounts reflect the differences in their ontologies. Merleau-Ponty's ontology is predicated on the thesis of the ontological primacy of phenomena, and, as I have sought to show, he understands phenomena as both immanent and transcendent. Thus, the lived body, as a phenomenon, includes both the immanent agency of my conscious life and the transcendence of worldly objects: "I apprehend my body as a subject-object, as capable of 'seeing' and 'suffering' " (PP 95; PP-F 111). It is not the case for Merleau-Ponty, as Sartre contends, that the body-subject is ontologically disjunct from the body-object; it is rather the case that the same lived body manifests itself in both roles. There is, as explicated earlier in the section on the tacit cogito, a fundamental reflexivity in the lived body's relations with worldly objects such that every contact with a thing is at the same time a presence to itself: I cannot touch an object without at the same time being touched by it. Consequently, the phenomenon of grasping does not pose the problem for Merleau-Ponty that it poses for Sartre. I can pick up a ball or catch it when it is thrown to me because I can see what I am doing: the corporeal intentionality that allows my fingers to curl around the ball as it impacts on my palm (that is, the local intelligence manifested by my body in its active role as subject) can be coordinated with the vision I must have of my hand as worldly object if I am to position it in the ball's path. This eye-hand coordination would be impossible without corporeal reflexivity, if my body were not aware of itself as it interacts with the worldly objects among which it dwells.

Corporeal reflexivity, however, is tacit, horizonal, pre-thematic: what happens when the body thematizes itself? This is the domain in which the double sensations of classical psychology take place, and to which Sartre refers as the third ontological dimension of the body.

> My body . . . is recognized by its power to give me 'double sensations': when I touch my right hand with my left, my right hand, as object, has the singular property of being able to feel too. [But] the two hands are never simultaneously in the relationship of touched and touching to each other. When I press my two hands together, it is not a matter of two sensations felt together as one perceives two objects placed side by side, but of an ambiguous set-up in which both hands can alternate the roles of 'touching' and being 'touched.' (PP 93; PP-F 109)

Although appeals to first-hand experience are seldom convincing in philosophical debate, perhaps because expectations typically color the nature of experience, it is still worthwhile to try the little experiment. If Sartre were correct, there could be no question about which hand is playing which role: one hand would clearly be subject and the other object, and there would be no confusion because the two roles are distinct and incommunicable, because, for Sartre, they belong to mutually exclusive ontological domains. But, for Merleau-Ponty, ambiguity prevails: the roles do not coincide, they alternate—in such a way that one is confounded in the attempt to assign separate roles to separate hands. A local anaesthetic applied to one of the hands might result in an experience more conformable to the Sartrean model—and demonstrate thereby its inapplicability to the norm of everyday life.

The idea of role reversal, expressed in the *Phenomenology of Perception* as alternation, occurs in *The Visible and the Invisible* (where it is given the thematic attention it does not receive in the *Phenomenology*) under the heading of reversibility. The thesis of reversibility occupies a central position in Merleau-Ponty's explicit ontology, and will be given the consideration it warrants in the chapter devoted to that subject. Here I want only to point to the fact that the ontology of the later work is prefigured in the earlier one, and to show how Merleau-Ponty's treatment of double sensations in the *Phenomenology* follows from the ontological standpoint implicit in his middle period and informs his understanding of the lived body.

Sartre contends that I can see through my eyes or see them as objects, "but I cannot 'see the seeing' " (BN 304). When I look at myself in a mirror, I can see my eyes reflected there, and I can also see their perspective on me and the things around me. Moreover, I can meet my eyes in the mirror or avoid my own look. My own look in the mirror is an unusual case of Sartre's look, but it fulfills his description insofar as it is a look in which I am objectified. My own mirrored look is tamer than the look of an other, to be sure, because it is subject to my volition in a way that the other's look is not—but it can still be disquieting. As Merleau-Ponty says (borrowing a phrase from Sartre), "even for the adult the image is never a simple reflection of the model; it is, rather, its 'quasi-presence'" (CRO 133). The point here is that there is a sense in which I can see myself seeing: the eyes in the mirror are seeing eyes; when I meet their gaze, I feel the impact of their look, and it is quite different from the look of eyes in a photograph or the dead eyes of a corpse. The magical properties of the mirror afford a special instance of corporeal reflexivity; the mirror allows me to see my visibility and my vision. In de-centering my experience of my body, it provides a concrete and vivid model for the corporeal reflexivity operative throughout the spectrum of my bodily experience: the body that sees has to be visible, and cannot be the subject of vision without a tacit awareness (made explicit with the mirror) of its own status as object. This is evident in the futility of the voyeur's project: he would see while remaining unseen, but his strategies of self-concealment betray the awareness that defeats his telos of omniscience. He cannot hide his visibility from himself.

The ontological implications embedded in the issue of double sensation are revealed in stark clarity in the case of sexual desire. The goal of desire, according to Sartre, is "to get hold of the other's free subjectivity through [her] objectivity-for-me" (BN 382). In order to do this, I must make the other's consciousness available to my grasp; I must bring about the incarnation of the other. As Sartre describes it, the dialectic of desire proceeds as follows. When I desire an other, my own consciousness is "troubled": it becomes "clogged in my flesh." My desire brings about my incarnation: "the being which desires is consciousness making itself body" (BN 389). In this state, I wish to arouse desire in the other, to induce her consciousness to become flesh. I do this by means of the caress (BN 390). But, if I succeed in ensnaring the other's freedom in her facticity, I must nonetheless fail in my attempt to possess it. "Desire stands at the origin of its own failure inasmuch as it is a desire of *taking* and of *appropriating*" (BN 398). I seek to incarnate the other's consciousness in order to possess it, but as soon as I attempt to grasp the other's flesh or to appropriate it through penetration, two transformations occur which subvert my project: my body, becoming the active instrument of my intentions, awakens from the swooning passivity of incarnation, my disturbance disappears, and my body becomes being-for-itself (first ontological dimension); at the same time, my grasping reduces the other's body to "an instrument in the midst of the world," and causes it to fall "from the level of *flesh* to the level of pure object" (second ontological dimension) (BN 398). Thus, when I grasp/penetrate the other's body, I do not get what I want—I am left holding a mere object from which consciousness has fled—and my own desire "has become abstract" in transcending its disturbance (BN 398). "Desire is itself doomed to failure" (BN 396).

Sartre's account of desire pivots on the notion of flesh, consciousness incarnated, but there is no place for flesh in any of his three ontological dimensions of the body. His ontology renders the notion of flesh inconceivable. "Being-for-itself can only be entirely body or entirely conscious-ness: it cannot be *united* with a body" (BN 305; BN-F 368). Yet, without the intersection of immanence and transcendence, without the incarnation of consciousness in the body's flesh, desire and the caress cannot be. You must inhabit your body for it to be the object of my desire, and when I caress your body it must be you that I touch—otherwise erotic love would be but mystified necrophilia.

Merleau-Ponty appropriates the notion of flesh from Sartre and grants it a privileged place in the explicit ontology of *The Visible and the Invisible* where he describes it as an irreducible (VI 147; VI-F 193–94). For Sartre, as for any thinker operating within the presuppositions of the dualist tra-dition, flesh can only be the union of contradictories; for Merleau-Ponty, however, the element of flesh is an instantiation of the thesis of the on-tological primacy of phenomena: it is the concrete coincidence of imma-nence and transcendence in the phenomenon of the lived body.

Before leaving the topic of the lived body, I would like to dispel a mis-conception that crops up regularly in the secondary literature on Mer-leau-Ponty. This is the mistaken thought that the body functions for Merleau-Ponty as the transcendental ego does for Kant and Husserl, that it is to be conceived as the agency underlying the organization of experience or as the foundation of transcendental constitution. It must be granted that grounds for this interpretation can be found in Merleau-Ponty's writing.

> Our body, to the extent that it moves itself about, that is, to the extent that it is inseparable from a view of the world and is that view itself realized, is the condition of possibility . . . of all the expressive operations and all the acqui-sitions which constitute the cultural world. (PP 388; PP-F 445)

This is the meaning-bestowing function of the body, the power of organ-izing experience grounded in bodily motility and its perceptual synthesis. As such, as the condition for the possibility of the constitution of a cultural world, the body bears a functional resemblance to the transcendental ego.

But this is only half of the total picture. One must keep in mind that the body also has an interrogative function: it is a questioning of the world, and its motility is a response to the questions the world raises. I move in response to the demand of things to be seen as they are, as they need to be seen to respond to the reflexive questions that arise between us. The active, constituting, centrifugal role of the body, its transcendental opera-tion, is inconceivable apart from its receptive, responsive, centripetal role before the givenness of the world, its existence as flesh amidst the flesh of the world. The body does not synthesize the world *ex nihilo*; the body seeks understanding from the bodies with which it interacts. Once it is understood that categorial activity presupposes corporeality, that re-cognition presup-poses perception which presupposes an encounter of bodies, then it be-comes clear that the body cannot be reduced to a pure transcendental agency. Or, again, once transcendental agency is understood as requiring corporeality, it becomes evident that the Kantian/Husserlian model of a purely immanent constituting consciousness requires radical modification. Some elaboration may be helpful here to integrate this point with fundamental arguments set forth earlier.

Although there is a centrifugal aspect to bodily intentionality, explicated above under the heading of sedimentation, this should not be conceived as the imposition of form on the data of experience. This interpretation would leave Merleau-Ponty vulnerable to the charges he levels against intellectualism: if the sensuous matter of experience is conceived as receiving its meaning from the supervenient activity of some immanent agency of intentionality, be that regarded as pure consciousness or incarnate consciousness, then the problem of organization becomes insoluble. Unless the matter of experience is pregnant with form, unless the parts of the phenomenal world are conceived (in accordance with the principle of autochthonous organization) as intrinsically related and primordially meaningful, then the assignment of one meaning rather than another or the imposition of this form rather than that must be regarded as an arbitrary fiat and utterly groundless. (See chapter 4 above.)

The possibilities sedimented in lived space through the centrifugal aspects of bodily intentionality must be conceived as *founded* upon the interdependent structures of motility and phenomenal space; that is, they presuppose a process of learning. Phenomenal space for the adult is articulated by possibilities founded in a bodily 'I can,' but this 'I can' must be understood in the context of genetic phenomenology as an acquisition, won through effort, in which the body develops habitual strategies for dealing with its environment. In the midst of a tennis match, I may see a particular configuration of game space—my position, my opponent's position, and the vector of the ball—as an opportunity to place the ball beyond his reach and win the point, that is, the possibility of slam may be apparent on the court, but this organization of space is not imposed by my bodily intentions, although they are complicit in it; it is rather that I have attuned myself to the limits of my abilities. Nor is the primal institution of game-space itself an arbitrary fiat: the conventional demarcation of space depends as much on the earth as it does on the bodies that inhabit it. Here, then, is the crucial point: because the lived body is a body, a worldly object among other worldly objects, it cannot perform the functions ascribed to transcendental consciousness. The body's freedom is circumscribed by phenomenal space, time, and objects around it which serve both to ground and to limit its 'I can,' whereas a pure consciousness would meet no such resistance and be free to constitute its world to suit itself; its very needs would be elective.

The lived body is not a transcendental subject; it is a phenomenon situated among other phenomena within the world horizon. If my body occupies a privileged position for me, that must be understood as a limitation, not as grounds for endowing it with some version of the incipient omniscience associated with pure transcendental subjectivity. The fact is that I do not constitute the world; I interpret it, I attempt to understand it. Nor do these interpretations absolutely predelineate my experience: error, frustration, disappointment, cognitive and practical failure all serve to inform me that my finite understanding, albeit grounded, is nonetheless outstripped by the transcendence of the world.

The apparent privilege of the phenomenal body experienced by the person whose body it is derives from one of the lived body's capacities: thematic reflection, the explicit cogito. As explained in the previous section, however, this capacity is founded upon corporeal reflexivity which itself is prepersonal or anonymous. The relevant revelation provided by thematic reflection is the awareness of occupying a viewpoint, a limited perspective. It is, as I have argued, a strange reversal—more accurately, an outright mistake—to infer from the finitude of one's perspective that one is the origin of the constitution of one's world. That mistake, as I have also tried to show, is based on the prior mistake of regarding the cogito as independent of its embodiment; that is, the mistake of conceiving consciousness as separate or separable from its body and its world. Merleau-Ponty's account of the incarnation of consciousness in the lived body corrects these mistakes and, in the process, delivers a devastating blow to the idealisms generated by transcendental philosophy.

Still, it would seem that the phenomenal body, the body I live, cannot simply be placed on a par with other phenomenal objects. It would seem that the very attention devoted to it in these pages bespeaks an ontological significance that other phenomena do not have. Consider the following passage from the *Phenomenology* which concludes one phase of Merleau-Ponty's discussion of double sensation.

> The body catches itself from the outside engaged in a cognitive process; it tries to touch itself while being touched, and initiates 'a kind of reflection'[6] which is sufficient to distinguish it from objects, of which I can indeed say that they 'touch' my body, but only when it is inert, and therefore without ever catching it unawares in its exploratory function. (PP 93; PP-F 109)

The distinction between the body and objects Merleau-Ponty draws here is based on the corporeal reflexivity which is an essential attribute of percipient bodies and absent from the objects of the world which are not capable of perception. The phenomenal body can see: its ability to sense other things depends upon its ability to sense itself, and this anonymous tacit cogito is the foundation for the explicit cogito, the emergent experience of selfhood and subjectivity which sets the body apart from objects. This is ontologically significant: it is the basis of the subject-object dualism Merleau-Ponty was striving to overcome in his own thought.

I have commented earlier on the tension in the *Phenomenology* between the thesis of the ontological primacy of phenomena which rejects the categories of dualist thought and the language of consciousness and object which tends to preserve a latent dualism. Here we arrive at the crux of the matter. The question is whether Merleau-Ponty's emphasis on the phenomenal body as the subject of perception can be reconciled with his attempt to articulate a non-dualistic ontology, that is, an ontology that does not trade upon an ontological disjunction between subject and object, consciousness and thing. My standpoint on this issue has been adumbrated frequently in earlier portions of this text: although the *Phenomenology* contains language that sustains dualistic interpretations, its central thought is that phenomena are ontologically primary, that the phenomenal world is the fundamental reality which grounds all conceptualization including the concepts of subject and object, and that 'phenomenon' names an original order of being which must be conceived in non-dualistic terms. However, the tension in the *Phenomenology* needs to be resolved. On one hand, it is legitimate to say that both lived body and perceptual object are phenomena, and that, although the one incorporates a reflexivity absent from the other, this does not entail an ontological disjunction within the domain of phenomena. On the other hand, because this difference between conscious bodies and inanimate things has long been construed as entailing some form of dualism, it is necessary to show that subsuming both under the heading of phenomena is more than a definitional fiat.

There is a progressive realization evident in the development of Merleau-Ponty's thought from the *Phenomenology of Perception* to *The Visible and the Invisible*. In the *Phenomenology*, Merleau-Ponty takes the position that I perceive things and that things can be said to "perceive" me inasmuch as I am perceptible from the positions they occupy. In "Eye and Mind," he takes up this thought that there is a metaphorical sense in which the things I see also "see" me (EM 167; EM-F 31–32),[7] but he does not elaborate the metaphor or develop the thought into a thesis. In *The Visible and the Invisible* the metaphor recurs: "the seer and the visible reciprocate one another and we no longer know which sees and which is seen" (VI 139; VI-F 183), but here it is developed into a thesis, the thesis of reversibility. This thesis is central to the explicit ontology Merleau-Ponty was formulating in his last work, and I shall offer an explication of it in chapter 9, which is devoted to that subject. The point that is relevant here, however, is that the reversibility thesis marks the culmination of a continuously emergent thought: Merleau-Ponty's attempt to purge his ontology of dualistic categories, his attempt to recast the traditional disjunction between perceiver and perceived, his attempt to understand the differences between seer and seen within the framework of a genuinely phenomenological ontology—this endeavor is evident throughout his works and acquires thematic prominence in his middle and late periods. If there is a relation of reversibility between perceiver and perceived—between the body as sensing and the body as sensed, between my body and yours, between the phenomenal body and other worldly phenomena—then the ontological wedges traditionally driven to split these pairs and force the members of the sundered couples into mutually exclusive domains of being must be withdrawn, and the language of subject-object disjunction replaced with that of communion and reciprocity. The fundamental relatedness of seer and seen must be made conceivable.

The perceptual capabilities of the lived body do not remove it from the phenomenal world or transform it into a transcendental subject. The body is flesh. It is as flesh that it perceives the world and itself. But the flesh of the body is the flesh of the world. How we are to conceive flesh, what it means to think it "as an element, as the concrete emblem of a general manner of being," remains to be seen. But, even now, this much is clear: the ontological significance of Merleau-Ponty's phenomenology of the lived body resides in the fact that his investigation of embodiment led him to the notion of flesh which, in turn, provided an exemplar for phenomena. It is ultimately through one's own body that one is able to begin to understand the world.

Part Three

The Explicit Ontology of
The Visible and the Invisible

NINE

The Reversibility Thesis[1]

The ontology of *The Visible and the Invisible* calls for understanding. What would this ontology be? What would it take as its task? In one of the earlier working notes (January 1959), Merleau-Ponty describes the project he intends to undertake as that of defining an "ontology [which] would be the elaboration of the notions that have to replace . . . those of subject, object, [and] meaning" (VI 167; VI-F 221), that is, the categories of traditional ontology.[2] His replacement notions are expressed in novel terms—brute/ wild/savage Being, the flesh, the chiasm/intertwining, etc.—and the novelty of the terms requires an interpretation of the ontology they articulate: an interpretation which would understand this new ontology in comparison to traditional ontology, on the one hand, and in relation to the ontology implicit in Merleau-Ponty's earlier work, on the other. One may speak in the singular of traditional ontology inasmuch as the ontologies of the Western tradition are characteristically dualistic: they presuppose a bifurcation of being into disjunct and mutually exclusive spheres of immanence (the sphere of consciousness, subjectivity, being-for-itself) and transcendence (the sphere of things, objectivity, being-in-itself). This bifurcation, as I have sought to show, inevitably results in skepticism and solipsism, which is why its notions have to be replaced. Hence the requirement to compare Merleau-Ponty's new ontology to the traditional one: does the new resolve or merely recapitulate the problems of the old? The second requirement, comparison of Merleau-Ponty's later, explicit ontology with his earlier, implicit ontology,[3] has its ground in the need to understand the direction of his thought. If there is a radical change in direction, if *The Visible and the Invisible* approaches the problems of dualism in a manner incompatible with that of the earlier works, then the doctrine of those works will be undermined by his later thinking and will have to be revised or abandoned. Preeminently at stake here are Merleau-Ponty's doctrine of the lived body, his thesis of the ontological primacy of phenomena, and its correlate, the thesis of epistemological primacy of perception.

In the interpretation to be offered here, I shall contend (a) that the reversibility thesis set forth in *The Visible and the Invisible* is crucial to understanding both his novel terminology and his strategy for resolving the problems of dualistic ontology, (b) that the antecedents of the reversibility thesis are clearly evident in the *Phenomenology of Perception*; and (c) that the ontology of the later work explicates the ontology implicit in the earlier work. I shall argue that there is a consistent development of a unitary standpoint rather than a turn or break in the continuity of Merleau-Ponty's thought.

My principal reference in this part, *The Visible and the Invisible,* is the work left unfinished when Merleau-Ponty died suddenly in May of 1961. Claude Lefort, who edited the manuscript for publication, provides in his foreword and editorial note (VI xi-xxxix; VI-F 337–60, 7–14) information regarding the state of the manuscript and his own editorial precepts and decisions. This need not be recapitulated, but I think it might be useful for me to comment on those aspects of this work that have a bearing on my approach to it and to Merleau-Ponty's *oeuvre* as a whole.

The published version of *The Visible and the Invisible* is sixty per cent coherent text and forty per cent working notes. I call the first "coherent text" because it comes to us in the familiar form of sequential prose organized into arguments which are structured to support a complex but unitary philosophical standpoint. The text is not without ambiguity—which is entirely appropriate, given Merleau-Ponty's views on the phantom of univocity—but it contains no irresolvable inconsistencies. The working notes, however, are fragmentary, episodic, and sometimes contradictory; they are arranged chronologically, and shift back and forth among a wide spectrum of themes and subject matters. Hence, although the coherent text is clearly not a finished text, I have chosen to regard it as a much more definitive guide to Merleau-Ponty's later thought than the working notes. Where I refer to the working notes, it is only to illumine a point, and not to substantiate an interpretation.

Lefort has divided the first part (the coherent text) of *The Visible and the Invisible* into four chapters and an appendix. The first chapter, "Reflection and Interrogation," accomplishes two tasks: (a) it reorients the problem structure of the *Phenomenology*; and (b) it recasts the critique of traditional philosophy from the double-pronged thrust against intellectualism and empiricism to a unified critical analysis of objective or reflective thought, that is, the kind of thinking hitherto characterized as *la pensée de survol* or high-altitude thinking. Yet, this reorientation and recasting constitute a development of the problematic of the *Phenomenology*, not an abandonment of it. The problem structure of *The Visible and the Invisible* centers around perceptual faith and the main threats to its validity: illusion, perspective, and the problem of intersubjective variation posed by the existence of others. This, I contend, should be understood as continuous with the defense of the thesis of the primacy of perception against the threats to its validity Merleau-Ponty presents in the *Phenomenology*. The critique of reflective thought stresses the flaws common to empiricist and intellectualist thinking (that is, their unacknowledged presupposition of perceptual faith coupled with their inability to account for it, their espousal of the thesis of determinate being, their tendency to reify abstractions, etc.), but does not neglect the differences between them. In fact, Merleau-Ponty presents this critique in two phases, the first directed against scientific objectivism (that is, empiricism), and the second directed against idealistic subjectivism (that is, intellectualism). My point here is that the paramount goal of Merleau-Ponty's work remains the same—his intent is to carry Western philosophy beyond the dualism of subject and object—but in the later work he states in explicit terms what was only implicit earlier; the solution to the problems of Western philosophy calls for a new ontology, a genuinely phenomenological ontology. It will come as no surprise to the reader that I agree with both the diagnosis and the prescription. And I agree further that the task of setting forth that ontology is the single most important task confronting philosophers today. That is why I have undertaken the project at hand.

The second chapter, "Interrogation and Dialectic," is primarily a critique of Sartrean dialectic (although, since Sartre draws heavily from Hegelian dialectic in the formulation of his own thought, Merleau-Ponty takes up the latter, as well) which evolves into a presentation of "hyperdialectic," that is, a presentation of the version of dialectic Merleau-Ponty has incorporated within his own standpoint. The third chapter, "Interrogation and Intuition," presents a critique of Husserlian eidetics (or essential intuition, *Wesenschau*), followed again by a positive statement of Merleau-Ponty's own reintegration of essence with fact. Sartre and Husserl, together with the Gestalt theoreticians, are the major influences on Merleau-Ponty's thought: it is for this reason that I have given them the attention they have received here. One must understand Merleau-Ponty's philosophy as an attempt to preserve the fundamental truth of the Franco-German phenomenological movement by incorporating it within the context of the ontology that is demanded by that truth, that is, as an attempt to rescue phenomenology from the undermining influences of the retreat to immanence that has characterized transcendental philosophy since its inception.

The fourth chapter of *The Visible and the Invisible* presents in twenty-six pages the germ of Merleau-Ponty's explicit ontology. Its title, "The Intertwining—The Chiasm" ["*L'entrelacs—le chiasme*"], names the reversibility designated by Merleau-Ponty as "the ultimate truth" (VI 155; VI-F 204). The figure called forth by these terms is that of the crossing and turning back on itself of the single thread that emanates from the spider's body when she spins her web. This web-matrix, the whole cloth, the flesh, of the world *is* an interweaving, an *elementary* knotting, which is always prior to its unravelling in language and thought. The world is primordially phenomenon, primordially woven and weaving: an autochthonous organization, a Gestalt-contexture. The figure of the interwoven is rich in implication and lends itself to flights of interpretation. The very brevity of this crucial text has produced an assortment of inventive reconstructions in the secondary literature—in philosophy as in astrophysics, paucity of data typically results in speculative extravagance. I want, however, to be as prosaic and straightforward as possible in identifying what I take to be the basic idea conveyed in the figure. First: the novel terms, chiasm/intertwining/flesh, all rest on the notion of reversibility: "the chiasm is that: the reversibility" (VI 263; VI-F 317). Second: reversibility, the *de facto*—*phenomenal*—interwovenness of things, is primordial, elementary, irreducible. Matter is pregnant with form: their intertwining is real, their conceptual separation is ideal. To conceive the phenomenon as the product of the coming together of discrete, really disjunct domains of different kinds of being (the physical and the mental, the transcendent and the immanent, etc.) is to reify abstractions, to commit Whitehead's fallacy of misplaced concreteness, to confuse the idealities constituted as separate entities in language with the realities manifest as phenomena. In short, the ontology explicitly stated in terms of chiasm/intertwining/flesh is the ontology implicit in the familiar doctrine of autochthonous organization. It is, as I shall continue to argue, a genuinely phenomenological ontology, an ontology based on the thesis of the ontological primacy of phenomena.[4]

1. THE IDEA OF A PHENOMENOLOGICAL ONTOLOGY

A phenomenological ontology is an ontology in which being or reality is conceived as phenomenon. Husserl, Heidegger, and Sartre have each espoused this thesis, the thesis of the ontological primacy of phenomena, although there are radical differences in their conceptions of phenomena. Husserl defined phenomena within the standpoint of the *epoché* as self-givenness or immanence.[5] Heidegger conceived the 'phenomenon' of phenomenology as "what . . . shows itself in itself."[6] And Sartre reverted to a neo-Cartesianism in which the phenomenon was to be understood in terms of the dialectical interplay of the "trans-phenomenal phenomena" of being-for-itself and being-in-itself.[7]

In the case of Merleau-Ponty, the ontological thesis of the primacy of phenomena has to be interpreted in conjunction with its epistemological correlate, the thesis of the primacy of perception. "The perceived world is the always presupposed foundation of all rationality, all value and all existence."[8] For Merleau-Ponty, the real world is the perceived world is the phenomenal world. This, the standpoint of the *Phenomenology of Perception*, is elaborated in *The Visible and the Invisible* under the heading of "perceptual faith." Perceptual faith names our belief in the veracity of perception, a belief "that our vision goes to the things themselves" (VI 28; VI-F 48). "It is our experience . . . of inhabiting the world by our body, of inhabiting the truth by our whole selves, without there being need to choose nor even to distinguish between the assurance of seeing and the assurance of seeing the true, because in principle they are one and the same thing" (VI 28; VI-F 49). In perceptual faith, the correlative theses of the primacy of phenomena and the primacy of perception are not posited as philosophical principles; they are rather lived through in the mode of unwavering *Urdoxa*.

Perceptual faith is, nonetheless, "faith . . . and not knowledge" (VI 28; VI-F 49), which raises the question concerning the validity of its taking the truth of perception for granted. Merleau-Ponty answers this question obliquely in his recurrent adversion to the threat of illusion. Illusion constitutes a threat to perceptual faith because it provokes the reflective query as to whether all our perceptual experience might be as mistaken as our moments of illusion. In all his responses to this threat, one theme is dominant: illusion, always discovered after the fact in the self-correction of perception, does not warrant skepticism with regard to the validity of perception (VI 41: VI-F 65).

Merleau-Ponty argues that it is not illusion that prohibits us from naively taking for granted that what we perceive is nothing other than what is; rather, he claims, it is the variance from our own of other perspectives which undermines our naive confidence and provokes the reflective awareness that one's own perspective is only that—one's own perspective—and therefore somehow inadequate. But: inadequate in comparison to what? Inadequate in comparison to the ideality of a general perspective capable of accommodating and reconciling all individual variations. This ideal generality is, above all, ideal: that is, it is a generality that is expressed in language, constituted in thought, and projected by culture. It is, in Merleau-Ponty's terms, an invisible which stands in a tensed relation of identity-and-difference with the visible. Here we encounter the core problematic of *The Visible and the Invisible*.

Merleau-Ponty casts and recasts the question of the relation of the visible and the invisible several times in the course of the extant manuscript, and the terms themselves are continually reworked and redefined. The basic ontological question is whether the differentiation of the visible and the invisible commits Merleau-Ponty to a new dualism. He repeatedly rejects the monistic resolution: that an apparent difference between visible and invisible can be resolved by a real identity. This notion of coincidence is rejected in favor of a fundamental identity-and-difference which he expresses in a series of familiar metaphors: dihiscence, fission, divergence (*écart*), chiasm, intertwining. There is here no 'monism of the phenomenon,' but there is no dualism, either. There is, instead, flesh, which Merleau-Ponty describes "as an element, as the concrete emblem of a general manner of being" (VI 147; VI-F 193–94)—and which, through its essential characteristic of reversibility, is intended to subtend the monism/dualism polarization.

2. REVERSIBILITY AND ITS VICISSITUDES

The notion of reversibility is modelled on the phenomenon of touch.[9] Its domain is then extended to encompass vision, perception in general, intersubjectivity, reflection, and language. Although Merleau-Ponty does not acknowledge the fact, the notion undergoes some structural changes as it shifts from domain to domain. I think it may be possible to eliminate some misunderstanding of the term by thematizing its vicissitudes and distinguishing the concomitant modifications of the idea.

Let me begin with a brief resumé of the issue of double sensations explicated earlier (chapter 8, 2 above) because it provides the specific problem-context in response to which Merleau-Ponty gradually developed the general thesis of reversibility.

(i) Touch

> We are dealing with two essentially different orders of reality. To touch and to be touched, to feel that one is touching and to feel that one is touched— these are two species of phenomena which it is useless to try to reunite. . . . In fact they are radically distinct, and they exist on two incommunicable levels. (BN 402–403)

This is taken from the passage in *Being and Nothingness* where Sartre is at work distinguishing the first two "ontological dimensions" of the body: (1)"my body for-me" (which he says "belongs . . . to the structures of the non-thetic self-consciousness," BN 434, that is, belongs within the sphere of subjectivity), and (2) "the body-for-others" (which he says is equivalent to the Other's body for me, BN 445, hence belongs within the sphere of objectivity). For Sartre, touching is accomplished by the body-as-subject; being touched is something that happens to the body-as-object; and the two dimensions of bodily experience constitute "two essentially different orders of reality."[10]

It is evident that this disjunction of touching and being touched results in a dualistic conception of embodiment in which the body-subject has no common ground, no point of intersection, with the body-object. My experience of touching my own body, under Sartre's analysis, would be qualitatively equivalent to that of touching yours: an unacceptable conclusion, given the kind of internal feedback loop which makes solitary masturbation, for example, so different from caressing another.

In the *Phenomenology of Perception*, Merleau-Ponty criticizes Sartre's account of touching and raises the question of the unity underlying my experience of touching and being touched (PP 106n; PP-F 124n). In his answer (PP 93; PP-F 109—quoted here in chapter 8), we find a foreshadowing of the reversibility thesis, although it is not named as such or developed thematically. What Merleau-Ponty describes in this passage as alternation, he will later (in *The Visible and the Invisible*) describe as reversibility, but the essential aspects of the description will not change. That is, he will deny both (a) that the touching and being touched are radically disjunct and (b) that they are simultaneous or coincident.[11] He will argue, instead, that there is an essential ambiguity, an alternation or reversibility in which the touched hand feels itself touching and *vice versa*.

The basic model of reversibility is that of one hand touching another.

And it is clear in this model that between "my body touched and my body touching, there is overlapping or encroachment" (VI 123; VI-F 165): the roles of touching and touched are *prima facie* reversible because, after all, they are roles played by a unitary sensor, my own body. Yet, this underlying unity does not produce an absolute identity: the touching hand does not coincide with the touched hand; there is already a de-centering, "a sort of dehiscence [that] opens my body in two" (VI 123; VI-F 165). This fission or non-coincidence is essential to perception: to perceive the thing, in this case my own hand, there must be a distancing of it. Perceiving something is different from being that thing (that is, coinciding with it): even in the case of touching my own body there is difference/distance/alienation within the identity/unity.

The ontological significance of this identity-within-difference needs to be stressed. Coincidence in self-perception is one of the grounds for the traditional isolation of the epistemological subject: it provides the basis for the theses of incorrigibility of first person experience and transparency in the sphere of immanence which lead to the radical bifurcation of interiority and exteriority or consciousness and thing/Other/world. Similarly, absolute disjunction of perceiving and being perceived also produces a discontinuity between being-a-subject and being-an-object. The only way to evade the trap of the polarizations of dualism is to take up the standpoint, adopted by Merleau-Ponty, of a fundamentally ambiguous identity-encompassing-difference. It is this ambiguity that Merleau-Ponty articulates in the thesis of reversibility.

Shifting now from the model of one hand touching another to that of hand touching worldly object, we find the same identity-within-difference underlying the thesis of reversibility, but it must be altered to allow for the differences between touching one's own body and touching bodies that are not one's own. On the side of identity, Merleau-Ponty claims that there is a continuity between my body and the things surrounding me in the world I inhabit. Indeed, I can touch worldly things precisely because I am myself a worldly thing. If I were an incorporeal being, I could not palpate the things around me or interrogate the world with my hands. My hand "takes its place among the things it touches, is in a sense one of them, opens finally upon a tangible being of which it is a part" (VI 133; VI-F 176). For me to touch the table, I must be touched by the table. Yet, there is also difference: touching the table and being touched by it is not the same as touching my right hand with my left and feeling with my right hand the pressure of my left. Reversibility obtains in both cases, but I cannot experience the table touching me in the same way the hand touched can take up the role of touching. The plain fact of the matter is that the table is neither part of my body nor sentient in the way my body is. There is an asymmetry in the reversibility thesis emerging here that needs to be investigated.

Before that investigation can begin, however, a more urgent problem must be confronted. It is the problem of all reflective analysis: the problem created by the fact that reflection corrupts its subject matter by introducing an ego in the midst of an experience which may not have been egologically structured. That is the case here. The 'subject' of perception, for Merleau-Ponty, is the anonymous body, the body prior to the reflective differentiation which identifies it as mine. Given this "hyperreflective"[12] consideration, one must ask whether it is legitimate to distinguish (as I just have) the experience of being touched by the table from the experience of being touched by myself. It is the ego introduced by reflection that makes/grounds these distinctions, that constitutes the world as exterior, alien, different. If one is faithful to the unreflective anonymity of perception, must one then refrain from distinguishing the touching-back of the table from the touching-back of the other hand? In short, the question here is whether the thesis of the anonymity of the perceiving body is compatible with the asymmetry in the reversibility thesis asserted above.

The context required for adequate treatment of this question is that of the self-Other dialectic. Since Merleau-Ponty approaches that dialectic from the standpoint of seeing rather than touching, I shall postpone discussion of the question of asymmetry until the fundamentals of the reversibility thesis as it applies to vision have been set forth.

(ii) Vision and synesthesia

Turning now to vision, I take up first the question of the relation of seeing and touching in the context of Merleau-Ponty's doctrine of synesthesia. My intent here is to show that the identity-within-difference of reversibility explains the synesthetic unification of the senses without obscuring their separability.

> Since the same body sees and touches, visible and tangible belong to the same world. . . . Every movement of my eyes—even more, every displacement of my body—has its place in the same universe that I itemize and explore with them, as, conversely, every vision takes place somewhere in the tactile space. There is double and crossed situating of the visible in the tangible and of the tangible in the visible; the two maps are complete, and yet they do not merge into one. The two parts are total parts and yet are not superposable. (VI 134; VI-F 177)

It is clear from this passage that, in his doctrine of synesthesia, Merleau-Ponty does not intend to conflate vision and touch (VI 217; VI-F 271). The perception of color is not typically a tactile experience. Yet, every colored surface has a texture. The senses are united in one body and open onto a unitary world, but to lose one of them is to lose a quality of experience that the remaining senses cannot restore. Vision and touch "are not superposable," but they are reversible: for the most part, I can touch what I see and see what I touch.

In the tactile sphere, the reversibility thesis maintains that to touch something is also and necessarily to be touched by it. What about vision? It is the case that seeing requires a body capable of being seen just as touching requires a body capable of being touched. The eye, as much as the hand, must be a part of the world it perceives; it must obey the same laws of motility, and adjusts its own 'I can' to the demands of the vision it interrogates. But, beyond this, is it the case that to see something is also and necessarily to be seen by it?[13]

The passage most frequently cited in critical writing addressed to this point is the one in "Eye and Mind" where Merleau-Ponty speaks of a reversal of roles between the painter and the visible spectacle he paints. In this context, Merleau-Ponty quotes a painter's comment: " 'In a forest, I have felt many times over that it was not I who was looking at the forest. I felt, on certain days, that it was rather the trees that were looking at me' " (EM 167; EM-F 31).

Following this and speaking in his own voice, Merleau-Ponty suggests that there is a point at which "one no longer knows who sees and who is seen, who paints and who is painted" (EM 167; EM-F 32).

Here, again, we confront the question of asymmetry. Do the trees see the painter as the painter sees the trees? Or is there an asymmetry such that the painter's seeing of the trees is different from his being seen by them?[14] At stake here is the question of the fundamental meaning of the reversibility which Merleau-Ponty labelled "ultimate truth" (*vérité ultime*) in the last words he wrote.[15] If Merleau-Ponty's single most important goal was to conceive a non-dualistic ontology, and if the notion of chiasm/intertwining is the critical thought in that endeavor, and, finally, if the reversibility thesis provides the inner meaning of chiasm/intertwining—then it is worth whatever effort is required to see through the term to the reality it is intended to disclose.

The passage just quoted from "Eye and Mind" prima facie supports the view that reversibility names a relationship of symmetry (aRb = bRa)—I see the tree, the tree sees me—in which the relational term, the verb 'to see,' retains a univocal meaning. If one adopts this view, one is obliged to redefine the verb 'to see' in such a way that it becomes meaningful to speak of beings, like trees, which see without having eyes. It would also then be necessary to understand human vision in such a way that our eyes are not essential to that seeing. I reject this view, not only because it is manifestly implausible, but because it does not do justice to the full spectrum of Merleau-Ponty's writing on the subject—or to the phenomenon of reversibility.

The passage in which Merleau-Ponty quotes the painter speaking of being seen by the trees leads into a discussion of the mirror image. The trees 'see' the painter in a manner comparable to that in which the mirror 'sees' the painter: that is, the trees, like the mirror, let him become visible; they define a point of view on him which renders visible for him something that otherwise would remain invisible—his outside, his physiognomy, his carnal presence. The trees and the mirror function as Other. They provide, at the level of perception, the literal reflection that will culminate, at the level of the cogito, in the figurative reflection of thought turned on itself. This is the manner in which the reversibility of perception anticipates and grounds the movement to the reflexivity which is the apex and paradigm of the invisible for Merleau-Ponty.

Of course, trees do not have reflecting surfaces and mirrors do not see as we do. We are speaking here in similes. The troublesome aspect of the passage at hand, and others like it, is that Merleau-Ponty appears to want to force the simile to the point of literal assertion: he says, in *The Visible and the Invisible*, repeating the language of "Eye and Mind," that "the seer and the visible reciprocate one another and we no longer know which sees and which is seen" (VI 139; VI-F 183). Why does he insist on this counter-intuitive manner of formulating his thought? Why does he not say that it is *as if* the trees see me?

The answer, I believe, is that he is trying to de-center his ontology. To say that it is *as if* the trees see me is to project my consciousness into the standpoint of the trees; it is to make transcendental consciousness ubiquitous and digest the transcendence of the world in the maw of immanence. This is contrary to Merleau-Ponty's intent in the later works where he wants to give consciousness an outside which limits it and makes it visible as a body which can be seen from external points of view. His stated task in *The Visible and the Invisible* is to bring the results of the *Phenomenology of Perception* to "ontological explicitation," but the one flaw that he repeatedly says needs to be corrected is that, in the earlier work, he "retained in part the philosophy of 'consciousness' " (VI 183; VI-F 237).[16] In sum, I think we must try to understand this movement of his thought as part of his continuing effort to free phenomenology from its historical confinement within the sphere of immanence by restoring to phenomena the transcendence they manifest in the perceptual domain.

A brief historical digression may be helpful here, to clarify the point at hand and to unify this phase of the argument with earlier phases.

In the attempt to keep this manuscript within the bounds of reasonable length, I have virtually ignored the impact of Hegel on Merleau-Ponty's philosophy[17] (although Hegel's mute presence in the dialogue between Sartre and Merleau-Ponty can hardly have gone unremarked to the discerning reader), but this silence must now be broken. As noted earlier (chapter 6, 1 above), there is a correlation between Merleau-Ponty's treatment of the tacit cogito or corporeal reflexivity and his doctrine of reversibility. At the unreflective level of perceptual experience, for example, when I touch things in the process of manipulating them, there is an essential reflexivity: to touch the thing is to be touched by it; to feel the thing is to feel its touch on my hands. This is the tacit cogito, and its historical source is Hegel (who, in turn, discovered it by recognizing that something like the Kantian 'I think' is at work beneath the level of predicative judgment, that is, at the level of sensuous immediacy).[18] Hegel argues that, from the standpoint of consciousness, the experience of the thing is consciousness's experience of itself.[19] Again, from the standpoint of consciousness, what the thing is in itself *is* what it is for consciousness.

At the level of perception, however, consciousness perceives the thing as other than itself, as a separate and independent reality. At the level of perception, "the object . . . is the real truth, is the essential reality; it is, quite indifferent to whether it is known or not."[20] That is, consciousness at the level of perception is unreflective, unaware of its own role in constituting the object. It is not until consciousness reaches the level of self-consciousness that it becomes aware that the otherness of the object manifesting itself perceptually is an otherness for consciousness, a meaning constituted by consciousness and attributed to the object or, again, an immanent modification of consciousness rather than a transcendent reality. It is at this level that desire emerges with the explicit telos of self-certainty or the elimination of difference: the otherness of the object must be overcome in order that consciousness may unify itself, that is, effect the unity of self-consciousness and object-consciousness. This is ultimately achieved at the culmination of the Hegelian dialectic with an absolute reduction to immanence, where all that *is* is consciousness conscious of itself as the sole and unitary origin, preserver, and destiny of all things: this is the coincidence of the real and the rational in the apotheosis of *Geist,* the return of the Absolute unto itself.

Now, it is just this overcoming of difference, this transformation of the otherness/difference grounded in transcendence by means of reducing it to an immanent meaning constituted by consciousness, that Merleau-Ponty rejects: the perceptual world transcends the world as thought; the phenomenon transcends its apprehension. We perceive the real, we think the ideal, and the former cannot be reduced to the latter. But—here the familiar dilemma arises again—is it not the case that to perserve the difference between transcendent things and the immanent consciousness of things is to introduce an ontological bifurcation between thing and consciousness and project oneself back into the framework of traditional dualism? If there is a difference, must it not be an ontological difference?

It is in response to the challenge of this dilemma that Merleau-Ponty sets forth the thesis of reversibility as a correlate to the tacit cogito. The doctrine of the tacit cogito states that there is a corporeal reflexivity operative at the level of perception: to touch the thing is to feel the thing touching me. But what is taking place here is the contact of two bodies (one or both of which may be sentient), and not an (inconceivable)[21] encounter of immaterial, non-extended consciousness with a material, extended thing. There is an identity of the touching and the touched (the touching is the being touched), but there is also the difference Merleau-Ponty calls dehiscence/divergence/ *écart* (the touched thing is separate from, independent of, more than the touching that reveals its presence and conceals what lies beyond its touch). In the reduced sphere of immanence, from the standpoint of transcendental consciousness, there is a strict identity: the touched thing is and only is what is revealed in the touching (the being of the object is identical with that which is manifest to the subject). But if this contact, this touching/being-touched, is understood as the contact between two bodies, bodies which are both flesh but separate from each other, then neither body need be reduced to what becomes manifest to one at the moment of contact. Phenomenal bodies—fleshly things—transcend their apprehension.

In sum, then, the moment of dehiscence/divergence/*écart* in the reversibility relation sustains the difference lost in the Hegelian version of the tacit cogito because it acknowledges the corporeal element essential to that reflexive identity of touching and touched which precludes the reduction of flesh to *Geist*. Or, to state the same conclusion in other terms, the difference between phenomena and their apprehension by consciousness which is finally overcome in the Hegelian dialectic cannot be overcome in Merleau-Ponty's "hyperdialectic" because Merleau-Ponty conceives phenomena as corporeal, as manifestly transcending their manifest adumbrations: the phenomenon is the thing we perceive, but we perceive that we do not perceive the entirety of its being. To touch something is not to coincide with it.

(iii) The body as exemplar sensible

We have traced the vicissitudes of reversibility from the basic model of touch, through vision and synesthesia, to arrive now at the body in its totality as flesh. The body is designated by Merleau-Ponty as "exemplar sensible" (VI 135; VI-F 178–79), and this, presumably, means that he takes it as the prime example of sensibles in general. If the body is conceived as flesh, then to take it as exemplary of all sensibles is to conceive of everything sensible as being somehow flesh. Indeed, the equations of wild Being and perceived world, of the "generality of the Sensible in itself" and flesh, are explicitly drawn by Merleau-Ponty (VI 139, 170; VI-F 183, 223). The implication here is the same problematic attribution of sentience to perceptibles such as trees that we have encountered throughout this study. And the why of this attribution remains unresolved. "Carnal being," says Merleau-Ponty, is to be conceived as "a prototype of Being" (VI 136; VI-F 179)—but why?

To find the answer we must learn to think of the relation of body to world as relation of flesh to flesh after the model of one hand touching the other—but we must think this folding of the flesh back on itself as decentered, as taking place at a level prior to the emergence of conscious, I-centered, personal reflection. At the level of perceptual faith, where I do not see, but "one perceives in me" (PP 215; PP-F 249), it is misleading to think of a body-subject in relation to a world-object; it is more accurate to think of an anonymous perceptual unfolding, dehiscence, *écart* (VI 142; VI-F 187–88). It is this "Visibility in itself" (VI 139; VI-F 183) that Merleau-

Ponty proposes to call flesh, and to name thereby the wild Being that is prior to subject-object differentiation. "The flesh of the world . . . is indivision of this sensible Being that I am and all the rest that feels itself [*se sent*] in me" (VI 255; VI-F 309).

It may be well, at this stage in the argument, to pause and consolidate the findings.

(a) Note, first, the recurrence of the reflexive voice: "a certain visible . . . turns back upon [*se retourne sur*] the whole of the visible" (VI 139; VI-F 183); "the sensible Being . . . that feels itself [*se sent*] in me." This is the language of reversibility and it is through this reversibility that we must understand chiasm/intertwining and flesh.

(b) There is a strong continuity linking the notion of Gestalt in the *Phenomenology of Perception* and that of flesh in *The Visible and the Invisible*: both terms serve the same structural function in Merleau-Ponty's ontology as he makes apparent in a working note dated September, 1959 (that is, just after completing the first half of the manuscript, but before undertaking the work in the second half where he begins to thematize the concepts associated with the flesh and the chiasm). "The Gestalt . . . implies the relation between a perceiving body and a sensible, i.e. transcendent i.e. horizonal i.e. vertical and *not perspectival* world" (VI 209; VI-F 259, emphasis added).

(c) As indicated by the key words "not perspectival," the problem that kept the *Phenomenology of Perception* in thrall to the "philosophy of 'consciousness'" was that of conceiving Gestalten in accordance with the perspectivalist strain in that work. Yet, already with the notion of autochthonous organization—which was developed in the *Phenomenology* (PP441; PP-F 503)—Merleau-Ponty foreshadowed the notion of the flesh, that is, the notion of the Visible articulating itself through reversibility. And, even in the later work, the notion of Gestalt still plays the important role of mediating the movement out of silence to expression (VI 206; VI-F 259).

(d) It was argued in the preliminary phases of this chapter that it is no longer illusion (as it was in the *Phenomenology*) but rather the variance from one's own of other perspectives that undermines our confidence in perception. There has to be some way of resolving the differences between the view of things I have here-now and the viewpoints occupied by others in different places and times. For a phenomenological ontology, a relativism with regard to perspective is a relativism with regard to truth and other values. This challenge has to be met if Merleau-Ponty's non-dualist ontology is to succeed in overcoming the skepticism and solipsism that beset dualist ontologies and mark their ultimate failure.

(iv) Alterity: the other and differentiation.

The question of the bridge between my experience and the experience of the other is the question that broaches upon solipsism. If one makes an ontological disjunction between seer and seen, body as subject and body as object (as did Sartre), then solipsism is the inevitable result. On the other hand, if one speaks in the language of coincidence of an identity of seer and seen, the consequence would be "some huge animal whose organs our bodies [that is, my body and the bodies of others] would be, as for each of our bodies, our hands, our eyes are the organs" (VI 142; VI-F 187).

The solution to the problem of other bodies must be found within the identity-within-difference structure of reversibility. My right hand, being touched by my left, can reverse the roles and touch the left one back. My body, being seen by the Other, can reverse the roles and take up the Other's vantage on itself. Here the Other functions as my mirror: he de-centers me, lets me see myself from another vantage. I do not coincide with the Other, but his experience of my being is not the undisclosable secret Sartre would make of it, either. In the language of the *Phenomenology*, it is the 'I can' of motility that allows me to take up the Other's vantage point. In *The Visible and the Invisible*, this 'I can,' this "mediation through reversal" (VI 215; VI-F 268), is subtended by the "ultimate notion" of flesh: the being of which Other and I are discernable parts, but which grounds the commonality which allows our roles to be reversed.

The major difference between Merleau-Ponty and his antecedents in the phenomenological tradition on this point lies in the fact that the commonality between Other and me is grounded in the flesh that we both visibly/ obviously are, rather than in the transcendental consciousness some have found it necessary to posit as the One underlying the manifold of perspectives. As Merleau-Ponty puts it, we must "no longer make belongingness to one same 'consciousness' the primordial definition of sensibility," we must rather understand sensibility in both myself and the Other as "the return of the visible upon itself, a carnal adherence of the sentient to the sensed and of the sensed to the sentient" (VI 142; VI-F 187).

There is a difference between the logic of the generality of the flesh and that of the oneness of consciousness. I can experience the Other's flesh without merging with it, but—in the case of the Other's consciousness— either I cannot experience it at all, or, if somehow I could, I would become lost in it and lose my singularity.

Note, however, this vicissitude in reversibility: the right hand touching left hand model has to be altered here as it was in the case of hand touching table. Shaking hands with the Other is not the same as shaking hands with oneself. There is reversibility in both cases, but his experience of my right hand as object is inaccessible to me in a way that my left hand's experience of my right hand is not. There is a limit to the 'I can.' There is dehiscence, fission, *écart*. There is a bridge and an intertwining, but there is not an identity. The anonymity of the flesh prior to reflective differentiation is not the absolute anonymity of complete indefinition: there is an inchoate estrangement such that when, at the level of reflective personal awareness, the differentiation between self and Other is thematized, it will be a grounded differentiation, a differentiation grounded in the fission of the flesh and not simply a fiat of consciousness which has made the unhappy choice of alienation.

Now it is time to recognize that we have arrived at a solution to the problem of symmetry versus asymmetry in reversibility. So far, we have cast the problem in terms of trees—other beings that are not sentient in the way we are—and asked if it was an implication of the reversibility thesis that my seeing the trees entailed the trees seeing me, in a univocal sense of seeing. Now we ask, with regard to the Other—another being who is sentient as I am—whether my seeing him entails his seeing me. In the case of the Other, the question of modality of sentience is eliminated: both trees and other humans are sensitive to light, but the Other is sensitive to light as I am, that is, by means of the same organs of vision. And yet it is clear that the reversibility is not symmetrical: we cannot see ourselves exactly as Others see us and, Robert Burns notwithstanding, no Lord could give us the gift of being able to do so. Because that would entail living his body while, at the same time, retaining my own incarnate being; that is, it would entail being his body while still being mine. Nor is this a matter of level of awareness such that reversibility would be symmetrical at the level of un-reflective perceptual faith and become asymmetrical at the level of reflection. Indeed, it is the very desire to see ourselves as Others see us that motivates the development of reflective awareness. The point to be driven home is that flesh must be understood as primordially dehiscent.

But what about the earliest phases of life when the infant lives in an indistinction of perspectives such that it does not (and probably cannot) differentiate its flesh from its mother's flesh? Surely here there is true anonymity and symmetrical reversibility: no difference between being touched by Mother and being touched by its own spasm of undirected movement. Only within the standpoint of the philosophy of transcendental consciousness can one make the inference from (a) lack of conscious dif-ferentiation to (b) lack of differentiation altogether. The fact is that the infant cannot live its mother's flesh. At least since parturition, the infant is a discrete body and lives its separateness. Its mouth recognizes the tran-scendence of Mother right from the start. Whatever we may speculate about the immanent quality of infantile awareness, it is clear from the outside that the infant's body is a quest for nurture—for food, warmth, soothing sounds and touches—from a transcendent source.[22]

In Merleau-Ponty's view, the rudiments of the self-Other distinction are sedimented in the infant's world by the age of six months.[23] At this point, if not from birth, the significance of the Other will reside in a continuum of 'like-me-but-not-me' which will develop to include the full range of ex-perience from interpersonal solidarity to alienation. The "transfer of cor-poreal schema" which is Merleau-Ponty's term for the "pairing" (Husserl) that goes on at the prereflective level and accounts for the immediate iden-tification of an Other as a being like unto oneself who is experiencing the same world but from over there—this prereflective level transfer of sense is a *transfer*, an identification, not an identity. All of which means that the otherness of the Other, his difference from me, is part of the meaning he has at the most primordial and unreflective levels of experience. And that means that his look, my being seen by him, remains for me inaccessible (or accessible only indirectly).

Sartre was wrong in equating my body-for-others with the Other's body-for-me because there is a fundamental difference in the way in which these two are experienced *by me*—even at the prereflective level before the self-Other differentiation becomes thematic. That differentiation is the modicum of truth to be found in Sartre's own doctrine of the look: I feel myself being seen from a vantage I can approximate but can never live. The Other is, indeed, my mirror, but I cannot see through the eyes I see in the mirror. Whence I conclude that the reversibility between 'I see the Other' and 'the Other sees me' is asymmetrical. I see him in what Husserl would call a fulfilled intention. But his seeing of me is something I experience in an "analogizing apperception" which must always remain an unfulfilled intention.

Merleau-Ponty thematically expresses his awareness of this point.

> To begin with, we spoke summarily of a reversibility of the seeing and the visible, of the touching and the touched. It is time to emphasize that *it is a reversibility always immanent and never realized in fact.* My left hand is always on the verge of touching my right hand touching the things, but I never reach coincidence.[24]

And later in the same paragraph:

> Likewise, I do not hear myself as I hear the others, the sonorous existence of my voice is for me as it were poorly exhibited; I have rather an echo of its articulated existence, it vibrates through my head rather than outside. *I am always on the same side of my body*; it presents itself to me in one invariable perspective. (VI 147–48; VI-F 194; emphasis added)

Here, then, is the answer to the question posed at the beginning of this part of the chapter. There I asked whether the thesis of the anonymity of the perceiving body is compatible with a fundamental asymmetry within the reversibility thesis. Now we know that it is, because the anonymity of the body is infected with the germ of mineness from the very start, and this is so because "I am always on the same side of my body"—a fact which grounds an *Existentiale* structuring our existence from birth.

Given this asymmetry, the problem of the trees seeing me is easily resolved. In the presence of the trees, if I am sensitive to it, I can experience my being seen as I experience my being seen in the presence of an Other. The trees can function as the mirror that lets me experience my own visibility. *Qua* visible, the trees and I are made of the same stuff: flesh. The indistinction between seeing and being seen lies within the sphere of my own—as yet unreflected—experience: my seeing is continuous with my being seen; I could not be one without the other, and there is no line of demarcation that can be drawn between the being of my body as subject and that of my body as object. Even though they do not and cannot coincide—"either my right hand really passes over to the rank of being touched, but then its hold on the world is interrupted, or it retains its hold on the world, but then I do not really touch *it*" (VI 148, VI-F 194)—they are nonetheless reversible and that reversibility places them within the same ontological category: *voyant-visible*, flesh which is reversibly seeing and seen.

What of the flesh of the trees? "Where are we to put the limit between the body and the world, since the world is flesh?" (VI 138; VI-F 182). Must we attribute seeing to the trees and mountains of the world in order to preclude an ontological bifurcation within the flesh between myself who can see and the other things which, literally speaking, cannot?

There is no need either to attribute seeing to mountains and trees or to introduce an ontological bifurcation within the flesh of the world. There is flesh which is sensitive to light, flesh which is not, and degrees of sensitivity linking the extremes. We need not convert the animals, vegetables, and minerals of the world to humanity to overcome ontological dualism. Trees and mountains do not see; they are blind witnesses to my own visibility. The body as exemplar sensible does not function as an example of sensibility in inanimate things. The human body is that particular kind of flesh that allows the flesh of the world to double back on itself and be seen. The fact remains that there would not be human vision without human bodies. "The flesh of the world is not *self-sensing* as is my flesh—It is sensible and not sentient" (VI 250; VI-F 304).

(v) Reversibility and reflection: the invisible

What, finally, is this reversibility and how does it resolve the problems of ontological dualism?

The problems of dualism chosen for emphasis here are the problems of solipsism and skepticism. In the preceding section, the response to solipsism opened by the reversibility thesis was set forth. The Other's world is my world because the two views are reversible. His viewpoint is a locus in the Visible that I can occupy: it is not closed off to me, although I cannot live his experience of it and alienation remains a grounded possibility.

Skepticism results from dualism because the bifurcation of being into spheres of immanence and transcendence, consciousness and thing, drives an epistemological wedge between knower and known: consciousness-of-a-thing and the thing itself are relegated to mutually exclusive orders of being such that there is no standpoint from which they can be compared.

The representation (consciousness-of-a-thing) may be adequate to the thing or it may not; but this cannot be determined if there is no access to the thing which is not already mediated by consciousness. How does reversibility address this problem?

> We must not think the flesh starting from substances, from body and spirit—for then it would be the union of contradictories—but we must think it . . . as an element, as the concrete emblem of a general manner of being. (VI 147; VI-F 193)

Flesh is, then, elementary. Perception is the relation of flesh to itself that Merleau-Ponty describes with the images of reversibility. How does perception reach its object? Perception is the flesh touching-seeing-feeling itself. There is no representation at the level of perception: there is only flesh in touch with itself.

We have to learn to think of perception as we live it in perceptual faith, that is, as a relation between sensibles in which the flesh of the perceiver necessarily admits of being perceived. That is the essence of the reversibility relation: not that the tree I see sees me, but that I am visible from the standpoint of the tree as it is from mine because we are both made of the same stuff: the flesh of the world. Thus conceived, perception is a worldly event and not a private occurrence that takes place within an invisible sphere of immanence.

How is this a response to skepticism?

It undermines the clout of the two major threats to the validity of perception. Those threats are illusion and perspective. Illusion is undermined because it is no longer the non-coincidence of immanent representation with transcendent reality, but rather a phase in the perceptual event of worldly unfolding that Merleau-Ponty calls interrogation. Interrogation is linked to reversibility in that the demand of seeing—that the seen reveal itself—has as its necessary correlate a demand of the seen—that the seer move his body as Vision requires to let the scene be seen. Illusion, correctly understood, is but a moment of this interrogating adjustment.

The threat of perspective is more complex, but it comes to rest in the conflict or dissonance of competing viewpoints. The response to this threat offered by the reversibility thesis is the possibility of exchange. This is the possibility, guaranteed in principle although not always easy to carry out, that an initial dissonance move in the direction of an ideal harmony by reversing positions. I can take up your position in worldly space, as you can take up mine—and, in the figurative space of understanding, a similar kind of exchange can be approached through the gestures of communication. The ground of this possibility lies in the fact that we are both flesh of a unitary world and not monadological transcendental egos each constituting a world of his own in which he reigns supreme as original creator and final judge of truth and value.

What of this 'figurative space of understanding'? What of the traditional spheres of privacy and immanence? How does the reversibility thesis bear upon what Merleau-Ponty calls the invisible?

Here we encounter the last of the vicissitudes of reversibility: the reversibility of the visible and the invisible. Here reversibility is to be conceived as reflection, reflection in the dual sense of mirroring and of thought. Language is the medium in which the world is reflected, that is, mirrored and thought. This is not a variation of Wittgenstein's early picture theory of language. A picture is a representation. Mirrors do not re-present the world or replicate it in a domain apart; they reflect what is before them in the same world in which they are, themselves, located and visible. Language does not duplicate or copy the world; it is, rather, the manner in which the world's intelligibility/meaning/sense (*sens*) unfolds.

In the compressed five-page treatment (VI 151–55; VI-F 198–204) that constitutes the totality of Merleau-Ponty's teaching on the subject of reversibility in language and thought, he draws an analogy between musical ideas and musical notation, on one hand, and carnal ideas and linguistic notation (or semeiology), on the other. The meaning of a musical phrase depends on its carnal experience: the sense of the phrase has to be heard, and is only apparently detachable in the form of notation. Although signs of language admit of a kind of detachability not to be found in musical notation—that is, there is an ideality of thought which tends toward a kind of purity not to be found in musical notation—still, the ideality of language in thought remains conditioned by the carnal texture of the world it reflects. The idea is the ideality *of* the visible: "it is the invisible *of* this world, that which inhabits this world, sustains it, and renders it visible" (VI 151; VI-F 198). The point here is that language is in service to the world from which it is derived. The thesis of the primacy of perception remains in force.

The element of reversibility enters with the notion of illumination of the visible by the invisible. Just as the overlooked (hence invisible) glint of light on the eyes of a portrait bring that painting to visible life, so does the invisible ideality of language illumine the world and make its intelligibility apparent.

Heidegger says that it is language, not man, that speaks. Merleau-Ponty writes that "language is everything, since it is the voice of no one, since it is the very voice of the things, the waves, and the forests" (VI 155; VI-F 204). They are both making the same point: language grows out of the *écart/* dehiscence and folding back upon itself or reversibility of the flesh of the world. Language is "another flesh" (VI 153; VI-F 200).

Merleau-Ponty is saying more than that language is referential, that it exhibits a fundamental of-ness. He is asserting a double referentiality in the thesis of reversibility. One moment of this referentiality has just been explicated: the visible world referring to itself through another flesh, another visibility; the flesh of language is the world illuminating itself through us, the body that speaks both aloud and silently to itself. The other moment of referentiality has to do with the *Gestaltung* of signs, the autochthonous organization of words. As we have seen, the body's seeing depends upon its own visibility, its touching depends on its being touched. In an analogous way, "the sense [*sens* or meaning] upon which the arrangement of sounds opens reflects back upon the arrangement" (VI 154; VI-F 201). And, again, "if my words have a meaning, it is not *because* they present the systematic organization the linguist will disclose, it is because that organization, like the look, refers back to itself" (VI 154; VI-F 202).

Two basic strains in Merleau-Ponty's philosophy of language converge here. There is the familiar strain that, in authentic speech, language articulates itself according to the demands of the as yet unspoken aspect of the world that seeks expression. To this is now coupled the thought, heralded in earlier work but not thematically explicated, that the organization of signs is meaningful because it is self-referential. The analogy with vision and touch is helpful in understanding this vicissitude of reversibility, but is only an analogy: that is, in addition to the isomorphism, there is also a difference between language and perception which has to be understood as well. What is peculiar to the reversibility of language?

The autochthonous organization of language mirrors the autochthonous organization of the world (VI 155; VI-F 203). The meaning structure of language reflects the meaning structure of the world because what is made intelligible in language is the world's innate intelligibility (the λογος of the world). It is the meaning of the world detaching itself from the world (but never completely, for the bond of reference can never be broken) to illumine the world and, at the same time and necessarily, to illumine itself. This relation of reciprocity in which neither of the relata is intelligible apart from the other is the relation of reversibility.[25] It is an asymmetrical relation, as was its progenitor in Merleau-Ponty's thought: the *Fundierung* relation with its two moments of expression and sedimentation. The found*ing* term is the transcendent ground, the world; and the found*ed* term is the linguistic significance which returns to the world and sediments in it the meaning drawn from it in expression. What differentiates the reversibility of language from the reversibility of touching and seeing is the detachability of the linguistic sign in thought. (If there is a perceptual counterpart to the detachability of language, it would be the quasi-autonomy of the—misnamed—image of dreams and waking revery.)

Reflection or thought manifests the same double referentiality of reversibility that exists in language. In reflection, I become other to myself: this is the familiar specular relation in which the terms are asymmetrically reversible. The reflecting role is exchangeable with the reflected (when I speak silently to myself I can take up either of the dehiscent roles: the erstwhile spoken-to can currently speak) but some role, some persona, is always momentarily alienated, perceived from the outside. The remaining moment of the double referentiality is the reciprocity of thought and linguistic sign. This is, again, a relation of reversibility and not the identity that positivistic psycholinguists would make of it. There is not a coincidence of thought and sign (or token or representation); the two remain distinct. Evidence for this lies in the "significative intention,"[26] the hungry hiatus of thought in need of the word that will come to fulfill and complete it. Ultimately, thought will have to be conceived as the relation of signs to themselves: the signs that demand other signs to make themselves intelligible. Reversibility here manifests itself as exchangeability or translatability. The mark of a thought that has found itself is freedom from a particular formulation, that is, the ability to think itself in other terms. Yet, distinct as it is from language, thought remains tied to it. Translation of a thought into other terms which resonate with the first does not betoken complete liberation: thought needs its hold on words to keep itself from evanescing. The meaning of the thought lies in the reversibility of its formulations, and cannot exist apart from this exchange.

3. IMPLICATIONS OF THE REVERSIBILITY THESIS

Before tabulating the results of this study, it would be well to note that it is incomplete. The reversibility thesis has not been fully articulated. The role of reversibility in the linguistic aspect of our relations with Others, the exchange of ideas which is at the same time the genesis of ideas, has not been broached. Nor has the relevance of reversibility to an understanding of emotional exchange been mentioned, although a moment's thought could summon a glimpse of how Merleau-Ponty's reversibility thesis might provide what is lacking in Sartre's account of the look and the "double reciprocal incarnation" of sexual desire.[27] There is also the organizational difficulty which arises out of my decision to discuss the reversibility thesis before setting forth an interpretation of Merleau-Ponty's teaching on the subject of language. Yet, as is apparent in the pages immediately preceding this one, the topics of reversibility and language intersect. Accordingly, I have had to presuppose some familiarity with Merleau-Ponty's philosophy of language in the latter phases of my treatment of the reversibility thesis. In the next and concluding section of this chapter, I shall attempt to provide a more complete account of Merleau-Ponty's understanding of language. Within that context, I shall be able to return to the issue of reversibility, language, and Others, and fill in the blanks that have to be left here. Notwithstanding this incompleteness, however, there are some points I hope to have made, and I will conclude by recapitulating those that strike me as most important.

First in order of magnitude is the role of reversibility in Merleau-Ponty's attempt to resolve the ontological problems he took up in *The Visible and the Invisible*. The reversibility of subject and object in perception allows

Merleau-Ponty to contend that both roles are played by an elemental reality —flesh—without requiring him to collapse the distinction between them.

Secondly, in tracing the vicissitudes of reversibility from the basic model of touching-touched through the complexities of synesthetic reflexivity in alterity, thought, and language, I hope to have forestalled a simplistic or reductionistic understanding of the phenomenon. There are differences as well as similarities in my relations to myself, Others, and worldly things, and both must be appreciated if we are to avoid attributing to Merleau-Ponty such literally false claims as that trees see me.

Along these lines, a third conclusion centers on the fundamental asymmetry of reversibility. I see the Other and the Other sees me; but I do not experience my being seen as he does. A literal reversal of roles is impossible. Although looking presupposes being visible, seeing and being seen remain divergent, non-coincidental. I live my body ecstatically, but it is the only body I'll ever live.

This leads to my fourth conclusion: the thesis of reversibility articulates the notion of transfer of corporeal schema beyond the basic idea of pairing Merleau-Ponty appropriated from Husserl, and provides a deeper understanding of his account of intersubjectivity.

In the fifth and final place, I hope to have shown that the ontology being developed in *The Visible and the Invisible* is firmly rooted in Merleau-Ponty's earlier work and, specifically, that the central thesis of reversibility grows out of his critique in the *Phenomenology of Perception* of Sartre's ontological disjunction between body-subject and body-object. To be more specific, I have attempted to substantiate my claim that the thesis of the primacy of phenomena which grounds the implicit ontology of the *Phenomenology* culminates in the doctrine of the element of flesh wherein the term 'flesh' occupies in the explicit ontology of *The Visible and the Invisible* the same conceptual space as the term 'phenomenon' (or 'Gestalt') occupied in the earlier work. 'Phenomenon,' 'Gestalt,' and 'flesh' name the same fundamental reality: "the always presupposed foundation of all rationality, all value and all existence."

There are, I think, two basic reasons for this terminological shift: (a) the term 'phenomenon' invites the specter of subjectivism, the conception of being-for-a-subject/consciousness, traditionally associated with it; and (b) it also leads interpreters to misunderstand Merleau-Ponty's philosophy as another version of post-Kantian transcendental philosophy when, in fact, it is an attempt to break away from the reduction to immanence while preserving the truths revealed by transcendental thought. What Merleau-Ponty calls "the philosophical lie" of transcendental thought (or the philosophy of reflection) is its claim that the structures of thought/cognition are prior to experience (this claim providing the basis for the central notion of transcendental constitution and its putative apodicticity/universality) whereas, in fact, "it is essential to the reflective analysis that it start from a *de facto* situation" (VI 44; VI-F 69).[28] The transcendental thought of the philosophy of reflection takes its departure from the phenomenal world of perceptual faith, and it also takes its measure from that world; that is, to the extent that transcendental philosophy succeeds in revealing the structures of meaning constitutive of the phenomenal world, that success is measured against the standard of actual experience. Transcendental thought "by principle leaves untouched the twofold problem of the genesis of the existent world and of the genesis of [its own] idealization" (VI 46; VI-F 70). Its lie is to regard itself as founding, when it is founded in actuality.

But there is a profound truth to transcendental philosophy's core notion of constitution. That truth centers around the phenomenon of sedimentation, the settling of culture into things, and account must be made of it. To render this account, Merleau-Ponty (like many of his contemporaries and ours: Foucault, Lacan, Derrida) follows the path of language opened up by Saussure and Heidegger. It is in the working of language that we shall find the means by which sedimentation operates. Transcendental consciousness is displaced as the origin and master of the constitution of meaning, and the realization dawns that thought is governed by language rather than the reverse. Merleau-Ponty differs from these contemporaries, however, in his execution of "the linguistic turn."

Transcendental philosophy located the ground of meaning in mind or consciousness and conceived the latter as *sui generis*: the question of its origin was bracketed, banished to the realm of the inexplicable noumenon, elevated to the level of theological mystery—all of which amount to the same. Now language has taken the (transcendental) place of consciousness in some contemporary minds as the origin of meaning. But the question of its own origin has once again been bracketed, banished, mystified. It is once again the question that cannot be asked, the ἄρρητος which, if voiced, exiles the questioner to the realm of metaphysical foundations and onto-theologic. The reason for the banishing in both cases is the same: the inner logic of transcendental reasoning precludes accounting for the genesis of its own originary term, be it consciousness or language. The result is a philosophy based on the foundation of a fundamental dogma which disallows questions regarding foundations by referring them to a doctrine of perpetual absence.

Merleau-Ponty's philosophy of language is frankly foundational in a sense disallowed by currently dominant strains in contemporary Continental thought. His 'foundationalism' is a consequence of his ontology, but, like that ontology, it is not a naive foundationalism; that is, it is not set in the context of the tradition of metaphysics whose 'end' is so widely heralded. Indeed, as I shall try to show in the following section, Merleau-Ponty's philosophy of language, albeit foundational, is informed by a genuinely radical critique of the transcendental philosophy upon which the 'ending' metaphysics rests and thereby succeeds (where its contemporary competitors fail) in overcoming the difficulties of onto-theo-logic. For Merleau-

Ponty, language is founded upon the phenomenal world which is its origin, referent, and measure. For his competitors, the foundations of language are lost in the obscurity of a perpetual absence. The Perpetually Absent is a traditional name for an ambivalently transcendent godhead.

To cast the issue in somewhat finer terms, the task ahead is to explicate the transcendental function of language (that is, sedimentation) without lapsing on the one hand, into the transcendental presuppositions of traditional metaphysics or rebounding, on the other, into the dogmatic mystification of post-hermeneutic skepticism.

TEN

Language

Foundation and Truth

Far from possessing the secret of the being of the world, language is itself a world, itself a being—a world and a being to the second power, since it does not speak in a vacuum, since it speaks *of* being and *of* the world and therefore redoubles their enigma instead of dissipating it. *The philosophical interrogation concerning the world therefore does not consist in referring from the world itself to what we say of the world*, since that interrogation repeats itself again within language.[1] To philosophize is not to cast the things into doubt in the name of words, as if the universe of things said were clearer than that of brute things, as if the real world [*le monde effectif*] were a canton of language [and] perception a confused and mutilated speech. (VI 96–97; VI-F 132: emphasis added)

"The philosophical interrogation concerning the world . . . does not consist in referring from the world itself to what we say of the world." Here, in a phrase, is the thought that separates Merleau-Ponty from those of his contemporaries who are currently in vogue. As stated here, it is a critical thought, a negative thought: it says that it is a mistake to put language in the place of the world as the ultimate theme of philosophical interrogation. The positive thought that is its correlate has already been set forth a number of times: "the perceived world is the always presupposed foundation of all rationality, all value, and all existence" (PriP 13). The issue, as noted earlier, centers on the question of foundations: either language is founded on something prior to it which serves as its ground, origin, measure, and referent—or language refers only to itself and any appeal to a foundation which would serve as its ground, origin, or measure is an appeal to onto-theology.

Merleau-Ponty speaks to this issue, but his speaking was silenced a quarter-century ago, hence he did not—could not—address himself to such key texts as Derrida's *De la Grammatologie*[2] which was published in 1967, six years after Merleau-Ponty's untimely death. It is, then, somewhat unusual for me to set Merleau-Ponty's teaching on language in the context of a debate that had barely begun when he died. Unusual, perhaps, but necessary, because the debate has still barely begun. Yet, as will become apparent, the question of foundations is crucial: on it depends the nature and validity of philosophical interrogation itself. To abandon the foundations of philosophical discourse is, *ipso facto*, to project oneself into relativism and skepticism with regard to truth and value. And relativism, no matter how guarded, how sophisticated, how virtuosic its expression may be, has always the same consequence—rhetorical noise accompanied by philosophical silence—for, although one can always attack, one can never defend: absent foundations of some sort, there can be no grounds for espousing one viewpoint rather than another, and one can lay claim only to consistency, never truth.

The debate over foundations is, then, consequential. That is one reason for entering it. But the decisive reason is that it is in the context of this debate that the force of the validity of Merleau-Ponty's standpoint becomes apparent. In the pages that follow, I shall defend the claim that Merleau-Ponty's phenomenology of language is a direct consequence of his phenomenological ontology and, as such, provides a response to the two forms of the retreat to immanence most prevalent in Continental thought today: (a) post-hermeneutic skepticism, and (b) semeiological reductionism. 'Post-hermeneutic skepticism' is my term for the standpoint, consequent upon a certain reading of Heidegger, that Being is forever imprisoned within the house of language, that there is no access to either Being or beings which is not mediated by language. 'Semeiological reductionism' is my term for the position that has grown out of a certain interpretation of Saussure and holds that signifiers refer exclusively to other signifiers, that there is no signified that is not itself within the chain of signifiers.[3] Beneath the differences between these two standpoints is the common result: from neither vantage is it deemed possible to pass beyond the immanent sphere of language to a transcendent (that is, extralinguistic) reality. And that means that there is no conceivable *terminus ad quem* which might be reached by disputants in a controversy, no transcendent ground which could serve to substantiate one view and discredit the others: discourse could lead only to further discourse and terminate, if at all, by fiat of violence or fatigue.

1. POST-HERMENEUTIC SKEPTICISM AND SEMEIOLOGICAL REDUCTIONISM

Post-hermeneutic skepticism

The problem posed by Heidegger in the section of *Being and Time* devoted to "Understanding and Interpretation" is essentially a variant of the problem of truth which emerges from the thesis of subjectivity: if the world, as I understand it, is necessarily the-world-as-I-understand-it, and if my understanding of the world is necessarily an interpretation biased by presuppositions, then truth becomes a problem. The truth, as I understand it, is always only my interpretation, and the biases which structure that interpretation undermine its claim to objectivity, that is, its claim to express what is as *it* is.

In *Being and Time*,[4] these biases are explicated in terms of the "fore-structure" of fore-having (*Vorhabe*), fore-sight (*Vorsicht*), and fore-conception (*Vorgriff*): understanding is biased by a structure of pro-jection or anticipation which is inherent to it. This projection of pre-suppositions is explicated in terms of the "totality of involvement" (*Bewandtnisganzheit*) which informs the primordial sphere of readiness-to-hand (*Zuhandenheit*). The telic nature of our involvement with things thus results in a projection of meaning which constitutes the intelligibility of things or our understanding of them. This, in turn, produces a circularity intrinsic to understanding: we understand things in terms of a prior interpretation; what we seek to understand thematically is always already caught up in a prethematic context of understanding. The hermeneutic circle is a result of the fore-structure intrinsic to understanding; that is, it is a result of the inherent structure of understanding that it always projects a context of meaning or involvement ahead of itself.

In *Being and Time*, this problematizing of truth consequent upon the projective structure of understanding is not directly associated with language. Later, however, Heidegger makes the connection between truth and language that recasts the problem posed by the hermeneutic circle in a linguistic framework. In "The Origin of the Work of Art" (1935–36), Heidegger concludes that "art is by nature an origin: a distinctive way in which truth comes into being, that is, becomes historical."[5] Art brings truth into being by fixing it in place, by thematizing it. This act of thematization is ποίησις, poetic creation. "*All art*, as the letting happen of the advent of the truth of what is, is, as such, essentially poetry" ("Origin," p. 72). Heidegger grants to poetry—"the linguistic work, the poem in the narrower sense"— a "privileged position in the domain of the arts" because "language alone brings what is, as something that is, into the Open for the first time" ("Origin," p. 73). This thought had been expressed earlier (in 1935) in *An Introduction to Metaphysics*: "it is in words and language that things first come into being and are."[6] And it reaches culmination later (in 1946) with Heidegger's statement in "What Are Poets For?" that "language is the precinct [templum], that is, the house of Being."[7] Truth happens in art, above all in poetry, where the thematizing of language brings things into being. Truth is ἀλήθιᾰ—unforgetfulness, unconcealment—and it is in language that the unconcealment of things happens. Yet every disclosure, every revelation, is, at the same time, a concealment; language covers things over in the very process of thematization or unconcealment. Furthermore, we live in a time of fallenness, a time of spiritual decline, a time when "language in general is worn out and used up" (IM, p. 42). Our time is characterized by a "flight of the gods" (IM, p. 37): the gods who "bring us to language"[8] have fled, and the poet—the one who stills himself, listens, and turns to the gods for his measure—faces an abyss.

We live in a time when language has become exhausted, when "Being has become little more than a mere word and its meaning an evanescent vapor" (IM, p. 41). We live in a time of "idle talk [which] destroys our authentic relation to things" (IM, p. 11). Idle talk dissembles, conceals things, and dissembles that dissemblance, conceals that concealment, by its very taken-for-grantedness. And this fallen, exhausted, dissembling language which subverts our relation to Being has taken us over. "Man acts as though he were the shaper and master of language, while in fact language remains the master of man."[9]

The problem of truth posed by the hermeneutic circle of projective understanding has now become a problem of language. We are mastered by a fallen language that dissembles our relations to things, conceals Being, and covers over its dissemblance by the very quality of ordinariness that betokens its exhaustion. Language, which grounds our understanding of things, is itself grounded in an abyss, an *Ab-grund*, an absence of ground: the gods, to whom the poets, the original speakers of truth, listen for their measure, have fled and darkness prevails. Truth is grounded in language, but the ground of language has fallen away leaving an *Ab-grund*.

If this were the totality of Heidegger's teaching on the subject of language and truth, he would be rightly seen as a skeptic, even a nihilist: this view, as set forth here, imprisons man within a dissembling language and denies him any relation to Being independent of language by means of which that dissemblance can be rectified. If one attributes all meaning to the transcendental function of language—if one regards language as entirely centrifugal, as the sole ground of constitution and the source of all *Sinn-gebung* or projection of meaning—but denies that language originates in this world to which it refers, then one has severed language from any transcendent ground and foreclosed the possibility of measuring its truth.

Heidegger, however, is neither skeptic not nihilist. Language, for him, remains a grounded phenomenon. One may dispute the legitimacy of his appeal to Being or to presence, or one may find in his later elaboration of the concept of appropriation (*Ereignis*) a promising answer to the question of the ground of the "Saying of language."[10] I favor the latter, but this is not yet the place to argue the point. (See my conclusion, "Abyss and Logos.") The issue at hand is that of post-hermeneutic skepticism. And the point I hope to have made is that if one fastens upon the *problem* of truth posed by Heidegger's hermeneutic understanding of language and, at the same time, rejects the legitimacy of his or any other *solution*—if any appeal to a ground is *ipso facto* discredited as a relapse into traditional metaphysics and onto-theology—then one is committed to both skepticism and nihilism. I have characterized this position as *post*-hermeneutic skepticism to signal the fact that it is a position taken, not by Heidegger, but by those who have followed the path of his thinking to a crucial juncture and then departed from it.

Semeiological reductionism

Semeiology is the science of signs. Semeiological reductionism is the attempt to reduce all science to semeiology. This is a radical formulation of the position, but the position is itself necessarily radical—so radical as to be untenable—although its adherents have avoided direct confrontation with its ultimate consequences. It is difficult to defend the claim that the laws of physics, biology, psychology, sociology, etc. are reducible to the laws governing the relations of signs within societies,[11] but that is an ineluctable implication of the position currently dominating mainstream Continental thought.

The premise that transforms semeiology into semeiological reductionism is the premise that signs refer exclusively to other signs, that signs cannot refer to extralinguistic realities; for example, phenomena to which we have cognitive access in non- or pre-linguistic modes, preeminently in the mode of perception. Or, to state this premise in a positive form, semeiological reductionism holds that all cognitive modes are thoroughly permeated by or conditioned upon language and that this is a result of the fact that meaning or significance, the object of cognition, is generated exclusively in and by sign systems, that is, by language, broadly or narrowly conceived. Note that this premise does not entail denial of the existence of things independent of language, nor does it entail denial of our ability to perceive these things: it contends only that our cognition of things is inextricably mediated by language or, again, that human cognition is imprisoned within the immanence of language.

Although Saussure did not explicitly espouse the standpoint of semeiological reductionism, his influential *Course in General Linguistics*[12] is, for the most part, compatible with that standpoint[13] and might justly be regarded as its primary antecedent. Saussure was a linguist, not a philosopher; he chose to speak as a scientist and to avoid the domain of metaphysics. Except for a brief critique of "the superficial notion" that language is "nothing more than a name-giving system" (*Course*, p. 16), in which he argues that "the linguistic sign unites, not a thing and a name, but a concept and a sound-image,"[14] we find little in Saussure that betrays an ontological commitment. Indeed, elements of scientific realism—

the social fact alone can create a linguistic system . . . (*Course*, p. 113),
language is a social institution . . . (*Course*, p. 91)

—are unselfconsciously mixed with elements of a language-based transcendental idealism.

no individual . . . could modify in any way the choice [of a given signifier for the idea that it represents]; and what is more, the community itself cannot control so much as a single word; it is bound to the existing language. (*Course*, p. 71)

Saussure writes of both the "internal" and the "external" elements of language—for example, the systematic relations among phonemes operative within the organism of language and such influences impinging on language from without as political history, geography, enthnography, and so forth—but he does not discourse on the relation of word and thing.

There are three fundamental tenets in Saussure's thought, however, which lend themselves to the development of semeiological reductionism. First is the thesis of cognitive dependency, the thesis that thought is dependent on language.[15] The second is Saussure's renowned definition of the primary linguistic entity, the sign, and the association of signifier (*signifiant*, sound-image) and signified (*signifié*, concept).[16] And the third tenet is the thesis of opposition or difference which is the basis for Saussure's diacritical theory of language, and which maintains that the delimitation of a linguistic unit (or isolable sign) requires the differentiation of a signifier from all others in the chain of sound-images and a concurrent and correlative differentiation of the signified from all others in the chain of concepts (*Course*, p. 104). Here Saussure stresses the point that this identity by opposition can *only* be established through the correlation of signifier and signified: the "slice of sound" in a spoken chain is identifiable only if it is correlated with a discrete concept and, *vice versa*, a given concept is isolable only if it is correlated with a discrete signifier or sound-image (whence follows the first tenet, the thesis of cognitive dependency).[17] The correlation of a given signifier with a given signified is entirely arbitrary (that is, not grounded in onomatopoeia or some concatenation of natural signs) and depends on linguistic "values that owe their existence solely to usage and general acceptance" within a community (*Course*, p. 113).

These three tenets alone do not entail semeiological reductionism, although they take us to its brink. Their cumulative effect is to assert that cognition depends on language and that the signs constituting the linguistic system cannot be divorced either from that system as an organic whole or from the communal values that establish themselves within the system. The premise that must be added to arrive at the reductionist position is the premise that signs refer only to other signs within the system and do not depend upon any grounding in an extralinguistic reality which would account for their origin, measure, and ultimate reference.

This premise does not appear in Saussure's theorizing. Indeed, it is excluded by the central notion of linguistic value which stipulates a social grounding as necessary for language.[18] This, as noted earlier, is the scientific realism of Saussure at work.

But the reductionist premise that confines cognition within the immanence of language finds a hospitable host in Saussure's theory, specifically in the operative equivocity of his notion of the signified. Following the convention of the use-mention distinction, it is the case that, for Saussure, 'tree' signifies tree. He states this in two ways.[19]

[A] 'arbor' signifies tree.

[B] 'arbor' signifies ☨.

Now 'tree' in [A] and '☨' in [B] function as signifiers for tree; neither is a tree, but both represent the concept, one by means of a word, the other by means of a picture. Trees cannot appear in texts, in written (or spoken) discourse. Suppose, *per impossibile*, Saussure could have included a real tree in his text. Or, suppose it occurred to him to use an indexical term, for example, 'this page' signifies this page, the one on which these words are written. Would he have done so? I think he would have. I think that is why he used the picture, ☨. But I must leave the point moot. The point that is not moot, however, is that the signifiers 'tree' and '☨' in [A] and [B] above are ambiguous, *essentially ambiguous*, because they can be taken to refer either to a concept or to a thing. There is no way, within discourse alone, that one can resolve this ambiguity.

Of course, one can say

[C] 'this page' signifies this page, the one on which these words are written.

But the reductionist can always point out that the words 'this page, the one on which these words are written' are themselves signs and not this page, the one on which these words are written. Indeed, that is the ploy employed by semeiological reductionism. It underlies the claim that there is no egress from the chain of signifiers, no access to a transcendent reality, because signs are necessarily defined by reference to other signs and derive any meaning they can have therefrom. Even ostensive definitions such as [C] remain locked within the chain of signifiers according to the reductionist claim.

The question of semeiological reference is at least as old as the medieval dispute over nominalism and realism—anticipations of it are evident in *Cratylus* (386–90)—and one might expect contemporary philosophers to have realized that neither of the traditional standpoints is defensible: nominalism cannot account for the origin of signs, and realism cannot account for the transcendental function (or sedimentation) of language; some third alternative is required. Yet semeiological reductionism is but thinly veiled nominalism. What gives the version current in Continental thought its appearance of novelty is the synthesis of neo-Husserlian transcendental idealism with neo-Saussurean semeiology. And that, simply stated, is the synthesis of Saussure's thesis of cognitive dependency with Husserl's thesis that all meaning originates within the sphere of immanence. The result is the attribution to Language, as a trans-personal, historically evolving agency of cultural constitution, all the functions of sense-bestowing Husserl attributed to the transcendental ego. Language thus takes on the character of a groundless ground. It is a ground because it is the origin of all meaning or value and the ultimate object of cognition. But it is, itself, groundless since the meaning bestowed by a given sign is arbitrary, cannot be read off the signifier, but must be defined by reference to other signs, which in turn require definition by reference to yet other signs, and so on: no sign is meaningful apart from its inclusion within the entire system. Yet the system itself has no referent, no source of meaning. The signs refer only to each other, but each signifier is itself devoid of meaning: where then does the system acquire its meaning? Saussure posited a social ground for language with his notion of communal value—which, one may assume, is a mediate reference to the world through the structures of social praxis. However, this ground has been forsaken in the reduction to immanence which re-verses Saussure's ordering of priorities by positing language as the source of all value, including communal value. This leaves the sign system with no appeal except to itself, and gives it the character of a groundless absolute: a self-generating system that can speak only about itself. Furthermore, since the system is, itself, historically evolving, each synchronic slice must be understood diachronically, in the context of its antecedents, and this pro-jects the search for grounds back into a linguistic prehistory where darkness necessarily prevails. The sign system, hence every individual sign within it, is adrift in the ἄπειρον.

This conclusion runs contrary to the beliefs of Saussure, who outlined a method of retrospective induction that could produce positive results in the search for historical grounds (*Course*, p. 213). From the standpoint of semeiological reductionism, however, "true reconstruction" is an impossibly optimistic conception. Given the absence of genuine foundations, there can be only partial de-constructions, that is, the dismantling of a linguistic struc-ture held to be apriori within the present synchrony in order to reveal the accidents influencing its genesis. De-construction thus typically functions to produce an exposé, a scandal, a nexus of fissures in the edifice of received belief. Unlike its Heideggerian predecessor, destruction,[20] de-construction does not offer even a qualified promise that the clearing away of intervening assumptions (that is, the history of Western ontology) will open the way for a disclosure of truth. Destruction is pointed toward the revelation of grounds; de-construction seeks to reveal their absence.

The question of the relation of language and history is central to the problematics of both hermeneutics and semeiology. If one answers that question with the model of a closed circuit in which the nature of language is determined by historical accident and our understanding of history is determined by the vagaries of language, then one has locked oneself within a groundless immanence with no opening on truth and no possibility for any accumulation or refinement of knowledge. As Merleau-Ponty puts it,

history cannot be our only approach to language, because language would then become a prison. It would determine even what one could say about it [21] and, being always presupposed in what is said about it, it would be incapable of any clarification. Even the science of language, enveloped in its present state, would be unable to reach a truth of language, and thus objective history would destroy itself. (PW 24; PW-F 35)[22]

Post-hermeneutic skepticism and semeiological reductionism: these are alternate routes to a neo-Socratic ignorance: a position that defends no position, but attacks from whatever vantage is expeditious at the moment. Indeed, since even in this philosophical counterpart of guerilla warfare every attack must originate somewhere, since every exposure of falsity betrays the latency of truth, those who engage in it must be careful to shift ground, to obscure their bases of operation, to betray their allies as a matter of principle, to erase the signs of having occupied some position, however momentarily. It is a dance that requires a level of virtuosity worthy of Socrates at the height of his casuistical power.

But just as Socrates's profession of ignorance was a rhetorical device which could not withstand critical scrutiny, so does the skeptical retreat to the abyss display its own bad conscience with regard to the impossibility of referring beyond the chain of signifiers. The statement which denies the possibility of referring within language to things lying beyond language must make the reference it denies is possible—and then put that reference under erasure.

This is a path that has already been investigated—perhaps most carefully by Wittgenstein, in his *Tractatus*. At the end of that book, he finds that he has spoken of things that cannot, according to this own theory, be expressed in language. And so he puts his words under erasure.

My propositions serve as elucidations in the following way: anyone who understands me eventually recognizes them as nonsensical, when he has used them—as steps—to climb up beyond them. (He must, so to speak, throw away the ladder after he has climed up it.)[23]

Later, in the *Philosophical Investigations*, Wittgenstein realizes that the ladder cannot be thrown away: if his theory requires him to erase what it forced him to say, then it is the theory that must be thrown away because it embodies a contradiction. In the case of the *Tractatus*, the theory held that *"the limits of my language* mean [*bedeuten*] the limits of [my] world" (*Tractatus*, prop. 5.6). But the theory required Wittgenstein to speak of the relation between language and world in order to explain what it means for any proposition (including the one just cited) to be true (*Tractatus*, props. 2.223, 2.224, 4.022). And that requirement entails a reference beyond language to what language shows. The showing of language, its ownmost function, requires a passage beyond the chain of signifiers, a reference beyond the immanent sphere of language: the showing of language depends upon a cognitive, but prelinguistic, opening upon the world; it depends upon the perception of phenomena. "There are, indeed, things that cannot be put into words. They *make themselves manifest*" (*Tractatus*, prop. 6.522). "What we cannot speak about we must pass over in silence" (*Tractatus*, prop. 7). That is Wittgenstein's concluding proposition in the *Tractatus*. But the silence of which he speaks there is broken in the *Investigations* where it becomes the theme of his inquiry. And it is to this silence before speech, this silence within speech, this realm that transcends language and provides its enabling context, that Merleau-Ponty turns in his interrogation of language.

2. MERLEAU-PONTY'S EARLY GESTURAL THEORY OF LANGUAGE.

If there had been no mankind with organs of phonation or articulation and an apparatus for breathing—or at least with a body and the capacity to move himself—there would have been no speech and no ideas. (PP 390–91; PP-F 448)

Merleau-Ponty's chapter on language in the *Phenomenology* is entitled "The Body as Expression and Speech." It concludes the series of chapters in part one where Merleau-Ponty sets forth his theory of the lived body, and his treatment of language is subservient to that end. Later, he weights matters differently: language is taken as an autonomous theme from 1949 (*Consciousness and the Acquisition of Language*)[24] through the mid-fifties. Finally, in the last works, the problems of language are treated within the context of Merleau-Ponty's overriding concern with ontology. There are shifts of emphasis during the phases of this development, but one fundamental idea remains constant: language comes into being within the phenomenal world and could not exist without it or the human bodies interacting within it. Language is thus a founded phenomenon, a phenomenon founded upon human embodiment within the world, and must be understood within this context.

Language is founded. But how and upon what is it founded? This is the problem of origins, a problem that should be faced by any theoretical account of language, but one that is evaded by many. For instance, those theories which espouse the theses of post-hermeneutic skepticism or semeiological reductionism—specifically, the thesis to which both are committed that human cognition is confined within the immanent sphere of language, that any apprehension of meaning presupposes the mediation of language—are forced by that commitment into an implicit denial of the possibility of the evolution of language from phases in the development of humanity marked by the absence of language. If all cognition presupposes language, then it is impossible for a pre- or non-linguistic form of life to learn to signify, that is, to use signs. If one contends that all learning presupposes the use of concepts, that is, the significations of signs, then one is committed to some version of the doctrine of innate ideas.

This difficulty with the problem of origins has beset transcendental philosophy since the time of Kant. If understanding presupposes identification or recognition, and that in turn presupposes subsumption under a concept, then there can be no understanding prior to conceptualization, hence no possibility of explaining how our ancestors in the evolutionary chain learned the use of concepts. One is thus committed to some form of conceptual nativism. If, alternatively, conceptualization is conceived to be contingent upon language use, as is now generally believed, then one is committed to some form of linguistic nativism.[25] I have taken Kant as my example here, but the same argument applies to all who adopt a purely transcendental standpoint. Husserl, for instance, is committed to nativism with his doctrine of the "innate apriori" or its correlate, the theory of an eidetic language with a pure apriori grammar. With some stretching, transcendentalism can accommodate an evolution *within* language (for example, through conflicts in a plurality of sign systems), but it cannot allow for the evolution *of* language (or languages).[26]

Merleau-Ponty was neither an archaeologist nor an anthropologist, and nowhere in his writings can one find an empirical theory purporting to account for the evolution of language. What we do find, however, is an account of language that is designed to leave room for the possibility of the genesis of language from prelinguistic origins—coupled with speculation about the role of the body in that genesis. This speculation centers around the notion of the bodily gesture and the correlative idea of "singing the world."

(i) *Bodily gesture*. Two important points belong under this heading. The first is that the gesture, or something like it, is necessary to bridge the gap between prelinguistic and linguistic phases in the evolution of the significantly speaking animal. The gesture, or something like the gesture: that is, something capable of providing a third alternative in the traditional dilemma of natural signs versus conventional signs. Theories based on the notion of natural signs founder on the problem of explaining the plurality of existing languages when the differences between these languages would seem[27] to preclude the possibility of a common source. This, the problem of irreducible differences, also besets theories based on onomatopoeia (which may be viewed as a subset of natural sign theory). Conventional sign theories, among them Saussure's, assert that the relation between signifier and signified is entirely arbitrary, hence founder on the problem of primal institution. They can offer no explanation (indeed, are committed to the thesis that none can be given) as to *how* a given sound or mark is bound to a given meaning or signification.[28] Now, since that act of binding signifier to signified *is* the origin of language, conventional sign theories cannot *in principle* address the problem of origins. Furthermore, if one adopts Saussure's thesis that signifier and signified cannot exist in separation from each other, then the problem of origins becomes devastating: language must always have been; it could not have begun to be, because that beginning would require an inconceivable act: the act of an original binding of two elements that cannot exist as elements. More on this shortly.

The gesture is neither a natural sign nor a conventional sign, although it bears some resemblance to both since it occupies an intermediate position between the two. Unlike the conventional sign, the gesture is intrinsically meaningful, but unlike the natural sign, the gesture is not limited to one meaning. Thus, gestures (for example, a smile) always mean something, but, depending upon the context, can mean several things. The plurality of possible meanings allows for the possibility of the same gesture being institutionalized with different meanings within different cultural contexts and thereby acquiring conventional limitation and rigidity. Thus the oriental smile differs from the occidental smile, but in neither cultural context can the smile indicate a direction (in the manner of a pointing finger): like all gestures, the smile is meaningful because it delineates a relatively narrow range of significance.[29] Words, according to Merleau-Ponty, are linguistic gestures that have acquired institutional limitation within the conventions of a culture. One difference between the linguistic and the non-linguistic gesture is that the latter operates within the context of the natural world which is open to all, and the former operates also within a cultural background which is limited to its denizens.

> Verbal gesticulation . . . aims at a mental setting which is not initially given to everyone, and which is precisely its function to communicate. But here what nature does not provide, cultural background does. Available meanings, that is to say former acts of expression, establish between speaking subjects a common world, to which the present new word refers as the gesture refers to the perceptible world. (PP 186; PP-F 217)

There is a resonance of the ostension model vibrating between the lines of this text which some will find troublesome. (I do not: ostension, like gathering, is one of the myriad ways in which languages and gestures refer to the world. Reference must accommodate ostension as a possible modality; the mistake occurs when it is taken to be the sole and *original* modality.) Also, the question of the origin of the cultural world, required as the context for verbal gesticulation, is here left unanswered. It is clear from the sequel to the passage just quoted that Merleau-Ponty regards the available meanings constituting the cultural background for novel expression to have been built up from prior acts of expression which have been sedimented in the form of a culture.[30] Merleau-Ponty does not address himself specifically to the incipient conflict between Saussure, who presupposes community as a condition for language, and Heidegger, who claims that it is language (ποίησις) that gathers all things, hence founds the community of man. Nonetheless, it is clear from what he does say that he regards some primitive form of intersubjectivity (that is, community) as a necessary condition for the emergence of language (PW 42; PW-F 59–60).

Returning to the central issue, the question of the relation of sound or image to meaning, Merleau-Ponty states his position in straightforward terms: "The linguistic gesture, like all the others, delineates its own meaning." He goes on to say that "one is forced to accept" this idea "if one wishes to understand the origin of language" (PP 186; PP-F 217). The claim being made is clear, and is never retracted in Merleau-Ponty's later writing: in order to be able to conceive of language as having an origin, we must conceive the sign as originally meaningful, and as deriving that meaning from its own physiognomy—*and* from its reference to the world.

Whether one accepts the gestural theory of language (and it is difficult to think of an alternative if one acknowledges the force of Merleau-Ponty's claim that the role of the body must be crucial in the evolution of language) the overriding point remains: unless words are understood to be originarily meaningful in relation to a world, there is no conceptual space for resolution of the problem of origins, and the evolution of language remains inconceivable.

The second point to be stressed under the heading of bodily gesture has already been broached: the gestural theory is based on the denial of an original dissociation of signifier and signified (that is, token and meaning). As I have tried to show, Saussure is ambivalent on this point: (a) he states that signifier and signified constitute an indissoluble unity, but (b) he also says that the correlation of a given signifier with a given signified is ultimately arbitrary. One cannot have it both ways. In my judgment, Saussure is led to trivialize (a) the first point in order to develop the conventional theory of language based on (b) the second. That is, he can maintain (b) if (a) is trivialized to mean that no physical sound or mark *can function as a signifier* unless it is associated with a concept. But that is far different from the claim made by Merleau-Ponty that sounds and gestures emanating from human bodies are intrinsically meaningful.

This point is decisive. If one asserts that the relation of sound/mark and meaning is arbitrary, and this assertion is central to any convention theory of language, then signs can have only the meaning we assign to them in a deliberate act of linguistic institution. But the critique of the ostension model, as set forth by Wittgenstein[31] and others, shows that linguistic institution (that is, the act of bringing about an arbitrary connection between signifier and signified, the explicit adoption of a signifying or naming convention) necessarily presupposes the framework of a relatively sophisticated sign system as a condition for the possibility of any such act. Thus, within convention theories, the establishment of convention presupposes the prior existence of convention: language, if it exists, must always have been.

Furthermore, if one assents to the conventionalist thesis that signifiers can have only arbitrarily assigned significance, then we could find in a chain of signifiers only those meanings we were already prepared to attribute to them. Consequently, we could never learn anything from listening to another or reading his words. Signs could only provide the occasion for entertaining thoughts previously acquired. Thus convention theory founders on the problem of communication.[32]

Heidegger is no doubt correct in contending that the discourse in which most of us spend most of our time is idle chatter (*Gerede*),[33] and there is little doubt as well that Merleau-Ponty's distinction between originating or creative expression and secondary or institutionalized language owes as much (or more) to Heidegger's distinction between authentic and inauthentic speech as it does to Saussure's distinction between *la parole* and *la langue*:[34] Merleau-Ponty readily acknowledges that our discourse is predominantly inauthentic and is conducted within the parameters of convention where the ritualized exchange of familiar clichés involves neither the creative effort of expression nor the struggle to understand a novel thought. Although conventional theories can explicate conventional discourse, however, they cannot account for the institution of conventions. That is, they founder on the problem of origins—precisely because they dissociate signifiers from signification, sound/mark from meaning. In primal expression, originating speech, the token must convey its meaning, must say what it means, apart from instituted conventions: to appeal to convention to explain the establishment of convention is to beg the question of origins. The linguistic gesture (or something like it, something that has an inherent meaning, as 'ouch' means ouch) is required to explain how man became man, the being capable of signification.

(ii) *Singing the world.* The difficulty here, as already noted, is that some people say "ouch" when they are hurt and others say "aie" or something else. But the plurality of languages is troublesome only if one seeks univocity in natural language theory. Merleau-Ponty's gesture theory not only admits the possibility of gestures having many possible meanings, it requires a thesis of ambiguity or (limited) multivocity. As explained earlier, Merleau-Ponty's general doctrine of perceptual ambiguity follows from his adoption of the Gestalt theoretical thesis of contextual relevancy: the meaning of a perceptual theme is dependent in part upon the context in which it emerges. Since a gesture is a perceptual theme, the doctrine of ambiguity applies: the meaning of a gesture is contingent in part upon its context.

Although the doctrine of ambiguity accounts for the possibility of a given gesture or verbal gesticulation having differing meanings in different contexts, another premise is required to allow a given meaning to find expression in differing gestures. There is a considerable acoustic and physiognomic difference between 'green' and '*vert*'—does this not argue in favor of the conventionalist claim that the relation of signifier to signified is arbitrary? Here is Merleau-Ponty's response.

> If we consider only the conceptual and delimiting meaning of words, it is true that the verbal form—with the exception of endings—appears arbitrary. But it would no longer appear so if we took into account the emotional content of

the word, which we have called above its 'gestural' sense, which is all-important in poetry, for example. It would then be found that the words, vowels, and phonemes are so many ways of *singing the world*, and that their function is to represent things, not as the naive onomatopoeic theory had it, by reason of an objective resemblance, but because they extract, and literally express, their *emotional essence*. (PP 187; PP-F 218; emphasis added)

It is difficult, to be sure, to resurrect examples here—'green' and *'vert'* hardly suggest the emotional essence of the color now, after centuries of institution in the secondary (or inauthentic) language[35]—but this need not undermine the credibility of the idea. The passage from the speaking word (*la parole parlante*) of creative expression to the spoken word (*la parole parlée*) of instituted and sedimented languages (PP 197; PP-F 229)—a passage which all words make, even those protected by taboo and social prohibition, and which grants to poets the perennial task of revivifying language— drains the emotional essence from the word and leaves only the shell of its signifier. It is this passage, this process of impoverishment, that lends credibility to the conventionalist thesis, for once a word has lost its guts, it takes on the appearance of a mere token only arbitrarily associated with some meaning.

Different languages, then, say approximately the same thing in different ways, not because different conventions sprang up unaccountably in dif- ferent places, but because the human body can sing the world—and, cor- relatively, live the world—in different ways. *Approximately* the same thing can be said in different languages, but not precisely the same thing, because the emotional overtones, being bound to the sounds and traces of primal expressions, do not survive translation into other sign systems.[36] Conven- tion theory cannot, in the last analysis, explain this limit to translation because it can only appeal to a system of *de facto* associations when it is exactly those associations that need to be explained.

In sum, then, Merleau-Ponty's early gestural theory of language sets forth an alternative to the conventionalism upon which post-hermeneutic skep- ticism and semeiological reductionism rest. His refutation of the conven- tionalist position turns on the assertion that "the word has a meaning" (PP 177; PP-F 206) which I have sought to explicate and defend in the context of the problem of origins.[37] I have chosen this context because I regard it as timely and decisive in the current debate over the nature of language. The problem of origins also provides a link to the next phase of Merleau- Ponty's interrogation of language and an example of his anti-reductionist, synthesizing rather than polarizing, style of thought. Instead of taking sides in the natural language versus conventionalism debate, Merleau-Ponty seeks a position capable of accommodating the truths to be found at the extremes without committing the errors of extremity and reduction. As I have tried to depict in the simple diagrams below, Merleau-Ponty's speculations on the genesis of language allow for both a natural origin of language grounded in the phenomenal world/lived body and the evolution of convention in later phases of its development.

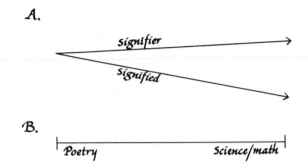

A.

signifier

signified

B.

Poetry   *Science/math*

   In the first or diachronic diagram [A], there is an idealized depiction of the movement from primitive gestures wherein there is a coincidence of sound/mark and meaning (for example, 'ouch' means ouch), through a process of increasing separation in which signifier becomes only conventionally related to signified. The earlier phases provide the context which enable the processes of linguistic institution to take place in later phases. Each later phase thus builds upon the acquisitions of earlier phrases—and this process, traced in reverse, provides the basis for etymology and what Saussure calls "retrospective induction" or reconstruction.
   The second or synchronic diagram [B] is a flat projection of the first: not a collapse of history into the present, but a depiction of the spectrum of language—from gesture to algorithm—at any given time. Toward the left end, there are the uses of language which depend on the proximity of signifier and signified (that is, the uses such as poetry or slang which trade on signs that retain much of their gestural or existential significance). And, toward the right, there are the uses which are highly abstract and artificial or conventional.
   The general thrust of Merleau-Ponty's theory of language is that, in both diagrams, the uses of language which occur toward the right originate within, and ultimately derive their significance from, uses occurring on the left. This is a consequence of the correlative theses of the ontological primacy of phenomena and epistemological primacy of perception which maintain that the perceived world is the ground, measure, and referent of all meaning and cognition. This point is aptly illustrated in the analogy Merleau-Ponty often draws between linguistic signs and musical notation (PP 182, 188; PP-F 213, 219): just as the notes on the score are meaningless apart from their reference to sounds, so are the words of a language meaningless apart from their reference to a world.
   As Merleau-Ponty says, "strictly speaking . . . , there are no conventional signs" (PP 188; PP-F 219), because the signifiers of our languages do not

refer only to hard-edged and determinate concepts. The illusion of transparency arises from second-order or constituted languages where the long-standing institution of the association between this signifier and this signification grants the sign a *de facto* autonomy and freedom from inherence in the world. But *homo sapiens* was not born with a dictionary in his hand: words have deeper roots; even the sophisticated inventions of technical language have origins which stretch back beyond the fiat of a new coinage. If Heidegger is right, 'phenomenology' is an outgrowth of 'φῶς' (light)[38] and that is only a recent ancestor, ancient Greek being relatively young as languages go. Whether or not Heidegger is right in this specific case, there is wisdom in his general technique of etymological retrieval: the full meaning of a word does not reside completely in its contemporary use; the synchronic context is itself illumined by the diachronic context,[39] and the origin of the word has a bearing on current use.[40] (This is one of the main points depicted in diagram [A].) There are no conventional signs, strictly speaking, because all conventional usage is grounded in an original, expressive singing of the world.

So far, I have considered Merleau-Ponty's treatment of the problem of origins from the standpoint of what might be called "archaeological speculation."[41] The problem of origins can also be approached from the standpoint of developmental or cognitive psychology, and it is this approach that governs Merleau-Ponty's writing on language in the late forties and early fifties. I have noted that Merleau-Ponty was not an archaeologist, but he was, in fact, a cognitive psychologist. Hence this territory was, for him, familiar ground. One may wonder, then, why he never finished or published the major work on language he undertook in this period: *The Prose of the World*.[42] Claude Lefort, who decided to edit and publish this unfinished manuscript, suggests that Merleau-Ponty "deliberately abandoned" the work (PW xi; PW-F i). Lefort's reconstruction is as follows.

> From 1952 to 1959 a new task imposes itself, and [Merleau-Ponty's] language is transformed. He discovers the delusions in which 'philosophies of consciousness' are trapped and from which his own critique of classical metaphysics has not saved him. He begins to confront the necessity of providing an ontological foundation for the analyses of the body and perception that had been his starting point. (PW xix; PW-F xi)

I concur in this assessment and agree, too, that the movement which carries Merleau-Ponty toward the new book—*The Visible and the Invisible*—is "both more violent and more faithful to the early inspiration " than the *Prose of the World* manuscript.

The task here, then, is that of (a) explicating the conception of language set forth in Merleau-Ponty's writings during the period which followed the publication of the *Phenomenology* in 1945 until the transition to the new voice of *The Visible and the Invisible*, (b) explaining why and how this conception needed to be modified, and finally (c) offering an interpretation of the emergent theory of language as it appears in Merleau-Ponty's last works. As I hope now to show, the earlier conception is based on the notion of *Fundierung* or foundation (and is flawed by its dependence on the notion of consciousness), and the later conception is oriented around the ideas of reversibility and intertwining.[43]

3. THE *FUNDIERUNG* MODEL OF LANGUAGE

The notion of *Fundierung* plays a central role in the *Phenomenology* where it underlies not only Merleau-Ponty's treatment of language but his accounts of time, reason and fact, reflection and the prereflective, thought and perception, etc. (PP 394; PP-F 451). As it applies to language, the foundation relation can be diagrammed as shown.

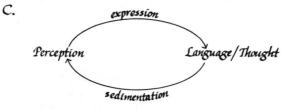

Perception is the originary or found*ing* term: the perceptual world is the ground of the meaning expressed in the verbal gesticulation which subsequently gives rise to instituted language. The concepts of language provide the means of thinking. Thought is thus found*ed* on perception through the mediation of expression, specifically, the bodily acts of gesture and speech. This, in a crude nutshell, is the scheme of Merleau-Ponty's response to the problem of origins.

The reciprocal movement of the *Fundierung* relation, sedimentation, accounts for the transcendental function of language and thought: the categories of thought and language return to the perceptual world to structure it, organize it, and enrich it with deposits of meaning and possibility. Since we are born into a world of instituted language, we find the perceptual world *already* structured, organized, and laden with meaning. This is the point stressed by post-hermeneutic skepticism and semeiological reductionism: for us, all cognition of the world is always already mediated by language, and this mediation amounts to confinement within a sphere of linguistic immanence. I have tried to show that this view leaves no theoretical room for the origination of language because it denies the possibility of anything like the expression function depicted in diagram [C] above, that is, the possibility of moving from sub- or pre-linguistic apprehension of meaning to expression by means of signs. For the same reason, the standpoints named above cannot account for the *motivation* of creative speech: they preclude the possibility of anything like a significative inten-tion, a meaning or intent in search of a linguistic expression.

The *Fundierung* relation is one of asymmetrical reciprocity. The founding term has an originality or priority, that is, the founded term is derived from it, but is not, as Merleau-Ponty points out (PP 394; PP-F 451), "simply derived," because it is through the founded term (the sign or category) that the original or founding term (the meaning or intent) is expressed. (We shall find a similar asymmetrical reciprocity in the reversibility model.)

In the *Phenomenology*, the founding term is conceived as the silence that is prior to expression and categorial thought. This silence receives the name of tacit cogito: the prereflective, prethematic presence to ourselves that is at the same time our presence to the world. It is consciousness at the level of perception. It is existence. It is "subjectivity conceived as inherence in the world" (PP 405, PP-F 464). And it is the foundation of language/thought/knowledge.

> The consciousness which conditions language is merely a comprehensive and inarticulate grasp upon the world . . . , and though it is true that all particular knowledge is *founded* on this primary view, it is true also that the latter waits to be won back, fixed and made explicit by perceptual exploration and by speech. Silent consciousness grasps itself only as a generalized 'I think' in face of a confused world 'to be thought about.' (PP 404; PP-F 462–63; emphasis added)

Several points are pertinent here. (1) Silence is prior to speech and founds it. (2) The silence of the tacit cogito ruptures the seal of immanence by virtue of being an opening upon the world. (3) But at the same time, it is not an unconsciousness because the perceptual opening on to the world must also be presence to itself. (4) It is, as Merleau-Ponty puts it, "a meeting of the human and the non-human" (PP 403; PP-F 462); that is, it is the conjunction of immanence and transcendence which is necessary for con-sciousness to be consciousness of something other than itself. (5) Finally, the meaning that is brought to speech is not a meaning that is constituted by the categories of language and thought.[44] This last point needs to be stressed because it is what, above all, separates Merleau-Ponty from those contemporary Continental philosophers who seek to project us back into a sphere of linguistic immanence.

The doctrine of the silent or tacit cogito allows Merleau-Ponty to resolve the truth of the thesis of subjectivity[45] with the truth of the transcendence of the world: presence to world is, at the same time and necessarily, an anonymous (that is, prereflective) presence to oneself.[46]

The two sides of the *Fundierung* relation enable Merleau-Ponty to do justice to both sides of the realism/empiricism versus transcendentalism/intellectualism polarity without embracing the reductionism that follows if one is forced to choose between the two sides because they are held to be mutually exclusive. On the one hand, the transcendent reality of body and world grounds the movement of expression.[47] On the other hand, the world is not immune to culture, nor does it sustain culture on its surface as an overlay which can be lifted to reveal a stratum of pure nature without the imprint of the human body.[48]

Expression alters the world by reconfiguring it to favor a given view or attitude or interpretation. The sediments of expression are meanings which inhabit the world in such a manner that "what is expressed [i.e., the world] is always inseparable from experience" (PP 391; PP-F 448). This, then, leaves us with the question whether it makes any sense to assign a temporal ordering, a relative priority, between nature and culture, or perception and expression in the unfolding of worldly significance.

Merleau-Ponty's answer to this question is complex,[49] but the *Fundierung* model appears as a constant refrain and leaves little room for doubt: "The sensible gives back to me what I lent to it, but this is only what I took from it in the first place" (PP 214).[50] And again:

> There is an autochthonous significance [*sens*] of the world which is constituted in the dealings which our incarnate consciousness has with it, and which provides the basis of every deliberate *Sinngebung*. (PP 441; PP-F 503)

The act of expression is a "deliberate *Sinngebung*" and it is founded on the worldly significance revealed to us in perception.

The problem, of course, is that perception here is still conceived as an act of consciousness. The perceptual world has not yet taken on the character of the wild/brute/savage being that we encounter in *The Visible and the Invisible;* it has broken from the sheer immanence of Husserl's *Lebenswelt*, but it is still tied to the concept of consciousness. The *Fundierung* model, intended to undercut the world-consciousness polarity, still trades on it.[51]

Now, as I have repeatedly argued, the consequences of philosophies of immanence are solipsism and skepticism. Husserl was well aware of this and sought to evade the skepticism that would undermine his project of rigorous science by attempting to reconfigure his phenomenological ontology along the lines of a theory of transcendental intersubjectivity. One could then speak of objectivity and truth with reference to the rationality and universality of a human world, but still operate within the sphere of immanence (that is, without removing the brackets around the transcendent world): "natural world" would then refer to the world constituted by transcendental consciousness as natural.

In the period under consideration (roughly 1949–52), Merleau-Ponty eleborates his *Fundierung* model to bring out the social or intersubjective underpinnings of language which were implicit in his earlier writing but insufficiently stressed. In this way, he recapitulates the Husserlian program,[52] but does not pay sufficient heed to his own critique of Husserl's account of intersubjectivity—in which he (Merleau-Ponty) demonstrated that the concrete and fundamental structures of intersubjectivity (apprehension of other human beings as both other and human or like unto oneself, communication, etc.) presuppose grounding in the transcendent realities of human bodies and the natural world. As explained in chapter 7 above, recognition of other selves as selves presupposes incarnation as a condition for transfer of corporeal schema, and communication presupposes a transcendent ground of truth as the basis for reconciling divergent perspectives. Since, then, resolving the problems of intersubjectivity requires a move beyond the sphere of immanence, one cannot evade the skepticism that undermines the philosophies of immanence by redefining objectivity and truth in the context of a theory of transcendental intersubjectivity.

One might argue that Merleau-Ponty's emphasis on the social or communal world as the basis for expression signals a growing awareness of the need for a transcendent ground (since communality presupposes that grounding). Or one might argue that the shift from individual to group consciousness is not much of an improvement (since consciousness remains at the core of the problematic). The two views are not incompatible. In any case, the *Fundierung* model underlies Merleau-Ponty's understanding of language during the time he was writing *The Prose of the World,* but it is modified as indicated in the diagram shown.

The point I want to illustrate here is that communality is presupposed on both sides of the *Fundierung* relation: expression presupposes community in the institution of language (the individual, even the poet, needs the complicity of the community to institute new usage); and sedimentation (or sublimation),[53] being the transformation of the perceptual world by culture, clearly requires communal participation in a given way of seeing things.

A key text in the interpretation of Merleau-Ponty's writings during the period now being considered is the letter[54] he sent to Martial Gueroult in 1952 at the time of his candidacy to the Collège de France in which he describes his work since 1945 and outlines his current projects. These projects involve working out "a new type of relation between mind and truth" which is based on "experience of the perceptual world." The questions to be raised will require not only a theory of truth but also a theory of intersubjectivity. He goes on to say that he is "now working on two books dealing with a theory of truth (PriP 7), and later names them as "The Origin of Truth" and "Introduction to the Prose of the World." "The Origin of Truth" became *The Visible and the Invisible*,[55] the project that displaced that of *The Prose of the World* and led to its abandonment. But it is the latter that concerns us now, and in his description of it to Martial Gueroult, we find the familiar *Fundierung* model recast in the context of knowledge and communication, that is, in the context of intersubjectivity.

> It seems to me that knowledge and the communication with others which it presupposes not only are original formations with respect to the perceptual life but also they preserve and continue our perceptual life even while transforming it. Knowledge and communication sublimate rather than suppress our incarnation, and the characteristic operation of the mind is in the movement by which we recapture our corporeal existence and use it to symbolize instead of merely to coexist. This metamorphosis lies in the double function of our body. Through its 'sensory fields' and its whole organization the body is . . . predestined to model itself on the natural aspects of the world. But as an active body capable of gestures, of expression, and finally of language, it turns back on the world to signify it. (PriP 7)

The movement toward symbolization is the movement toward language; the double function of the body is the asymmetrical reciprocity of expression and sedimentation/sublimation hitherto named as *Fundierung*. My point here is that the *Fundierung* model, modified to emphasize the dimension of communication (that is, intersubjectivity as mediated by language), lies at the core of Merleau-Ponty's overview of his work during the period under consideration.

The *Fundierung* model provides a clear link between Merleau-Ponty's emergent theory of language and the development of his ontology. Merleau-Ponty's ontology, as I have argued, is based on the thesis of the ontological primacy of phenomena. The *Fundierung* model grants a primacy to expression, the originating function of language; that, in turn, is described as an "ultimate fact,"[56] and this ultimate fact of expression is based on the correlate to Merleau-Ponty's ontological thesis, that is, it is based on the epistemological thesis of the primacy of perception.[57] The perceived world, the phenomenal world, is what makes knowledge possible, and this origin, this making possible, is accomplished by language, specifically by the ultimate fact of expression which establishes truth. But what of sedimentation: does it cohere with the ontological thesis at hand, or does it amount to a counter-thrust?

If, contrary to the viewpoint taken here, we are always already in language, if the idea of the first words of the first speaker (or writer, marker, leaver of traces) is a bankrupt fantasy, if expression is always the coherent deformation of already available forms of expression, if it is impossible to penetrate the layers of sediment—then it would seem that we are imprisoned in linguistic immanence and that there is no stratum of meaning that is not already mediated by signifiers.

Perhaps the first point to make in response to this familiar challenge is that old or acquired usages must have been new once. The simple induction that follows upon this observation forcefully renews the problem of origins and leads to the consequences set forth earlier.

But let us consider the act of expression synchronically, contemporaneously, that is, within the context of established language and without raising the question of origins. How does genuine expression take place in the present?

Merleau-Ponty's account centers around the notion of the "significative intention" which precedes and directs my verbal expression. He distinguishes it sharply from the model of encoding a clearly formulated thought: in genuine expression, it is not a matter of reproducing a formula, it is rather an attempt to formulate, an attempt to discover what it is that one wants to say (S 89; S-F 112). I am drawn toward signification by something that needs to be said and which imposes on me the task of finding words for it in order to learn, myself, what it is that I want to say. Merleau-Ponty describes this something that needs to be said in the categories of silence as "a mute presence which awakens my intentions without displaying itself before them" (S 89; S-F 112). In the process of filling this gap, phrases recommend themselves to me from the store of sedimented language, and I try them on until I find one that fits the gap and fulfills the intention. It is not simply a question of finding the missing piece in a puzzle, however, the words that fill the gap are altered in the process of insertion. This is the coherent deformation that constitutes the speaker's (or writer's) style and is the result of re-contextualization: the ordinary meaning of words is changed when they are incorporated within the context of an individual's novel usage.[58] It is not that the words exhaust the intention or capture it or embody it; it is rather that they transcend themselves toward a signification which is conveyed by allusion. There is *"a surpassing of the signifying by the signified which it is the very virtue of the signifying to make possible"* (S 90; S-F 112).

What is this allusive reference beyond itself that allows the sedimented language to transcend itself toward new meaning and fulfill significative intentions? A first-level answer is that the spoken or written words refer to other words which are absent from the text but which can be filled in by an interpreter—as Merleau-Ponty fills in the murderous intent of Julien Sorel when he makes his way toward Verrières and Madame de Renal in Stendahl's novel, *The Red and the Black*. "The desire to kill is . . . not in the words at all. It is between them, in the hollows of space, time, and signification they mark out, as movement in the cinema is between the immobile images which follow one another" (S 76; S-F 95). But this is only a first-level answer because it leaves unanswered the question as to what it is that allows the interpreter to fill the fissures in the text; that is, it leaves unanswered the question as to how allusion works, what it is that tells the interpreter what the author conveys through his silence and omission.

The answer to this latter question is "that statements purport to unveil the thing itself, that language surpasses itself toward what it signifies" (S 81; S-F 101). In the sequel to this passage, Merleau-Ponty definitively states his rejection of the thesis of linguistic immanence.

> Signs do not simply evoke other signs for us and so on without end, and *language is not like a prison we are locked into* or a guide we must blindly follow; for what these linguistic gestures mean, and gain us such complete access to that we seem to have no further need of them to refer to it, finally appears at the intersection of all of them.[59]

What appears at the intersection of all these linguistic gestures—and transcends them all—is meaning or signification. And this meaning ultimately derives from and refers to the phenomena of the perceptual world.

The passage quoted above is taken from Merleau-Ponty's essay, "Indirect Language and the Voices of Silence," a revised version of the third chapter of *The Prose of the World* ("The Indirect Language") which he rewrote and published in the summer of 1952. It is the only portion of that abandoned work that Merleau-Ponty did publish, and that fact lends authority to its contents. It also lends authority to other portions of *The Prose of the World* manuscript which amplify or bulwark the thoughts of the published essay. There is one such portion of *The Prose of the World* which explicates the correlation I have been attempting to draw here between the concept of the significative intention, the thesis of the transcendence of meaning/signification, and the ontological/epistemological primacy of the phenomenal/perceptual world. The text to which I refer is in the second chapter, "Science and the Experience of Expression," and the following excerpts from it will, I trust, substantiate my interpretation of Merleau-Ponty on this point.

> There is indeed an interior of language, a *signifying intention* which animates linguistic events and . . . makes language a system capable of its own self-recovery and self-confirmation.[60] . . . The signification of signs derives at first from this configuration in current usage, from the style of human relations that emanate from them, [but] only the *blind and involuntary logic of things perceived*, totally suspended in our body's activity, could lead us to a glimpse of the anonymous spirit which, in the heart of language, invents a new mode of expression. (PW 36–37; PW-F 52, emphasis added)

In footnotes to these passages, Merleau-Ponty writes the following.

> All this only makes clear the transcendence of signification in relation to language.

[There are] no limits to language, no structure of language. . . . These limits and values *exist*; quite simply, *they are of a perceptual order*: there is a *Gestalt* of language. . . .[61] *In the end language must signify something and not always be language about language.* But signification and the sign belong to the perceptual order, not to the order of absolute spirit. (PW 37; PW-F 53, emphasis added)

The "anonymous spirit" inhabiting language and drawing it toward novel or creative expression is not to be attributed to the "absolute spirit" of a universal transcendental consciousness standing behind speech, but rather belongs to "the blind and involuntary logic of things perceived," what Merleau-Ponty frequently names as "the allusive logic of the perceived world" (S 57; S-F 71).

To state the case succinctly, the meaning that transcends my words and motivates my intentions to signify is grounded in the meaning that emanates from the perceived world. The doctrine of sedimentation, far from undermining the thesis of the primacy of perception, substantiates it: the sedimented language, the store of knowledge originally wrested from the perceived world, does not screen us from the world; rather it provides the means of articulating the world and adding to that store. Speaking of the moment at which the significative intention draws from the repository of sedimented language the words it needs, Merleau-Ponty says: "at this moment something has been *founded* in signification; an experience has been transformed into its meaning, has become truth. Truth is another name for sedimentation." (S 96; S-F 120, emphasis added).

The significative intention is anterior to the sedimented language; it is something which is waiting to be said, thus something that has not yet been said: it is a mute plea for words, but not just any words—only the words that will do it justice and give it the name that is properly its own. This point is decisive in the case against the thesis of linguistic immanence: if there were not something prior to language which makes a claim on language—if the gap constituting the significative intention were not a *determinate* gap, one which narrowly delimits the range of words that can fill it—then any language, any set of signs, any chain of signifiers would suffice. We could say anything because we would be talking about nothing. Language must refer to something beyond itself if it is to be capable of truth. Since Merleau-Ponty claims that "the least use of language implies an idea of truth" (PriP 10), we may infer that it implies referentiality as well. This interpretation need not rest on inference, however, since Merleau-Ponty has stated his position unequivocally: "In the end language must signify something and not always be language about language."

4. REFERENCE AND TRUTH

Merleau-Ponty approaches the dual issue of reference and truth in his essay on "Indirect Language and the Voices of Silence." The problem structure

of the essay centers on two apparently irreconcilable aspects of the referentiality of language. There is the infra-referentiality of Saussure's diacritical model and the extra-referentiality of Merleau-Ponty's *Fundierung*
model. The first contends that signs have meaning only in reference to
other signs,[62] and the second holds that the meaning of signs (or sign
systems) derives ultimately from their reference to the world. The problem
is complicated by the tension between Merleau-Ponty's gestural theory of
language and Saussure's concept of phonemic opposition: whereas Merleau-Ponty contends that, at the basic level of gestural signification, sounds
embody meaning, he also states that "what we have learned from Saussure
is that, taken singly, signs do not signify anything and that each one of
them does not so much express a meaning as mark a divergence of meaning
between itself and other signs."[63] This latter issue is not taken up thematically as an issue: Merleau-Ponty continues to adhere to his doctrine of the
expressive gesture,[64] but does not take issue with the concept of phonemic
opposition—except to say in passing that it is "a difficult idea because common sense tells us that if term A and term B do not have any meaning
[*sens*] at all, it is hard to see how there could be a difference of meaning
between them" (S 39; S-F 49). Indeed, if "the writer's act of expression is
not very different from the painter's," and if "hidden in the empirical language there is a language to the second power in which signs once again
lead the vague life of colors" (S 45; S-F 56), if, in sum, the expressive sound
of a phoneme constitutes its identity and differentiates it from all others
as the anguish in the yellow rent of Van Gogh's Golgotha sky (S 55; S-F
69) differentiates it from cool blues, hot oranges, and even other less tor-
mented shades of yellow—then common sense is right and the diacritical
meaning of phonemes is parasitic upon their physiognomies.

Nor is the former issue (infra-referentiality versus extra-referentiality)
explicitly discussed and resolved. For most of the essay the two conflicting
viewpoints glide along side by side sharing equally in Merleau-Ponty's ap-
proval until suddenly he seems to turn his back on the first to embrace the
second, but without thematically explaining why. This calls for critical attention. First: note the apparently irreconcilable opposition between the
two views.

Infra-referentiality—We always have to do only with sign structures whose
meaning [*sens*] *being nothing other than* [*n'étant rien d'autre que*] the way in which
the signs behave toward one another and are distinguished from one another,
cannot be set forth independently of them. (S 42; S-F 52–3, emphasis added)

Extra-referentiality—At the very moment language fills our mind up to the
top without having the smallest place for thought not taken into its vibration,
and exactly to the extent that we abandon ourselves to it, *it passes beyond* [*il
passe au-delà*] the 'signs' toward their meaning [*sens*]. (S 43; S-F 54, emphasis
added)

Second: recall the decisive move toward extra-referentiality at the end of the essay. "Language goes beyond [*se dépasse*] itself toward what it signifies. . . . Signs do not simply evoke other signs for us and so without end, and language is not like a prison" (S 81; S-F 101). How are we to account for this in the absence of a thematic argument?

A word on the genesis of the essay may be germane. As noted above, the published version is a revision of the third chapter of the interrupted manuscript entitled *The Prose of the World*. Comparing the two versions, many significant differences come to light, but two are particularly relevant here. The sentences announcing the decisive move toward extra-referentiality appear in both versions, but the passages explaining that move are omitted in revision and do not appear in the published version. Here they are.

> To signify, to signify something: this decisive act is . . . only accomplished when the constructions[65] are applied to the perceived as the source of signification or expression. The perceived object, with its viscous significations, has a twofold relation to what is understood. On the one hand, it is only the sketch or fragment of meaning which calls for a repetition that fixes the perceived object and finally makes it *exist*. On the other, the perceived object is the prototype of meaning and alone accomplishes the actual truth of what is understood. . . . There is . . . nothing that we can actually and effectively think without relating it to our field of presence, to the actual existence of the perceived object—and in this sense the field of presence contains everything. There is no truth that can be conceived only outside the field of presence, outside the limits of some situation or some structure. We are able to sublimate this situation . . . , but we cannot cut the roots which implant us in a situation. (PW 106–07; PW-F 151)

This is as strong a statement of the primacy of perception as can be found in Merleau-Ponty's works. It has the effect of grounding all convention, all formal thought, all signs (even the mathematical signs of the algorithm) in the perceived world. For this reason, it destroys any claim to full autonomy which might be made on behalf of a sign system and thereby undercuts the thesis of infra-referentiality. But—these passages were not included in the published version of the essay.

The second difference relevant to this discourse is the entire first section of the published version, which was added in the process of revision. This is the section that establishes the problematic, that counterpoises infra- and extra-referentiality.

How to explain these differences? How to understand the peculiar parallel treatment of apparent opposites?

The main portion of the essay, the long midsection which dominates both versions, is devoted to a discourse on painting and an exploration of its parallel to language. The governing hypothesis is that both are based on the world of silence, the mute realm of existence prior to expression. In the course of the early version, the parallel is asserted in a straightforward way. "Everything . . . that is true of painting is also true of language." "Language is painting as painting is language" (PW 69n; PW-F 97n). The basis for asserting the parallel is that language and painting are both forms of expression founded on the silent world of perception.

> All perception, and all action which presupposes it, in short, every human use of the body, is already *primordial expression*. This means that perception is . . . the primary operation which first constitutes signs as signs. Perception makes what is expressed dwell in signs, not through some previous convention, but through the eloquence of their very arrangement and configuration. (PW 78; PW-F 110: S 67; S-F 84)

By the end of the essay, however, the parallel between language and painting has broken down, and broken down in several ways. "Language speaks, and the voices of painting are the voices of silence" (PW 102; PW-F 145; S 81; S-F 101). So the essay whose early version began with the premise that "the parallel [between painting and language] is in principle legitimate" (PW 47; PW-F 66) is rewritten with a problem-setting introduction that proposes to try out the parallel in order to "perceive what may in the end make that parallel impossible" (S 46–47; S-F 58–59).

What is it that makes the parallel impossible? There is little in painting that corresponds to the sedimentation of language.[66] Sedimentation—"the presence of all presents in our own" (S 96; S-F 120)—gives language a historical character different from that of painting, but, more to the point, it grants a ductility to the word (S 81; S-F 101) that is nowhere equalled in painting. It is the sedimented language of acquired usage that recedes before the thing, bows to its meaning, renders itself unobtrusive, creates the illusion of a transparent signification: in short, sedimentation allows a transcendence of the signifier toward the signified. To be sure, painting has a tradition, many traditions, and those traditions confer an accessibility to past acquisitions (perspective, chiaroscuro, the techniques of rendering light, texture, etc.), but one does not see through the painting to its meaning as one does in language. This, to be sure, is a relative difference, a relative privilege of language over painting,[67] but it is decisive. It means that language refers in a way that painting does not; it embodies truth in a way that painting does not.

Both language and painting derive from and ultimately refer to the perceived world. This thesis is constant throughout Merleau-Ponty's career. But the manner in which he conceives the reference of language to world does change. And that change, brewing from the time of the *Phenomenology*, bubbles to the surface in the revision of "The Indirect Language" with the breakdown of the painting-language parallel.

Linguistic signs are diacritical in a way that dabs of color are not; they refer to each other in a way that the elements of a graphic composition do not. Certainly, the addition of a line or a dab of paint will alter a painting—even more dramatically than the addition of a word (other than 'not') will change a piece of prose—and Merleau-Ponty comments on this (S 45; S-F 57). But that 'not' is crucial; it changes the value of the terms in its domain.

This difference illumines a passage that, apart from it, would seem to be a kind of *bêtise* foreign to Merleau-Ponty. "Man does not paint painting, but he speaks about speech."[68] One thinks immediately of Velázquez's *Las Meninas* and what Foucault and others have written about its self-referentiality . . . and wonders how Merleau-Ponty could have ignored the whole genre of artists painting themselves painting.[69] But this misses the point—the point that there is a self-referentiality intrinsic to language which derives from the diacritical nature of signs, and which has no direct counterpart in painting precisely because the analogy between words or phonemes and color dabs breaks down when faced with the realization that colors, like the infant's babbling sounds,[70] are not signs the way that words or phonemes are.[71]

In the introductory section of "Indirect Language and the Voices of Silence" which recasts the problematic of the earlier version, Merleau-Ponty correlates the diacritical nature of language with a certain totalizing effect: if "the terms of language are engendered only by the differences which appear among them," then it would seem that one would have to "go from the whole of the speaker's language to the whole of the hearer's language," and this poses the problem that "one would have to know the language in order to learn it" (S 39; S-F 49). That is, if terms mean what they do only by virtue of their organization, their places within the whole, then one would have to apprehend the entire Gestalt in order to understand the place/meaning of a given term, and to learn how language works, what words do, what the speaking of language-users is intended to accomplish. But this is not so much the case with painting: a picture can be seen as such (if not fully appreciated) apart from its place within a totality of paintings. Merleau-Ponty's closing comments in the essay indicate that he regards the relation of a painter to the overall tradition of painting to be quite different from that of a writer to his tradition: a painter rivals his predecessors; a writer takes up the universal task of a total accumulation of truth.[72] There is, again, a sedimentation in language, a reprise of its history necessary for each renewal, which does not occur in painting.

The thought I am trying to convey, the thought that marks the difference between the two versions of the essay, the thought that brings together the apparently disparate themes of infra-referentiality and extra-referentiality is this: it is its infra-referentiality, its diacritical nature, that marks the relative difference between language and painting and grants language the privilege of totalizing, of sedimenting its acquisitions, and thereby making a greater claim to truth. But truth requires extra-referentiality: speech and writing, if true, are true *about* something, ultimately about the world. The point is that language can refer to the world in its own unique way because it refers to itself in its own unique way. Despite the appearance of conflict between them, infra-referentiality and extra-referentiality are correlates.[73]

With this thought a host of others falls into place. First in order of magnitude is the reconciliation, indeed interdependence, of the immanent aspect of language (the universe within constituted by infra-referentiality)[74] and its transcendent aspects (its origination within and ultimate return to the perceived world, its extra-referentiality). This means that one can do full justice to one aspect without denying or ignoring the other; that is, one can avoid the reduction to immanence characteristic of post-hermeneutic skepticism and semeiological reductionism. In second place, the problems of origination, learning, and communication which seemed insurmountable if language is conceived as closed in on itself now can be resolved by recourse to the reference to a communal world precluded by the thesis of linguistic immanence. Other, less obvious, points might also be made, but this is not the time to catalogue gains, because the account is not fully rendered.

The correlation of infra-referentiality and extra-referentiality requires a development beyond the *Fundierung* model of language because that model tends to ignore infra-referentiality, to presuppose it without explicating how the two moments interdepend. For this reason, "Indirect Language and the Voices of Silence" remains a transitional work, for it still depends on the concept of *Fundierung* (or *Stiftung*) to correlate the immanent dimension of language with the transcendent, what "comes from" within and what "comes from" without (S 58–59; S-F 73–74). The transition from the *Fundierung* model to the reversibility model, or the incorporation of the former within the latter, is certainly foreshadowed in this period, as is evident in the following quotation from *The Prose of the World*.

> It is true that language is founded, as Sartre says, but not on an apperception; it is founded on the phenomenon of the mirror, ego–alter ego, or the echo, in other words, of a carnal generality: what warms me, warms him; it is founded on the magical action of like upon like (the *warm* sun *gives warmth* to me), on the fusion of me embodied—and the world. This foundation does not prevent language from coming back dialectically over what preceded it and transforming the purely carnal and vital coexistence with the world and bodies into a coexistence with language. (PW 20n; PW-F 29n)

The evolution of the *Fundierung* model into the reversibility model is not yet complete in this passage, but the transition has clearly begun. Two aspects of this transition should be highlighted. As indicated above, during this phase of his thought, Merleau-Ponty is attempting to correlate a theory of truth with a theory of intersubjectivity, and the *Fundierung* model of language is the medium of this correlation. Truth is founded in language through the moment of expression, but expression is now being reconceived under the heading of communication (that is, under the heading of intersubjectivity), whereas previously expression had been understood primarily as a thematization of the tacit cogito (that is, as an outward manifestation of the prereflective contact of self with self which is the correlate of any cognition of the world). The development of the intersubjective foundations of expression portends no radical shift in Merleau-Ponty's thinking. As explained above (chapter 6, 1), the tacit cogito is not sheer interiority; corporeal reflexivity is always mediated through other persons and the world. This thought is now correlated with Merleau-Ponty's emergent understanding of language: thus, my cognition of the world is now seen as mediated through an act of expression which is a contact with others. Expression is founded on communication; I discover my truths by seeing them mirrored in others. A thought, a way of seeing things, a truth—as Saussure says—is nebulous until it is formulated in language; now it is clearer why this is so: when my groping words awaken a recognition in others, when words come to fill my significative intention and communicate it to another, something is established which then has life of its own and becomes more visible to me. A cultural object is born which mirrors my existence in the eyes of another and allows that inchoate existence to realize itself for itself. The cultural object, founded as it is upon the world, has density and depth: it admits of exploration and elaboration as its relations to other cultural objects—equally founded upon the world, hence always already caught up in that matrix—become thematized.

The second aspect of the transition to the reversibility model requiring comment has to do with a movement from specificity to generality. In the specific context of communication, reversibility is conceived as a relation of self and other or ego and alter-ego: carnal generality here refers only to the flesh of human bodies. When, in *The Visible and the Invisible* reversibility is extended beyond the human domain, the element of flesh acquires a generality that encompasses the full range of phenomena; flesh becomes conceived as the flesh of the world. This move toward generality is required to overcome the subject or consciousness orientation which Merleau-Ponty regarded as the major flaw in his earlier work. Instead of constructing a theory of truth about the world in correlation with a theory of intersubjectivity, Merleau-Ponty now proposes to base both on an ontology. As I have attempted to show, however, this move should be understood as a fulfillment or acknowledgment of the implications of the long-standing theses of the epistemological primacy of perception and the ontological primacy of phenomena.

The question that impels Merleau-Ponty to explicate his ontology, to interrogate the implicit and render it explicit, is, above all others, the question of the locus of truth. Through the earlier works, we have traced a movement in which the locus of truth has shifted from the tacit cogito or individual existence through communication and expression to intersubjective existence. But, although truth is always grounded in a reference to the world which remains its origin and measure, it has been conceived as located somehow apart from the world in the domain of consciousness or the sphere of the (individual, then collective) subject. The meaning that we take from the world in expression and project back into it through sedimentation becomes somehow detached from the world in the process. The detachment is never conceived as a separation: the logos of the perceived world is refracted in the emergent logos of language, but language remains a corporeal, that is, worldly, phenomenon. Still, the coherent deformation that takes place in this refraction implies a difference between the world and the world "according to man." What we express in creative uses of language is a perspective upon the world. These perspectives are collected in the sedimentation of culture. Thus the palimpsest of sedimented language is a history of human truth. This is the insight of the *Fundierung* model. However, the very referentiality of language which is required to ground its claim to truth introduces an incipient dualism between perspective and culture, between nature and man. The union of fact and reason, announced in the thesis of autochthonous organization and the doctrine of matter-pregnant-with-form, is threatened by the detachment that takes place when language transforms the world into its truth and converts things into their meanings. Latent in these formulations are the vestiges of the transcendental subject and the transcendent world.

These vestiges, once recognized and acknowledged, call for an ontological critique. They call for supercession in a refined ontology capable of preserving the difference required for reference and truth, the difference between language and world, but they require that difference to be conceived in a way that does not vitiate truth by encysting it within systems of signs that have lost contact with the world and can no longer point to anything but themselves.

5. REVERSIBILITY AND LANGUAGE

The primary task of twentieth-century philosophy is to think the thought that will supersede ontological dualism. *The Visible and the Invisible* names the task in its title: it is the task of thinking the 'and.' "The visible" refers to more than perceptual objects and "the invisible" refers to more than thoughts or ideas, but that 'more' can be bracketed for the moment to allow a general characterization of the work. How are thought *and* thing, perceptual object *and* idea, world *and* meaning to be brought together into a *universe* that encompasses them both without contradiction, but holds them far enough apart to allow for the referentiality upon which the possibility of truth and falsity depends? Our century has given its answer: it has named the place of the 'and' as language: ideas and objects come together in words or signs. Language is now more than the medium of philosophical discourse, it is its sanctuary.

But language is only the beginning of an answer. A good beginning, I think, but no more than that—or even less—until the how of language's magical healing is understood. Thought and thing come together in language. Dualism has been overcome. And we are free now to exult in our medium. We have found the *tertium quid*. There, exactly there, is the problem: we now have a third thing. We have forgotten Occam's advice and indulged in the proliferation of entities. As long as the how of language's healing remains magical, we shall have succeeded only in compounding the problem of the rift between thought and thing by adding another rift: the one that isolates language from everything else. So long as we discourse only about discourse, so long as we install ourselves within language and refuse on principle to consider its place in the universe which gave it birth and continues to nurture it, so long, in short, as we continue to ignore the ontological question that brought language into prominence in this century, we shall have succeeded only in postponing our future instead of stepping into it.

Language, it is said, embodies culture. But there is a history of culture which must move forward since we are able to read it backward. Were the circle of linguistic immanence truly impermeable, there would be no history of culture. Fortune, however, dictates otherwise, and the new Eleaticism will impede growth no more successfully than did the old.

Merleau-Ponty is one of those who see beyond the circle and perceive the life of language among the things that feed it.

> Language is a life, is our life and the life of things. Not that *language* [*le langage*] takes possession of life and reserves it for itself: what would there be to say if there existed nothing but things said? It is the error of semantic philosophies[75] to close up language as if it spoke only of itself: language lives only from silence; everything we cast to the others has germinated in this great mute land which we never leave. (VI 125–26; VI-F 167)

There would, indeed, be nothing to say (at least, nothing new) if nothing existed but things said: philosophy in this mode would become a glass bead game like Hesse's in which virtuosity results in recognition but no accomplishment. What would it be to master language—and nothing else? It would be an impossibility: for to understand language is to understand what language is about. Those blind from birth may speak cogently about colors, but it would be a mistake to assume that they truly understand what they say.

So—language is grounded: language originates in the world and refers ultimately to the world. Beyond what we say, there is always "the mute experience from which we draw what we say" (VI 88; VI-F 121). To speak of language, then, we begin with its ground.[76] And we return to the ground. But something happens in between. Expression takes place and founds another world, a world of meaning. The perceptual world, the visible world, is now doubled in the world of ideas, the invisible world.

Now there are two worlds. But these are not the two worlds of classical dualism because they are related rather than mutually exclusive. The invisible world mirrors the visible world upon which it is founded. By tracing the *Fundierung* relation, we have seen expression as the picking out or gathering of something to say of something (τò λέγειν) which then becomes sedimented as a cultural acquisition, a meaning. Things become converted into their meanings in a process which has some resemblance to Aquinas's *conversio ad phantasma*, but here the intelligible species is conveyed by language as the medium of the active intellect. With language, we do something to the world that makes it intelligible and thereby changes it.

We do something to the world with language. Subject transforms object with instrument. This is the language of traditional ontology: immanence, transcendence, and mediation. And that is a problem that must be addressed.

There is another problem requiring attention. The discussion of the *Fundierung* relation addressed the question of truth without considering its correlate, falsity. In *The Visible and the Invisible* (as throughout his work), Merleau-Ponty subsumes questions of truth and falsity under the general heading of partiality.[77] In an earlier discussion of this subject (chapter 5, 1 above), partiality was conceived as an attribute of phenomena, a manner in which their temporality unfolds, and as an earmark of their reality or transcendence. Over against the partiality of phenomenal unfolding, there is the idea of totality, an idea which has an experiential base. What makes us dissatisfied with the partiality that is consequent upon temporality and finitude, and draws us toward the ideal of full adequation, is "the prepossession of a totality which is there before one knows how and why, whose realizations are never what we would have imagined them to be, and which nonetheless fulfills a secret expectation within us, since we believe in it tirelessly" (VI 42; VI-F 65–66). This prepossession is, of course, an aspect of the perceptual faith; it is, specifically, that horizonal sense of the world's style, the manner in which it presents itself as a totality enveloping every partial unfolding, a totality which grounds our ideal of objectivity or full adequation, and thereby orients us toward truth.

It has been characteristic of transcendental philosophy since Kant to shift the ideal of truth away from objectivity, which requires a transcendent ground, and toward intersubjectivity, which was mistakenly conceived to be achievable within the sphere of immanence. This tendency, as noted earlier, is particularly evident in the work of Husserl. And it is characteristic of Merleau-Ponty to seek to preserve the insights of both models by eliminating the polarization that conceives them as mutually exclusive. As I have sought to show, intersubjective accord requires a transcendent ground (to mediate conflicts in perspective) and objectivity requires intersubjective accord (as a measure of its validity). How this mediation and measuring take place brings us back to the theme of language and the problem mentioned above.

The threats to perceptual faith are illusion[78] and perspective or intersubjective variation. It is the latter that concerns us here. It is through the variation or differences in individual perspective that one is forced to an awareness of the partiality, hence relative falsity, of one's naive belief in the objectivity or truth of his view of the world. At the level of perceptual faith we are unreflective, hence unaware that our view is but a view: awareness of perspective occurs at the level of reflection. The problem of truth now becomes a problem of reconciling individual differences, and this endeavor generates the ideal of universality. The ideal of universality, as Merleau-Ponty realized when testing the parallel of the linguistic arts and painting, is a telos inherent in the basic project of speech and expression (PP 391–92; PP-F 448–49). It is not the case that universality resides in an eidetic language prior to the existing languages that imperfectly realize it; it is rather the case that universality, intersubjective concordance, lies in front of existing languages as the telos that draws them forward.[79]

That language embodies that telos has been a constant thesis in Merleau-Ponty's thought, but *how* it approximates that goal does not get explained until the last writings, the ones that announce the theme of reversibility and the project of articulating its underlying ontology.

Here, then, we arrive at the nexus of the problematic. There are the two problems—the problem of transcending the language of dualism and the problem of coordinating truth and intersubjectivity—and there is the emergent ontology with its refinement of the *Fundierung* model into the reversibility model. How Merleau-Ponty deploys the latter in his approach to the former: this is the concluding task to which I now turn.

Let us begin with a transitional idea, the idea of dialectic. In Hegel, as in Merleau-Ponty,[80] dialectic is the process of reconciling differences and moving from partiality to universality, that is, toward truth. Dialectic also performs an essential ontological function for both philosophers, since it effects the mediation of in-itself and for-itself. Thus dialectic addresses both of the problems before us.[81]

But what is dialectic? Dialectic is not, for Merleau-Ponty, what it was for Hegel and Sartre. He criticizes Hegelian and Sartrean dialectics on the grounds that (a) they superimpose a purely formal structure on experience (instead of attending to the mutable formations which are immanent within the matter of experience and emerge amidst the contingency of history), and (b) they polarize the terms in dialectical tension by conceiving them through an external logic of negation (instead of conceiving that tension as an ambiguous dynamic, a process of change through time in which concrete differences overcome themselves precisely because the differences impede an inherent telos of unity at work from the start). The idea Merleau-Ponty regards as crucial to "good dialectic" or "hyperdialectic" is "the profound idea of *self-mediation,* of a movement through which each term ceases to be itself in order to become itself, breaks up, opens up, negates itself in order to realize itself" (VI 92; VI-F 126). This description of dialectical self-mediation resonates with earlier descriptions of expression as the process through which things are converted into their meanings: both are processes of change, but change which, rather than altering the character of things, results in things realizing themselves and fulfilling a promise implicit in their earlier identities.

Still, this is metaphorical and vague: what is it for something to be converted into its meaning, to cease to be itself in order to become itself? Merleau-Ponty does not provide the details, but it may be possible to extrapolate them from what he says elsewhere. Meaning is grounded in the world; there is a nascent logos of the perceived world, a logic in contingency (S 88; S-F 110); things are pregnant with meaning: these are familiar doctrines and they all point to the need for expression as the transition from pregnancy to birth, from latency to realization. In the *Phenomenology*, Merleau-Ponty suggests that the generality of worldly meaning is grounded in the typicality of the world and only later becomes the generality of the concept (PP 403; PP-F 462). In *The Prose of the World*, he says that it is the peculiarity of speech to reveal relations between things and within things (PW 140–41; PW-F 195), that is, as I interpret it, speech reveals the relations constitutive of both outer and inner horizons. Then, corresponding to the generality of the logos of the perceived world, there is Merleau-Ponty's notion of "a unity of language across languages" (CAL 88), "a concrete universality which realizes itself only gradually and finds itself treating the expressive desire [for unity] which animates languages rather than the transitory forms which are its result" (CAL 93). Finally, there is the radical thesis that "there is only, strictly speaking, a single language in development" to which Merleau-Ponty appends (in a footnote) the phrase, "existential universal, existential eternity" (PW 39; PW-F 56).

As I ponder them, these themes point to the idea of an emergent *ratio*: a rationality in things that becomes evident when it is unified in language. Or, rather, *to the extent* that it is unified in language—for both language and world are unfolding in time. This process of unification, while manifestly progressing and achieving, remains open-ended, a regulative ideal. Unity and rationality: these terms have been correlates since the time of Parmenides. What is novel in Merleau-Ponty's use of them is the reconciliation he effects with their traditional rival, Heraclitean change. Emergent unity, emergent rationality: achieved through the process of thematizing and accumulating relationships in the expression and sedimentation of language. If "speech is the vehicle of our movement toward truth" (PW 129; PW-F 181), it carries out this movement by unifying the relations evident in the world's typicality and by unifying the perspectives of the particular individuals inhabiting the world. But these two moments are not separate and distinct: the unification of perspectives both presupposes a unitary world as a basis for reconciliation and furthers that unification in the movement toward objectivity, that is, in the movement toward the ideal of an impartial logos. Hence, it is through the mediation of language, of expression and sedimentation, that Merleau-Ponty demonstrates the inner relation of truth and intersubjectivity.

But this mediation is not yet dialectical, not yet self-mediation, and it is still cast in the ontologically ambivalent language of subjectivity and perspective. The thought that is needed to understand Merleau-Ponty's hyperdialectic, and shed the vestiges of traditional ontology, is that of reversibility. The basic idea, explicated earlier (chapter 9, 2 above), is that of the flesh of the world folding back on itself, reflecting itself, and thereby sustaining an historical process which constitutes itself as a contingently emergent *ratio*. This folding back on itself of the flesh is the self-mediation of hyperdialectic, and its privileged, but not exclusive, means is language. Understanding what this means leads us into the final phases of explication and interpretation.

The interpretation of reversibility set forth in the first division of this chapter centered on the body and its unique capacity to sense other things by sensing itself. The tacit cogito, the 'inside of thought,' was revealed to be founded on corporeality: the idea is what I know ($o\hat{\iota}\delta\alpha$); it derives from what I see ($\epsilon\check{\iota}\delta\omega$); and my seeing is dependent on my corporeal visibility as my touching is dependent upon feeling myself touched. Thus, I can think the world because I can see it, and I can see it because I am of it. But my seeing is not *my* seeing: seeing is originally prepersonal, prereflective, anonymous; hence, at this original level, the personal pronoun can be dropped. Seeing is a relation of worldly flesh to itself, the relation of reversibility, hence we no longer need treat perception "as the operation of a 'subject' in whatever sense one takes the term" (VI 23; VI-F 41). Perception is now the anonymous folding back of the flesh of the world onto itself which renders the world visible: it no longer need be conceived dualistically as a relation of immanent subjectivity to transcendent thing. This is genuinely a relation of self-mediation; and it is genuinely dialectical because the relatedness of flesh to itself, being itself the emergent phenomenon, is conceived as prior to any abstract reification of discrete relata (for example, subject and object). Nor is there an abstract or formal negation at work in this phenomenal unfolding: perception is no longer the impossible coming together of a subjective for-itself with an objective in-itself where each is conceived through the negation of the other. There is, instead, the dynamic dehiscence of flesh folding back on itself and unfolding through time. Dehiscence or *écart* is not a supervenient structure of formal, abstract negation; it is rather an emergent self-realization concretely developing in accordance with the specific character of the given phenomenon: sexual history, for example, realizes itself according to its own demands, and they are not reducible to or even isomorphic with the demands of economics.[82] Similarly, as is becoming increasingly apparent in our own time, the ecological demands of the flesh of the world are realizing themselves in ways that could not be predelineated by any dogmatic formalism. The point I am trying to establish here is that the dialectics of the reversibility of flesh permit one to conceive historical process, change, and unfolding without adopting the standpoint of an ontology which is committed to dualism because it is committed to the bifurcation of a core polarity or a fundamental formal structure centered on negation. This point coincides with the earlier one regarding perception: it is possible to do conceptual justice to both history and perception without lapsing into the framework of dualistic ontology, and Merleau-Ponty has demonstrated this with his ontology of flesh.

Still, there remains the problem of emergent intelligibility, the problem of the relations of language and phenomena, idea and flesh, the problem of the invisible significance of the visible domain of perception. Let us approach this problem by recalling that perception is always perception of a Gestalt, that is, of a meaning, of something significant. That significance is the ground of the ideality that is liberated from things by being snared in language. Yet it remains an ideality of things, a worldly ideality. "We will therefore have to recognize an ideality that is not alien to the flesh, that gives it its axes, its depth, its dimensions" (VI 152; VI-F 199). In one sense, all ideality is worldly, for there is no other source and ideas do not spring up *ex nihilo* (VI 88; VI-F 121). And, in another sense, all ideas are worldly because "they would not be given to us *as ideas* except in a carnal experience" (VI 150; VI-F 197), that is, in a perception of the world and the words spoken, written, and heard within it. Still, there is a detachability of some kind: the detachability that grounds Platonic heavens, logical entities, eidetic realms, and the like. It is this detachment of meaning from things, this conversion of things into meanings which return to enlighten them, that has to be explained.

So far, we have seen that it is language that grounds the constitution of ideality, and that the signs which inform the world are signs that originate within the world: in short, we have seen how the asymmetrical expression-sedimentation circuit of *Fundierung* accounts for the relation between visible *sens* and invisible significance. But now this account must be refined. Now the expressive act of the speaking subject must be reconceived as a prepersonal act that may be appropriated in reflection but which takes place in a kind of *ek-stasis* of the flesh. We must conceive expression as a vicissitude in the reversibility of flesh.

The two aspects of reversibility Merleau-Ponty names in the last words of *The Visible and the Invisible* describe language as being both "the expression of experience by experience" and "the voice of no one . . . , the very voice of things."[83] The task for us is to understand how it can be both, and the key to that understanding is the notion of flesh. Note that expression is not attributed to a personal agency, a subject, but rather is attributed to experience. Experience is an event in the contact of flesh with flesh, sentient flesh with flesh that may or not be sentient. Experience expresses itself in language and the language that speaks is the voice of things. Things demand expression, the world demands its song and predelineates the lyrics. There is a parallel between this genesis of ideality and the meaning that evolves in the unfolding of history.

> It is asked '*Where* is history made? Who makes it? What is this movement which traces out and leaves behind the figures of the wake?' It is of the same order as the movement of Thought and Speech, and, in short, of the perceptible world's explosion within us. Everywhere there are meanings, dimensions, and forms in excess of what each 'consciousness' could have produced; and yet it is men who speak and think and see. We are in the field of history as we are in the field of language or existence. (S 20; S-F 28)

These words are contained in the "Introduction" to *Signs* which Merleau-Ponty wrote in 1960 while he was engaged in composing *The Visible and the Invisible;* consequently, I think it is legitimate to infer that his description of Speech and Thought as "the perceptible world's explosion [*éclatement*] within us" is intended to resonate with the notion of dehiscence or *écart* that is, the fission of the flesh that produces an apparently detachable domain of meaning.

'Meaning' in English can be rendered as either *sens* or *signification* in French. Both terms are used extensively by Merleau-Ponty and, although there is no sustained convention employed, *sens* typically refers to the meaningfulness of the perceptual world, the nascent logos of things or, "wild meaning"; and *signification* refers to the meaning liberated by language. The question at hand concerns the relation of the two. On one side, they are the same because language is "the very voice of the things," and, on the other, they differ because it is "men who speak" and in speaking generate the invisible region of ideality. This sameness and difference must be thought together, not as an impossible or mystical union of contradictories, nor as irreconcilables which together constitute a reluctantly dualistic ontological difference, but rather as correlative aspects of a unitary unfolding. There is the world and there is the world according to man. The thesis of subjectivity reflectively reminds us that, for man, they must be the same; and the world itself perceptually reminds us that, even for man, they must be different: the world according to man transcends man. There is one world, one flesh: we are in it and of it; our history is its history. The unity of the world is an unremitting thesis in Merleau-Ponty which subtends all differentiations. This is familiar doctrine.

What is strange, what stresses our understanding, is the thesis that attempts to think the sameness and difference in one thought: the thesis of reversibility. With reversibility Merleau-Ponty attempts to think the how of the relation of visible things and invisible ideas. This thinking is philosophy: "philosophy is the reconversion of silence and speech into one another" (VI 129; VI-F 171), or again, "philosophy is the perceptual faith questioning itself about itself" which is necessary "because the existing world exists in the interrogative mode" (VI 103; VI-F 139). We interrogate the world: the world questions itself through us: these statements are exchangeable because we are as much world as are trees and mountains, because our doing is as much the world's transformation of itself as is the carving of a canyon by a river or the implosion of a red giant.

But, how concretely are we to think the transformation of the world that takes place when language converts things into their meanings? The words that constitute the answer to this question are known, but what is the meaning of 'the reversibility of the flesh'? The clue to the meaning sought here is the body. (The body as lived, not the words 'the body' written here: without the first, the second have no meaning.) We have already seen that the body in its gestural function provides the conceptual space for an answer to the question of language origins. We have also seen the role of the body, as seer-seen or sentient-sensible, in the development of the concept of reversibility. Now we turn once again to the body in search of a better understanding of the enigma of expression and how it is illumined by the reversibility of flesh.

Throughout the course of his interrogation of language, Merleau-Ponty recurrently draws an analogy between body and language. In *Consciousness and the Acquisition of Language*, for example, he writes that "language functions with respect to thought as the body does with respect to perception" (CAL 91–92). Here Merleau-Ponty is still (1949) caught up in the categories of consciousness and subjectivity, but the analogy

language : thought :: body : perception

is not limited to that framework. Two years later, this analogy is expanded in the section of "On the Phenomenology of Language" entitled "The quasi-*corporeality*[84] of the signifying" where Merleau-Ponty uses the notion of corporeal intentionality to explicate how "language ... effects the mediation between my as yet unspeaking intention and words ... in such a way that my spoken words surprise me myself and teach me my thought" (S 88–89; S-F 110–11): expression is not a reflective 'I think,' but an 'I can' grounded in bodily intentionality.

When Merleau-Ponty undertakes the project of *The Visible and the Invisible*, the body-language analogy is enriched with the notions of flesh and reversibility. There is, he writes, a question as to how flesh, our flesh and the flesh of things, "by a sort of folding back" exhibits "a visibility, a possibility that is not the shadow of the actual but its principle," how one passes from extension to thought (which are "the obverse and reverse of one another"), how or "by what miracle a created generality, a culture, a knowledge come to add to and recapture and rectify the natural generality of my body and of the world" (VI 152; VI-F 199–200). The question is left as a question: "It is now too soon to clarify this surpassing that does not leave its field of origin" (VI 153; VI-F 200), but the form of an answer is given.[85]

Let us only say that the pure ideality is itself not without flesh nor freed from horizon structures: it lives of them, though they be another flesh and other horizons. It is as though the visibility that animates the sensible world were to emigrate, not outside of every body, but into another less heavy, more transparent body, as though it were to change flesh, abandoning the flesh of the body for that of language. (VI 153; VI-F 200)

There are other steps remaining in the development of the analogy, but it might be well to pause and consider what has been presented so far. First, note that the thesis of the primacy of perception remains in full force: ideality is derived from visibility and remains tied to it, never achieving complete emancipation from the flesh or purity of spirit. Note also that meaning is founded, that worldly *sens* remains the foundation of the *significations* of language. And, in the third place, note that although the passage from the visible to the ideal involves a detachment from the flesh of things it nonetheless remains attached to another flesh, the flesh of words (that is, signifiers of some kind): ideas are bound always to carnality. I stress these points to reinforce my claim that Merleau-Ponty's execution of the linguistic turn is continuous with his earlier standpoint, that he does not abandon his phenomenological ontology for one predicated on an ontological or epistemological ultimacy of signs.

The next step in the development of the body-language analogy is to elaborate the structure of reversibility that constitutes its *ratio*.

Just as my body sees only because it is a part of the visible in which it opens forth, the sense upon which the arrangement of sounds opens reflects back upon that arrangement. . . . As also, if my words have a meaning, it is not *because* they present the systematic organization the linguist will disclose, it is because that organization, like the look, refers back to itself. As there is a reversibility of the seeing and the visible, and as at the point where the two metamorphoses cross what we call perception is born, so also there is a reversibility of the speech and what it signifies; the signification is what comes to seal, to close, to gather up the multiplicity of the physical, physiological, linguistic means of elocution, to contract them into one sole act, as the vision comes to complete the aesthesiological body. And, as the visible takes hold of the look which has unveiled it and which forms a part of it, the signification rebounds upon its own means. (VI 154; VI-F 201–202)

Here, in this crucial text, several strands of Merleau-Ponty's philosophy of language come together. There is an analogy between body and language, not only because both are somehow flesh, but because they both exhibit the reversibility that is definitive of flesh: as the body senses things by sensing itself (corporeal reflexivity), so an arrangement of signifiers signifies something by referring back to that very arrangement. There is a reflexivity of language that is analogous to corporeal reflexivity: just as its own reflexivity allows the body to sense things by sensing itself, so the infra-referentiality of a chain of signifiers endows it with the power of extra-referentiality, the power to refer beyond itself to the meaning of things. Such is the claim being made, but how is it to be understood? How does the organization of a chain of signifiers refer to itself and thereby refer beyond itself? This is a difficult question—one which calls for venturesome interpretation—for Merleau-Ponty says little more on the subject than I have already quoted.

Let me begin with the reminder that Merleau-Ponty privileges the domain of creative language, authentic expression, words that search out and convey a novel and elusive thought. This is where language speaks; sedimented language obscures this original speaking because its signification, being commonly available, precedes the discourse. In authentic discourse (for example, when one reads a philosopher for the first time) there is a point at which one begins to understand, when the commonplace significations of his words are coherently deformed to take on the meaning they have to acquire to unify his text, to make it comprehensible and meaningful. This falling into place of the signifiers, this *Gestaltung*, occurs for the reader as it does for the writer when the thought seeking expression succeeds in announcing itself. The words make sense only when the words make sense. This is not a mere tautology: it is the function of the words to *make* sense and they succeed in this function only when that signification returns to illumine the organization of the chain of signifiers that brought it to light. There is a paradox here which calls for thought.

What happens when a new text begins to make sense, when words that were initially connected only by juxtaposition begin to resonate with each other and display such a cohesive unity that none could be altered without disturbing the meaning of the whole? We read the text sequentially, word by word, phrase by phrase, sentence by sentence. But these elements do not acquire their proper meaning as parts until they are seen in the context of the whole that it is their purpose to convey. How, then, do we arrive at the whole—since understanding it is presupposed for the elements that convey it to perform their function?

This is the problem Merleau-Ponty addresses in the opening pages of "Indirect Language and the Voices of Silence" and, as we have seen, he argues there that extra-referentiality (the meaning of the whole that refers beyond the chain of signifiers) depends upon infra-referentiality (the cohesive interrelatedness of the elements in the chain). Now we see that it works the other way as well: infra-referentiality also depends on extra-referentiality in the way that the parts of a Gestalt contexture acquire their significance *as parts* only by virtue of being seen in relation to the whole. The conclusion Merleau-Ponty draws in the essay at hand is that there is an "immanence of the whole in the parts" (S 41; S-F 51)[86] which grounds the unification. And this imminence/immanence of the whole in the parts is but another name for the Gestalt-theoretical doctrine of autochthonous organization, the automatic falling into place of the parts that compose a Gestalt.

The doctrine of auto-organization, explicated in chapter two above, is rich with implication. It is the basis of Merleau-Ponty's solution to the problem of organization generated by perceptual atomism, and it is also the basis of his claim that the world horizon is the ultimate context of understanding and thereby functions as the ideal toward which finite cognition strives. But what concerns us here is its role in the body-language analogy, and specifically its relation to the thesis of the reversibility of flesh. The analogy between body and language is grounded in the reversibility that allows both of them to resonate with the world in the generation of meaning: it is worldly *sens* which is reflected in the signification of both body and language. Intentionality is incarnate in both body and language. In one case, Merleau-Ponty speaks of corporeal intentionality; in the other, he speaks of the significative intention. In both cases the intention, the process of apprehending/constituting meaning, is grounded in a response to the world, and in both cases the meaning taken from the world returns to the world to inform it. This is the circuit of expression and sedimentation, but now it is conceived as a relation of flesh to itself rather than as a relation of consciousness to thing.

The aboriginal expression is the gesture, a bodily response to worldly meaning which gathers parts of the world into a unity, and their *Gestaltung* makes sense only because the parts were imminently/immanently a whole. But that unity is now available through the gestures to another. If it is recognized—which recognition presupposes the other's apprehension of that unity in the world's autochthonous organization—if it is acknowledged and corroborated by the other, it is on the way toward institution, already functioning as the concurrence on which community is founded. Yet, founding that instituted concurrence presupposes a prior concurrence: the incipient communality grounded in bodily isomorphism, generality of bodily needs and praxis, and transfer of corporeal schema—all of which are present in primitive form among the higher primates.

The evolution of conventional language from primitive gesticulation, as depicted in diagram [A] of section 2 above, involves the increasing separation of sound/mark/signifier from meaning/signified. But that detachment is never complete: the sign never loses its corporeality; its flesh is another body which is "less heavy" and "more transparent," yet nonetheless worldly flesh. The sign can signify only because it is flesh and because it refers ultimately to the world which remains its origin and final measure. To attempt to detach world and language, to sever the bond of life between them, and to assume that the latter can digest the former without leaving a trace of its nutrition is to perpetuate the hybris of the *Geist* that has long sought in vain to be self-sufficient and immortal.

The text (VI 154; VI-F 201–202) quoted at length some pages back is crucial in yet another way: it provides an answer to what Ricoeur calls "the challenge of semeiology." Ricoeur:

> A renewed phenomenology of meaning cannot be content with repeating descriptions of speech which do not acknowledge the theoretical status of linguistics and the primacy of structure over process which serves as an axiom for linguistics.[87]

Structure, in this context, is held (by structuralists) not only to be prior to process (that is, speech), but also to be autonomous: "It is scientifically legitimate to describe language as being essentially an autonomous entity composed of internal dependencies, in a word, a structure."[88] Ricoeur's objection to Merleau-Ponty's phenomenology of speech is that "it rushes past the objective science of signs and moves too quickly to speech" ("Question," p. 247) instead of "patiently [disentangling] semantics from semeiology" and then building "the level of the utterance on the phonological, lexical, and syntactical levels" ("Question," p. 253).

There are several flaws in Ricoeur's hasty interpretation of Merleau-Ponty—including his characterization of sedimentation in terms of "the old psychological notion of *habitus*" ("Question," p. 249)—but the one that is relevant here is apparent in his demand that the semeiological function (which he characterizes as "opposing sign to sign") be patiently disentangled from the semantic function ("representing the real by signs") ("Question," p. 252). As I have just demonstrated, for Merleau-Ponty, these two functions are interdependent and cannot be disentangled. Semeiological infrareferentiality depends upon semantical extra-referentiality, and *vice versa*. Ricoeur fastens on Merleau-Ponty's early phenomenology of the speaking subject and completely ignores the culmination of that line of thought in the later works. He refers only to the *Phenomenology* and *Signs*; *The Visible and the Invisible* is not cited, the central thesis of reversibility is not mentioned, and the displacement of the subject by Merleau-Ponty is left unremarked in an essay devoted to that subject.

Ricoeur's challenge prompts James Edie to voice a query of his own (in his "Foreward" to *Consciousness and the Acquisition of Language*).

> The question which we are forced to address to Merleau-Ponty is whether his theory of language, which seems to be exclusively concerned with *words* as they occur in concrete acts of usage, does justice to the role of syntax in the production of meaning and, secondly, what the relation of syntax (if it is given a status independent of *la parole*) is to speech acts. (CAL xxxii)

Edie allows that an answer might be given from "within the resources of [Merleau-Ponty's] own thought" (CAL xxxii) and I think it would be appropriate to attempt such an answer here. The point at stake, once again, is that syntax is not independent of speech, nor is speech autonomous with respect to syntax. Syntax, "the systematic *organization*" of words disclosed by the linguist, is inseparable from the *words* organized, as the organization or structure of the whole is inseparable from its parts. Where Merleau-Ponty differs from the structural linguist lies not in any neglect of syntax, but rather in his denial that it is prior to originating, expressive speech. The autonomy of syntax is a misconception arising from the assumption that the sedimented language is the whole of language. The point here is that the so-called laws of syntax are culled out of sedimented language after the fact of its institution in expression, and even then are subject to transformation depending upon changes in usage which are themselves "lawful" only in retrospect and impossible to predict (hence are not lawful in the sense of being obedient to the laws of science). There is, however, another sense in which all of speech, including expressive speech, is lawful: it is lawful not because it is always responsive to law (that is true only of sedimented speech), but because in its originating act it is legislative: it institutes the laws of usage and does so in response to the demand of wild meaning, that is, in response to the demand of the world to be sung anew. Expression is certainly attuned to syntax—"the *arrangement* of sounds" or written signifiers is crucial in the disclosure of meaning—but that attunement is not bound by former usage: if it were, novel transformations could not occur, nothing new could be said, and any attempt to account for the genesis of syntactical rules would have to be abandoned in favor of some form of nativism (which, indeed, is the posture to which structuralism is committed).

To conclude this discussion of the body-language analogy and bring the chapter to a close, let us turn to one further text in which those strands of this complex discourse which are still loose may be woven together.

> Like the flesh of the visible . . . speech is a relation to Being through a being, and like it, it is narcissistic, eroticized, endowed with a natural magic that attracts the other significations into its web, as the body feels the world in feeling itself. *In reality there is much more than a parallel or an analogy here, there is solidarity and intertwining.* . . . No longer are there essences above us, like positive objects, offered to a spiritual eye; but there is an essence beneath us, *a common nervure*[89] *of the signifying [signifiant] and the signified [signifié], adherence and reversibility of one another*—as the visible things are the secret folds of our flesh, and yet our body is one of the visible things. (VI 118; VI-F 158)

Speech is a relation to Being through a being. The being is the chain of signifiers; what then is Being? Speaking in another but similar context, Merleau-Ponty characterizes the level of the idea as "the invisible *of* this world, that which inhabits this world, sustains it, and renders it visible, its own and interior possibility, the Being of this being" (VI 151; VI-F 198). So: speech is a relation to ideality through a chain of signifiers, and the ideality inhabits the world and renders it visible. Speech is the body of thought. But now the body-language analogy is strengthened: more than analogues for each other, body and language intertwine, that is, they are reversible. What does this mean?

The analogy we have been considering is this—

body : perception :: language : thought.

The ground or *ratio* of the analogy is reversibility; the relation of body and perception and the relation of language and thought are analogous because the relation in both cases is the relation of reversibility. At the end of the passage quoted, Merleau-Ponty asserts that the reversibility relation obtains between two other terms that figure significantly in this discourse: signifier [*signifiant*] and signified [*signifié*]. Hence, we can extend the analogy as follows—

body : perception :: language : thought ::
signifier : signified :: being : Being.

In each case, the relation uniting the dyads is the relation of reversibility, reversibility in one of its vicissitudes. It would be a mistake, as I argued in the first division of this chapter, to understand the central term—reversibility—in a univocal way. The usage is deliberately homonymous or, better, ambiguous. The reversibility of one hand touching another is not identical to the reversibility of touch and vision. Yet, if they are not isomorphic, they are at least homologous: the point of extending the analogy is that we learn something more about the original dyads by adding the new ones. The relation of signifier to signified is that of reversibility. So is the relation of self to other (as is evident in the transfer of corporeal schema, the projection and introjection of negative and positive traits, etc.). And this analogical juxtaposition of

signifier : signified :: self : other

illumines the nature of communication (see chapter 7 and chapter 9, 3 above). However, there can be no question of reducing the relations obtaining in one dyad to these obtaining in another: that would be an empty formalism, indeed, and would overlook the emergent nature of the logos that is embodied in "the profound idea of self-mediation" (VI 92; VI-F 126), and the "plurality of relationships" constituting the essential ambiguity of Merleau-Ponty's hyperdialectic (VI 94; VI-F 129).

Notwithstanding this ambiguity of reversibility which results from the range of its vicissitudes, there is a constant that needs, finally, to be stressed: in all cases, the reversibility relation obtains within the folding back on itself of one flesh. That is the ontologically consequential thought. There is one flesh, the flesh of the world, which manifests itself in manifold ways from the sentient to the nonsentient, from silence to speech, from the mundane to the symbolic, that is, throughout the plenitude of phenomenal unfolding. This is Merleau-Ponty's response to the bifurcations of dualist thought: not simply to assert a monism of the phenomenon in an act of dogmatic contention, but rather to show how the bifurcated domains, collected now under the comprehensive titles of visible and invisible, can be healed without rendering them static and impermeable There is dehiscence, *écart*, difference in the distancing of my body from anothers, in the divergence of the signified from the signifier that sustains it, in the isolation of a being from the Being which encompasses it—but in all these cases the reversibility of the terms grounds an intertwining that makes them interdependent rather than mutually exclusive and gathers them in the folds of the flesh of one world.

It is in this sense that the body-language analogy is more than analogy; moreover, it is in this sense that all the analogues named are more than analogues. The solidarity that is constituted by their intertwining is the solidarity of the interrelatedness of all things within the unity of one world seeking to express itself in a single language.

Here is the truth of the philosophies of linguistic immanence which is obscured by their misguided reductionism. That truth is the ideal of a single language, a single chain of signifiers, capable of encompassing the totality of Being, the totality of the signified. What is misguided in their manner of thinking this ideal is to conceive it as behind us, as though all there could ever be were predelineated in language—whereas, if Merleau-Ponty is right, just the reverse in this case.

> In a sense, if we were to make completely explicit the architectonics of the human body, its ontological framework, and how it sees itself and hears itself, we would see that the structure of its mute world is such that all the possibilities of language are already given in it. (VI 155; VI-F 203)

The point is that the single language is before us as the ideal that draws us into speech, communication, and the attempt to overcome particular differences in the movement toward a universal truth. This truth is, indeed, predelineated, not in language, but in its ground, origin, and measure—the world it seeks always to approximate in its song. Nor is this vacuous, wild-eyed, book-ending lyric: the point follows strictly from the asymmetrical reversibility of signifier and signified. The chain of signifiers derives its significance, its inner cohesion, its meaningfulness from the autochthonous organization of the world to which it refers. Its infra-referentiality derives from its extra-referentiality: a chain of signifiers can make sense only if the world to which it ultimately refers is sensible. Granted, it illumines that world, articulates it, institutes its meaning,[90] and founds its truth—but it does not create that truth; it only lets it be seen.

In the beginning, there was the world.

Conclusion

Abyss and Logos

> As a matter of principle, fundamental
> thought [*la pensée fondamentale*] is bottom-
> less. It is, if you wish, an abyss.
> (S 21; S-F 29).

What is this abyss that ungrounds contemporary Continental thought and subtends post-hermeneutic pessimism? We inherited it from Heidegger—who found it in Nietzsche. The earliest progenitor I can find is Anaximander's τὸ ἄπειρον (which arrives after the cosmogonical idea of χάος reported by Hesiod and differs significantly from it), although it might be more accurate to seek the abyss beneath the totality of human efforts at cognition—as the motivation of that effort and its sustaining force.

1. NIETZSCHE

[The hermit] will doubt whether a philosopher could *possibly* have "ultimate and real" opinions, whether behind every one of his caves there is not, must not be, another deeper cave—a more comprehensive, stranger, richer world beyond the surface, an abysmally deep ground behind every ground, under every attempt to furnish "grounds" [*ein Abgrund hinter jedem Grunde, unter jeder "Begründen"*].[1]

What is this *Abgrund* Nietzsche projected behind every ground? Alphonso Lingis finds chaos. Quoting the passage above, he writes:

What could function as ground—as ratio and as foundation—for the order of essences is the stability of ultimate unity, is God or the transcendental ego, both of which Nietzsche declares to be dead. The Will to Power is an abyss [*Abgrund*], the groundless chaos beneath all the grounds, all the foundations, and it leaves the whole order of essences groundless.[2]

Here, at the beginning of his essay on Nietzsche's will to power, Lingis takes up the currently standard[3] interpretation of the Nietzschean abyss. According to this interpretation, there can be but one ground, one kind of ground: an absolute ground. The proper name of this ground is 'God' and 'transcendental ego' is its recently revealed cognomen. Nietzsche is the one who confronts us with the death of God and seeks to dispel all the illusions that have covertly nurtured themselves on His name and our desire for that antidote to finitude. Thus Nietzsche forces us to awareness of the abyss beneath our feet, the abyss that betrays the illusory Being of all grounds.

Under this interpretation, Nietzsche's abyss is easily understood: it is the absolute negation of the absolute. It is non-God: sheer absence in the place of the plenitude of presence. 'God and abyss,' thus, names a binary opposition—which induces us to take sides: theism or atheism, onto-theology or nihilism, metaphysics or anti-metaphysics.

Is this abyss Nietzsche's abyss? Or has it overlooked the rope? "Man is a rope, tied between beast and overman—a rope over an abyss."[4] Zarathustra is here expounding the doctrine of overman. Who is Zarathustra's overman?

> The overman is the meaning of the earth. Let your will say: the overman *shall be* the meaning of the earth! I beseech you, my brothers, *remain faithful to the earth* . . .
> Once the sin against God was the greatest sin; but God died, and those sinners died with him. To sin against the earth is now the most dreadful thing, and to esteem the entrails of the unknowable higher than the meaning of the earth.[5]

The overman is the meaning of the earth. Does the overman take his meaning from the earth or does the earth derive its meaning from the overman? For Nietzsche, the answer must be: not either but both. An exclusive disjunction would force upon Nietzsche a dilemma—naive realism or unmotivated transcendental constitution—both of whose lemmas he has explicitly attacked and repudiated. The overman is neither a philosopher of Nature nor a metaphysically comfortizing Apollonian dreamer. The overman is a Dionysian participant in the tragedy of his finitude who seeks the truth of his own condition, and thereby changes it. The overman is the meaning of the earth, and the meaning he gives to the earth is the meaning he has drawn from it. The overman is faithful to the earth: the earth is what he esteems rather than the unknowable God above it—or the equally unknowable void that would be beneath it were the earth to have no meaning or value.

The spontaneous assertion of meaning grounded in sheer nothingness is the prerogative of an unthinkable divinity. And humans who, despairing of God, set out to manufacture meaning from the void—those who undertake the project of unmotivated transcendental constitution—are deceiving themselves. Their self-deception consists in a refusal of finitude: a wilful denial of their own need/desire/motivation, its grounding in the earth and flesh, and the world's obtrusion into autistic fantasy. These are the all-too-human; they are unfaithful to the earth; their project is not to be confused with that of the overman.

Nietzsche was too earthly to pronounce the death of God only to give birth to his shadow, to replace absolute light with absolute darkness, to elevate and preserve the thesis by asserting the antithesis. The thought which Nietzsche attempted to think in a radical and consistent way was the thought of becoming—and this is a thought that lies beyond the impossible dialectics of Being and non-Being. What, then, is Nietzsche's abyss?

The symbol of the abyss shares with all symbols the character of over-determination; hence it would be a mistake to search for univocity. The etymology of the term, especially in German, suggests the basic metaphor of groundlessness. The question raised by the arguments just set forth is that of the character of this groundlessness. Lingis is, I think, correct in maintaining that Nietzsche repudiated all theological senses of ground—including the covertly theological sense of grounding employed by Kant in his appeal to the transcendental unity of apperception.[6] However, the denial of an absolute ground is not equivalent to the absolute denial of all grounds.

Unless, of course, one tacitly assents to the postulate that it is *essential* to the notion of ground or foundation that it be absolute. This postulate informed Kant's thinking as it informs the thought of all those who posit apodicticity as a criterion for philosophical verity.[7] And, given the evidence and arguments presented above, I think it is valid to infer that this postulate informs the interpretation of Nietzsche currently in vogue. But, by 1886,[8] it is evident that Nietzsche has begun to challenge this postulate. Indeed, in such recurrent Nietzschean doctrines as overman and his fidelity to the earth, I find a deliberate attempt on Nietzsche's part to think the thought of finite, non-absolute grounds.

Finite truths are grounded in the kinds of evidence available to finite minds. Such evidence is never complete, never perfect, although it admits of degrees of adequacy.[9] The inevitability of a future implies the unfolding of new evidence and, thereby, the possibility that accepted truths will have to be modified. Reflection on this gives rise to cognitive anxiety. One symbol for this anxiety is the symbol of the abyss. This essentially negative symbol has a positive correlate in Nietzsche's thought: the symbol of overman, the one to whom the rope over the abyss leads, the one who symbolizes the greater truths grounded in the evidence of future unfolding, the one who ventures into other, deeper caves in search of "a more comprehensive, stranger, richer world beyond the surface" of his own present opinions. To be sure, that stranger, richer world will also be a world of becoming and, as such, offer grounds only for further opinion: this anxious reflection is the abyss, the "*Abgrund hinter jedem Grunde, unter jeder 'Begründen.'*"

2. HEIDEGGER

The meaning of Being can never be contrasted with beings [*Seienden*], or with Being as the "ground" which gives beings support; for *a "ground" becomes accessible only as meaning*, even if it is itself the abyss of meaninglessness [*der Abgrund der Sinnlosigkeit*][10]

Here, in *Being and Time* (1927), grounding is conceived as an activity carried out by Dasein: any ground posited by Dasein is necessarily a ground interpreted within the context of Dasein's understanding, hence is relativized to that standpoint. Given the ontology of *Being and Time*, that is, fundamental ontology,[11] all grounds are *meanings* mediated by the existential structures (*Existenzialen*) of Dasein. Two years later (1929), Heidegger elaborated his standpoint on the question of grounds and the abyss as follows.

> Grounds have their un-reason [*Un-wesen*], because they arise from finite freedom; [and] the latter cannot rid itself from what arises from it. . . . *Freedom is the ground of grounds*. . . . As *this* kind of ground, however, freedom is the *abyss* of Dasein.[12]

The abyss is grounded in Dasein, specifically in its correlative structures of finitude and freedom. For any ground posited by Dasein, there is the possibility of positing another, competing ground. Given the finitude of Dasein, there can be no absolute certitude (that is, no apodicticity) in the comprehension of grounds or in the choice among competing grounds.

So far, then, there is a similarity between the thinking of Nietzsche and Heidegger on the question of *Grund* and *Abgrund*. In both cases, the abyss symbolizes cognitive insecurity with regard to the grounding of human truths. The similarity extends to the accounts they give for the origins of this insecurity: here both Nietzsche and Heidegger appeal to the finitude[13]—specifically, the temporality—of human existence. The facticity of our past, our concrete history, locates us within the framework of a flawed global understanding that has always to be reappropriated and transcended;[14] and the future necessarily opens us to the unfolding of evidence that may require modification of cherished beliefs hitherto accepted as grounded truths.

As Richardson points out,[15] however, the notion of abyss changes as Heidegger's thinking matures and takes the turn from his earlier to his later period.

In "The Origin of the Work of Art" (1935–36),[16] Heidegger writes of a rift (*Riß*) between world and earth which figures significantly in the "establishing of truth in the work [of art]."

> Truth establishes itself in the work. Truth is present only as the conflict between lighting and concealing in the opposition of world and earth. Truth wills to be established in the work as this conflict of world and earth. . . . The conflict is not a rift as a mere cleft is ripped open; rather, it is the intimacy with which opponents belong to each other. This rift carries the opponents into the source of their unity by virtue of their common ground. It is a basic design, an outline sketch, that draws the basic features of the rise of the lighting of beings. [*Er ist Grundriß. Er ist Auf-riß, der die Grundzüge des Aufgehens der Lichtung des Seienden zeichnet.*] This rift does not let the opponents break apart; it brings the opposition of measure and boundary into their common outline.[17]

That rift and abyss occupy the same conceptual space in Heidegger's thought is evident in the similarity of the images evoked by the terms, and in the fact that they perform analogous functions in discourse devoted to the issue of truth and its grounding or establishment. However, an important change has taken place: instead of conceiving the abyss as grounded in the finitude of Dasein, Heidegger has de-centered his ontology and reconceived the abyss, here named as rift, as intrinsic to Being.

The transcendental idealism latent in the Dasein-centricity of fundamental ontology (which, like all idealisms, tacitly nurtures itself on the ontological dualism it is designed to overcome) has been amended in the direction of a more genuinely phenomenological ontology. The abyss no longer names a difference between immanent subject and transcendent world; as rift, it now names a difference within the phenomenal domain: the difference between lighting and concealment, between measure and boundary, between the "dawning" world and the "self-closing" earth. This difference must, indeed, be seen as an ontological difference, but this ontological difference does not demarcate two mutually exclusive domains; it points, rather, to a difference within a unitary sphere.

The conflict between world and earth—like analogous tensions between immanence and transcendence, the revealed and the concealed, the invisible and the visible—designates the circumstances that make the happening of truth both a task and an historical event. Conceived in this way, as an intimate strife, as a conflict within a unitary sphere, the rift/abyss emerges as a symbol for the correlativity of truth and untruth which need not be confused with the notion of absolute groundlessness. No longer is the finitude/freedom of Dasein the sole origin of untruth, no longer does the absolute distance between finite man and infinite God split the domain of knowledge into abyssally separated spheres of nescience and omniscience; rather, the recognition that human existence is integral with the unfolding of Being has led to the incorporation of that existence within the overall dialectic of concealment and unconcealment in the intimate strife of earth and world. As I have tried to show elsewhere,[18] Heidegger, in his later works, regards man as a vehicle or conduit of truth rather than as its fabricator. Language speaks through the poet, and truth happens as an historical event. But that unconcealment is correlated with concealment in a twofold way: (a) the unconcealment presupposes a prior concealment (in the withholding of self-secluding earth), and (b) the lighting of one aspect of Being obscures other adumbrations which withdraw into the concealment of obscurity.

The rift or abyss, therefore, is as much a condition for truth as it is a source of error and untruth. It is a symbol not for absolute groundlessness but for the intrinsic obscurity of all grounds. The obscurity of grounds resides in the transcendence of the earth as the repository of our (willed or not) primordial faith in "the self-secluding factor that juts up in the Open."[19]

The question, deferred earlier,[20] which now must be confronted is the question of the λόγος. What is the role of language in the interplay of *Grund* and *Abgrund*?

In 1950 and 1951, fifteen years after writing "The Origin of the Work of Art," Heidegger gave a lecture on "Language"[21] in which he said:

> Language is—language, speech. Language speaks. If we let ourselves fall into the abyss denoted by this sentence, we do not go tumbling into emptiness. We fall upward, to a height. Its loftiness opens up a depth.[22]

Why does the assertion that language is language, that language speaks, denote an abyss? But first: what is meant here by 'abyss'? "We speak of an abyss where the ground falls away and a ground is a lacking to us, where we seek the ground and set out to arrive at a ground, to get to the bottom of something."[23] This characterization of the abyss follows another question: "Is language itself the abyss?" And that question is raised in the context of an assertion made by Hamann in a letter to Herder: "Reason is language, λόγος."[24] Hamann seeks a ground for reason, finds it in language, and then implies that this realization opens an abyss.

If reason is grounded in language, and language is itself groundless, then, indeed, we do face an abyss—an abyss constituted by the groundlessness of language. But: is language itself groundless, is language itself the abyss? What is Heidegger's answer to this question? And what is ours?

Any question posed about the ground of language must be posed, and answered, in language. In the search to get to the bottom of language, we arrive again at language. Here is the thought that takes us to the brink of the thesis of linguistic immanence, that is, to the brink of the abyss of utter groundlessness. Language is grounded in X. Language is X. Whatever can be put in the place of X is—language. Hence the formula: language is language. *Die Sprache ist: Sprache.* Here is where the thinking of post-hermeneutic skepticism stops.

But Heidegger's thinking does not stop here. He takes us to the brink of the abyss at the *beginning* of his essay on "Language," where the threat of the abyss is raised as a question. The essay ventures into the abyss opened by the formula in order, as Heidegger suggests, to reach a height, to open a depth. Where is Heidegger's thought at the end of the essay?

The essay ends with no further reference to the abyss—because, in the course of the essay, Hamann's 'abyss' has been replaced with 'rift' (*Riß*) which Heidegger uses to interpret the poem by Trakl around which the discourse of the essay centers. The line in the poem that evokes the notion of rift is this: "Pain has turned the threshold to stone."[25] Heidegger says of "the threshold" that it "sustains the middle in which the two, the outside and the inside, penetrate each other."[26] And of "the pain" Heidegger writes:

> But what is pain? Pain rends. It is the rift. But it does not tear apart into dispersive fragments. . . . It settles the between, the middle of the two that are separated in it. Pain joins the rift of the dif-ference. Pain is the dif-ference itself.[27]

The interplay of the German terms *reißen-Riß* and *scheiden-Schied*, stressed throughout this paragraph,[28] culminates with an identification: pain is the rift [pain≡rift]; pain is the dif-ference itself [pain≡dif-ference]; hence (my inference) there is an identity between rift and dif-ference.[29]

"Rift" retains the same significance here in "Language" as it had in the essay on "The Origin of the Work of Art," although two minor modifications have occurred. The characterization of the rift as pain is reminiscent of the thesis of the finitude of Dasein (but Heidegger is careful to warn us that "we should not imagine pain anthropologically":[30] this is not a reversion to Dasein-centricity). And, second, although the rift remains characterized as an intimacy that both separates and gathers together, it is now world and things that are joined in the rift, and the play of light and dark is now a play of brightness and pain.[31]

In "The Origin of the Work of Art," the rift, as the intimate strife between world and earth, names the place of the Open (*das Offene*)[32] in which truth establishes itself in the work of art. Heidegger then goes on to assert that "*all art*," as the letting happen of the advent of the truth of what is, is, as such, *essentially poetry*."[33] And he makes it clear that "the *linguistic* work, the poem in the narrower sense, has a privileged position in the domain of the arts."[34] Thus, a strong connection between the rift and language has already been made.

In the essay at hand, "Language," this connection is made even more explicit. Language, as the happening of truth, happens as the appropriation (*Ereignis*) of the dif-ference. It happens as the stilling which is the calling of world and things into "the middle of their intimacy." That is, language is the calling of world and things into "the rift that is the dif-ference itself."[35]

Toward the beginning of his essay on "Language," Heidegger takes up the question posed by Hamann's characterization of language as an abyss. This is the question—encapsuled in the formula, *die Sprache ist: die Sprache; die Sprache spricht*—whether language is groundless, a bottomless abyss. Note that this is Hamann's question, Hamann's challenge: an hypothesis taken up by Heidegger for consideration, but kept at a distance. At the end of the essay, the formula has changed: no longer is it the barren "language is language"; "language speaks"; now it is "language speaks as the peal of stillness"; "language, the peal of stillness, is, inasmuch as the dif-ference takes place." And the abyss of groundlessness has now been replaced by the rift, which is not the utter absence of ground, but the *Unter-Schied*: the middle, the threshold, the intimacy that preserves a separation, the interpenetration of world and things.[36]

Nor is this rift which is the dif-ference itself a mere mediating term between world and things.

> The dif-ference does not mediate after the fact by connecting world and things through a middle added on to them. Being the middle, it first determines world and things in their presence [Wesen], i.e., in their being toward one another [Zueinander], whose unity it carries out.[37]

The middle, the place of the rift that is the dif-ference between world and things, "first determines world and things in their *Wesen*," that is, in their essence or rationale.[38] What does this mean? How does it bear on the question of the abyss?

Throughout this discourse, two ways of understanding 'abyss' have been counterpoised: (a) the abyss of utter groundlessness and (b) the of dif-ference, of intimate separation. In the weighing of these two models, two separate issues have demanded consideration. There is the exegetical question regarding Heidegger's stance: to which model does he subscribe? And there is the question of validity: which model, if either, commands our assent?

Both issues depend on the prior question as to whether the two models are genuinely different. The view that appears to prevail today, which I have characterized as 'post-hermeneutic skepticism, is that there is really only one model, that of (a) utter groundlessness, and that the notion of (b) dif-ference is but another formulation of that model. I think that this view is mistaken, that the two models are profoundly different, that Heidegger subscribes to the latter, and that he is correct in doing so.

As I have attempted to show, the conception of the abyss as utter ground-lessness depends upon an ontological dualism in which there is an exclusive disjunction between the world as it is in itself (or for an infinite or divine or absolute understanding) and the world as perceived by finite under-standing. That exclusive disjunction *is* the abyss as conceived in model (a). As I have also sought to show, both Nietzsche and Heidegger entertained that conception, but moved resolutely away from it—because both recog-nized to need to do justice to the domain of finite truth which is rendered unintelligible by the ontological dualism implicit in the model of utter groundlessness.

When the issue of the abyss resurfaces in the context of philosophical discourse attuned to the complex role of language in the process of human understanding, the same ontological issue arises: does language reveal truth about the world, or is the domain of language (as the domain of human understanding) radically disjunct from the domain of transcendent reality? The thesis of linguistic immanence, the thesis that language can refer only to itself, the thesis that the only grounding asserted for language must necessarily be limited to further uses of and appeals to language, names language as the abyss of groundlessness—because finite cognition is con-fined to the domain of language and the latter can appeal to no ground other than itself. This is the threat to finite truth (or reason) posed by Hamann that Heidegger takes up in the opening pages of his essay on "Language."

In the passage last quoted, Heidegger explicitly repudiates the thought that there is an abyss that renders the horizon of finite understanding disjunct from things themselves. There is no need of a mediating term between world and things, because the middle where they interpenetrate in intimate strife is prior to their separation into disjunctive and mutually exclusive domains. It is precisely in language that the *Wesen* of world and things, that is, their correlation or "being toward one another" (*Zueinander*), is determined (*ermittelt*). It would be a clearcut *petitio* to assert that the disjunction performed by language is presupposed by language.[39] Yet language is implicated in the taking place, the happening or event (*das Ereignis*), of the dif-ference between world and things. This is what remains to be understood.

This, the final phase of our tracing of the development of the abyss through Heidegger's writing takes us to the period 1957-59 when Heidegger delivered a series of lectures[40] which provides the context in which a resolution of the abyss-logos problematic can be found in his eleboration of the term *Ereignis* or appropriation.

I have been attempting to show that Heidegger does not subscribe to the thesis of linguistic immanence or any other thesis that entails the view that language is groundless. My main line of argument has centered on the point that the abyss Heidegger finds beneath language is not to be understood as groundlessness, but is rather to be understood through the terms he uses to describe it: specifically, rift (*Riß*) and dif-ference (*Unter-Schied*). These terms have been characterized as naming a middle, an intimate strife, a between, a correlation (*Zueinander*) or gathering (*Versammlung*) which preserves separation while unifying. This characterization, I have argued, does not describe a nothingness, an utter absence of grounds. If, however, the abyss does not designate the groundlessness of language, does it, then, name a peculiar kind of ground upon which language may be said to rest? This question calls for more groundwork.

The formula, "language speaks," has been amended to say "language speaks as the peal of stillness." In "The Way to Language," a further development occurs. "*Language* speaks. Language first of all and inherently obeys the essential nature of speaking: it says. Language speaks by saying, this is, by showing."[41] How does this statement inform the question of grounds? Heidegger has already said: "*The essential being of language is Saying as Showing [Das Wesende der Sprache ist die Sage als die Zeige].*"[42] Have we here a clearcut statement on Heidegger's part concerning the ground of language? Not quite. The key term is derived from '*Wesen*,' and that word, like the Greek οὐσία, is 'essentially' ambiguous. Indeed, Heidegger is very circumspect about the question of grounds. "On what does the being of language rest, that is, where is it grounded? Perhaps we are missing the very nature of language when we ask for grounds."[43] In the pages that follow this query about the question of grounds, Heidegger changes the terms of his discourse in a twofold shift. First, he identifies "the moving force" ("*das Regende*") of the *Wesen* of language[44] as "appropriation" ("*das Eriegnen*");[45] then he argues that, although appropriation is not to be conceived in the traditional ways of thinking of grounds (that is, in terms of cause and effect or antecedent and consequence), it grants/gives/confers (*gewähren*) more than grounding does.[46]

The immediate conclusion to be drawn from this is that "the being of language [*das Sprachwesen*] . . . rests on appropriation [*im Ereignis beruht*]," [47] or that its origin lies in the nature or mode of appropriation. [48] "Language is the house of Being because language, as Saying, is the mode of appropriation." [49] But: what is appropriation?

The German term, *Ereignis*, is a compound of *'eignen'* the verb 'to own,' and the prefix *'er-'* which betokens the beginning of action or the reaching of its end. One might think of appropriation as 'the achievement of belonging to.' When, in "The Way to Language," Heidegger brings the term into play, he refers to two earlier works, *Identity and Difference* and *Being and Time*. In the former, he offers a definition of sorts: "appropriation is that realm, vibrating within itself, through which man and Being reach each other in their nature [*Wesen*]," and, again, "appropriation appropriates man and Being to their essential togetherness [*ihr wesenhaftes Zusammen*]." [50] The second reference is to the section (44) of *Being and Time* devoted to "Dasein, Disclosedness [*Erschlossenheit*], and Truth," and, I think, is intended to provide the background for understanding his claim that appropriation alone "is what gives us such things as a 'there is,' a 'there is' of which even Being itself stands in need to come into its own as presence [*als Anwesen*]." [51] The point of this latter reference is that appropriation underlies disclosedness by granting presence: it is Heidegger's account of what has traditionally been called givenness. And he treats it as an ultimate. "There is nothing else from which the appropriation itself could be derived, even less in whose terms it could be explained." [52]

It is now time to assemble the pieces. The context is the issue of logos and abyss, language and the question of grounds. We started with the notion of abyss and traced it through the language of rift and dif-ference to arrive at the idea of a gathering or middle that "first determines world and things in their presence," but preserves the tension between them. This idea was then correlated with Heidegger's teaching on language, and the question arose as to the role of language in the determination of world and things. And it turned out that it is in language that the *Wesen* of world and things is determined and, then, that the *Wesen* of language, in turn, rests on appropriation. Appropriation, however, is not to be conceived as a ground in the traditional sense, although it is an ultimate and grants/gives more than grounds as traditionally (that is, *metaphysically*) conceived do. [53]

Here I rest my case. Language is not an *Abgrund*, an abyss in the sense of total absence of grounds. Language originates in and rests on appropriation, whether we choose to call appropriation the *ground* of language or not. Indeed, I think it is entirely appropriate to think of appropriation as the ground of language—as long as 'ground' is not conceived in the traditional or metaphysical sense (that is, as the divine Absolute, or as that Absolute dissimulates itself in the guise of universal, atemporal, Transcendental Consciousness or Reason).

The quest of thinking always remains the search for the first and ultimate grounds. Why? Because this, that something is and what it is, the persistent presence of being [*das Wesende des Wesens*], has from old been determined to be the ground. As all nature [*Wesen*] has the character of a ground, a search for it [*Wesen*] is the founding and grounding of the ground [*das Ergründen und Begründen des Grundes*].[54]

These words appear in an essay written roughly a year before the essay on "The Way to Language," and Heidegger may have radically altered his position during that time without signalling the change in a thematic way. He may also have quietly renounced his statement six months earlier in "The Principle of Identity" that the abyss we have been seeking to understand "is neither empty nothingness nor murky confusion, but rather: *das Er-eignis*," that is, appropriation.[55] But if Heidegger had, in fact, made such an unadvertised turnabout, it is highly unlikely that he would have directed his reader to the earlier account of appropriation in "The Principle of Identity" as he does in "The Way to Language."[56]

The search for the ground is the search for *das Wesende des Wesens*. The *Wesen* of world and things is determined by language whose own *Wesen* rests ultimately on appropriation—through which we are to think the origin of the *Wesen* (*Wesensherkunft*) of Being. It is valid, I think, to infer from this that *das Wesende des Wesens* is named by 'appropriation.' And appropriation has been explicitly named as the abyss that is *not* empty nothingness (*leere Nichts*).

Heidegger does not leave us confronting nothingness, but he does not leave us fulfilled, either. He leaves us with a word, 'appropriation,' which designates the place where answers to our questions are to be sought. Appropriation names the realm in which world and things are gathered into their *Wesen* and *Anwesen*, the realm through which man and Being reach each other in their *Wesen*, the realm in which we might seek to find the unity of the fourfold, and so forth. But this language, in its tireless self-referentiality, threatens to evanesce, to disappear in a vapor. Why? "We human beings remain committed to and within the being of language, and can never step out of it and look at it from somewhere else."[57]

This is not a version of the thesis of linguistic immanence—although it approaches its threshold of pain—because, for Heidegger, language is also extra-referential: it speaks of things and shows things which lie beyond itself. But we human beings reach these things, according to Heidegger, only insofar as we and they are appropriated to each other by language. We are not the masters of language, rather the reverse is the case: we must wait upon language to show us what it will. Our relation to language, and hence to world and things, is thus "determined by destiny: whether and in what way the nature of language, as the arch-tidings of appropriation, will retain us in appropriation."[58]

Here, as is always and deliberately the case in Heidegger, when we pursue the philosophical quest to our limits we arrive in the domain of poetry. Ultimately, and because it is an ultimate, we cannot understand appropriation: our ultimate thinking, which directs itself to the as yet unspoken, is ultimately a thanking.

> All reflective thinking is poetic, and all poetry in turn is a kind of thinking. The two belong together by virtue of that Saying which has already bespoken itself to what is unspoken because it is a thought as a thanks [*weil es der Gedanke ist als der Dank*].[59]

Yet, this that is named by 'appropriation' and specifies the place where we might hope to find an answer to the question of abyss and logos merits further interrogation, further attempts to understand, to get to the center or "middle" designated by the rift/abyss that is not nothing.

3. MERLEAU-PONTY

> The progress of the interrogation toward the *center* is not the movement from the conditioned unto the condition, from the founded unto the *Grund*: the so-called *Grund* is *Abgrund*. But the abyss one thus discovers is not such by *lack of ground [faute de fond]*, it is upsurge of a *Hoheit* which supports from above (cf. Heidegger, *Unterwegs zur Sprache*), that is of a negativity that *happens to the world [une négativité qui* vient au monde].[60]

The affinity between Heidegger and Merleau-Ponty resonating in this text deserves exploration, but here I will limit myself to an enumeration of the salient points.

(i) The traditional search for a ground ends in an *Abgrund*, an empty nothingness, because that search was prefigured to find nothing other than The Absolute in some guise or other: God,[61] the unconditioned or *causa sui*, the onefold root of the principle of sufficient reason, the coincidence of the Rational and the Real in an infinite Transcendental Consciousness, etc. Merleau-Ponty's radical critique of empiricism and intellectualism disposes finally of both the transcendent absolute and the immanent absolute. The rejection of traditional metaphysics is clearcut in both thinkers (although Merleau-Ponty does not subscribe to the view that metaphysics is at an end).

(ii) Fundamental thought is bottomless or abyssal, not because the lack of an absolute leaves an absolute lack, but because the depth can never be plumbed by finite thinking. Or, to shift the spatial metaphor, because every height reached draws us higher: the discovery of every grounded meaning is at the same time an opening on to further meanings still to be dis-covered. The philosophical point here is that the open-endedness of inquiry does not betoken an intrinsic futility but, rather, ensures its perpetuity as a (if not The) meaningful endeavor.

(iii) The call to language that motivates abyssal or fundamental thought is a call that originates from beyond language in an unspoken, or silence, that appropriates us or demands a *Saga*, a singing expression. Something wants to be said, something that will evanesce unless it is said, something that can never be finally said, but always requires renewal. Merleau-Ponty adopts Husserl's term, 'significative intention,' to designate this presence of an absence, this elusive meaning in search of a place in language. Heidegger appeals to Stefan George's poem, "The Word," and speaks of the name that may or may not emerge from the bourn of fate.[62]

Beneath these three important affinities is a deeper one which addresses the major concern of this work—ontology —and, I trust, justifies concluding it as I am. This book began with an extended treatment of Cartesian and post-Cartesian influences on Western thought, and is now ending with an extended treatment of Heideggerian and post-Heideggerian influences on the same tradition. The problematic in both cases centers on the ontological problem of dualism. The thesis defended throughout is that Merleau-Ponty's ontology provides an alternative to the skepticism, the abyss of groundlessness, that logically and historically follows from dualism and infects the cultures in which it is sedimented. Merleau-Ponty's ontology articulates the phase through which our culture will have to pass if it is to emerge on the far side of this abyss.

The godly are arrayed against the ungodly; both are armed with weapons dull and deadly: mediation is unthinkable. And the ground beneath the absolute and its shadow has still to be thought by those whose voices prevail.

One sect of the thinkers whose thoughts now guide the drift of our culture has taken its departure from an interpretation of Heidegger that is as mistaken as it is pervasive. Their guiding thought is that all meaning derives from language—whose own source is forever lost to us, and is therefore effectively (if not actually) non-existent. I have sought to show that this thought is both false and falsely attributed to Heidegger, who did, indeed, teach that the *Wesen* and *Anwesen* of world and things depends somehow on language, but also taught that language depends on appropriation.

Whence, then, the falsity? The falsity, the misguidance, depends on the peculiar coincidence of the 'somehow,' '*Wesen/Anwesen,*' and 'appropriation.'

(i) The 'somehow'

Heidegger's account leaves the realm of the discursive when it approaches the question of the how of appropriation. "*Die Sprache spricht,*" he said, and then asking himself how, replied with *Ereignis*, the mutual appropriation, or belonging together, of word and thing. Earlier (May 1958), he used another term.

> The same word, Λόγος, the word for Saying, is . . . also the word for Being, that is, for the presencing of beings [*das Anwesen des Anwesenden*]. Saying and Being, word and thing, belong to each other in a veiled way, a way which has hardly been thought and is [*unausdenkbar*] *not to be thought out to the end.*[63]

"Die Sprache spricht." Das Ereignis ereignet. In the end, thinking remains "delivered over to the mystery of the word."[64]

But this is not to say that Heidegger preserves silence when it comes to the explication of such ultimate terms as *Ereignis* and *Λόγος.* Instead, he provokes us with poetry replete with references to other ultimates such as fates, gods, and destiny; which leaves the way open for our latterday guides to claim that the logic of ultimates leaves but two alternatives, God or the abyss He left behind upon departing this world, and that, although neither may be thinkable ultimately, ultimately only one is *eigentlich.*

I have argued that, with the notion of appropriation, Heidegger has named the ontological space subtending sheer immanence and absolute transcendence, and thereby undercut the logic of ultimates that endows the abyss of groundlessness with its spurious credibility. This is the basis of a rapprochement with Merleau-Ponty. More than that, if we can find in Merleau-Ponty a discursive account of the how of appropriation to supplement Heidegger's poetic thinking/thanking, we might open the way for a more appropriate sequel to Heidegger's fundamental thinking.

The resonance between them enfranchises them both.

(ii) 'Wesen/Anwesen'

'*Wesen,*' like '*οὐσία,*' straddles the ontological difference (*die ontologische Differenz*) or, in other words, designates the unity of the dif-ference (*der Unter-Schied*). In terms perhaps all too plain, '*Wesen*' speaks simultaneously of *esse* and *essentia,* of existence and meaning, of *Sein* and *Sosein,* of things and how they are understood, of beings, Being, and their relation to language: that is undoubtedly why Heidegger employs the term so frequently. But the term embodies a question, as it must to function as it does. The question it embodies is thematically raised in every one of Heidegger's writings on language. And in every one of these writings, Heidegger steadfastly refuses to hazard an answer.

The question: does the *Wesen* of things derive exclusively from language, or is the *Wesen* of things grounded exclusively in the things themselves?

Heidegger refuses to answer the question as it is posed for two reasons— one of which, I think, is entirely legitimate. That reason is that the posing of the question restricts the answer to a choice between two equally unacceptable alternatives: semeiological reductionism or naive scientific realism. The other reason, frequently stated as such, is that to answer the question, one would have to occupy a standpoint outside language, and that we cannot do.

'*Anwesen*' is also ontologically ambiguous in a way that recapitulates the ontological ambiguity of its root: presence can be interpreted to be relative to or independent of language. And that is also a question which Heidegger repeatedly asks and repeatedly refuses to answer.

The ontologically bivalent notions of *Wesen* and *Anwesen* call for a resolution of the polar tension between immanence and transcendence contained within them. Somehow, we have to be able to correlate the *Wesen/Anwesen* of language with that of things instead of regarding them as mutually exclusive. We have to see *how* language and things come together and inform each other. The name Heidegger gives to this belonging to each other is 'appropriation.' But when the question of the how of appropriation arises, the traditional aporias of *Wesen* and *Anwesen* are relegated to poetry. Heidegger's writings on the subject are *Holzwege* which fetch up at the bourn of the norn.

And that, as I have argued, is what allows some writers to label the metaphysics of presence crypto-onto-theo-logic.

That it need not be thus, indeed, *must* not be thus can be demonstrated within the context of Merleau-Ponty's ontology. Can be, moreover, has been—throughout the course of this book. To see this more clearly, only one further preparatory step need be taken.

(iii) 'Appropriation'

Appropriation [*das Ereignen*] is not the outcome (result) of something else, but the giving yield [*die Er-gebnis*] whose giving reach alone is what gives us such things as a "there is" [*ein «Es gibt»*], a "there is" of which even "Being" [*«das Sein»*] stands in need to come into its own [*sein Eigenes*] as presence [*als Anwesen*].[65]

In this passage, Heidegger attributes the givenness of things—one aspect of the gift to which Heidegger responds with thinking/thanking—to appropriation, and asserts that presence depends upon that givenness. In earlier passages, we have seen Heidegger maintain that the being of language (*Sprachwesen*) rests on the giving yield (*Er-gebnis*) of appropriation. And I have argued that *das Wesende des Wesens* is named by 'appropriation,' that is, that 'appropriation' is Heidegger's term for that in virtue of which all that *is* and is meaningful—*is* and is meaningful.

This is clearly the ancient province of the gods. The gods that created all things, endowed them with meaning, and named them—all in the aboriginal speech act.

Yet we live in a time when the gods have either died or fled. Where, to paraphrase Nietzsche's question, are we to find something capable of filling the god-hole—when anything capable of filling the god-hole must, perforce, take the shape of a god, named as such or not?

Back, once again, to the initial dilemma: inauthentic god or authentic abyss. Man requires a measure, or so it has always seemed. Thus, he must fabricate his measure from nothing. Then deceive himself about what he has done. Or admit that he has no measure at all, and try, if he can, to live without one.

The dilemma is a false dilemma. The fleeing and dying gods have left behind the ground from which they emerged—and the questions to which they were a tentative and errant answer. That is their source and their sustenance during their brief span and ours. All gods came into being at some time and in some way. The creation of symbols does not occur *ex nihilo*, nor do symbols create themselves—although it is an essential tenet of all theologies to deny the truth of these denials. Indeed, this is the quintessential tenet of the voguish crypto-onto-theo-logic which deifies the system of symbols by treating it as effectively *causa sui*.

So: we must reject the false dilemma and return to the question of the how of appropriation, the whence of givenness and meaningfulness, the "non-metaphysical" ground of word and thing.

In part three above, I have set forth Merleau-Ponty's teaching on this matter: the early model based on the notion of *Fundeirung*, and the later model based on the notion of reversibility. It provides an answer to the question now before us, the question of the unitary tension relating the *Wesen/Anwesen* of things and of language.

Heidegger refuses to answer the question of the correlation between the *Wesen* of things and the *Wesen* of language because, I think, he does not want to lay claim to knowledge that things have abiding meanings apart from those imparted/revealed by language. This commitment to the transcendental function of language has its proximal source in the progression of thought that proceeds from Kant through Hegel to Husserl and beyond. An X can be (re-)identified as an X only through the mediating concept of X-ness. Lacking the concept, the percept is blind. Or, in Saussure's terms, "nothing is distinct before the appearance of language."[66] This is one horn of a dilemma. The other derives from what I have been calling 'the problem of organization' (chapter 4 above): if the thing (or phenomenon or perceptual theme) has no meaning (or *sens*) apart from that imparted by the concept or linguistic sign, then there is no warrant for assigning just this concept to just that thing, or for returning to just that element in the perceptual field (as opposed to some other) to (re-)identify *it* as a member of the class or category designated by the concept. Also on this horn of the dilemma is the problem of the *esse* of the referent: signs discriminate among things; they do not create them. Now, if it is truly the case that "we human beings . . . can never step out of language," this dilemma becomes devastating because it denies forever the possibility of understanding how word and thing became appropriated to each other, how the word ever emerged from prelinguistic silence, how the thing ever acquired its identity. *Somehow*, in the passage from prelinguistic animal to significantly speaking human, language came to interpose itself between man and world—where it resides as an impermeable barrier between us and the beings among which we dwell.

But, surely, this one-sided. Even from the human vantage, it is not only signifiers that distinguish Jack from Jill and oak from pine: we *see* the difference; is given to us.

The boundary that primordially separates person from person and tree from tree is the edge of the Gestalt that defines each as a perceptual theme. That is a given, an irreducible feature of the givenness of things. And there are mountains of evidence to attest to the fact that this primordial discrimination is constant across a wide range of divergent forms of life, be they linguistic, prelinguistic, or non-linguistic. When my dog's nose tells her there is a woodcock in the vicinity and she imparts this information to me in the tensed rigidity of her pointing stance, the bird that suddenly flushes from cover defines itself by its motion and cry. And if it turns out to have been a grouse instead of a woodcock, I must adjust my reflexes and linguistic anticipations to its demands. Regardless of whether I have constituted this copse as woodcock territory, if the bird is a grouse, it will have the smell of a grouse and fly the way that grouse fly. 'Grouse' informally denotes a natural type that is determined by DNA and subsequently designated in language. My dog and I *perceive* that natural type as such—and communicate about it, more or less effectively, through gestures.

Of course, our whole autumnal ritual is prefigured by culture and takes place within a horizon of sedimented linguistic structures. At one level of discourse, my setter and I are artifacts—products of human connivance and contrivance. And, so is the bird in its *Wesen* as an instance of its type and as quarry, trophy, and food. All three of us *be* as we are in this annual *pas de trois* because our roles have been choreographed through centuries of interlocking primal and derivative institution. And for all of this, I am, indeed, thankful. I am the recipient of a form of life.

But I need not invoke the gods to understand it. There is an historical explanation which culminates in the world of organisms feeding upon one another and learning, in some prehistoric era, to talk about and ritualize the process. This is what the *Fundierung* model allows us to conceptualize: how the phenomenal world, aboriginally present to percipient organisms, eventually expressed itself through some of those organisms in the evolution of language.

Stop. Wait. This is an account, to be sure, although a mundane one, but—is it the truth? Opinion supported by λόγος, a story. One among many such stories. All of them constructed in language. All of them providing conceptual space into which the days of our lives may be fitted, one way or another. The stories differ, command different audiences, who, in differing times and places, have shown themselves to be willing to live according to the stories they were born into, and to die in defense of them. Poets, inhaling the breath of the gods, construct the stories, and in them we communicants find our destinies. Take this bread, flesh of my flesh, consume it, make it your flesh, and we shall be one in life everlasting.

There is truth, human truth, that is, finite, limited truth, in this story, as there is in all such world-historic stories. There is also error in the story, as in all others. The error is implicit in the limit, which is necessary to the story, defines it as this story and not another.

In the beginning, the absolute beginning, there was χάος—in absolute need of meaning, having none of its own. Then there was the word, the λόγος, the speech act of the gods, that conferred meaning upon it all. And the story was told, through divine inspiration, to the poets, prophets, and thinkers,[67] who gave it and its sanctions to us. This is our story. There are others. Beneath this story of ours, prior to it, there is χάος, as there is beneath all such stories; because all the stories, all the λόγοι, impart all the meaning and order there is to be had. Ultimately.

First darkness. Then the λόγος, which imparts the light. Without the λόγος, no light. The only light there *is* is the light of the λόγος. Apart from this λόγος, there is only another. Apart from all λόγος, there is only darkness, the abyss of *leere Nichts, Sinnlosigkeit*.

That, too, is a story, today's story; it has its own logic. That logic, clearly seen, is nothing other that onto-theo-logic.

The story about stories that I, inspired by Merleau-Ponty, would tell, is also only a story, and, like all the others, bound by its limits to errancy.[68] But, unlike today's story, its logic is not onto-theo-logic; that is, its λόγος is not conceived as effectively *causa sui*. Furthermore, this story that I am about to tell lays claim to truth. Like all stories, it is opinion expressed in and supported by λόγοι. But the λόγοι of the story refer beyond themselves to a prelinguistic λόγος,[69] the "latent logos" or "autochthonous *sens*" of the perceptual world "where there are non-linguistic significations,"[70] the "λόγοσ 'ενδιάθετος which calls for the λόγοσ προφορικός" (VI 170; VI-F 224). In short, the words of this story refer to a ground of meaning against which their truth may be measured and assessed.

My story begins, not with χάος, but with the indefinite, τὸ ἄπειρον. This need not be an absolute beginning, because it does not attempt to answer the question of its own ultimate origin; it simply says that, prior to any relatively defining state of affairs (such as, for example, a "big bang"), there was a relatively undefined state of affairs (perhaps an im-mense cloud of hydrogen atoms, or perhaps some other state of affairs lacking even the *mens* or measure afforded by the notion of hydrogen atom). *Tὸ ἄπειρον* is neutral with regard to the antinomy of ultimate causal origins. This story is the story of becoming, and wherever one starts the telling of it, one leaves open the question of a prior tale. All story-tellers know that there are better stories to come, but we all tell the best one we know.

The indefinite defines itself, perhaps in the genesis of molecular structures of increasing complexity, perhaps in another way: we should not define τὸ ἄπειρον in exclusively physical terms. It is even probable that Anaximander, himself, did not do so: (a) if Heidegger is to be believed, φύσις was not an exclusively material principle for the Presocratics; and (b) if Anaximander was as accomplished a thinker as he doubtless was, he would not have contradicted himself by asserting that that from which the inchoate πέρᾶς has not emerged is limited or bounded in any way (as it would have to be if it were to exclude whatever might be conceived as non-physical or immaterial). Nor should we make the unwarranted inference from indefinite to infinite (and thence on to absolute). Indeed, with Kirk and Raven, "we may legitimately doubt whether the concept of infinity was apprehended before questions of continuous expansion and continuous divisibility were raised by Melissus and Zeno."[71] In any case, the genuinely hermeneutic nature of the problem before us, compounded by the fortuitous fragmentation in fact as well as principle (all texts are fragmentary insofar as all texts are necessarily allusive), frees us from doxography for ἀλήθειἄ: my concern here is the story that demanded telling from Aniximander rather than his adequacy to the call.

The indefinite defines itself. The flesh of the world articulates itself through itself. Becoming happens. Forms emerge from the indefinite which was pregnant with them; they emerge, combine, recede, and give way to new forms. They give ground to the πέρᾱς, and thereby provide an emerging, changing measure. The earth moves and mountains rise, only to be carved by glaciers and eroded by rain.

The flesh of the world also articulates itself through that part of itself which we, ourselves, are. Through itself is also through us: we who are both fleshly and articulate, the flesh of the world that has discovered the signs of its (and our) self-referentiality. "Egg shell" refers to egg shell refers to birth and death, to becoming and our becoming. "Egg shell" can refer to egg shell (a) because egg shells, being what they are, differ from clam shells, and (b) because 'egg,' being what it is, differs from 'clam.' *Both* conditions, extra- as well as infra-referentiality, must be met. That is the logic of language, which recapitulates the logic of the world, the same logic of the world that allows us to infer egg from egg shell, and to continue that chain of inference through to the birth and death processes of all things caught up in the logic of becoming; that is, all things subject to "the assessment of time"; that is, all things.

4. Τὸ ἄπειρον

The source of coming-to-be for existing things is that into which destruction, too, happens 'according to necessity; for they pay penalty and retribution to each other for their injustice according to the assessment of Time,' as [Anaximander] describes it in these rather poetic terms.[72]

The negativity that Merleau-Ponty associates with the abyss and describes as something that "happens to the world" can be understood in terms of the destruction mentioned above by Anaximander—which Nietzsche interprets as "penance" for the "wrong" of coming-to-be as an individuated existing thing[73]: the law of becoming is that all things which come into being must also pass away. It can also be understood as the very process of individuation, as the negativity that differntiates one positive thing from another.

In the context of the interpretation of the abyss being developed here, however, these two thoughts of negativity coalesce into one. The connecting idea is that of the abyss as symbol for the cognitive anxiety which is the human correlate to the process of becoming. It is through words that things which are destined to pass away may abide. That is one of the chief virtues of language: in differentiating, it also preserves. But that is also one of the greatest flaws inherent in language: it is the source of the illusion of atemporality and immutability. The thought, sometimes attributed to Heraclitus, that all things change except the logos, is mistaken concerning the logos, for it changes too. Those who have studied the histories of words and ideas know this to be the case—and those who pursue such studies with an understanding of the problems of hermeneutics know it even better: retrieval is always and necessarily projection. The point here is that the differentiations of language, the orderings of meaning, are as destined to change as the things whose differentiations they thematize and sediment. There is the authentic abyss, in the midst of the reversibility of the visible and the invisible. This abyss is not sheer emptiness, it is replete with emergent meaning.

The ground shifts in its *Wesen* and *Anwesen*. The story about stories is that old stories must give way to new ones if only because the old ones changed the world by reflecting it from the vantage of a time. So, also, must this story give way in time. But only, I hope, after it has done its job: the job of changing the world by convincing it that stories—philosophical ones, at least —have a job to do, which, like all jobs, can be done more or less well. The better ones tell the truth as best it can be told.

Such reflections take us beyond Merleau-Ponty, backward and forward in time, and into the realm of the frankly metaphysical, the proper habitat for a book on ontology. That may be troublesome to others, but is not to me. Nor was it to Merleau-Ponty, who saw metaphysics "at the horizon of the sciences of man" and conceived it as the task of thematizing the context that scientific theorizing always presupposes.

> There can be no rivalry between scientific knowledge and the metaphysical knowing which continually confronts the former with its task. A science without philosophy would literally not know what it was talking about. A philosophy without methodical exploration of phenomena [i.e., science] would end up with nothing but formal truths, which is to say, errors.[74]

Metaphysics is currently enjoying a rest while the world discovers, once again, that it does not coincide with theology. For the moment, while Continental thought lags on its errant and creative path, both science and metaphysics are out of vogue, literally in disfavor, because the stink of gods is upon them. And that is an historical oddity, since both kinds of knowing, that attuned to themes and that attuned to horizons—as attempts to understand, rather than sacrifice possible knowledge for impossible belief—have always been opposed to the dictates of the λόγοι of gods.

This leaves us, you and I, with a choice. Abandon science and philosophy in the name of a de-construction that resurrects gods in the place where they are least welcome; or seek the λόγος that is the very voice of things.

Abyss and logos: Abyss beneath the logos/ Or logos within the abyss.

Notes

INTRODUCTION

1. Since I am writing in English, I shall refer to page numbers in the English translations of Merleau-Ponty's works using the initials listed in the table of abbreviations. I shall also provide references to the French editions, and mark them with the suffix -F appended to the short title. Thus, 'PP 28; PP-F 36' refers to page 28 of *Phenomenology of Perception*, trans. Colin Smith (London: Routledge and Kegan Paul, 1962), and page 36 of *Phénoménologie de la perception* (Paris: Gallimard, 1945). In some instances, I have provided my own translations or modified the translations given in the English editions.

2. "For the philosopher, . . . the juxtaposition 'subjectivity *in* the world as object' and at the same time 'conscious subject *for* the world,' [contains] a necessary theoretical question, that of understanding how this is possible. The epoché . . . leads us to recognize, in self-reflection, that the world that exists for us, that is, our world in its being and being such, takes its ontic meaning entirely from our intentional life." Edmund Husserl, *The Crisis of European Sciences and Transcendental Phenomenology*, trans. David Carr (Evanston: Northwestern University Press, 1970), pp. 180–81.

3. Martin Heidegger, *Being and Time*, trans. Macquarrie and Robinson (New York: Harper and Row, 1962), sect. 7A.

PART ONE

ONE

1. Descartes, *Rules for the Direction of the Mind*, in *The Philosophical Works of Descartes*, ed. and trans. Haldane and Ross (New York: Dover, 1955), Vol. I, Rule IV, p. 9.

2. "It were better not to study at all than to occupy one's self with objects of such difficulty, that, *owing to our inability to distinguish true from false*, we are forced to regard the doubtful as certain; for in those matters any hope of augmenting our knowledge is exceeded by the risk of diminishing it. Thus . . . *we reject all such merely probable knowledge* and make it a rule to *trust only what is completely known and incapable of being doubted*." (Rule II, PWD 3. Emphasis added.)

3. "None of the mistakes which men can make . . . [is] due to faulty inference; they are caused merely by the fact that we found upon a basis of poorly comprehended experiences, or that propositions are posited which are hasty and groundless." (Rule II, PWD 5.)

4. "The imagination can act on the senses by means of the motor power applying them to objects, while they on the contrary can act on it, depicting on it the images of bodies." (Rule XII, PWD 39.)

5. "*No direct experience can ever deceive the understanding if it restrict its attention accurately to the object presented to it, just as it is given to it* either at firsthand or by means of an image; and if it moreover refrain from judging that the imagination faithfully reports the objects of the senses, or that the senses take on the true forms of things, or in fine that external things always are as they appear to be; for in all these judgments we are exposed to error." (Rule XII, PWD 44. Emphasis added.)

6. "If we consider a body as having extension and figure, we shall indeed admit that from the point of view of the thing itself it is one and simple. For we cannot

from that point of view regard it as compounded of corporeal nature, extension and figure, since *these elements have never existed in isolation from each other.* But relatively to our understanding we call it a compound." (Rule XII, PWD 40. Emphasis added.)

7. Descartes, *Meditations on First Philosophy*, in *The Philosophical Works of Descartes*, ed. and trans. Haldane and Ross (New York: Dover, 1955), Vol. I, Meditation III, p. 160.

8. "My principle task in this place is to consider, in respect to those ideas which appear to me to proceed from certain objects that are outside me, what are the reasons which cause me to think them similar to these objects." (Med. III, PWD 160.)

9. "This proposition: I am, I exist, is necessarily true each time that I pronounce it, or that I mentally conceive it." (Med. II, PWD 150.)

10. Descartes's distinction between "objective" and "formal" existence corresponds roughly to the distinction I have been drawing between immanence and transcendence: thoughts are immanent (exist in the objective mode) and their referents are transcendent (exist formally).

11. "I am certain [by virtue of the coincidence in question] that I am a thing which thinks; but do I not then likewise know what is requisite to render me certain of a truth? Certainly in this first knowledge there is nothing that assures me of its truth, excepting the clear and distinct perception of that which I state, which would not indeed suffice to assure me that what I say is true, if it could ever happen that a thing which I conceived so clearly and distinctly could be false; and accordingly it seems to me that already I can establish as a general rule that all things which I perceive very clearly and very distinctly are true." (Med. III, PWD 158.)

12. "If the objective reality of any one of my ideas is of such a nature as clearly to make me recognize that it is not in me either formally or eminently, and that consequently I cannot myself be the cause of it, it follows of necessity that I am not alone in the world, but that there is another being which exists, or which is cause of this idea." (Med. III, PWD 163.)

13. "Whatever God produces by means of secondary (i.e., created) causes, God can produce and conserve immediately and without their aid." William of Ockham, *Quodlibeta* VI, qu. 6, in *Philosophical Writings*, trans. Boehner (Indianapolis: Bobbs-Merrill, 1964), p. xix.

Descartes's early training in theology is evident in the *Meditations* and, indeed, major strains of his argument must be interpreted in this context. Specifically, the maxim of Ockham's quoted above underlies the hyperbolic doubt generated by the hypothesis of the evil genius.

Descartes's epistemology holds that our ideas are caused by things. His theology holds that things are caused by God. Hence, God is the origin of our ideas, but "by means of secondary causes." The force of the maxim, in the present context, is that God can produce in us the idea of a thing "immmediately" and without the "aid" of the "secondary" or mediating cause; that is, God can produce the idea in the absence of the thing.

The evil genius is the God of the scholastics in all respects except the benevolence that would prevent him from deceiving us by causing us to have ideas which purport to represent things when in reality those things are not present. And that is how the proof of God's benevolence can function in Meditation VI to banish the specter of the evil genius and thereby ground our belief that corporeal things exist conformable to our (clear and distinct) ideas of them. "Since God is no deceiver, it is very manifest that He does not communicate to me these ideas immediately and by Himself, nor yet by the intervention of some creature in which their reality is not formally, but only eminently, contained." (Med. VI, PWD 191.)

14. "Whence then come my errors? They come from the sole fact that, since the will is much wider in its range and compass than the understanding, I do not restrain

it within the same bounds, but extend it also to things which I do not understand."
(Med. IV, PWD 175–76.)

15. The Cartesian strategy, after three centuries of elaboration and refinement, reaches culmination in Wittgenstein's *Tractatus*—which is at once its purest expression and the *reductio* that refutes it.

16. The general meanings of the terms 'opacity' and 'translucency' will, I hope, have been conveyed by their usages in the foregoing discussion and by their metaphorical significance as well. In a more rigorous mode, however, 'opacity' might be explicated in terms of the other-sidedness of perceptual objects: objects given to me in perception do not reveal themselves completely; to the extent that there is always a side I cannot see (or an inside I cannot feel, or a past and future not present), there is always some opacity preventing the attainment of a *perfectly* adequate comprehension. Thus, opacity is a necessary feature of the way in which perceptual objects are given. 'Transparency' refers to the opposite aspect of givenness, the revealing as opposed to the obscuring aspect. Although perceptual objects do not have the complete transparency of thoughts (which have no sides, hence no hidden other side or inside), they are somewhat transparent—admittedly a forced usage—insofar as they are at least partially disclosed.

17. *An Essay Concerning Human Understanding*, ed. A. C. Fraser (New York: Dover, 1959). Book I is entitled "Neither Principles nor Ideas Are Innate."

18. E.g., extension, figure, motion, etc. (*Essay*, II, V).

19. "Simple ideas, when offered to the mind, the understanding can no more refuse to have, nor alter when they are imprinted, nor blot them out and make new ones itself, than a mirror can refuse, alter, or obliterate the images or ideas which the objects set before it do therein produce." (*Essay*, II, I, 25.)

20. "In [the reception of simple ideas] the understanding is merely passive; and whether or no it will have these beginnings, and as it were materials of knowledge is not in its own power. For the objects of our senses do . . . obtrude their particular ideas upon our minds whether we will or not." (*Essay*, II, I, 25.)

21. "It is not in the power of the most exalted wit or enlarged understanding, by any quickness or variety of thought, to invent or frame one simple idea in the mind." (*Essay*, II, I, 25.)

22. *A Treatise of Human Nature*, ed. Selby-Bigge (Oxford: Oxford University Press, 1964), I, IV, 6, p. 253.

23. William Warren Bartley, III, *The Retreat to Commitment* (New York: Knopf, 1962), p. 112.

24. It is noteworthy that Hume offers here the same list of possible causes of perceptions as that given by Descartes in the *Meditations*: the imagination, the object, and God.

25. "There can be nothing more certain than that the idea we receive from an external object is in our minds: this is intuitive knowledge. But whether there be anything more than barely that idea in our minds, whether we can thence certainly *infer* the existence of anything without us, which corresponds to that idea, is that whereof some men think there may be a question made; because men may have such ideas in their minds, when no such thing exists, no such object affects their senses." (*Essay*, IV, II, 14.)

26. "[The] uniting principle among ideas is not to be consider'd as an inseparable connexion; . . . nor yet are we to conclude, that without it the mind cannot join two ideas; for nothing is more free than that faculty: but we are only to regard it as a gentle force, which commonly prevails . . . nature in a manner pointing out to everyone those simple ideas, which are most proper to be united into a complex one." (*Treatise*, I, I, 4, 10–11.)

27. "According to my definitions, necessity makes an essential part of causation; and consequently liberty, by removing necessity, removes also causes, and is the

very same thing with chance. As chance is commonly thought to imply a contradiction, and is at least directly contrary to experience, there are always the same arguments against liberty or free-will." (*Treatise*, II, III, 1, 407.)

28. "They are not identical insofar as Hume bases his principles of synthesis on an inductive or psychogenetic model and Descartes bases his on a deductive or logical model.

29. "The Philosopher and His Shadow," in *Signs*, trans. R. C. McCleary (Evanston: Northwestern University Press, 1964), pp. 159–81.

30. *Cartesian Meditations*, trans. Dorian Cairns (The Hague: Nijhoff, 1960), p. 8.

31. Husserl characterizes the grasping of absolutely indubitable evidence as "a grasping of something itself that is, or is thus, a grasping in the mode 'it itself,' with full certainty of its being, a certainty that accordingly excludes every doubt. . . . An *apodictic* evidence, however, is not merely certainty of the affairs . . . evident in it; rather it discloses itself, to a critical reflection, as having the signal peculiarity of being *at the same time the absolute unimaginableness* (inconceivability) of their *non-being*, and thus excluding in advance every doubt as 'objectless,' empty." (CM 15–16.)

32. "The universal sensuous experience in whose evidence the world is continuously given to us . . . is obviously not to be taken forthwith as an apodictic evidence, which, as such, would absolutely exclude . . . the possibility of its non-being. Not only can a particular experienced thing suffer devaluation as an illusion of the senses; the whole unitarily surveyable nexus, experienced throughout a period of time, can prove to be an illusion, a coherent dream." (CM 17.)

33. Husserl, *The Paris Lectures*, trans. Peter Koestenbaum (The Hague: Nijhoff, 1967), p. 9. (These lectures, presented at the Sorbonne in February of 1929, were expanded later that year into the original manuscript of *Cartesian Meditations*.)

34. Husserl, *The Idea of Phenomenology*, trans. Alston and Nakhnikian (The Hague: Nijhoff, 1964), pp. 2–3. (Lectures presented in Göttingen in April and May of 1907.)

35. Husserl, *The Crisis of European Sciences and Transcendental Philosophy*, trans. David Carr (Evanston: Northwestern University Press, 1970), p. 181.

36. "Evidence denotes a universal primal phenomenon of intentional life, namely . . . the quite preeminent mode of consciousness that consists in the *self-appearance*, the *self-exhibiting*, the *self-giving*, of an affair . . . in the final mode: 'itself there,' 'immediately intuited,' 'given originaliter.' For the [transcendental] Ego that signifies: not aiming confusedly at something, . . . but being with it itself." (CM 57.)

37. "Everything that is exists for me only as the intentional objectivity of my cogitations." (PL 31.) *"Transcendence is an immanent mode of being, that is, one that constitutes itself within the ego*. Every conceivable meaning, every thinkable being— regardless of whether it is immanent or transcendent—falls within the realm of transcendental subjectivity. The idea of something outside this realm is a contradiction. . . . To conceive of the universe of true being as being something outside of the universe of possible consciousness . . . is sheer nonsense." (PL 32.)

38. As will become more apparent in the sequel, to refrain from ontological assertions is not to resolve the issues and problems that call for such assertions. This is especially clear when one faces up to the task of explaining the *genesis* of the meaning 'transcendent thing.'

39. "The natural, objective world-life is only a particular mode of the transcendental life which forever constitutes the world, [but] in such a way that transcendental subjectivity, while living on in this mode [that is, that of the natural attitude], has not become conscious of the constituting horizons and never can become aware of them. It lives in 'infatuation,' so to speak, with the poles of unity without being aware of the constituting multiplicities belonging essentially to them." (*Crisis* 175–76.)

40. "In the *epoché* and in the pure focus upon the functioning ego-pole . . . it

follows *eo ipso* that nothing human is to be found, neither soul nor psychic life nor real psychophysical human beings." (*Crisis* 183.)

41. See *Crisis*, sect. 28, where Husserl argues that "all praxis . . . presupposes the being of this world" and hence necessarily proceeds upon the assumption (or prejudices) intrinsic to the natural attitude.

42. In sect. 45 of the *Crisis*, the *epoché* is described as bringing us to the attitude of "fully 'disinterested' spectators."

43. "The 'transcendental' *epoché* is meant, of course, as a habitual attitude which we resolve to take up once and for all. Thus it is by no means a temporary act." (*Crisis* 150.)

44. See Husserl's discussion of hyletic data in sect. 85 of *Ideas I*.

45. And, were Husserl to abandon this tenet, he would have to concur with Merleau-Ponty's judgment (PP xiv) that the transcendental reduction cannot be completed.

46. "The constitutive systems . . . by virtue of which such and such objects and categories exist for [the ego] are themselves possible only within the frame of a genesis in conformity to [eidetic] laws." (CM 75–76.)

47. "Deduction . . . cannot by us be erroneously conducted." (Rule III, PWD 7.) "Association is . . . a title . . . for a conformity to eidetic laws on the part of the constitution of the pure ego. It designates a realm of the 'innate' Apriori, without which an ego as such is unthinkable." (CM 81.)

48. Husserl does not, himself, seem to regard the necessity of eidetic law as precluding the possibility of error and illusion; in fact, he explicates the latter in terms of the disappointment of expectation (or lack of an anticipated harmonious fulfillment) which occurs when the unfolding multiplicities intended as adumbrations of a synthetic whole do not cohere with the index (i.e., the principle of the series) which should unify them. Nonetheless, it is difficult to understand how it is possible for us to experience this disappointment when our anticipations (which are bound by the necessity of eidetic law or universal a priori) are constitutive of experience. Nor have I found Husserl addressing himself to this problem. *That* Husserl regards the experience of error as compossible with that of apodictic essential intuition is not contested; *how* they can be regarded as such is: hence, the dilemma stated here would seem to confound him as well as Descartes.

Two

1. That the two paradoxes ultimately refer to the same difficulty becomes evident when it is noted that immanence is the condition for the perfectly adequate form of knowledge Meno assumed in posing his dilemma, and that transcendence is the condition for the utter ignorance constituting the dilemma's other horn.

2. "The definition of consciousness . . . can be formulated in the perspective of the for-itself as follows: 'The for-itself is a being such that in its being, its being is in question insofar as this being is essentially a certain way of *not being* a being which it posits simultaneously as other than itself.' " Jean-Paul Sartre, *Being and Nothingness*, trans. Barnes (New York: Philosophical Library, 1956), p. 174. Hereafter cited as BN. For the most part, I adhere to Barnes's translation. In the few instances where I depart from it, I supply the French text from *L'être et le néant* (Paris: Gallimard, 1943).

3. Sartre, *The Transcendence of the Ego*, trans. Williams and Kirkpatrick (New York: Noonday Press, 1957), pp. 42–54.

4. At this point in his text, Sartre has not yet introduced the convention of parentheses to distinguish thetic consciousness *of* an object from non-thetic (or horizonal) consciousness (of) itself.

5. "It is impossible to construct the notion of an object if we do not have origi-

nally a negative relation designating the object as that which *is not* consciousness." (BN 173.)

6. "The for-itself . . . causes itself to be defined by what it is not." (BN 177.) "Every revelation of a positive characteristic of being is the counterpart of an ontological determination as pure negativity in the being of the for-itself." (BN 179.)

7. This distinction of first order negation (negation *simpliciter*) from second order negation (negation of negation) is my own: the distinction exists in Sartre's text, but the labels are my addition.

8. In his chapter on "Bad Faith" Sartre argues that consciousness must be aware (of) its deception of itself. "That which affects itself with bad faith must be conscious (of) its bad faith since the being of consciousness is consciousness of being." (BN 49.)

9. To posit an object absolutely would be to conceive it as a determinate 'this' existing in itself, but that would entail conceiving the entirety of being-in-itself as determined in itself to be itself forever more.

10. The context is a critique of what Merleau-Ponty calls "objective thought"— but it is clear here and elsewhere that Merleau-Ponty regards Sartre as an objective thinker.

11. Jean-Paul Sartre, *Nausea*, trans. Alexander (New York: New Directions Publishing Corp., 1964), p. 172. Sartre's original text reads as follows: "Je compris qu'il n'y avait pas de milieu entre l'inexistence et cette abondance pâmée. Si l'on existait, il fallait exister *jusque-là*. "*La Nausée* (Paris: Gallimard, 1938), p. 181. The corresponding text in Merleau-Ponty's *Phénoménologie* reads: "Tout ce qui existe existe comme chose ou comme conscience, et il n'y a pas de milieu" (PP-F 47).

12. Sometimes Sartre capitalizes 'In-itself,' 'For-itself,' 'Being,' etc., and sometimes he does not. So far as I can tell, there is no convention consistently employed.

13. "C'est dehors, sur l'être qu'il y a un monde qui se découvre à moi." (BN-F 269.)

14. See VI 98–99/VI-F 133–34 where Merleau-Ponty argues that "Descartes and Cartesianism had finally pushed this thinking thing which only half *is* over to the side of Being," and that Sartre has "overcompensated" in the same way for the idealistic tendency of his own thought.

15. "What is given in not consciousness or pure being; it is . . . experience, in other words the communication of a finite subject with an opaque being from which it emerges but to which it remains committed." (PP 219; PP-F 253.)

16. "The unity of either the subject or the object is not a real unity, but a presumptive unity of the horizon of experience. We must rediscover, as anterior to the ideas of subject and object . . . that primordial stratum [*couche*] at which both things and ideas are born." (PP 219; PP-F 254.)

17. "Objective thought . . . knows only alternative notions; starting from actual experience, it defines pure concepts which are mutually exclusive: the notion of *extension*, which is that of an absolute externality of one part to another, and the notion of *thought* which is that of a being wrapped up [*recueilli*] in himself . . . the notion of *cause* as a determining factor external to its effect, and that of *reason* as a law of intrinsic constitution of the phenomenon. . . . The perception of our own body and the perception of external things provide an example of *non-positing* consciousness, that is, of consciousness not in possession of fully determinate objects. . . . These phenomena cannot be assimilated by objective thought." (PP 49; PP-F 60–61.)

THREE

1. Merleau-Ponty, "The Primacy of Perception and Its Philosophical Consequences," trans. Edie, in *The Primacy of Perception*, ed. Edie (Evanston: Northwestern University Press, 1964), p. 13.

2. "Because Being appears as ground, beings are what is grounded; the highest being, however, is what accounts in the sense of giving the first cause. When metaphysics thinks of beings with respect to the ground that is common to all beings as such, then it is logic as onto-logic. When metaphysics thinks beings as such as a whole, that is, with respect to the highest being which accounts for everything, then it is logic as theo-logic. . . .

"The deity enters into philosophy through the perdurance of which we think at first as the approach to the active nature of the difference between Being and beings. The difference constitutes the ground plan in the structure of the essence of metaphysics. The perdurance results in and gives Being as the generative ground. This ground itself needs to be properly accounted for by that for which it accounts, that is, by the causation through the supremely original matter—and that is the cause as *causa sui*. This is the right name for the god of philosophy. Man can neither pray nor sacrifice to this god." Martin Heidegger, *Identity and Difference*, trans. Stambaugh (New York: Harper and Row, 1969), pp. 70–72.

3. Or *différance*.

4. In *Physics*, I, 1, 184a, Aristotle distinguishes between "things which are more knowable and obvious to us" and "those which are clearer and more knowable by nature"; and then proceeds upon this epistemological basis to drive an ontological wedge: "the same things are not 'knowable relatively to us' and 'knowable' without qualification."

5. "The ipseity [of the thing] is never *reached*: each aspect of the thing which falls under our perception is still only an invitation to perceive beyond it, still only a momentary halt in the perceptual process. If the thing itself were reached, from that moment it would be arrayed before us and stripped of its mystery. It would cease to exist as a thing at the very moment when we thought to possess it. What makes the 'reality' of the thing is therefore precisely what snatches it from our grasp. The aseity of the thing, its unchallengeable presence and the perpetual absence into which it withdraws, are two inseparable aspects of transcendence." (PP 233; PP-F 269–70.)

6. "The subject of sensation is neither a thinker who takes note of a quality, nor an inert setting which is affected or changed by it, it is a power which is born together with a certain existential environment or synchronizes itself with it." (PP 211; PP-F 245.)

FOUR

1. *Treatise*, I, II, 1, p. 27.

2. G. T. Fechner, *Elemente der Psychophysik* (Leipzig, 1860).

3. Weintraub and Walker, *Perception* (Belmont, Calif: Brooks/Cole Pub. Co., 1966), p. 77. Also, see J. A. Swets, "Is There a Sensory Threshold?" *Science* 134 (1961), 168–77.

4. See R. A. McCleary and R. S. Lazarus, "Autonomic Discrimination without Awareness: An Interim Report," *J. Pers.* 18 (1949), 171–79.

5. W. Metzger, "Optische Untersuchungen am Ganzfeld," *Psychologische Forschung* XII (1930).

6. Kurt Koffka, *Principles of Gestalt Psychology* (London: Routledge and Kegan Paul, 1935), p. 120.

7. J. F. Corso, *The Experimental Psychology of Sensory Behavior* (New York: Holt, Rinehart, and Winston, 1967), pp. 550–51.

8. Aron Gurwitsch, "Some Aspects and Developments of Gestalt Psychology," in his *Studies in Phenomenology and Psychology* (Evanston: Northwestern University Press, 1966), p. 16. Hereafter cited as "Aspects."

9. "Aspects," p. 20.

10. Gurwitsch, *The Field of Consciousness* (Pittsburgh: Duquesne University Press, 1964), pp. 123–127. Hereafter cited as *Field*.

11. *Field*, p. 91.

12. Koehler, "Ueber unbemerkte Empfindungen und Urteilstäuschungen," *Zeitschrift für Psychologie*, vol. 66 (1913); also *Gestalt Psychology* (New York: Liveright, 1947), pp. 91ff.

13. "It may be . . . safely stated in a general manner that a dualistic account of perception and the adoption of the constancy hypothesis are closely connected." *Field*, p. 91.

14. Gurwitsch, "The Phenomenological and the Psychological Approach to Consciousness," in *Studies in Phenomenology and Psychology*, p. 103.

15. Rubin, *Synsoplevede Figurer* (Copenhagen, 1915). An abridged English translation appears in *Readings in Perception*, ed. D. C. Beardslee and Michael Wertheimer (Princeton: Van Nostrand, 1958), pp. 194–203.

16. Weintraub and Walker, *Perception*, p. 11.

17. "The word *Prägnanz* is of course ultimately connected with the Latin *impregnare*. The suggestion here, however, is not that of something being fertilized or made pregnant but rather of something being stamped or pressed into a particular shape (compare the word *prägen*, which is used primarily to refer to the minting of coins). Certain types of configurations, one might say, are particularly impressive; they carry a certain stamp or they strike us in particular ways." T. R. Miles, "Gestalt Theory," *Encyclopedia of Philosophy*, ed. Paul Edwards (New York: Macmillan, 1967), III, p. 320.

18. Koffka, *Principles of Gestalt Psychology*, p. 110.

19. David Katz, *Gestalt Psychology*, trans. Tyson (New York: Ronald Press, 1950), p. 40.

20. "Aspects," pp. 27–28.

21. Here Merleau-Ponty refers to Cassirer's *Philosophy of Symbolic Forms*, III.

22. For a more extended treatment of the issues at stake in this section, see M. C. Dillon, "Gestalt Theory and Merleau-Ponty's Concept of Intentionality," *Man and World*, Vol. 4, No. 4 (Nov. 1971).

23. Merleau-Ponty, *The Structure of Behavior*, trans. Alden L. Fisher (Boston: Beacon Press, 1963). *La Structure du comportement* (Paris: Presses Universitaires de France, 1942). In a footnote to the passage quoted, Merleau-Ponty cites a reference by Koffka to Wertheimer's principle of isomorphism which he (Koffka) regards as a solution to the problem of correlating physiological processes with conscious processes. Koffka writes the following. "What [Wertheimer] said amounted to this: let us think of the physiological processes not as molecular, but as molar phenomena. If we do that, all the difficulties of the old theory disappear. For if they are molar, their molar properties will be the same as those of the conscious processes which they are supposed to underlie. And if that is so, our two realms, instead of being separated by an impassable gulf, are brought as closely together as possible." Kurt Koffka, *Principles of Gestalt Psychology*, p. 56.

24. Gurwitsch refers to *The Structure of Behavior* and *Phenomenology of Perception* in *The Field of Consciousness*, pp. 169–173. And Merleau-Ponty refers to two early (1932 and 1936) essays by Gurwitsch in his *Phenomenology of Perception*, p. 47n and p. 384n. As will become evident shortly, however, they are separated by profound differences and did not collaborate.

25. Gurwitsch: "Gestalt theory has been led towards a strictly descriptive orientation by the dismissal of the constancy hypothesis. . . . We may interpret the dismissal of the constancy hypothesis as an incipient phenomenological reduction. We say 'incipient' because the dismissal of a specific assumption advanced on the basis of the . . . general conception of the orientation of psychology with respect to

physics does not *ipso facto* entail a departure from this general conception. Gestalt theory has not, in fact, abandoned it." (*Field*, pp.168–69. See also pp. 7, 170.)

Merleau-Ponty: "By taking the *Gestalt* as the theme of his reflection, the psychologist breaks with psychologism, since the meaning, connection and 'truth' of the percept no longer arise from the fortuitous coming together of our sensations as they are given to us by our psycho-physical nature, but determine the spatial and qualitative values of these sensations, and *are* their irreducible configurations. It follows that the transcendental attitude is already implied in the descriptions of the [Gestalt] psychologist, insofar as they are faithful ones." (PP 59; PP-F 72.)

26. Although Gurwitsch adheres to the ontological standpoint of Husserl's transcendental idealism, he departs from Husserl (as did Sartre before him) in rejecting the idea of the transcendental ego as the originating agency of conscious acts in favor of a "non-egological conception of consciousness." See *Studies in Phenomenology and Psychology*, chap. 11.

27. The most comprehensive and sustained critique of Husserl's ontology offered by Merleau-Ponty may be found in chapter 3 of *The Visible and the Invisible* entitled "Interrogation and Intuition."

28. Field, p. 171.

29. "For . . . everyday life, with its changing and relative purposes, relative evidences and truths suffice. But science looks for truths that are valid, and remain so, once for all and for everyone." (*Cartesian Meditations*, p. 12.)

30. Kirk and Raven, *The Presocratic Philosophers* (Cambridge: Cambridge University Press, 1957), fragment 347, p. 273 (from Simplicius, *Physics*, 145, 1).

31. "Sense, signification, and meaning do not denote real features or real constituents of the act of perception, but, on the contrary, an objective ideal unit, similar to the case of meanings of symbols." (*Field*, p. 176.) "Meanings . . . are ideal entities and units between which no temporal relations obtain." (P. 328.) "There is no time at all in the domain of meanings." (P. 329.)

32. See *Ideas* I, sects. 97–101, for further elaboration of this distinction. Also, Dagfinn Føllesdal provides an excellent discussion of some of its ramifications in "Husserl's Notion of Noema," *The Journal of Philosophy* LXVI, no. 20 (October 1969), pp. 680–87.

33. *Field*, pp. 114–16.

34. Ibid., p. 327.

35. Ibid., pp. 234–45.

36. Ibid., pp. 270–79. Also see "Phenomenology of Thematics and of the Pure Ego: Studies of the Relation between Gestalt Theory and Phenomenology" in *Studies in Phenomenology and Psychology*, pp. 253–58.

37. *Field*, p. 54.

38. Ibid., p. 31.

39. "Towards a Theory of Intentionality," *Philosophy and Phenomenological Research* XXX, no. 3 (March 1970), pp. 364–65.

40. "On the Intentionality of Consciousness," in *Studies in Phenomenology and Psychology*, pp. 136–37.

41, Ibid., p. 136.

42. Ibid., p. 137.

43. Husserl, *The Phenomenology of Internal Time-Consciousness*, ed. Heidegger, trans. Churchill (Bloomington and London: Indiana University Press, 1964), pp. 78–79.

44. Suzanne Cunningham, *Language and the Phenomenological Reductions of Edmund Husserl* (The Hague: Nijhoff, 1976), p. 73.

45. Robert S. Brumbaugh, *The Philosophers of Greece* (New York: Crowell, 1964), pp. 31–35.

46. *Philosophical Investigations*, trans. Anscombe (New York: Macmillan, 1953), paras. 65–67.

47. "If . . . we want to give an unprejudiced definition of gestalt psychology's philosophical meaning, we would have to say that, by revealing 'structure' or 'form' as irreducible elements of being, it has again put into question the classical alternative between 'existence as thing' and 'existence as consciousness,' has established a communication between and a mixture of, objective and subjective, and has conceived of psychological knowledge in a new way, no longer as an attempt to break down these typical ensembles but rather an effort to embrace them." Merleau-Ponty, "The Metaphysical in Man," in *Sense and Non-Sense*, trans. H. L. and P. D. Dreyfus (Evanston: Northwestern University Press, 1964), p. 71. "Le metaphysique dans l'Homme" in *Sens et non-sens* (Paris: Editions Nagel, 1966), pp. 150–51.

PART TWO

FIVE

1. I have found it convenient to divide Merleau-Ponty's scholarly career into three periods: early, middle, and late. The early period (up to 1944) centers around *The Structure of Behavior* and is dominated by psychological theory. The middle period (1945–1958), the longest and most productive, begins with the publication of the *Phenomenology of Perception* and takes up a wide range of issues from politics to aesthetics from a phenomenological perspective. The late period (1959–1961), cut off by Merleau-Ponty's sudden death, covers the time when he was working on *The Visible and the Invisible* and includes the writing of "Eye and Mind." For someone primarily interested in Merleau-Ponty's political thought and the changes in his attitude toward Marxism, other temporal boundaries might be more fitting.

2. The issue of intersubjectivity, here treated summarily, will be explored in depth in chapter 7 below.

3. Literally, thought that "flies over" everything; figuratively, high altitude thinking.

4. This thought is anticipated in the *Phenomenology*: "We are not in some incomprehensible way an activity joined to a passivity." (PP 428; PP-F 489.)

5. "Indirect Language and the Voices of Silence," S-75; S-F 93–94.

6. See PP 280–98; PP-F 324–44.

7. Gurwitsch criticizes Merleau-Ponty for "maintaining the existence of 'privileged perceptions' " on the grounds that this is at variance with his (Merleau-Ponty's) thesis that the *sens* of a thing is inseparable from its phenomenal appearance. (*Field*, p. 300.) His thought seems to be that Merleau-Ponty cannot make a qualitative distinction between perceptions without appealing to extra-perceptual (i.e., non-phenomenological or objective) criteria.

Merleau-Ponty does not, however, define optimal perception in terms of variables such as distance, angle, lighting, and so forth which are conceived and measured objectively (i.e., absolutely or non-perspectivally). On the contrary, the optimal perception of a thing is determined phenomenally and differs for each perceptual theme. We experience the theme falling into place, becoming less problematical and more determinate. The relevant variables are internal coherence (of parts to whole) and contextual relevancy (of theme to horizon), and they are defined phenomenologically. Indeed, the so-called objective variables are grounded upon the phenomenal ones insofar as they depend upon the experience of tending toward stability and phenomenal constancy.

See PP 12, 230–35 (PP-F 19, 265–71) for further exposition of the thesis of optimal perception.

Six

1. Merleau-Ponty's customary term is *"l'irréfléchi"* which is usually and quite properly translated as "the unreflective." For reasons that will become apparent in my text, I sometimes refer to this as "the prereflective" as a reminder that the possibility of thematic reflection is intrinsic to perception.

2. The notion of *Fundierung* or foundation, which is central to the implicit ontology of the *Phenomenology*, will be discussed in a later chapter devoted to language—because language is the context most appropriate to its explication.

3. "The sensible forms of being which lie around me, the paper under my hand, the trees before my eyes, do not yield their secret to me, rather is it that my consciousness takes flight from itself and, in them, is unaware of itself" (PP 369; PP-F 423).

4. Sartre's account of the body exacerbates rather than relieves the contradiction at the core of his notion of the prereflective cogito. See chapter 8, "The Lived Body," below which contains a critique of Sartre's position on this issue.

5. "The Child's Relations with Others," trans. William Cobb, in *The Primacy of Perception*, ed. James M. Edie (Evanston: Northwestern University Press, 1964). "Les relations avec autrui chez l'enfant" from the series *Les Cours de Sorbonne* (Paris: Centre de Documentation Universitaire, 1960).

6. "Merleau-Ponty and the Psychogenesis of the Self," *Journal of Phenomenological Psychology* Vol. 9, No. 1–2 (Autumn 1978).

7. "Erotic Desire," *Research in Phenomenology* Vol. XV, 1985. See also "Merleau-Ponty on Existential Sexuality: A Critique," *Journal of Phenomenological Psychology* Vol. 11, No. 1 (Spring 1980).

8. "It is the function of language to cause essences to exist in a state of separation which is in fact merely apparent, since through language they still rest upon the antepredicative life of consciousness." (PP xv; PP-F x.)

Seven

1. Edmund Husserl. *Cartesian Meditations*, trans. Dorion Cairns (The Hague: Nijhoff, 1960). Henceforth cited as CM.

2. Merleau-Ponty, "The Child's Relation with Others," trans. William Cobb, in *The Primacy of Perception*, ed. James M. Edie (Evanston: Northwestern University Press, 1964). "Les relations avec autrui chez l'enfant" from the series *Les Cours de Sorbonne* (Paris: Centre de Documentation Universitaire, 1960). Henceforth cited as CRO.

3. "Properly speaking, neither the other ego himself, nor his subjective processes or his appearances themselves, nor anything else belonging to his own essence, becomes given in our experience originally. If it were, if what belongs to the other's own essense were directly accessible, it would be merely a moment of my own essence, and ultimately he himself and I myself would be the same." (CM 109.)

4. "In the last resort, the actions of others are, according to [the theory of analogical inference], always understood through my own; the 'one' or the 'we' through the 'I.' But this is precisely the question: . . . how can I know that there are other I's, how can consciousness which, by its nature, and as self-knowledge, is in the mode of the I, be grasped in the mode of Thou, and through this, in the world of the 'One?'" (PP 348; PP-F 400–401.)

5. One might argue that the self-other distinction is also absent from the sphere of prereflective engagement, hence that there is a kind of syncretism which is not lost with the passage beyond infancy. Although I could cede this point without diminishing the force of my argument, I am not disposed to do so, but would argue, on the contrary, that the distinction in question is sedimented in the adult world

and operates, if only tacitly, even in prereflective modes (e.g., while competing in sports).

6. The point here—aptly illustrated in this critique—is that reflective analysis tends to attribute to the phenomenon it investigates a quality of self-consciousness that derives from the method of investigation and does not belong to the experience in question.

7. "If my body is to appropriate the conducts given to me visually and make them its own, it must itself be given to me not as a mass of utterly private sensations but instead by what has been called a 'postural' or 'corporeal schema.' This notion, introduced long ago by Henry Head, has been taken over and enriched by Wallon, by certain German psychologists, and has finally been the subject of a study in its own right by Professor Lhermitte in *l'Image de notre corps* (Paris, 1939)." (CRO 117.)

8. 'Cenesthesia,' the term just defined, should not be confused with the notion of synesthesia which refers to the inseparability of the senses and the blending of sensory contents.

9. Given the doctrine of cenesthesia, "the consciousness I have of my body is impenetrable by you. You cannot represent yourself in the same way in which I feel my own body; it is likewise impossible for me to represent to myself the way in which you feel your body. How, then, can I suppose that, in back of this appearance before me, there is someone who experiences his body as I experience mine?" (CRO 114).

10. The very term, 'intersubjectivity,' perpetuates a Cartesian bias because it implicitly conceives human sociality as communion among conscious subjects: conceived in this way, the structures of being-with presuppose an intellectualist anthropology. Merleau-Ponty's use of the term betrays once again the fact that the *Phenomenology of Perception* is a transitional work. Although he succeeds, as I have tried to show, in resolving the Cartesian/Husserlian problem of solipsism—and does so by moving beyond the ontological presuppositions that generate the problem—Merleau-Ponty's middle period account of intersubjectivity suffers because it is still conceived as an account of *intersubjectivity*.

11. For detailed discussion of this and other relevant points, see M. C. Dillon, "Merleau-Ponty and the Psychogenesis of the Self," *Journal of Phenomenological Psychology* Vol. 9, No. 1–2 (Autumn 1978).

12. And thereby perpetuates Lacan's initial *méconnaissance*. See Lacan, "The mirror stage as formative of the function of the I as revealed in psychoanalytic experience," in *Écrits*, trans. Sheridan (New York: Norton, 1977), p. 2, and "Aggressivity in psychoanalysis," also in *Écrits*, p. 19.

Wilden's commentary on "the alienation revealed by the *stade du miroir*" is particularly lucid on this point. See Anthony Wilden, *Lacan and the Discourse of the Other*, in Jacques Lacan, *Speech and Language in Psychoanlysis*, trans. Wilden (Baltimore: Johns Hopkins University Press, 1981), pp. 164–77. I might observe, however, that Wilden's structuralist interpretation of the mirror stage leads him to waffle on the issue of the priority of self-alienation to the self-other dialectic (Wilden, p. 174) in the face of Lacan's clear assertion: "This jubilant assumption of his specular image by the child at the *infans* stage . . . would seem to exhibit in an exemplary situation the symbolic matrix in which the *I* is precipitated in a *primordial* form, *before it is objectified in the dialectic of identification with the other*, and before language restores to it, in the universal, its function as subject." (Lacan, "The mirror stage . . . ," p. 2. Emphasis added.)

My argument in support of the position that the earliest phases of self-recognition/alienation (e.g., the mirror stage) presuppose the prior context of alienating encounters with an other is set forth in "Merleau-Ponty and the Psychogenesis of the Self."

13. "At two or three months one observes that deliberately looking at the child makes him smile. At that moment there will be in the child at least one perception of a look as of something that makes him complete." (CRO 124.)

14. "I understand all the more easily that what is in the mirror is my image for being able to represent to myself the other's viewpoint on me; and, inversely, I understand all the more the experience the other can have of me for seeing myself in the mirror in the aspect I offer him." (CRO 139.)

15. I was tempted to include a chapter on love in this work because I believe that the opening of that domain to philosophical understanding is one of Merleau-Ponty's most significant contributions to Western thought, but I have decided not to do so. Merleau-Ponty did not write extensively on the subject of love, although his scattered remarks are seminal and his writing on intersubjectivity, especially his responses to Sartre's pessimism, begs for completion. I intend to undertake a study of love predicated on the ontology articulated herein, but that is a project that demands an autonomy it could not have in the present context. I can, however, refer the reader to pilot essays in which I have attempted to sketch the implications of Merleau-Ponty's ontology for a theory of love. See "Toward a Phenomenology of Love and Sexuality," *Soundings* Vol. LXIII, No. 4 (Winter 1980); and "Erotic Desire," *Research in Phenomenology* Vol. XV, (1985).

EIGHT

1. Schneider is "a patient whom traditional psychiatry would class among cases of psychic blindness" (PP 103; PP-F 119). His motor disorders, to be discussed below, "are related to far-reaching disorders of sight, which in turn arise from the occipital injury which lies at the root of his condition" (PP 113; PP-F 131).

2. Gelb and Goldstein, "Über den Einfluss des vollständigen Verlustes des optischen Vorstellungsvermögens auf das taktile Erkennen" in *Psychologische Analysen hirnpathologischer Fälle* (Leipzig: Barth, 1920), Chap. II, pp. 157–250.

Goldstein, "Über die Abhängigkeit der Bewegungen von optischen Vorgängen," *Monatschrift für Psychiatrie und Neurologie* (Festschrift Liepmann, 1923).

Goldstein, *Zeigen und Greifen* (Nervenartzt, 1931).

For other works by Gelb and Goldstein cited by Merleau-Ponty see the bibliography of the *Phenomenology of Perception*.

3. Heidegger, *Being and Time*, trans. Macquarrie and Robinson (New York: Harper and Row, 1962), sect. 17, pp. 107–114.

4. Although this is not one of Merleau-Ponty's examples, he does provide extended support for this point. See PP 138–39 /PP-F 161–62 (where he argues that cases of apraxia and psychic paralysis remain unintelligible unless we acknowledge that "motility is not the handmaid of consciousness"), PP 139–142/PP-F 162–66 (where he demonstrates that we have a "motor 'memory' " which is not representational), and PP 142–45/PP-F 166–70 (where he shows that there can be no successful account of the genesis of habit which does not allow for motor significance). "It is the body which understands in the cultivation of habit." (PP 144; PP-F 169.)

5. Sartre, *Being and Nothingness*, trans. Barnes (New York: Philosophical Library, 1956). Hereafter cited as BN. Where I have altered Barnes's translation, reference to the French language text—*L'être et le néant* (Paris: Gallimard, 1943)—is provided, using the abbreviation BN-F.

6. Merleau-Ponty refers here to Husserl's *Cartesian Meditations*.

7. "Eye and Mind," trans. Dallery, in *The Primacy of Perception*, ed. Edie (Evanston: Northwestern University Press, 1964), p. 167. *L'Œil et l'esprit* (Paris: Gallimard, 1964), pp. 31–32.

PART THREE

NINE

1. An early version of this chapter was published under the title, "Merleau-Ponty and the Reversibility Thesis," *Man and World* Vol. 16 (1983).

2. See VI 22–3; VI-F 41. "Our purpose is . . . to show that the being-object and the being-subject conceived by opposition to it and relative to it do not form the alternative, that the perceived world is beneath or beyond this antinomy, that the failure of 'objective' psychology is—conjointly with the failure of 'objectivist' physics—to be understood not as a victory of the 'interior' over the 'exterior' and of the 'mental' over the 'material,' but as a call for the revision of our ontology, for the re-examination of the notions of 'subject' and 'object.' "

3. See VI 176; VI-F 230 "I must show that what one might consider 'psychology' (*Phenomenology of Perception*) is in fact ontology." Also, in another working note written during the same month (February 1959) as the above, Merleau-Ponty speaks of the "necessity of bringing the results of the *Phenomenology of Perception* to ontological explicitation." (VI 183; VI-F 237).

4. Chapter five of *The Visible and the Invisible*, which Lefort titles "Preobjective Being: The Solipsist World" and treats as an appendix, is, in my view, properly to be regarded as an introduction to a critique of the ontological presuppositions which prevent Husserl and Sartre from delivering adequate accounts of intersubjectivity and keep them, despite efforts to the contrary, within the solipsistic sphere of immanence. See chapter 4 above.

5. "To each psychic lived process there corresponds through the device of phenomenological reduction a pure phenomenon, which exhibits its intrinsic (immanent) essence . . . as an absolute datum." Edmund Husserl, *The Idea of Phenomenology*, trans. Alston and Nakhnikian (The Hague: Nijhoff, 1964), p. 35.

6. Martin Heidegger, *Being and Time*, trans. Macquarrie and Robinson (New York: Harper and Row, 1962), sec. 7A.

7. Jean-Paul Sartre, *Being and Nothingness*, trans. Hazel Barnes (New York: Washington Square Press, 1966), Introduction, pp. 21–24: "The Ontological Proof."

8. Maurice Merleau-Ponty, "The Primacy of Perception and Its Philosophical Consequences," trans. James Edie, in *The Primacy of Perception*, ed. James Edie (Evanston: Northwestern University Press, 1964), p. 13.

9. In taking up the issue of reversibility in seeing, Merleau-Ponty explicitly states that he will consider reversibility in vision as a variant of tactile reversibility. "What is this prepossession of the visible, this art of interrogating it according to its own wishes, this inspired exegesis? We would perhaps find the answer in the tactile palpation where the questioner and the questioned are closer, and of which, after all, the palpation of the eye is a remarkable variant" (VI 133; VI-F 174). And, again, "every reflection is of the model of that of the hand touching by the hand touched [*toute réflexion est du modèle de celle de la main touchante par la main touchée*]." (VI 204; VI-F 257, my translation.)

10. The equations of "my body for-me" with body-subject and "the body-for-others" with body-object are explicated in my essay "Sartre on the Phenomenal Body and Merleau-Ponty's Critique," *Journal of the British Society for Phenomenology* Vol. 5, No. 2 (May 1974).

11. There is a minor inconsistency in Merleau-Ponty's writings that should be noted here. In *L'Œil et l'esprit* (Paris: Gallimard, 1964), he writes that "my body is *simultaneously* seeing and seen" (p. 18, emphasis added). He goes on to say that my body "sees itself seeing" and "touches itself touching." This language of simultaneity and coincidence—written in the summer of 1960—conflicts with the later argu-

ments against simultaneity and coincidence in the latter part of the VI manuscript which he wrote the following fall and winter.

I view the passage in *L'Œil et l'esprit* as an oversight which went unnoticed/uncorrected because simultaneity/coincidence was not a thematic issue in that work. When, in *The Visible and the Invisible*, it did become an issue, Merleau-Ponty articulated the standpoint which I am taking to be his considered and (literally) final statement.

(Unless otherwise indicated, passages quoted from *L'Œil et l'esprit* are my own translations from the Gallimard edition. I shall provide page references to the Carleton Dallery translation in *The Primacy of Perception*, ed. James Edie [Evanston: Northwestern University Press, 1964] using the abbreviation, EM, and giving first the page number in the English translation and then the page number in the French edition.)

12. "Hyperreflection" (*"surréflexion"*) is the name given by Merleau-Ponty to that kind of reflection which would confront its own "ultimate problems" (VI 46; VI-F 70).

13. In this context, it is illuminating to raise the question of reversibility in regard to the other senses. Is it the case that to smell a sulfur spring is to be smelled by it? Or to hear a thunderclap—or to taste a wine? The *reductio* suggested here is not intended to undermine the reversibility thesis: the point, rather, is to guard against too literal an interpretation of it.

14. I am indebted to Alphonso Lingis for bringing this problem to focus for me. His paper on "The Visible and the Vision" (presented at the Seventh Annual Meeting of the Merleau-Ponty Circle, SUNY-Binghamton, October 1982) begins with the question of what Merleau-Ponty had in view "when he said, with painters, that it is not I that see the trees and the landscapes, but it is the trees and landscapes that look at me." Although my answer to this question differs from the one proposed by Lingis (notably on the question of asymmetry), his treatment of the psychoanalytic understanding of this issue, derived in part from Lacan, brilliantly thematizes the component of sexual desire in the reversibility of vision.

15. This characterization of the reversibility thesis as ultimate truth in Merleau-Ponty's last written words is discussed by Claude Lefort in the "editor's foreword" to the English translation (VI xxix-xxx)—which is the "postface" to the French text (VI-F 356–57).

16. See also VI 200; VI-F 253. "The problems posed in *Ph.P* are insoluble because I start there from the 'consciousness'-'object' distinction."

17. I understand that, as I write this, Professor Theodore Geraets of the University of Ottawa is working on a study of the Hegelian antecedents of Merleau-Ponty's thought.

18. See Baillie's comment at the beginning of the section [B] on Self-consciousness: " 'consciousness of self' is the basis of the consciousness of anything whatsoever. This is Hegel's re-interpretation of the Kantian analysis of experience." G. W. F. Hegel, *The Phenomenology of Mind*, trans. Baillie (New York: Harper and Row, 1967), p. 217.

19. "What the object immediately [is] *in itself*—whether mere being in sense-certainty, a concrete thing in perception, or force in the case of understanding—it turns out, in truth, not to be this really; but instead, this inherent nature (*Ansich*) proves to be a way in which it is for an other [i.e., for consciousness] . . . . And it is *for* consciousness that the inherent nature (*Ansich*) of the object, and its 'being for an other' *are* one and the same." Ibid., pp. 218–19.

20. Ibid., p. 151.

21. "Inconceivable." How is one to conceive the space in which some extended thing *touches* something that has no extension (i.e., "takes up" no space)?

22. John O'Neill, in "The Specular Body: Merleau-Ponty and Lacan on Self and

Other" (also presented at the Seventh Annual Meeting of the Merleau-Ponty Circle), presents a particularly sensitive treatment of the process of infantile individuation. "The necessary separation of the infant and maternal bodies may be conceived *from the very start* as a *precipitation* of self and not-self in every motor and sensory behavior, involving social mediations, and possibly a critical moment such as the mirror stage," (P. 7, emphasis added).

23. "At six months . . . the child looks the other child in the face, and one has the impression that here, for the first time, he is perceiving another." Merleau-Ponty, "The Child's Relations with Others," trans. William Cobb, in *The Primacy of Perception,* p. 125.

24. This statement clearly rectifies an earlier passage in which Merleau-Ponty writes of "a veritable touching of the touch, when my right hand touches my left hand while it is palpating the things." (VI 134; VI-F 176.)

25. It is a consequence of the thesis of the primacy of perception that language must be conceived as grounded in phenomena and, specifically, as deriving the significance it articulates from the mute meaningfulness of the world. The autochthonous organization of the phenomenal world is the ground of worldly meaning. World is, thus, the primary or founding term of the asymmetrical relation of *Fundierung*, and the linguistic expression is founded and derivative. However, the world becomes intelligible for us only to the extent that its phenomena are seen in relation to one another. The ground of these relations lies in the—silent—autochthonous organization of phenomena, but the linguistic expression of the relations is the first step toward the ideal of unification which is the goal of understanding. In this view, transcendental constitution (i.e., the projection of linguistic schemata, ideal categories, or noemata) is not primordial but follows upon an original act of learning (akin to Husserl's "primal institution") which is a perceptual *Gestaltung*.

26. "On the Phenomenology of Language," in *Signs,* trans. McCleary (Evanston: Northwestern University Press, 1964), p. 89. "Sur la phénoménologie du langage," in *Signes* (Paris: Gallimard, 1960), p. 112.

27. I have undertaken this project in an essay on "Erotic Desire," *Research in Phenomenology* Vol. XV, 1985.

28. Merleau-Ponty's critique of Kantian transcendental thought is discussed in my article on "A priority in Kant and Merleau-Ponty" forthcoming in *Kant-Studien.*

Ten

1. "*L'interrogation philosophique sur le monde ne consiste donc pas à se reporter du monde même à ce que nous en disons, puisqu'elle se réitère à l'intérieur du langage.*" [VI-F 132.]

2. Jacques Derrida, *De la Grammatologie* (Paris: Les Editions de Minuit, 1967). *Of Grammatology,* trans. Spivak (Baltimore: Johns Hopkins University Press, 1976). It might be worthwhile to note here that Merleau-Ponty does address himself to Derrida—whose prominence in France was growing long before the publication of *Grammatology*—but he does not name Derrida in his reference to contemporary linguistics.

3. Although post-hermeneutic skepticism and semeiological reductionism emerge from the works of Heidegger and Saussure, neither of these figures, as I interpret the primary texts, espoused the standpoint derived from his thought.

4. Heidegger, *Being and Time,* trans. Macquarrie and Robinson (New York: Harper and Row, 1962), sect. 32, pp. 188–95.

5. Heidegger, "The Origin of the Work of Art," in *Poetry, Language, Thought,* trans. Hofstadter (New York: Harper and Row, 1971), p. 78. Subsequent reference to this work will be made in the main text using the short title, "Origin."

6. Heidegger, *An Introduction to Metaphysics,* trans. Manheim (New York: Double-

day, 1961), p. 11. Subsequent reference to this work will be made in the main text using the abbreviation, IM.

7. Heidegger, "What Are Poets For?" in *Poetry, Language, Thought*, p. 132.

8. Heidegger, "Hölderlin and the Essence of Poetry," trans. Scott, in *Existence and Being*, ed. Brock (Chicago: Regnery, 1949), p. 287. The original German language version of this essay was published in 1936.

9. Heidegger, ". . . Poetically Man Dwells . . . ," in *Poetry, Language, Thought*, p. 215.

10. "Language is the house of Being because language, as saying, is the mode of Appropriation." Heidegger, "The Way to Language," in *On the Way to Language*, trans. Hertz (New York: Harper and Row, 1971), p. 135. German language version published in 1959.

11. To the extent that semeiological laws are grounded in sociological laws, at least one science seems to defy the reduction.

12. Ferdinand de Saussure, *Course in General Linguistics*, ed. Bally and Sechehaye in collaboration with Reidlinger, trans. Baskin (New York: Philosophical Library, 1959). Subsequent reference to this work will be made in the main text using the short title, *Course*.

13. I say "for the most part compatible" because the scientific realism implicit in Saussure's appeal to sociology, history, physiology, etc. would be regarded as naive by contemporary proponents of semeiological reductionism.

14. That is, the sign unites a signified (concept) and a signifier (sound-image). *Course*, p. 66.

15. "Without the help of signs we would be unable to make a clear-cut, consistent distinction between two ideas. Without language, thought is a vague, uncharted nebula. There are no pre-existing ideas, and nothing is distinct before the appearance of language." *Course*, pp. 111–12.

16. "The linguistic entity exists only through the associating of the signifier with the signified. Whenever only one element is retained, the entity vanishes; instead of a concrete object we are faced with a mere abstraction." (*Course* pp. 102–103.) Also, see *Course*, pp. 65–67.

17. "Each linguistic term is a member, an articulus [joint, knuckle; turning point] in which an idea is fixed in a sound and a sound becomes the sign of an idea." *Course*, p. 113.

18. "The arbitrary nature of the sign explains . . . why the social fact alone can create a linguistic system. The community is necessary if values that owe their existence solely to usage and general acceptance are to be set up; by himself the individual is incapable of fixing a single value." *Course*, p. 113.

It is interesting to note the conflict with Heidegger here. The latter grants this power of linguistic institution to the poet—who stands apart from the community and listens to the gods.

19. Here I exchange Saussure's convention for the one I am employing, but, I trust, without altering his intent. See *Course*, pp. 66–67.

20. See *Being and Time*, sect. 6.

21. It is clear from the French text that the antecedent of "it"—in all four instances in this sentence—is "language."

22. Merleau-Ponty, *La prose du monde*, ed. Lefort (Paris: Gallimard, 1969). *The Prose of the World*, ed. Lefort, trans. O'Neill (Evanston: Northwestern University Press, 1973). Subsequent reference to this work will be made in the main text using the abbreviation, PW, for the English translation and PW-F for the French edition.

23. Ludwig Wittgenstein, *Tractatus Logico-Philosophicus*, trans. D. F. Pears and B. F. McGuinness (London: Routledge and Kegan Paul, 1961), prop. 6.54. Subsequent reference to this work will be made in the main text using the short title, *Tractatus*.

24. Merleau-Ponty, *Consciousness and the Acquisition of Language*, trans. Silverman

(Evanston: Northwestern University Press, 1973). Subsequent reference to this work will be made in the main text using the abbreviation, CAL.

25. It is true that adherents to the standpoints being criticized here generally eschew any notion of a "transcendental signified," that is, a concept or category presupposed by understanding and prior to language. However, it is equally true that they embrace the notion of a "transcendental sign system," that is, the notion that all cognition is mediated by language, hence presupposes language. It is this latter position that I contend is committed to a linguistic nativism.

26. As I have sought to show, post-hermeneutic skepticism and semeiological reductionism are committed to the transcendentalism that results in nativism. They are not, however, committed to the thesis of a single universal sign system embedded in the depths of the manifold of existing languages. Indeed, the currently governing models espouse a linguistic pluralism. But that does not free them from the nativism I contend is implicit in their views; rather, it compounds the nativism by presupposing a plurality of innate sign systems operative within different geographical sectors.

27. To me, at least. I am informed by my colleague, Paul Hopper, that contemporary linguists carefully refrain from assenting to this inference and prefer to allow theoretical room for the possibility of a common source.

28. If one asserts *that* signifier and signified are linked by the institution of a convention within a social context, one is also obliged to explain *how* this linkage might be established, how the originating speaker communicated his intent.

29. Gestures intrinsically have meaning, but the meanings they convey, although multi-determinable (or ambiguous), are not omni-determinable (which would make them meaningless): quite apart from convention, one perceives the gesture as expressing something finite, and the evolution of the situation (i.e., the context) provides the specification.

30. If the verbal gesture necessarily presupposes a sedimented *cultural* context, one must allow for the sedimentation of prelinguistic gestures as constituting the nascent culture or "form of life" within which the first words could appear.

31. In the opening arguments of his *Philosophical Investigations*, trans. Anscombe (New York: Macmillan, 1953). "So one might say: the ostensive definition explains the use—the meaning—of the word when the overall role of the word in language is clear." (Prop. 30, p. 14.) That is, when it is *already* clear: ostensive definition cannot explain the institution of a convention.

32. "The word possesses no virtue of its own; there is no power hidden in it. It is a pure sign standing for a pure signification. The person speaking is coding his thought. He replaces his thought with a visible or sonorous pattern which is nothing but sounds in the air or ink spots on the paper. Thought understands itself and is self-sufficient. Thought signifies outside itself through a message which does not carry it, and conveys it unequivocally to another mind which can read the message because it attaches the same signification to the same sign, whether by habit, by human conventions, or by divine institution. In any case, we never find among other people's words anything that we have not put there ourselves. Communication is an appearance; it never teaches us anything truly new. How could communication possibly carry us beyond our own powers of reflection, since the signs communication employs could never tell us anything unless we already grasped the signification?" (PW 7; PW-F 12–13.)

33. See *Being and Time*, sect. 35.

34. See Saussure, *Course in General Linguistics*, p. 14: "In separating language [*la langue*] from speaking [*la parole*] we are at the same time separating: (1) what is social from what is individual; and (2) what is essential from what is accessory and more or less accidental." That Merleau-Ponty alters this distinction for his own purposes (and, perhaps, misreads Saussure in the process) is convincingly argued

by James Edie in his "Foreword" to *Consciousness and the Acquisition of Language.* See pp. xxx-xxxi.

35. New slang coinages, oaths, obscenities, etc. might provide better examples since they retain some of the poetic clout of authentic expression, but, here too, familiar usage empties words of their emotional content.

36. PP 187; PP-F 218. See also CAL 99: "one can never exactly translate from one language into another."

37. Merleau-Ponty provides additional support for his thesis in detailed analyses of data taken from speech pathology in which, for example, he explicates several linguistic dysfunctions (aphasia, color amnesia) in terms of the deterioration of the meanings of words which, for the patient, have lost their "gestural or existential significance." (PP 192–93; PP-F 224–26; CAL 73.) Length restrictions preclude me from commenting on this and other interesting facets of the case he makes for his gestural theory.

38. See *Being and Time,* sect. 7A, p. 51.

39. As Merleau-Ponty points out in "On the Phenomenology of Language," in *Signs,* trans. McCleary (Evanston: Northwestern University Press, 1964), pp. 86–89. *Signes* (Paris: Gallimard, 1960), pp. 107–110. Subsequent reference to *Signs* will be made using the abbreviation, S, for the English translation and S-F for the French edition.

40. Thus it is illuminating, to cite an example with a direct bearing on the point at hand, to learn that the English 'idea' derives from the Greek οἶδα' (I know) which, in turn, is the present perfect of 'εἴδω' (I see). I should mention here, however, that Merleau-Ponty states that "etymology can . . . give a false idea of a word. In effect, when the meaning of a word is not behind but in front, this prospective meaning is not necessarily the result of past meanings." (CAL 84.) Properly understood, this does not undermine the bearing of etymology on contemporary usage. The context of this remark is a critique of ideal and universal grammar, i.e., the notion of a pure eidetic language which *precedes* all actual languages and of which they are imperfect realizations. Merleau-Ponty's point is that universality is the goal of language, the end toward which it strives, and not a prior condition of language. Ideality is thus in front of words, not behind them. (See, "On the Phenomenology of Language," (S 87; S-F 109.) But what is legitimately behind a current word usage is its origin: currency always indicates an attenuation of the force and vivacity of the founding/creative/authentic expression in originating speech. This can be retrieved in some measure through the techniques of etymology.

41. "We must rediscover the structure of the perceived world through a process similar to that of an archaeologist. For the structure of the perceived world is buried under the sedimentation of later knowledge." "An Unpublished Text by Maurice Merleau-Ponty: A Prospectus of His Work," trans. Arleen B. Dallery, in *The Primacy of Perception,* ed. Edie (Evanston: Northwestern University Press, 1964), p. 5. Subsequent references to *The Primacy of Perception* will be made using the abbreviation, PriP.

42. *Consciousness and the Acquisition of Language* is certainly an important document to consider in attempting to interpret Merleau-Ponty's thoughts on language during the period in question, but, as the translator, Hugh J. Silverman, is careful to point out, *Consciousness and the Acquisition of Language* "was not a carefully worked out or formally written book on the order of *The Structure of Behavior* or *Phenomenology of Perception.* Rather, it was a series of weekly lectures, transcribed by students and then approved by Merleau-Ponty himself." (CAL xxxv.) There is little or no conflict, however, between the course notes and what we have of *The Prose of the World;* indeed, several of the theses developed in the book have clearly grown out of the course.

43. I leave the term in its German form in order to distinguish the specific and technical meaning of *'Fundierung'* from the general and ordinary usage of 'foundation.' (Merleau-Ponty also uses the term, *'Stiftung'*—another appropriation from Husserl—to designate the founding/founded relation. *'Stiftung'* is usually translated as 'foundation' or 'establishment.')

44. The word's meaning is not compounded of a certain number of physical characteristics belonging to the object; it is first and foremost the aspect taken on by the object in human experience. . . . Here we have a meeting of the human and the non-human and, as it were, a piece of the world's behavior, a certain version of its style, and *the generality of its meaning as well as that of the vocable is not the generality of the concept, but of the world as typical.*" (PP 403; PP-F 462; emphasis added.)

45. The thesis of subjectivity is the thesis that the world, as I see it, is the world-as-I-see-it. See PW 117; PW-F 163–64: "The moment that we believe we are grasping the world as it is apart from us, it is no longer the world we are grasping, since we are there to grasp it. In the same way, there always remains, behind our talk about language, more living language than can ever be taken in by our view of it."

46. "This subjectivity [i.e., the tacit cogito], albeit imperious, has upon itself and upon the world only a precarious hold. *It does not constitute the world,* it divines the world's presence round about it as a field not provided by itself." (PP 403–04; PP-F 462; emphasis added.)

47. "What then does language express, if it does not express thoughts? It presents or rather it is the subject's taking up of a position in the world of his meanings. The term 'world' here is not a manner of speaking: it means that *the 'mental' or cultural life borrows its structures from natural life* and that the thinking subject must have its basis in the subject incarnate." (PP 193; PP-F 225; emphasis added.)

And again: "Our body, to the extent that it moves itself about, that is, to the extent that it is inseparable from a view of the world and is that view itself brought into existence, is the condition of possibility . . . of all expressive operations and all acquired views which constitute the cultural world." (PP 388; PP-F 445.)

48. "The spectacle perceived does not partake of pure being. Taken exactly as I see it, it is a moment of my individual history, and since sensation is a reconstitution, it presupposes in me sediments left behind by some previous constitution, so that I am, as sentient subject, a repository stocked with natural powers at which I am the first to be filled with wonder." (PP 215; PP-F 249.)

49. That is, he does not separate nature and culture into absolutely disjunct realms and state simply that one is built upon the other. The main point of the *Fundierung* model is to show the reciprocity (or intertwining) of the two. Indeed, Merleau-Ponty explicitly argues against the possibility of distinguishing within perception the natural component from the cultural component. See "Indirect Language and the Voices of Silence" where, in a discussion of the silent and the speaking arts, he argues that the painter is not able to say "what comes from him and what comes from things—because the distinction has no meaning." (S 58–59; S-F 73; emphasis added.)

50. *"Le sensible me rend ce qui je lui ai prêté, mais c'est de lui que je le tenais"* (PP-F 248).

51. "The world-structure, with its two stages of sedimentation and spontaneity [or creative expression], is at the center of consciousness" (PP 130; PP-F 152).

52. I should note that Saussure's emphasis on social foundations seems to have influenced Merleau-Ponty's thinking at this time.

53. Cf. PW 123–24; PW-F 173, where Merleau-Ponty describes his endeavor "to rediscover the paths of the sublimation which preserves and transforms the perceived world into the spoken world."

54. "An Unpublished Text" (PriP 3–11).

55. VI xxxiv.

56. "We must recognize as an ultimate fact this open and indefinite power of giving significance—that is, both of *apprehending* and conveying a meaning—by which man transcends himself towards a new form of behavior, or towards other people, or towards his own thought, through his body and speech." (PP 194; PP-F 226.) See also PP 389; PP-F 446–47.

57. "If . . . the truths of culture seem to us the measure of being, and if so many philosophies posit the world upon them, it is because knowledge continues upon the thrust of perception. It is because knowledge uses the world-thesis which is its fundamental sound [*qui en est le son fondamental*]. We believe truth is eternal because *truth expresses the perceived world* and perception implies a world which was functioning before it and according to principles which it discovers and does not posit. In one and the same movement knowledge roots itself in perception and distinguishes itself from perception. Knowledge is an effort to recapture, to internalize, truly to possess a meaning that escapes perception at the very moment that it takes shape there, because it is interested only in the echo that being draws from itself, not in this resonator, its own other which makes the echo possible." (PW 124; PW-F 174.)

58. "I express when, utilizing all these already speaking instruments [i.e., the modes of expression offered me by the given culture], I make them say something they have never said. We begin reading a philosopher by giving the words he makes use of their 'common' meaning; and little by little, through what is at first an imperceptible reversal, his speech comes to dominate his language, and it is his use of words which ends up assigning them a new and characteristic signification. At this moment he has made himself understood and his signification has come to dwell in me." "On the Phenomenology of Language" (S 91; S-F 113–14).

59. "Indirect Language and the Voices of Silence" (S 81; S-F 101, emphasis added).

60. This self-recovery and self-confirmation is the process of revivification of sedimented language when, as described earlier, it is taken up and transformed (or coherently deformed) in the process of genuine expression.

61. I think Merleau-Ponty's point here is that any limits that appear to structure language from within derive ultimately from the limits and structure of the perceived world. Thus, reversing Wittgenstein, the limits of my world mean the limits of my language. It is on this point that Ricoeur and Edie challenge Merleau-Ponty for failing to do justice to the "algorithmic aspect of language" brought out by the structuralists. See Edie's "Foreword " to *Consciousness and the Acquisition of Language* pp. xxxi–xxxii. In fact, Merleau-Ponty does address himself to this issue in "The Algorithm and the Mystery of Language" (PW 115–29; PW-F 161–81) where he argues that "the algorithmic expression is . . . secondary" (PW 128; PW-F 180) and derives from "the mute or operational language of perception" (PW 124; PW-F 175). I side with Merleau-Ponty on this issue. Indeed, it has been a major theme throughout this work that any form or logic appearing within experience emanates from within the perceptual world and is not superimposed upon it by a transcendental consciousness or Transcendent Source of a supervenient symbolic order. The issue of syntax and semantics will be taken up in section 5 below.

62. "Since the sign has meaning only insofar as it is profiled against other signs, its meaning is entirely involved in language." "Indirect Language and the Voices of Silence" (S 42; S-F 53).

63. "Indirect Language and the Voices of Silence" (S 39; S-F 49). He then amplifies this by saying that "contemporary linguistics conceives of the unity of language in an even more precise way by isolating, at the origin of words . . . , 'oppositional' and 'relative' principles to which the Saussurian definition of sign applies even more rigorously than to words, since it is a question here of components of language which do not for their part have any assignable meaning and whose sole function

is to make possible the discrimination of signs in the strict sense." "Indirect Language and the Voices of Silence" (S 40; S-F 50).

64. In fact, he appeals to it frequently in the course of the essay. See, for example, "Indirect Language and the Voices of Silence" (S 42; S-F 53–54): "Before there can be such ready-made significations [as those of instituted language], language must first make significations exist as guideposts by establishing them at the intersection of linguistic gestures as that which, by common consent, the gestures reveal."

65. That is, the constructions which formalize the signification. Merleau-Ponty is here using the example of an algorithm as a paradigm or test case of highly conventional or formalized signs, but, as he says, if his claim "is true of the algorithm, it is all the more true of language" (PW 107; PW-F 152). The critique of formal thought appears in "Indirect Language and the Voices of Silence," but without these passages on the algorithm.

66. See PW 69n; PW-F 97n: "the sedimentation of art collapses to the extent that it is achieved." Kisling's art is false (or a failure) exactly to the extent that it recapitulates the truths of Modigliani.

67. "In any case no language ever wholly frees itself from the precariousness of mute forms of expression, reabsorbs its own contingency, and wastes away to make the things themselves appear; [and] in this sense the *privilege* language enjoys over painting . . . remains relative." "Indirect Language and the Voices of Silence" (S 78; S-F 98).

68. *L'homme ne peint pas la peinture, mais il parle sur la parole.*" "Indirect Language and the Voices of Silence" (S 80; S-F 100).

69. Michel Foucault, *The Order of Things*, English translation of *Les Mots et les choses* (New York: Random House, 1970), chap. 1. I should note here that the self-referentiality of painting is a theme that Merleau-Ponty develops eight years later, in "Eye and Mind" (1960), when his reflections on painting go beyond the commentary on Malraux in "Indirect Language and the Voices of Silence" and present a more consolidated and distinctive viewpoint.

Artists have often mused upon mirrors because beneath this 'mechanical trick,' they recognized, just as they did in the case of the trick of perspective, the metamorphosis of seeing and seen which defines both our flesh and the painter's vocation. This explains why they have so often liked to draw themselves in the act of painting . . . , adding to what *they* saw then, what *things* saw of them.

Merleau-Ponty, "Eye and Mind," trans. Carleton Dallery, in *The Primacy of Perception*, ed. Edie (Evanston: Northwestern University Press, 1964). pp. 168–69. *L'Œil et l'esprit* (Paris: Gallimard, 1964), p. 34. Subsequent reference to this work will be made in the main text using the abbreviation, EM, for the English translation and EM-F for the French edition.

70. "[The] lack of relation between babbling and phonemic oppositions seems to indicate that possessing a sound as an element of babbling which is addressed only to itself is not the same as possessing a sound as a stage in the effort to communicate." "Indirect Language and the Voices of Silence" (S 40; S-F 50–51).

71. I exclude the question of ideograms or other such 'traces' as irrelevant to the issue at hand: paintings are not composed of ideograms.

72. "Precisely because painting is always something to be created, the works which the new painter is going to produce will be added to already created works. The new do not make the old useless, nor do they expressly contain them. They rival them. . . . Speech, not content to push beyond the past, claims to recapitulate, retrieve, and contain it in substance. And since without repeating it textually speech could not give us the past in its presence [sedimentation], it makes the past undergo

a preparation which is the property of language—it offers us the truth of it. . . . From the moment he seeks the truth, the philosopher does not think that it had to wait for him in order to be true; he seeks it as what has always been true for everyone. It is essential to truth to be integral, whereas no painting has ever pretended to be." "Indirect Language and the Voices of Silence" (S 79–80; S-F 99–100).

73. "With the first phonemic oppositions the child is initiated to the lateral liaison of sign to sign [infra-referentiality] *as the foundation* of an ultimate relation of sign to meaning [extra-referentiality]." "Indirect Language and the Voices of Silence" (S 40; S-F 51).

"It is because the sign is diacritical [infra-referentiality] from the outset, because it is composed and organized in terms of itself, that it has an interior and ends up laying claim to a meaning [extra-referentiality]." "Indirect Language and the Voices of Silence" (S 41; S-F 51).

"As far as language is concerned, it is the lateral relation of one sign to another [infra-referentiality] which makes each of them significant [extra-referentiality]." "Indirect Language and the Voices of Silence" (S 42; S-F 53).

"Its opacity, its obstinate reference to itself, and its turning and folding back on itself are precisely what make [language] a mental power; for it in turn becomes something like a universe [i.e., a sedimented totality], and it is capable of lodging things themselves in this universe—after it has transformed them into their meaning [i.e., through the founding act of expression]." "Indirect Language and the Voices of Silence" (S 43; S-F 54).

74. Or what some might call "inter-textuality."

75. I believe that it is clear from the context and substance of these remarks that what Merleau-Ponty here calls 'semantic philosophy' is what I have been referring to as 'semeiological reductionism.'

76. "There is being [*il y a être*], there is a world, there is something; in the strong sense in which the Greek speaks of τὸ λέγειν, there is cohesion, there is meaning. One does not arouse being from nothingness, *ex nihilo*; one starts with an ontological relief where one can never say that the ground be nothing." (VI 88; VI-F 121.)

77. "The philosophy of reflection is not wrong in considering the false as a mutilated or partial truth: its error is rather to act as if the partial were only a *de facto* absence of the totality, which does not need to be accounted for." (VI 42; VI-F 65.)

78. See chapter 5, 2 above where problems associated with illusion are discussed.

79. "Language is an entity, comparable to the Kantian idea, resulting from the totalization in an infinity of all the convergent means of expression." (CAL 93.) See also "Dialogue and the Perception of the Other" in PW, especially PW 142–44; PW-F 197–201.

80. This initial compatibility between Hegel and Merleau-Ponty should not lull us into ignoring fundamental differences between them. Ultimately, Merleau-Ponty will characterize Hegel's dialectic in plain terms as "bad dialectic" (VI 93–94: VI-F 127–29).

81. "The Hegelian dialectic is what we call by another name the phenomenon of expression, which gathers itself up and launches itself again through the mystery of rationality. And we would undoubtedly recover the concept of history in the true sense of the term if we were to get used to modeling it after the example of the arts and language. For the fact that each expression is closely connected within one single order to every other expression brings about the junction of the individual and the universal. The central fact to which the Hegelian dialectic returns in a hundred ways is that we do not have to choose between the *pour soi* and the *pour autrui*, between thought according to us and according to others, but that at the moment of expression the others to whom I address myself and I who express

myself are incontestably linked together." "Indirect Language and the Voices of Silence" (S 73; S-F 91–92).

82. Marxian feminists might contest this point. But then they would have to contend with the implications of Foucault's persuasive argument in favor of the inherence of real power and the empty nominalism of the abstract conception.

> "It seems to me that power must be understood . . . as the multiplicity of force relations immanent in the sphere in which they operate and which *constitute their own organization*; as the process which, through ceaseless struggles and confrontations, transforms, strengthens, or reverses them."
> "No doubt one needs to be nominalistic: power is not an institution, and not a structure."

Michel Foucault, *The History of Sexuality*, Vol. I, trans. Hurley (New York: Random House, 1980), pp. 92–93 (emphasis added).

83. "In a sense the whole of philosophy, as Husserl says, consists in restoring a power to signify, a birth of meaning, or a wild meaning, an expression of experience by experience, which in particular clarifies the special domain of language. And in a sense, as Valéry said, language is everything, since it is the voice of no one, since it is the very voice of the things, the waves, and the forests. And what we have to understand is that there is no dialectical reversal from one of these views to the other; we do not have to reassemble them into a synthesis: they are two aspects of the reversibility which is the ultimate truth." (VI 155; VI-F 203–204.)

84. Emphasis added.

85. "However we finally have to understand it, the 'pure' ideality already streams forth along the articulations of the aesthesiological body, along the contours of the sensible things." (VI 152; VI-F 200.)

86. The phrase in the French edition is "*cette imminence du tout dans les parties.*" '*Imminence*' is usually rendered as 'imminence' in English, as '*immanence*' is normally translated as 'immanence.' McCleary's translation of '*imminence*' as 'immanence' may or may not have been deliberate. As I understand the text, both meanings are apt: the imminence of the whole in the parts would depend on the immanence of the whole in the parts.

87. Paul Ricoeur, "The Question of the Subject: The Challenge of Semeiology," trans. Kathleen McLaughlin, in *The Conflict of Interpretations*, ed. Don Ihde (Evanston: Northwestern University Press, 1974), p. 251. Subsequent reference to this work will be made in the main text using the short title, "Question."

88. Here Ricoeur is quoting L. Hjelmslev, *Essais linguistiques* (Copenhagen, 1959), p. 21. See "Question," p. 250.

89. Nervure: a vein of a leaf, a tubular member of an insect's wing, derived from the medieval French term for the leather strap used to strengthen a shield.

90. This is the sense in which "truth is another name for sedimentation"—it has nothing to do with *habitus*—at the moment of expression "something has been founded in signification; an experience has been transformed into its meaning, has become truth." "On the Phenomenology of Language" (S 96; S-F 120).

Conclusion

1. Nietzsche, *Beyond Good and Evil*, trans. Kaufmann (New York: Random House, 1966), sect. 289, p. 229.

2. Alphonso Lingis, "The Will to Power," in *The New Nietzsche*, ed. David B. Allison (Cambridge, MA: The M.I.T. Press, 1985), p. 38.

3. Standard among those who have been influenced by Derrida's reading of Nietzsche.

4. Nietzsche, *Thus Spoke Zarathustra*, trans. Kaufmann, in *The Portable Nietzsche*, ed. Kaufmann (New York: Viking Press, 1954), I, Prologue, 4, p. 126.

5. *Zarathustra*, I, Prologue, 3, p. 125.

6. In the first *Critique*. That Kant's transcendental philosophy is implicitly theological becomes even more apparent in the second *Critique* where he argues for "The Existence of God as a Postulate of Pure Practical Reason" (*Critique of Practical Reason*, II, 2 ii).

7. E.g., that branch of the Cartesian tradition that proceeds though Kant to Hegel to Husserl and beyond.

8. See section 7 of the "Attempt at a Self-criticism" with which Nietzsche prefaced the 1886 edition of *The Birth of Tragedy* (trans. Kaufmann [New York: Random House, 1967], pp. 25–27). As late as 1882, Nietzsche writes as though the death of God casts us adrift in a void. See the aphorism on "The Madman": " 'Where is God gone?' he called out. 'I mean to tell you! *We have killed him*—you and I! We are all his murderers!' . . . 'Is there still an above and a below? Do we not stray, as through infinite nothingness? Does not empty space breathe upon us?' " (*The Joyful Wisdom*, trans. Common [New York: Ungar, 1960], III, aphorism 125, pp. 167–68.) Such passages can be interpreted as indications that Nietzsche subscribed to the postulate in question. However, in 1887—when Nietzsche published the second edition of *The Joyful Wisdom*—he added a fifth book in which he makes it clear that he no longer postulates the exclusive disjunction, either God or absolute groundlessness.

> Some have still need of metaphysics; but also the impatient *longing for certainty* which at present discharges itself in scientific, positivist fashion among large numbers of the people, the longing by all means to get at something stable . . . even this is still the longing for a hold, a support; in short, the *instinct of weakness*, which, while not actually creating religions, metaphysics, and convictions of all kinds, nevertheless—preserves them. . . . Belief is always most desired, most pressingly needed, where there is lack of will. . . . When a man arrives at the fundamental conviction that he requires to be commanded, he becomes 'a believer.' Reversely one could imagine a delight and a power of self-determining, and a *freedom* of will, whereby a spirit could bid farewell to every belief, to every wish for certainty, accustomed as it would be to support itself on slender cords and possibilities, and to dance even on the verge of abysses. Such a spirit would be the *free spirit par excellence*.

The Joyful Wisdom, V, aphorism 347, pp. 285–87. Here we see the third alternative to the fideism/nihilism disjunction: the slender ground of finite knowledge which allows us to dance on the *verge* of the abyss.

9. See chapter 5, 1–2 and chapter 10 above for an elaboration of the notion of finite truth and non-absolute grounds.

10. Heidegger, *Being and Time*, trans. Macquarrie and Robinson (New York: Harper and Row, 1962), I, 5, 33, pp. 193–94; emphasis added. I have altered the translation, rendering '*Seienden*' as 'beings' rather than as 'entities.'

11. The standpoint of "fundamental ontology" is the version of the thesis of subjectivity Heidegger adopted in that relatively early phase of his philosophical career. This 'Dasein-centricity,' in my view, constitutes a serious flaw in Heidegger's earlier work, the recognition and correction of which motivated his later turn (*Kehre*) to a language-oriented philosophy.

12. "*Der Grund hat sein Un-wesen, weil er der endlichen Freiheit entspringt. Diese selbst kann sich dem, was ihr so entspringt, nicht entziehen. . . . Die Freiheit is der Grund des Grundes. . . . Als dieser Grund aber ist die Freiheit der* Ab-grund *des Daseins.*" Heideg-

ger, *The Essence of Reasons/Vom Wesen des Grundes* [bilingual edition], trans. Malick (Evanston: Northwestern University Press, 1969), pp. 126–129. I have altered Malick's translation by rendering the German '*Grund*' as 'ground' rather than as 'reason,' and by modifying his wording of the first sentence of the passage quoted.

13. Cf. William J. Richardson, *Heidegger: Through Phenomenology to Thought* (The Hague: Martinus Nijhoff, 1963), I, III, 2, pp. 172–74.

14. Cf. Heidegger, *An Introduction to Metaphysics*, trans. Manheim (Garden City, N.Y.: Doubleday and Company, 1961), p. 79.

15. Richardson, *Heidegger*, p. 172n.

16. Heidegger, "The Origin of the Work of Art," in *Poetry, Language, Thought*, trans. Hofstadter (New York: Harper and Row, 1971). "*Der Ursprung des Kunstwerkes*," in *Holzwege* (Frankfurt am Main: Klostermann, 1950).

17. "Origin," pp. 62–63. "*Ursprung*," p. 51.

18. "Love, Death, and Creation," *Research in Phenomenology*, Vol. XI, 1981.

19. "The dawning world brings out what is as yet undecided and measureless [*Unentschiedene und Maßlose*], and thus discloses the hidden necessity of measure and decisiveness [*Maß und Entschiedenheit*].

"But as a world opens itself the earth comes to rise up. It stands forth as that which bears all, as that which is sheltered in its own law and always wrapped up in itself. World demands its decisiveness and its measure and lets beings attain to the Open of their paths. Earth, bearing and jutting, strives to keep itself closed and to entrust everything to its law." "Origin," p. 63. "*Ursprung*," p. 51. (Note the resonance of what Heidegger describes as the "as yet undecided and measureless" with what Anaximander called τὸ ἄπειρον.)

20. See above, chapter 10, 1.

21. "*Die Sprache*" in *Unterwegs zur Sprache* (Pfullingen: Neske, 1959). "Language" in *Poetry, Language, Though¹* trans. Hofstadter (New York: Harper and Row, 1971).

22. "*Die Sprache ist: Sprache. Die Sprache spricht. Wenn wir uns in den Abgrund, den deiser Satz nennt, fallen lassen, stürzen wir nicht ins Leere weg. Wir fallen in die Höhe. Deren Hoheit öffnet eine Tiefe.*" "Language," pp. 191–92. "*Die Sprache*," p. 13.

23. "Language," p. 191.

24. "*Vernunft ist Sprache*, λόγος." Johann Georg Hammann, *Schriften*, ed. Roth and Wiener (Berlin: Reimer, 1821), VII, pp. 151–52.

25. "*Schmerz versteinerte die Schwelle.*" From "*Ein Winterabend*" ["A Winter Evening"]. Georg Trakl, *Die Dichtungen. Gesamtausgabe mit einem Anhang: Zeugnisse und Erinnerungen*, ed. Kurt Horwitz (Zürich: Arche Verlag, 1946).

26. "Language," p. 204.

27. "Language," p. 204.

28. "*Doch was ist Schmerz? Der Schmerz reißt. Er ist der Riß. Allein er zerreißt nicht in auseinanderfahrende Splitter. Der Schmerz reißt zwar auseinander, er scheidet, jedoch so, daß er zugleich alles auf sich zieht, in sich versammelt. Sein Reißen ist als das versammelnde Scheiden zugleich jenes Ziehen, das wie der Vorriß und Aufriß das im Schied Auseinandergehaltene zeichnet und fügt. Der Schmerz ist das Fügende im scheidendsammelnden Reißen. Der Schmerz ist die Fuge des Risses. Sie ist die Schwelle. Sie trägt das Zwischen aus, die Mitte der zwei in sie Geschiedenen. Der Schmerz fügt den Riß des Unter-Schiedes. Der Schmerz ist der Unter-Schied selber.*" "*Die Sprache*," p. 27.

29. The inference presupposes that Heidegger means to assert an identity between pain and rift, and between pain and dif-ference. This presupposition/interpretation might well be contested. Nonetheless, the argument to follow can stand equally well on Heidegger's use of the genitive: the rift *of* the dif-ference [*der Riß des Unter-Schiedes*], and on Heidegger's reference to "the rift that is the dif-ference itself." "Language," p. 207. ["*Der Unter-Schied versammelt aus sich die Zwei, indem er sie in den Riß ruft, der er selber ist.*" "*Die Sprache*," p. 29.]

30. "Language," p. 205.

31. "The rift of the dif-ference makes the limpid brightness shine. Its luminous joining decides [*ent-scheidet*] the brightening of the world into its own. The rift of the dif-ference expropriates [*enteignet*] the world into its worlding, which grants things." "Language," p. 205.

32. "Origin," pp. 63–64. "*Ursprung*," p. 51.

33. "Origin," p. 72. Emphasis added. "*Alle Kunst ist als Geschehenlassen der Ankunft der Wahrheit des Seienden als eine solchen im Wesen Dichtung.*" "*Ursprung*," p. 59

34. "Origin," p. 73. Emphasis added. "[*Gleichwohl*] *hat das Sprachwerk, die Dichtung im engeren Sinne, eine ausgezeichnete Stellung im Ganzen der Künste.*" "*Ursprung*," p. 60.

35. "In stilling things and world into their own, the dif-ference calls world and thing into the middle of their intimacy. The dif-ference is the bidder. The dif-ference gathers the two out of itself as it calls them into the rift that is the dif-ference itself. . . .

"*Language speaks as the peal of stillness.* Stillness stills by the carrying out, the bearing and enduring, of world and things in their presence [*ihr Wesen*]. The carrying out of world and thing in the manner of stilling is the appropriative taking place [*das Ereignis*] of the dif-ference. Language, the peal of stillness, is, inasmuch as the dif-ference takes place. [*Die Sprache, das Geläut der Stille, ist, indem sich der Unter-Schied ereignet.*] Language goes on as the taking place or occurring of the dif-ference [*als der sich ereignende Unter-Schied*] for world and things." "Language," p. 207.

36. "Language," p. 202.

37. "Ibid.," p. 202. Emphasis added. "*Der Unter-Schied trägt Welt in ihr Welten, trägt die Dinge in ihr Dingen aus. Also sie austragend, trägt er sie einander zu. Der Unter-Schied vermittelt nicht nachträglich, indem er Welt und Dinge durch eine herzugebrachte Mitte verknüpft. Der Unter-Schied ermittelt als die Mitte erst Welt und Dinge zu ihrem Wesen, d.h. in ihr Zueinander, dessen Einheit er austrägt.*" "*Die Sprache*," p. 25.

38. It is well, I think, to reflect in English translations the important distinction between '*Wesen*' ('essence,' 'nature,' 'rationale,' occasionally 'being' [to signal its affinity with the Greek '*οὐσία*']) and '*Anwesen*' (usually and properly rendered as 'presence').

39. Some would contend that this *petitio* constitutes the basic structure of hermeneutic circularity. I believe this interpretation does violence to Heidegger's text, if only because it would render the hermeneutic circle vicious despite Heidegger's protests to the contrary.

40. I do not mean to suggest that Heidegger's philosophical writing during this period was limited to the three essays (listed below) to which I shall refer in what follows—nor do I mean to suggest by the word 'series' that these three lectures were grouped together in any explicit way by Heidegger.

"*Der Satz der Identität*" was delivered at the University of Freiburg im Breisgau on 27 June 1957. An English translation ("The Principle of Identity") accompanied by the German text appears in Heidegger, *Identity and Difference*, trans. Joan Stambaugh (New York: Harper and Row, 1969).

"*Das Wesen der Sprache*" was originally delivered as a series of three lectures at the University of Freiburg im Breisgau on 4 and 18 December 1957 and on 7 February 1958.

"*Der Weg zur Sprache*" was given as a part of a lecture series arranged in January 1959 by the Bavarian Academy of the Fine Arts and the Academy of Arts in Berlin.

"*Das Wesen der Sprache*" and "*Der Weg zur Sprache*" both appear in *Unterwegs zur Sprache* (Pfullingen: Neske, 1959) and English translations ("The Nature of Language" and "The Way to Language") appear in *On the Way to Language*, trans. Peter D. Hertz (New York: Harper and Row, 1971).

41. "The Way to Language," p. 124. "[*Indes*] *die* Sprache *spricht. Sie befolgt zuerst*

und eigentlich das Wesende des Sprechens: das Sagen. Die Sprache spricht, indem sie sagt, d.h. zeigt." "Der Weg zur Sprache", pp. 254–55.

42. "The Way to Language," p. 123. *"Der Weg zur Sprache,"* p. 254. Italicized in the German text.

43. *"Worin beruht, d.h. gründet das Sprachwesen? Vielleicht fragen wir, nach Gründen suchend, am Sprachwesen vorbei."* "The Way to Language," p. 125. *"Der Weg zur Sprache,"* p. 256.

44. I.e., "Saying as Showing."

45. *"The moving force in Showing of Saying is Owning. . . . This owning . . . which moves Saying as Showing in its showing we call appropriation."* "The Way to Language," p. 127.

"Das Regende im Zeigen der Sage ist das Eignen. . . . Das . . . Eignen, das die Sage als die Zeige in ihrem Zeigen regt, heiße Ereignen." *"Der Weg zur Sprache,"* p. 258.

I trust that any significant difference between 'Ereignis' and 'Ereignen' (both of which are rendered as 'appropriation') will emerge from the various contexts; I will not introduce a convention in English to distinguish between the noun and the gerund, but provide the German when appropriate.

46. "What appropriation yields through Saying is never the effect of a cause, nor the consequence of an antecedent. The yielding owning, the appropriation, confers more than any effectuation, making, or grounding." "The Way to Language," p. 127. (I have altered Hertz's translation here by rendering 'Gründen' as 'grounding' rather than as 'founding.' Also, I do not follow his convention of capitalizing 'appropriation.')

"Was das Ereignen durch die Sage ergibt, ist nie die Wirkung einer Ursache, nicht die Folge eines Grundes. Das erbringende Eignen, das Ereignen, ist gewährender als jedes Wirken, Machen und Gründen." "Der Weg zur Sprache," p. 258.

47. "The Way to Language," p. 130. *"Der Weg zur Sprache,"* p. 261.
48. "The Way to Language," p. 133. *"Der Weg zur Sprache,"* p. 265.
49. "The Way to Language," p. 135. *"Haus des Seins ist die Sprache, weil sie als die Sage die Weise des Ereignisses ist."* "Der Weg zur Sprache." p. 267.
50. "The Principle of Identity," pp. 37, 38. *"Der Satz der Identität,"* pp. 102, 103.
51. "The Way to Language," p. 127. *"Der Weg zur Sprache,"* p. 258.
52. "The Way to Language," p. 127.
53. In a footnote to "The Way to Language," Heidegger says that appropriation is difficult to think because thinking must overcome the view "that 'Being' is to be thought as appropriation." He goes on to say that "appropriation is different in nature, because it is richer than any possible metaphysical meaning of Being. Being, however, in respect of its essential origin, can be thought of in terms of appropriation." "The Way to Language," p. 129n. (I have altered Hertz's translation here.)

" . . . Das Ereignis ist wesenhaft anderes, weil reicher als jede mögliche metaphysische Bestimmung des Seins. Dagegen läßt sich das Sein hinsichtlich seiner Wesensherkunft aus dem Ereignis denken." "Der Weg zur Sprache." p. 260n.

54. "The Nature of Language," p. 71. *"Das Wesen der Sprache,"* p. 175.
55. "The Principle of Identity," p. 39. *"Der Satz der Identität,"* p. 104.
56. "The Way to Language," p. 127n. *"Der Weg zur Sprache,"* p. 258n.
57. "The Way to Language," p. 134. *"Der Weg zur Sprache,"* p. 266.
58. "The Way to Language," p. 135. *"Der Weg zur Sprache,"* p. 267.
59. "The Way to Language," p. 136. *"Der Weg zur Sprache,"* p. 267.
60. VI 250; VI-F 303. Here I have modified Lingis's translation. [The passage from *Unterwegs zur Sprache* cited by Merleau-Ponty in this working note dated May 1960 is quoted above.]
61. "God's being for us is an abyss." EM 177; EM-F 56.
62. "The Nature of Language," pp. 60–63. *"Das Wesen der Sprache,"* pp. 162–66.
63. "Words," trans. Joan Stambaugh, in *On the Way to Language*, p. 155. [I have

altered the translation and added emphasis.] "*Das Wort*," in *Unterwegs zur Sprache*, p. 237.

64. "Words," p. 156. "*Das Wort*," p. 238.

65. "The Way to Language," p. 127. [Here, again, I have altered Hertz's translation.] "*Der Weg zur Sprache*," p. 258.

66. Saussure, *Course in General Linguistics*, eds. Bally, Sechehaye, and Reidlinger, trans. Baskin (New York: Philosophical Library, 1959), p. 112.

67. I have taken this phrase, "poets, prophets, and thinkers," from a course bearing that name currently being offered at the State University of New York at Binghamton by Professor Dennis Schmidt.

68. To anticipate the critical riposte that the account (or story) of appropriation based on Merleau-Ponty's notions of *Fundierung* and reversibility is ultimately just as dependent on poetry as is Heidegger's, I might point out that the implicit tenet that all language comes to rest in some form of ποίησις or metaphor overlooks such significant (although, perhaps, non-ultimate) distinctions among uses and functions of language as those drawn above in the section (chapter 11, 3) devoted to the *Fundierung* model.

69. "We do not take Logos and truth in the sense of the Word" (VI 274; VI-F 328).

70. "There is a world of silence, the perceived world, at least, is an order where there are non-linguistic significations [*des significations non langagières*]—yes, non-linguistic significations." (VI 171; VI-F 225).

71. Kirk and Raven, *The Presocratic Philosophers* (Cambridge: Cambridge University Press, 1964), p. 109.

72. Simplicius, *Phys.* 24, 17, quoted in Kirk and Raven, *The Presocratic Philosophers*, p. 117.

73. Nietzsche, *Philosophy in the Tragic Age of the Greeks*, trans. Marianne Cowan (Chicago: Regnery, 1962), 4, p. 47.

74. "The Metaphysical in Man" (SNS 83, 97; SNS-F 146, 170–71).

Bibliography

Aristotle. *Physics*. Trans. Hardie and Gaye. *The Basic Works of Aristotle*. Ed. Richard McKeon. New York: Random House, 1941.

Bannan, John F. *The Philosophy of Merleau-Ponty*. New York: Harcourt, Brace and World, 1967.

Barral, Mary Rose. *Merleau-Ponty: The Role of the Body-Subject in Interpersonal Relations*. Pittsburgh: Duquesne University Press, 1965.

Bartley, William Warren, III. *The Retreat to Commitment*. New York: Knopf, 1962.

Beardslee, D. C., and Wertheimer, Michael, eds. *Readings in Perception*. Princeton: Van Nostrand, 1958.

Brumbaugh, Robert S. *The Philosophers of Greece*. New York: Crowell, 1964.

Corso, J. F. *The Experimental Psychology of Sensory Behavior*. New York: Holt, Rinehart and Winston, 1967.

Cunningham, Suzanne. *Language and the Phenomenological Reductions of Edmund Husserl*. The Hague: Nijhoff, 1976.

Derrida, Jacques. "La Forme et le Vouloir-Dire: Note sur la phénoménologie du langage." *Revue Internationale de Philosophie* XXI (1967).

————. *De la Grammatologie*. Paris: Les Editions de Minuit, 1967. [*Of Grammatology*. Trans. Spivak. Baltimore: Johns Hopkins University Press, 1976.]

————. "Différance." *Margins of Philosophy*. Trans. Alan Bass. Chicago: The University of Chicago Press, 1982.

————. "*Ousia* and *Grammē:* Note on a Note from *Being and Time*." *Margins of Philosophy*. Trans. Alan Bass. Chicago: The University of Chicago Press, 1982.

Descartes, René. *Rules for the Direction of the Mind*. Trans. Haldane and Ross. *The Philosophical Works of Descartes*. Eds. Haldane and Ross. New York: Dover, 1955.

————. *Meditations on First Philosophy*. Trans. Haldane and Ross. *The Philosophical Works of Descartes*. Eds. Haldane and Ross. New York: Dover, 1955.

De Waelhens, A. *Une Philosophie de l'ambiguïté: L'existentialisme de Maurice Merleau-Ponty*. Louvain: Nauwelaerts, 1967.

Dillon, M. C. "Gestalt Theory and Merleau-Ponty's Concept of Intentionality." *Man and World* 4 (1971).

————. "Sartre on the Phenomenal Body and Merleau-Ponty's Critique." *Journal of the British Society for Phenomenology* 5 (1974).

————. "A Phenomenological Conception of Truth." *Man and World* 10 (1977).

————. "Merleau-Ponty and the Psychogenesis of the Self." *Journal of Phenomenological Psychology* 9 (1978).

————. "Eye and Mind: The Intertwining of Vision and Thought." *Man and World* 13 (1980).

————. "Merleau-Ponty on Existential Sexuality: A Critique." *Journal of Phenomenological Psychology* 11 (1980).

————. "Toward a Phenomenology of Love and Sexuality." *Soundings* LXIII (1980).

————. "The Implications of Merleau-Ponty's Thought for the Practice of Psychotherapy." *Journal of Phenomenological Psychology* 14 (1983).

————. "Merleau-Ponty and the Reversibility Thesis." *Man and World* 16 (1983).

————. "Erotic Desire." *Research in Phenomenology* XV (1985).

————. "Apriority in Kant and Merleau-Ponty." *Kant-Studien* (forthcoming).

————. "Desire: Language and Body." *Post-Modernism and Continental Philosophy*. Eds. Silverman and Welton. Albany: SUNY Press (forthcoming).

————. "Merleau-Ponty and the Transcendence of Immanence: Overcoming the Ontology of Consciousness." *Man and World* (forthcoming).

Fechner, G. T. *Elemente der Psychophysik*. Leipzig: 1860.

Føllesdal, Dagfinn. "Husserl's Notion of Noema." *The Journal of Philosophy* LXVI (1969), 680–687.

Foucault, Michel. *Les Mots et les choses.* Paris: Gallimard, 1966. [*The Order of Things: An Archaeology of the Human Sciences.* New York: Vintage, 1973.]

———. *The History of Sexuality, Volume I: An Introduction.* Trans. Robert Hurley. New York: Vintage, 1980.

Gelb, A. and Goldstein, K. "Über den Einfluß des vollständigen Verlustes des optischen Vorstellungsvermögens auf das taktile Erkennen." *Psychologische Analysen hirnpathologischer Fälle.* Eds. Gelb and Goldstein. Leipzig: Barth, 1920.

Goldstein, K. "Über die Abhängigkeit der Bewegungen von optischen Vorgängen." *Monatschrift für Psychiatrie und Neurologie* (Festschrift Liepmann, 1923).

———. *Zeigen und Greifen.* Nervenarztt, 1931.

Gurwitsch, Aron. *The Field of Consciousness.* Pittsburgh: Duquesne University Press, 1964.

———. *Studies in Phenomenology and Psychology.* Evanston: Northwestern University Press, 1966.

———. "Towards a Theory of Intentionality." *Philosophy and Phenomenological Research* XXX (1970).

Hamann, Johann Georg. *Schriften.* Ed. Roth and Weiner. Berlin: Reimer, 1821.

Harries, Karsten. "Irrationalism and Cartesian Method." *Journal of Existentialism* VI (1966).

Hegel, G. W. F. *The Phenomenology of Mind.* Trans. Baillie. New York: Harper and Row, 1967.

Heidegger, Martin. *Sein und Zeit.* Tübingen: Max Niemeyer Verlag, 1967. [*Being and Time.* Trans. Macquarrie and Robinson. New York: Harper and Row, 1962.]

———. *Vom Wesen des Grundes.* Halle: Niemeyer, 1929. [*The Essence of Reasons.* Trans. Malick. Evanston: Northwestern University Press, 1969.]

———. *Einführung in die Metaphysik.* Tübingen: Niemeyer, 1953. [*An Introduction to Metaphysics.* Trans. Ralph Manheim. Garden City, NY: Doubleday, 1961.]

———. "Der Ursprung des Kunstwerkes." *Holzwege.* Frankfurt am Main: Vittorio Klostermann, 1963. ["The Origin of the Work of Art." *Poetry, Language, Thought.* Trans. Hofstadter. New York: Harper and Row, 1971.]

———. "Hölderlin und das Wesen der Dichtung." *Erläuterungen zu Hölderlins Dichtung.* Frankfurt am Main: Vittorio Klostermann, 1944. ["Hölderlin and the Essence of Poetry." Trans. Scott. In *Existence and Being.* Ed. W. Brock. Chicago: Regnery, 1949.]

———. "Wozu Dichter?" *Holzwege.* Frankfurt am Main: Vittorio Klostermann, 1963. ["What Are Poets For?" *Poetry, Language, Thought.* Trans. Hofstadter. New York: Harper and Row, 1971.]

———. "Die Sprache." *Unterwegs zur Sprache.* Pfullingen: Neske, 1959. ["Language." *Poetry, Language, Thought.* Trans. Hofstadter. New York: Harper and Row, 1971.]

———. " '. . . dichterisch wohnet der Mensch. . . .' " *Vorträge und Aufsätze.* Pfullingen: Neske, 1954. [" '. . . Poetically Man Dwells . . .' " *Poetry, Language, Thought.* Trans. Hofstadter. New York: Harper and Row, 1971.]

———. *Identität und Differenz/Identity and Difference.* Bilingual edition. Trans. Joan Stambaugh. New York: Harper and Row, 1969.

———. "Das Wesen der Sprache." *Unterwegs zur Sprache.* Pfullingen: Neske, 1959. ["The Nature of Language." *On the Way to Language.* Trans. Peter D. Hertz. New York: Harper and Row, 1971.]

———. "Das Wort." *Unterwegs zur Sprache.* Pfullingen: Neske, 1959. ["Words." Trans. Joan Stambaugh. *On the Way to Language.* Trans. Peter D. Hertz. New York: Harper and Row, 1971.]

————. "Der Weg zur Sprache." *Unterwegs zur Sprache.* Pfullingen: Neske, 1959. ["The Way to Language." *On the Way to Language.* Trans. Peter D. Hertz. New York: Harper and Row, 1971.]

Heidsieck, François. *L'Ontologie de Merleau-Ponty.* Paris: Presses Universitaires de France, 1971.

Hume, David. *A Treatise of Human Nature.* Ed. L. A. Selby-Bigge. Oxford: Oxford University Press, 1964.

Husserl, Edmund. *The Phenomenology of Internal Time-Consciousness.* Ed. Martin Heidegger. Trans. James S. Churchill. Bloomington: Indiana University Press, 1964.

————. *The Idea of Phenomenology.* Trans. Alston and Nakhnikian. The Hague: Nijhoff, 1964.

————. *Ideas: General Introduction to Pure Phenomenology.* Trans. W. R. Boyce Gibson. London: Allen and Unwin, 1931.

————. *The Paris Lectures.* Trans. Peter Koestenbaum. The Hague: Nijhoff, 1967.

————. *Cartesian Meditations.* Trans. Dorion Cairns. The Hague: Nijhoff, 1960.

————. *The Crisis of European Sciences and Transcendental Phenomenology.* Trans. David Carr. Evanston: Northwestern University Press, 1970.

Kant, Immanuel. *Critique of Pure Reason.* Trans. N. K. Smith. London: Macmillan, 1963.

————. *Critique of Practical Reason.* Trans. L. W. Beck. Indianapolis: Bobbs-Merrill, 1956.

Katz, David. *Gestalt Psychology.* Trans. Tyson. New York: Ronald Press, 1950.

King, Jeffrey H. *Phenomenology and Meta-Social Science.* Unpublished doctoral dissertation. State University of New York, University Center at Binghamton, 1983.

Kirk, G. S., and Raven, J. E. *The Presocratic Philosophers.* Cambridge: Cambridge University Press, 1964.

Koehler, W. "Ueber unbemerkte Empfindungen und Urteilstäuschungen." *Zeitschrift für Psychologie* 66 (1913), 51–80.

————. *Gestalt Psychology.* New York: Liveright, 1947.

Koffka, Kurt. *Principles of Gestalt Psychology.* London: Routledge and Kegan Paul, 1935.

Kwant, Remy C. *The Phenomenological Philosophy of Merleau-Ponty.* Pittsburgh: Duquesne University Press, 1963.

————. *From Phenomenology to Metaphysics: An Inquiry into the Last Period of Merleau-Ponty's Philosophical Life.* Pittsburgh: Duquesne University Press, 1966.

Lacan, Jacques. *Écrits: A Selection.* Trans. Alan Sheridan. New York: W. W. Norton, 1977.

————. *Speech and Language in Psychoanalysis.* Trans. Anthony Wilden. Baltimore: Johns Hopkins University Press, 1981.

————. "Merleau-Ponty: In Memoriam." Trans. W. Ver Eecke and D. de Schutter. *Review of Existential Psychology and Psychiatry* XVIII (1982–83).

Langan, Thomas. *Merleau-Ponty's Critique of Reason.* New Haven: Yale University Press, 1966.

Lefort, Claude. *Sur une colonne absente: Écrits autour de Merleau-Ponty.* Paris: Gallimard, 1978.

Levin, David Michael. "Tarthang Tulku and Merleau-Ponty: An Intertextual Commentary." *Dimensions of Thought: Current Explorations in Time, Space, and Knowledge.* Vol. I. Eds. Moon and Randall. Berkeley: Dharma Publishing, 1980.

————. "Sanity and Myth in Affective Space: A Discussion of Merleau-Ponty." *The Philosophical Forum* 14 (1982–83).

————. "Eros and Psyche: A Reading of Merleau-Ponty." *Review of Existential Psychology and Psychiatry* XVIII (1982–83).

Lingis, Alphonso. "The Visible and the Vision." Presented at Seventh Annual Meeting of the Merleau-Ponty Circle, State University of New York, University Center at Binghamton, October 1982.

———. "The Will to Power." *The New Nietzsche.* Ed. David B. Allison. Cambridge, MA: The M.I.T. Press, 1985.

Locke, John. *An Essay Concerning Human Understanding.* Ed. A. C. Fraser. New York: Dover, 1959.

Madison, Gary Brent. *The Phenomenology of Merleau-Ponty.* Trans. G. B. Madison. Athens, Ohio: Ohio University Press, 1981.

Mallin, Samuel B. *Merleau-Ponty's Philosophy.* New Haven: Yale University Press, 1979.

Mazis, Glen. "Touch and Vision: Rethinking with Merleau-Ponty Sartre on the Caress." *Philosophy Today* (1979).

McCleary, R. A., and Lazarus, R. S. "Autonomic Discrimination without Awareness: An Interim Report." *J. Pers.* 18 (1949), 171–79.

Merleau-Ponty, Maurice. *La Structure du comportement.* Paris: Presses Universitaires de France, 1942 [*The Structure of Behavior.* Trans. Alden L. Fisher. Boston: Beacon Press, 1963.]

———. *Phénoménologie de la perception.* Paris: Gallimard. 1945. [*Phenomenology of Perception.* Trans. Colin Smith. London: Routledge and Kegan Paul, 1962.]

———. *Sens et non-sens.* Paris: Nagel, 1966. [*Sense and Non-Sense.* Trans. H. L. and P. A. Dreyfus. Evanston: Northwestern University Press, 1964.]

———. "La Conscience et l'acquisition du langage." *Bulletin de psychologie* no. 236, XVIII 3–6 (1964). [*Consciousness and the Acquisition of Language.* Trans. Silverman. Evanston: Northwestern University Press, 1973.]

———. "Les Relations avec autrui chez l'enfant." *Les Cours de Sorbonne.* Paris: Centre de Documentation Universitaire, 1960. ["The Child's Relations with Others." Trans. William Cobb. In *The Primacy of Perception.* Ed. James M. Edie. Evanston: Northwestern University Press, 1964.]

———. "L'Expérience d'autrui." *Bulletin du Groupe d'études de psychologie de l'Université de Paris* (*1951–1952*). Paris: Centre de Documentation Universitaire. ["The Experience of Others." Trans. Fred Evans and Hugh J. Silverman. *Review of Existential Psychology and Psychiatry* 18 (1982–83).]

———. *La Prose du monde.* Ed. Claude Lefort. Paris: Gallimard, 1969. [*The Prose of the World.* Ed. Lefort. Trans. O'Neill. Evanston: Northwestern University Press, 1973.]

———. *Résumés de cours: Collège de France 1952–1960.* Paris: Gallimard, 1968. [*Themes from the Lectures at the Collège de France 1952–1960.* Trans. John O'Neill. Evanston: Northwestern University Press, 1970.]

———. *Signes.* Paris: Gallimard, 1960. [*Signs.* Trans. R. C. McCleary. Evanston: Northwestern University Press, 1964.]

———. *The Primacy of Perception.* Ed. James M. Edie. Evanston: Northwestern University Press, 1964.

———. *L'Œil et l'esprit.* Paris: Gallimard, 1964. ["Eye and Mind." Trans. Carleton Dallery. In *The Primacy of Perception.* Ed. James M. Edie. Evanston: Northwestern University Press, 1964.]

———. *Le Visible et l'invisible.* Ed. Claude Lefort. Paris: Gallimard, 1964. [*The Visible and the Invisible.* Ed. Lefort. Trans. Alphonso Lingis. Evanston: Northwestern University Press, 1968.]

Metzger, W. "Optische Untersuchungen am Ganzfeld." *Psychologische Forschung* XII (1930).

Miles, T. R. "Gestalt Theory." *Encyclopedia of Philosophy.* Ed. Paul Edwards. New York: Macmillan, 1967.

Nietzsche, Friedrich. *The Birth of Tragedy.* Trans. Kaufmann. New York: Random House, 1967.

——. *Philosophy in the Tragic Age of the Greeks.* Trans. Cowan. Chicago: Henry Regnery Company, 1962.

——. *The Joyful Wisdom.* Trans. Common. New York: Ungar, 1960.

——. *Thus Spoke Zarathustra.* Trans. Kaufmann. In *The Portable Nietzsche.* Ed. Kaufmann. New York: Viking Press, 1954.

——. *Beyond Good and Evil.* Trans. Kaufmann. New York: Random House, 1966.

Ockham, William (of). *Quodlibeta. Philosophical Writings* [of Ockham]. Trans. Boehner. Indianapolis: Bobbs-Merrill, 1964.

Olkowski, Dorothea E. "Merleau-Ponty's Freudianism: From the Body of Consciousness to the Body of Flesh." *Review of Existential Psychology and Psychiatry* XVIII (1982–83).

O'Neill, John. *Perception, Expression, and History: The Social Phenomenology of Maurice Merleau-Ponty.* Evanston: Northwestern University Press, 1970.

——. "The Specular Body: Merleau-Ponty and Lacan on Self and Other." Presented at Seventh Annual Meeting of the Merleau-Ponty Circle, State University of New York, University Center at Binghamton, October 1982.

Plato. *Meno.* Trans. W. K. C. Guthrie. In *The Collected Dialogues of Plato.* Eds. Edith Hamilton and Huntington Cairns. New York: Pantheon, 1961.

Richardson, William J. *Heidegger: Through Phenomenology to Thought.* The Hague: Nijhoff, 1963.

Ricoeur, Paul. *The Conflict of Interpretations.* Ed. Don Ihde. Evanston: Northwestern University Press, 1974.

Rubin, E. *Synsoplevede Figurer.* Copenhagen: 1915. ["Figure and Ground." Trans. and abridged by Michael Wertheimer. In *Readings in Perception.* Eds. Beardslee and Wertheimer. Princeton: Van Nostrand, 1958.]

Sallis, John, ed. *Merleau-Ponty: Perception, Structure, Language.* Atlantic Highlands, New Jersey: Humanities Press, 1981.

Sartre, Jean-Paul. *La Nausée.* Paris: Gallimard, 1938. [*Nausea.* Trans. Alexander. New York: New Directions, 1964.]

——. *The Transcendence of the Ego.* Trans. Williams and Kirkpatrick. New York: Noonday Press, 1957.

——. *L'être et le néant.* Paris: Gillimard, 1943. [*Being and Nothingness.* Trans. Hazel Barnes. New York: Philosophical Library, 1956.]

de Saussure, Ferdinand. *Course in General Linguistics.* Eds. Bally and Sechehaye in collaboration with Reidlinger. Trans. Baskin. New York: Philosophical Library, 1959.

Schmidt, James. *Maurice Merleau-Ponty: Between Phenomenology and Structuralism.* London: Macmillan, 1985.

Silverman, Hugh J. "Re-Reading Merleau-Ponty." *Telos* 29 (1976).

——. "Merleau-Ponty's Human Ambiguity." *Journal of the British Society for Phenomenology* 9 (1979).

——. "Merleau-Ponty on Language and Communication (1947–48)." *Research in Phenomenology* 9 (1979).

——. "Merleau-Ponty and the Interrogation of Language." *Research in Phenomenology* 10 (1980).

——. "Merleau-Ponty's New Beginning: Preface to *The Experience of Others.*" *Review of Existential Psychology and Psychiatry* XVIII (1982–83).

Singer, Linda. *The Mystery of Vision and the Miracle of Painting: A Critical Examination of Merleau-Ponty's Philosophy of the Visual Arts.* Unpublished doctoral dissertation. State University of New York, University Center at Binghamton (1981).

Swets, J. A. "Is There a Sensory Threshold?" *Science* 134 (1961), 168–177.

Trakl, Georg. *Die Dichtungen. Gesamtausgabe mit einem Anhang: Zeugnisse und Erin-nerungen.* Ed. Kurt Horwitz. Zürich: Arche Verlag, 1946.

Weintraub and Walker. *Perception.* Belmont, CA: Brooks/Cole Publishing Company, 1966.

Whitford, Margaret. *Merleau-Ponty's Critique of Sartre's Philosophy.* Lexington, KY: French Forum, 1982.

Wittgenstein, Ludwig. *Tractatus Logico-Philosophicus.* Bilingual edition. Trans. Pears and McGuinness. London: Routledge and Kegan Paul, 1961.

———. *Philosophische Untersuchungen/Philosophical Investigations.* Bilingual edition. Trans. G. E. M. Anscombe. New York: Macmillan, 1953.

Zaner, Richard M. *The Problem of Embodiment: Some Contributions to a Phenomenology of the Body.* The Hague: Nijhoff, 1964.

Name Index

Subject Index

Abyss (*Ab-grund*), 180, 185, 236, 242; and appropriation, 233–35; and Dasein, 227; and difference, 230–31; and God, 224–25; and groundlessness, 226, 230–31, 233, 237; and language, 229; and logos, 232, 233, 235, 244; and negativity, 242–43

Adumbration, 90–91

Alienation, 167; from body, 142; of consciousness, 47; self-alienation, 109, 110, 123, 125

Ambiguity: doctrine of, 190

Analyticity: and necessity, 12

Appearance, 54; and reality, 4, 9

Apperception: analogical, 116–17, 168; apperceptive transfer, 117; transcendental unity of, 226

Appropriation (*Ereignis*), 232, 237; and abyss, 233–35; and ground, 233–34; and language, 236; and meaning, 238–39

Art: truth in, 179, 227, 230

Atomism: logical, 12, 30, 31; perceptual, 59–62, 64, 65, 66, 68, 80–81

Becoming: 226, 242; and imperfect knowledge, 3; logic of, 242; primacy of, 95

Being, 156, 223; and appropriation, 233; being-for-itself, 38, 40, 44, 140, 156; being-in-itself, 40, 44, 156; determinate, 49, 97, 100; and knowledge, 2, 4; and language, 180, 221; meaning of, 226; and non-Being, 226; and nothingness, 37; order of, 54; as totality of signifiers, 223

Belief, 28

Body, 118, 122; bodily intentionality, 137–39, 147, 219; body-language, 217, 221, 221–22, 223; body-object, 158, 174; body subject, 174; child's experience of, 121–27; and consciousness, 105, 141, 145–46; and flesh, 35, 99, 101, 103, 106, 110, 112, 128, 131, 132, 139, 145, 145–46, 150, 164, 165, 166, 169, 170, 171, 213, 215, 216, 216–17, 219; intentionality of, 135, 136; and genesis of language, 187; lived body, 35, 114, 123, 131–32, 140, 143, 144, 146–47, 150, 153, 192, 216, 217; mind-body dualism, 37; as object, 122–23, 148, 166, 169; ontological dimensions of, 141, 142–47, 150, 153, 158; other's, 128–29; phenomenal, 139, 148, 149, 164; and solipsism, 113–14; spirit, 109; as subject, 123, 166, 169

British Empiricism, 21

Cartesianism, 6, 40, 50, 236; and certainty, 9, 18, 24, 27–28, 33, 49; cogito, 56, 102–103, 107–11, 113, 115, 124; and doubt, 13;

dualism, 5–6, 46–47, 47–48, 69; ego, 102–103; and empiricism, 5–6, 20; and intellectualism, 20, 26, 30; neo-Cartesianism, 156; *res cogitans*, 47–48, 102, 109; *res extensa*, 47–48; and skepticism, 24

Causation: universal, 15, 17

Certainty, 9, 18, 24, 27–28, 33, 49; criteria of, 14, 18–19, 22, 26; ground for, 24–25; and logical atomism, 12; transparency, 26; and truth, 9–10

Cogito, 14, 42, 102; Cartesian, 56, 102–103, 107–11, 113, 115, 124; cogitation, 118; cogitationes, 27; ego cogito, 27–28; existential, 108; explicit, 109, 148; indubitability of, 15, 107; prereflective, 38, 39, 140; tacit, 103, 104–105, 107, 110, 122, 124, 162, 163, 195, 213

Cognition: modes of, 28

Consciousness, 59, 85; alienated, 47; basic elements of, 18; and body, 105, 141, 145–46; categorical function of, 136; and cogito, 107–108; and constitution, 31, 147; eidetic laws of, 32; foundational, 104; and immanence, 28, 36, 38, 102, 134, 153; intentionality of, 28, 38, 70, 75, 92, 133; and intersubjectivity, 131; and meaning, 133–34; mythical, 96; and negativity, 39, 43, 140–41; object of, 38–39, 40, 86, 103, 163; phenomena of, 70; reality of, 107; pure, 147; self-consciousness, 46, 163; as sphere of ownness, 118–20, 122; structure of, 30; as subject, 102; synthesis of, 31; temporality of, 41; thetic, 38–39, 40, 142; of time, 75–76; transcendental, 130, 147, 162, 163–64, 175, 201, 235; world as object for, 18, 19, 33; worldly, 105

Constitution: and consciousness, 31, 147; formal structure of, 32; immanent, 90; and language, 77, 214; of meaning, 175, 219; transcendental, 70, 76, 174; and transcendence, 29; of the world, 32, 148

Contradiction: law of, 1

Dasein: existential structures of, 227; and ground, 226–27

Dialectic, 57; of Being and non-Being, 226; dialectical self-mediation, 211–12, 213; hyperdialectic, 46, 213; and negation, 45

Doubt: indubitability of the cogito, 15, 107; radical, 13

Earth, 225, 226; and world, 227, 230

Ego: alter ego, 113, 114, 117, 119, 207; cogitationes of, 27, 28; ego cogito, 27–28; ei-